your movie
SUCKS

roger ebert

**Andrews McMeel
Publishing, LLC**

Kansas City

10 11 RR4 10 9 8 7 6 5 4 3

ISBN-13: 978-0-7407-6366-3
ISBN: 0-7407-6366-0

Library of Congress Control Number: 2007923419
www.andrewsmcmeel.com

All the reviews in this book originally appeared in the *Chicago Sun-Times*.

attention: schools and businesses

Andrews McMeel books are available at quantity discounts with bulk
purchase for educational, business, or sales promotional use. For
information, please write to: Special Sales Department, Andrews McMeel
Publishing, LLC, 1130 Walnut St., Kansas City, Missouri 64106.

acknowledgments

● ● ● ● ● ● ● ● ●

Thanks above all to my wife, Chaz, and my assistants Carol Iwata and Greg Isaac for their invaluable contributions to this book. I owe deep gratitude to my editor, Dorothy O'Brien, who kept this project on track while being patient, cheerful, encouraging, and understanding. She is assisted by the equally patient Lesa Reifschneider.

At the *Chicago Sun-Times* I have been blessed with the expert editing of Michael Cooke, John Barron, Laura Emerick, Miriam DiNunzio, Teresa Budasi, Jeff Wisser, Darel Jevins, Avis Weathersbee, Jeff Johnson, and Marlene Gelfond. At Universal Press Syndicate I am indebted to Sue Roush, and to Michelle Daniel at Andrews McMeel Publishing.

Many thanks are also due to the production staff at *Ebert & Roeper*: my partner, Richard Roeper, and Don Dupree, David Plummer, Janet LaMonica, David Kodeski, Amanda Kammes, and Nancy Stanley. Last, but certainly not least, my gratitude to Marsha Jordan at WLS-TV.

introduction

· · · · · · · · ·

Some of these reviews were written in joyous zeal. Others with glee. Some in sorrow, some in anger, and a precious few with venom, of which I have a closely guarded supply. When I am asked, all too frequently, if I really sit all the way through those movies, my answer is inevitably: Yes, because I want to write the review.

I would guess that I have not mentioned my Pulitzer Prize in a review except once or twice since 1975, but at the moment I read Rob Schneider's extremely unwise open letter to Patrick Goldstein, I knew I was receiving a home-run pitch, right over the plate. Other reviews were written in various spirits, some of them almost benevolently, but of *Deuce Bigelow, European Gigolo,* all I can say is that it is a movie made to inspire the title of a book like this.

On the other hand, I learned a thing or two. Vincent Gallo's *The Brown Bunny* struck me, when I saw it at Cannes, as definitively bad. I engaged in an exchange of views with the director. When I saw his considerably shorter final cut, I had to concede that I could now see what he was getting at. A critic must be honest.

If a film of yours is included in this volume, take heart and be of good cheer. You may yet rank among the Gallos and not the Schneiders.

Roger Ebert

setting
the scene...
●●●●●●●●●

Deuce Bigalow: European Gigolo

(DIRECTED BY MIKE BIGELOW; STARRING ROB SCHNEIDER, EDDIE GRIFFIN; 2005)

Deuce Bigalow: European Gigolo makes a living cleaning fish tanks and occasionally prostituting himself. How much he charges, I'm not sure, but the price is worth it if it keeps him off the streets and out of another movie. *Deuce Bigalow* is aggressively bad, as if it wants to cause suffering to the audience. The best thing about it is that it runs for only seventy-five minutes.

Rob Schneider is back, playing a male prostitute (or, as the movie reminds us dozens of times, a "man-whore"). He is not a gay hustler, but specializes in pleasuring women, although the movie's closest thing to a sex scene is when he wears diapers on orders from a giantess. Oh, and he goes to dinner with a woman with a laryngectomy who sprays wine on him through her neck vent.

The plot: Deuce visits his friend T. J. Hicks (Eddie Griffin) in Amsterdam, where T. J. is a pimp specializing in man-whores. Business is bad because a serial killer is murdering male prostitutes, and so Deuce acts as a decoy to entrap the killer. In his investigation, he encounters a woman with a penis for a nose. You don't want to know what happens when she sneezes.

Does this sound like a movie you want to see? It sounds to me like a movie that Columbia Pictures and the film's producers (Jack Giarraputo, Adam Sandler, and John Schneider) should be discussing in long, sad conversations with their inner child.

The movie created a spot of controversy in February 2005. According to a story by Larry Carroll of MTV News, Rob Schneider took offense when Patrick Goldstein of the *Los Angeles Times* listed this year's Best Picture nominees and wrote that they were "ignored, unloved, and turned down flat by most of the same studios that . . . bankroll hundreds of sequels, including a follow-up to *Deuce Bigalow: Male Gigolo,* a film that was sadly overlooked at Oscar time because apparently nobody had the foresight to invent a category for Best Running Penis Joke Delivered by a Third-Rate Comic."

Schneider retaliated by attacking Goldstein in full-page ads in *Daily Variety* and the *Hollywood Reporter*. In an open letter to Goldstein, Schneider wrote:

Dear Patrick Goldstein, Staff Writer for the Los Angeles Times,

My name is Rob Schneider and I am responding to your January 26th front page cover story in the LA Times, *where you used my upcoming sequel to* Deuce Bigalow *as an example of why Hollywood studios are lagging behind the independents in Academy nominations. According to your logic, Hollywood Studios are too busy making sequels like* Deuce Bigalow *instead of making movies that you would like to see.*

Well, Mr. Goldstein, as far as your snide comments about me and my film not being nominated for an Academy Award, I decided to do some research to find what awards you have won.

I went online and found that you have won nothing. Absolutely nothing. No journalistic awards of any kind. Disappointed, I went to the Pulitzer Prize database of past winners and nominees. I thought, surely, there must be an omission. I typed in the name Patrick Goldstein and again, zippo—nada. No Pulitzer Prizes or nominations for a "Mr. Patrick Goldstein." There was, however, a nomination for an Amy Goldstein. I contacted Ms. Goldstein in Rhode Island; she assured me she was not an alias of yours and in fact like most of the world had no idea of your existence.

Frankly, I am surprised the LA Times *would hire someone like you with so few or, actually, no accolades to work on their front page. Surely there must be a larger talent pool for the* LA Times *to draw from. Perhaps, someone who has at least won a Cable Ace Award.*

Maybe, Mr. Goldstein, you didn't win a Pulitzer Prize because they haven't invented a category for "Best Third-Rate, Unfunny Pompous Reporter, Who's Never Been Acknowledged By His Peers"!

Patrick, I can honestly say that if I sat with your colleagues at a lunch-eon, afterwards, they'd say, "You know, that Rob Schneider is a pretty intelligent guy, I hope we can do that again." Whereas, if you sat with my colleagues, after lunch, you would just be beaten beyond recognition.

For the record, Patrick, your research is shabby as well. My next film is not Deuce Bigalow: Male Gigolo 2. *It's* Deuce Bigalow: European Gigolo, *in theaters EVERYWHERE August 12th, 2005.*

All my best,
Rob Schneider

Reading this, I was about to observe that Schneider can dish it out, but he can't take it. Then I found he's not so good at dishing it out, either. I went online and found that Patrick Goldstein has won a National Headliner Award, a Los Angeles Press Club Award, a RockCritics.com award, and the Publicists' Guild award for lifetime achievement.

Schneider was nominated for a 2000 Razzie Award for Worst Supporting Actor, but lost to Jar-Jar Binks. But Schneider is correct, and Patrick Goldstein has not yet won a Pulitzer Prize. Therefore, Goldstein is not qualified to complain that Columbia financed *Deuce Bigalow: European Gigolo* while passing on the opportunity to participate in *Million Dollar Baby, Ray, The Aviator, Sideways,* and *Finding Neverland.* As chance would have it, I *have* won the Pulitzer Prize, and so I am qualified. Speaking in my official capacity as a Pulitzer Prize winner, Mr. Schneider, your movie sucks.

Chaos

(DIRECTED BY DAVID DEFALCO; STARRING KEVIN GAGE, STEPHEN WOZNIAK; 2005)

Chaos is ugly, nihilistic, and cruel—a film I regret having seen. I urge you to avoid it. Don't make the mistake of thinking it's "only" a horror film or a slasher film. It is an exercise in heartless cruelty and it ends with careless brutality. The movie denies not only the value of life, but the possibility of hope.

The movie premiered in late July at Flashback Weekend, a Chicago convention devoted to horror and exploitation films. As I write, it remains unreviewed in *Variety*, unlisted on Rotten Tomatoes. As an unabashed retread of *The Last House on the Left* (itself inspired by Bergman's *The Virgin Spring*), it may develop a certain notoriety, but you don't judge a book by its cover or a remake by its inspiration. A few Web writers have seen it, and try to deal with their feelings:

"What is inflicted upon these women is degrading, humiliating and terrible on every level." —CAPONE, AIN'T IT COOL NEWS

"Disgusting, shocking, and laced with humiliation, nudity, profanity, and limit-shoving tastelessness." —JOHN GRAY, PITOFHORROR.COM

"What's the point of this s——t anyway?"
—ED GONZALEZ, SLANTMAGAZINE.COM.

But Capone finds the film "highly effective if painful and difficult to watch." And Gray looks on the bright side: DeFalco "manages to shock and disturb as well as give fans a glimpse of hope that some people are still trying to make good, sleazy, exploitation films." Gonzalez finds no redeeming features, adding, "DeFalco directs the whole thing with all the finesse of someone who has been hit on the head one too many times (is this a good time to say he was a wrestler?)."

I quote these reviews because I'm fascinated by their strategies for dealing with a film that transcends all barriers of decency. There are two scenes so gruesome I cannot describe them in a newspaper, no matter what words I use. Having seen it, I cannot ignore it, nor can I deny that it affected me strongly: I recoiled during some of the most cruel moments, and when the film was over I was filled with sadness and disquiet.

The plot: Angelica and Emily (Chantal Degroat and Maya Barovich) are UCLA students, visiting the country cabin of Emily's parents, an interracial couple. They hear about a rave in the woods, drive off to party, meet a lout named Swan (Sage Stallone), and ask him where they can find some ecstasy. He leads them to a cabin occupied by Chaos (Kevin Gage), already wanted for serial killing, Frankie (Stephen Wozniak), and Sadie (Kelly K. C. Quann). They're a Manson family in microcosm. By the end of the film, they will have raped and murdered the girls, not always in that order. Nor does the bloodshed stop there. The violence is sadistic, graphic, savage, and heartless. Much of the action involves the girls weeping and pleading for their lives. When the film pauses for dialogue, it is often racist.

So that's it. DeFalco directs with a crude, efficient gusto, as a man with an ax makes short work of firewood. Kevin Gage makes Chaos repulsive and cruel, Quann is effective as a pathetic, dimwitted sex slave, and the young victims are played with relentless sincerity; to the degree that we are repelled by the killers and feel pity for the victims, the movie "works." It works, all right, but I'm with Ed Gonzalez: Why do we need this s——t?

In response to this review, the following letter from the director and producer to me ran as an ad in the *Chicago Sun-Times*:

August 15, 2005
Dear Mr. Ebert:
Thank you for reviewing our film, Chaos, and for your thoughtful comments. However, there are some issues you raised that we strongly feel we need to address. First, it is obvious that our film greatly upset you. In your own words, "it affected [you] strongly," and filled you "with sadness and disquiet." You admitted that the film "works." Nevertheless, you urged the public "to avoid it, and you went so far as to resort to expletives: "Why do we need this s——t?", you asked.

As your colleague at the Chicago Daily Herald *commented, Chaos "marks the first real post-9/11 horror film," and "the horror reality has long ago surpassed the horror of Japanese movies and PG-13 films." Simply put, the* Herald *gets it and you do not.*

Natalie Holloway. Kidnappings and beheadings in Iraq shown on the Internet. Wives blasting jail guards with shotguns to free their husbands. The confessions of the BTK killer. These are events of the last few months. How else should filmmakers address this "ugly, nihilistic, and cruel" reality—other than with scenes that are "ugly, nihilistic, and cruel," to use the words you used to describe Chaos.

Mr. Ebert, would you prefer it if instead we exploit these ugly, nihilistic, and cruel events by sanitizing them, like the PG-13 horror films do, or like the cable networks do, to titillate and attract audiences without exposing the real truth, the real evil?

Mr. Ebert, how do you want twenty-first century evil to be portrayed in film and in the media? Tame and sanitized? Titillating and exploitive? Or do you want evil portrayed as it really is? "Ugly, nihilistic, and cruel," as you say our film does it?

We tried to give you and the public something real. Real evil exists and cannot be ignored, sanitized, or exploited. It needs to be shown just as it is, WHICH IS WHY WE NEED THIS S——T, to use your own coarse words. And if this upsets you, or "disquiets" you, or leaves you "saddened," that's the point. So instead of telling the public to avoid this film, shouldn't you let them make their own decision?

> *Respectfully,*
> *Steven Jay Bernheim*
> *Producer, Chaos*
> *David Defalco*
> *Director, Chaos*

And my response to the *Chaos* ad:

Dear Mr. Bernheim and Mr. Defalco,

Your film does "work," and as filmmakers you have undeniable skills and gifts. The question is, did you put them to a defensible purpose? I believed you did not. I urged my readers to avoid seeing the film. I have also urged them to see many films. Moviegoers make up their own minds. Like many at the screening I attended, I left saddened and disgusted. Michael Mirasol, a fellow critic, asked me why I even wrote a review, and I answered: "It will get about the audience it would have gotten anyway, but it deserves to be dealt with and replied to."

Yes, you got a good review from the Daily Herald, *but every other major critic who has seen the movie shares my view. Maybe we do "get it." As Michael Wilmington wrote in his zero-star review in the* Chicago Tribune, *the* movie "*definitely gave me the worst time I've had at a movie in years—and I wouldn't recommend it to anyone but my worst enemies. And from Laura Kern at the* New York Times: *"Stay far, far away from this one."* The line "why do we need this s——t" was not original with me; I quoted it from Ed Gonzalez at slantmagzine.com, who did not use any dashes in his version. I find it ironic that the makers of Chaos would scold me for using "coarse" language and "resorting to expletives."

But there is a larger question here. In a time of dismay and dread, is it admirable for filmmakers to depict pure evil? Have 9/11, suicide bombers, serial killers, and kidnappings created a world in which the response of the artist must be nihilistic and hopeless? At the end of your film, after the other characters have been killed in sadistic and gruesome ways, the only survivor is the one who is evil incarnate, and we hear his cold laughter under a screen that has gone dark.

I believe art can certainly be nihilistic and express hopelessness; the powerful movie Open Water, *about two scuba divers left behind by a tourist boat, is an example. I believe evil can win in fiction, as it often does in real life. But I prefer that the artist express an attitude toward that evil. It is not enough to record it; what do you think and feel about it? Your attitude is as detached as your hero's. If* Chaos *has a message, it is that evil reigns and will triumph. I don't believe so.*

You begin Chaos *with one of those sanctimonious messages depicting the movie as a "warning" that will educate its viewers and possibly save their lives. But what are they to learn? That evil people will torture and murder them if they take any chances, go to parties, or walk in the woods? We can't live our lives in hiding.*

Your real purpose in making Chaos, *I suspect, was not to educate, but to create a scandal that would draw an audience. There's always money to be made by going further and being more shocking. Sometimes there is also art to be found in that direction, but not this time. That's because your film creates a closed system in which any alternative outcome is excluded; it is like a movie of a man falling to his death, which can have no developments except that he continues to fall, and no ending except that he dies. Predestination may be useful in theology, but as a narrative strategy, it is self-defeating.*

I call your attention to two movies you have not mentioned: Ingmar Bergman's The Virgin Spring *(1960) and Wes Craven's* The Last House on the Left *(1972). As Gonzalez, despite his "coarse" language, points out, your film follows* Last House *so closely "that Wes Craven could probably sue Defalco for a dual screenwriting credit and win." Craven, also indebted to Bergman, did a modern horror-film version of the Bergman film, which was set in medieval times. In it, a girl goes into the woods and is raped and murdered. Her killers later happen to stay overnight as guests of the grieving parents. When they discover who they are, the father exacts his revenge. In the Craven version, there is also revenge; I gave the movie a four-star rating, because I felt it was uncommonly effective, even though it got many reviews as negative as my review of* Chaos. *Craven, and to a greater degree Bergman, used the material as a way of dealing with tragedy, human loss, and human nature.*

You use the material without pity, to look unblinkingly at a monster and his victims. The monster is given no responsibility, no motive, no context, no depth. Like a shark, he exists to kill. I am reminded of a great movie about a serial killer, actually named Monster *(2003). In it, innocent people were murdered, but we were not invited to simply stare. The killer was allowed her humanity, which I believe all of us have, even the worst of us. It was possible to see her first as victim, then as murderer.*

The film did not excuse her behavior, but understood that it proceeded from evil done to her. If the film contained a "warning" to "educate" us, it was not that evil will destroy us, but that others will do unto us as we have done unto them. If we do not want monsters like Aileen Wuornos in our world, we should not allow them to have the childhoods that she had. What I miss in your film is any sense of hope. Sometimes it is all that keeps us going. The message of futility and despair in Chaos *is unrelieved, and while I do not require a "happy ending" I do appreciate some kind of catharsis. As the Greeks understood tragedy, it exists not to bury us in death and dismay, but to help us to deal with it, to accept it as a part of life, to learn about our own humanity from it. That is why the Greek tragedies were poems: The language ennobled the material.*

Animals do not know they are going to die and require no way to deal with that implacable fact. Humans, who know we will die, have been given the consolations of art, myth, hope, science, religion, philosophy, and even denial, even movies, to help us reconcile with that final fact. What I object to most of all in Chaos is not the sadism, the brutality, the torture, the nihilism, but the absence of any alternative to them. If the world has indeed become as evil as you think, then we need the redemptive power of artists, poets, philosophers, and theologians more than ever. Your answer, that the world is evil and therefore it is your responsibility to reflect it, is no answer at all, but a surrender.

> *Sincerely,*
> *Roger Ebert*

The Brown Bunny Saga

CANNES, France, May 21, 2003—Coming up for air like an exhausted swimmer, the Cannes Film Festival produced two splendid films on Wednesday morning, after a week of the most dismal entries in memory. Denys Arcand's *The Barbarian Invasion*, from Quebec, and Errol Morris's documentary *The Fog of War*, about Robert McNamara, are in their different ways both masterpieces about old men who find a kind of wisdom.

But that is not the headline. The news is that on Tuesday night, Cannes showed a film so shockingly bad that it created a scandal here on the Riviera not because of sex, violence, or politics, but simply because of its awfulness.

Those who saw Vincent Gallo's *The Brown Bunny* have been gathering ever since, with hushed voices and sad smiles, to discuss how wretched it was. Those who missed it hope to get tickets, for no other film has inspired such discussion. "The worst film in the history of the festival," I told a TV crew posted outside the theater. I have not seen every film in the history of the festival, yet I feel my judgment will stand.

Imagine ninety tedious minutes of a man driving across America in a van. Imagine long shots through a windshield as it collects bug splats. Imagine not one but two scenes in which he stops for gas. Imagine a long shot on the Bonneville Salt Flats where he races his motorcycle until it disappears as a speck in the distance, followed by another shot in which a speck in the distance becomes his motorcycle. Imagine a film so unendurably boring that at one point, when he gets out of his van to change his shirt, there is applause.

And then, after half the audience has walked out and those who remain stay because they will never again see a film so amateurish, narcissistic, self-indulgent, and bloody-minded, imagine a scene where the hero's lost girl reappears, performs fellatio in a hard-core scene, and then reveals the sad truth of their relationship.

Of Vincent Gallo, the film's star, writer, producer, director, editor, and only begetter, it can be said that this talented actor must have been out of his mind to (a) make this film, and (b) allow it to be seen. Of Chloë Sevigny, who plays the girlfriend, Daisy, it must be said that she brings a truth and vulnerability to her scene that exists on a level far above the movie it is in.

If Gallo had thrown away all of the rest of the movie and made the Sevigny scene into a short film, he would have had something. That this film was admitted into Cannes as an Official Selection is inexplicable. By no standard, through no lens, in any interpretation, does it qualify for Cannes. The quip is: This is the most anti-American film at Cannes, because it is so anti-American to show it as an example of American filmmaking.

Interview with Vincent Gallo

August 29, 2004—Vincent Gallo and I have a history. In May 2003, I called his *Brown Bunny* the worst film in the history of the Cannes Film Festival. Then he put a hex on me to give me colon cancer. Now we're about to meet for the first time.

It was a little tense in the Lake Street Screening Room, following the screening of the re-edited, shorter version of *The Brown Bunny*. I heard Gallo was in the elevator. I heard he was in the hallway. I heard he was around the corner. Then there he was. The atmosphere lightened after he explained he had never wished colon cancer on me in the first place. He was misquoted. He actually specified prostate cancer.

"You know how that happened?" he asked. "I have prostatitis. I go to this guy doctor in California. He doesn't want to put me on antibiotics or whatever. But I get these things called a prostate massage."

"Are you taking flaxseed?" I asked him.

"I know all my nutritional things," he said. "I had been battling this prostatitis and a reporter who I didn't know said, 'I'm doing a story on Cannes and I want to know if you read what Roger Ebert said about your film.' I said, yeah, I read all about it. 'Well, do you have any comment?' And I said something like, 'Tell him I curse his prostate.' I said it in a joking way. And she converted it into a curse on your colon. At that point, I had become the captain of black magic."

"I don't believe in hexes," I said. "Besides, if I can't take it, I shouldn't dish it out."

"Right."

"Maybe by saying you made the worst film in Cannes history, I was asking for it."

"But I thought your response was funny when you responded with the colonoscopy line."

That was when I said the film of my colonoscopy was more entertaining than *The Brown Bunny*.

"I felt we were now on a humorous level," he said, "so I apologized. To tell you the weirdest story, I started getting these letters from cultist people criticizing me for going back on what they thought was like a genius thing I did. There was this guy in L.A. who approached me in a club and he was like, 'We're really disappointed in you.' And I asked why. And he said, 'Because we heard that you removed the curse from Roger Ebert.' I took one look at him and I thought, well, I did the right thing."

"Anyway, your aim was bad," I said, "because I had salivary cancer."

We had not yet actually discussed the Worst Film in the History of the Cannes Film Festival, so I broke the ice: "I've got to tell you, it's a different film now. I have to start over in the process of reviewing it because it's not the film I saw at Cannes. I think it's a better film."

The Brown Bunny involves several days in the life of a motorcycle racer named Bud Clay, who loses a race and drives his van cross-country while bugs collect on the windshield and he has sad, elusive encounters with lonely women. At the end of his odyssey, he seeks out his great former love, Daisy (Chloë Sevigny), and, like Gatsby, discovers that the light is out at the end of Daisy's pier.

"Did you know the lead-up to Cannes?" Gallo asked. "Did you know why it was shown at Cannes? Did you know what state it was in?"

I said I'd heard he let it be shown even though he wasn't finished with it.

That was the tip of the iceberg. Gallo's explanation of the pre-Cannes adventures of *The Brown Bunny* ran to 1,487 words (I know because I transcribed the interview). The highlights include:

- "I got involved in the film in a sacrificial way, beyond my normal self-abuse—like not eating, not sleeping, freaking out about unimportant things. Like, I had to use these Mitchell lenses, these Bausch & Lomb lenses, but I had to have them converted and it took a year. I was bringing all my good and bad habits into this project."

- "I had to postpone the racing sequences because I couldn't train in time and I was having problems with the motorcycles and I wasn't riding well."

- "Chloë had to shift her schedule a month and a half and I wanted to film her scene first because I wanted to sense the vibe of that scene and play off that vibe for the rest of the film. So the postponements cost me three months."

- "Curtis Clayton, who edited *Buffalo '66* with me, calls me every day—'It's the greatest, you've covered everything, the film looks great.' I just wanted him to look at the footage, tell me if anything was scratched or not usable, and then we would edit together. I finish shooting and he works one day with me, and he makes an odd face and says, 'You know, I've told you if I ever get my film financed I might not be able to finish this film.' I'm like, oh yeah, no problem, we should be done anyway. He says, 'Well, Ed Pressman called me while you were at lunch and said my film is green-lit.'"

"Curtis is a beautiful person with a lot of integrity, but he has a sort of smugness. He went, 'So I can work ten more days with you if you want, but that's it.' I said, 'Listen, if you felt you were even coming close, you should have brought me in on that. You cost me $150 grand just to look at my footage.' He goes, 'Well, I have the footage all arranged.'

"I said, 'You don't know the geography of America; I can't go by your things; I'm just gonna wipe the discs clean and I'll reload myself and I'll have it batch-digitized and I'll arrange everything in my way because I don't know if you had a foolproof system where you batch-digitized every frame of the film; you made so many mistakes in *Buffalo '66*—not intentional, but those things happen. I'm a fanatic and I wanna be sure that I have every frame of my picture.

"And we had a little tension, but he's not the kind of person you really have ordinary tension with so he just sort of left in a smug way. And I was freaked out because I could control everything else but I needed Curtis not even so much for his talent but for his voice of reason, his maturity, and his ability to keep me balanced, you know, allowing me to have a point of view and to take radical chances but with balance, you know.

"He leaves and for about two weeks I don't do anything; I'm nervous, very nervous. And I find an assistant who would be one of at least ten assistants, each of them leaving on a bad note because I was extremely unpleasant to work with."

What with one thing and another, the film seemed destined to be finished in September 2003. But then Thierry Fremaux, the artistic director of the Cannes Film Festival, asked to see it.

"I hadn't even cut the motel scene at this point, so not only is the film in rough cut, I haven't even got to the Chloë scene."

The Chloë scene. That would be the scene of graphic oral sex, which contrasts with the earlier scenes in the way pornography might contrast with a travelogue.

"I showed Thierry everything up until the motel scene; he asks if I will be able to finish the film in time for the festival. I say I don't know. I negotiate with the Japanese financiers that I'll rough through the motel scene—which will be good for me, because I've been stuck on it—and I'll make some fake ending because I was supposed to shoot the ending in April, which should have a motorcycle crash at the end."

Where you die?

"Yeah, where I die. A deliberate suicide. Not thinking clearly if I would use it because I had the same dilemma in *Buffalo '66*. I always write the film with the suicide and then I find a way out of it. The guy was gonna have a negative fantasy for a second of the van crashing. There were some shots of bunnies, there was the shot of him on the side of the road. I sort of clipped it together with the song."

The result was one of the most disastrous screenings in Cannes history. I refer to the press screening; at the public screening, reaction was more evenly divided between applause and boos, but the press hated the film. The impression got around that I led the boos, perhaps because the hex on my colon drew untoward attention toward me, but the British trade magazine *Screen International,* which convenes a panel of critics to score each entry, reported that *The Brown Bunny* got the lowest score in the history of its ratings.

Did I sing "Raindrops Keep Fallin' on My Head" at one point? To my shame, I did, but softly and briefly, before my wife dug her elbow into my side. By that point the screening was out of control anyway, with audience members hooting, whistling, and honking at the screen.

As it turns out, the French director Gaspar Noe was seated near me.

"He's not a great pal," Gallo said, "but I do know him, and he sort of twerks me on all the time. He loves to wind me up. And he came out of the screening and left like six messages on my voice mail. And he pinned it all on you, because he was sitting close to you and he presented it to me that you were orchestrating . . ."

But there were three thousand seats in that theater, I said. It got pretty demonstrative.

"Well," said Gallo, "because you asked and it needs to be answered clearly: Did I feel the film was finished at Cannes? No, of course not."

The next day at a press conference, I said, there was the impression you apologized for the film.

"*Screen International* falsely said I apologized for the film. What I said was this: Film has a purpose. It's not art. Real art is an esoteric thing done by somebody without purpose in mind. I've done that in my life and I'm not doing that making movies. I'm an entertainer. I love all movies. I don't divide them up into art films, independent films. *The Brown Bunny* was my idea of what a good movie would be.

"I'm not a marginal person. I don't pretend to be a cult figure. I'm just making a movie and I think the film is beautiful and I think, wow, everybody's gonna see how beautiful it is and when they don't agree with me, then in a sense I failed. I didn't fail myself because I made what I think is beautiful and I stand behind thinking that it's beautiful. I've only failed in this commercial way because I haven't entertained the crowd. If people don't like my movie, then I'm sorry they didn't like my movie. But I wasn't apologizing for it."

This new version, I said, is a lot shorter and in my opinion a lot better. It has a rhythm and tone that the Cannes version lacked.

"Seeing my film for the first time at Cannes," he said, "I was able to see what was wrong. It was clear that the Colorado and Utah piece was too long. There was also a dissolve where the film turned black for a minute. That was a mistake in the lab. Now if that mistake happened in a hundred other movies at Cannes, the audience would have been prepared to look past it. But because the film was so extreme and so untightened at that time, it really stood out."

What did you take out?

"What changed was the opening sequence. I shortened the race, which was a good four and a half minutes longer. The whole film at Cannes was exactly twenty-six minutes longer. The credits were three and a half minutes longer at the end, and one minute longer in the beginning. So that's about nine, ten minutes there. So there's sixteen more minutes of changes, and here's where the biggest chunk came. When he comes out of the Kansas motel, he does not wash the car, he does not change his sweater, and he does not go on that sequence through Colorado and Utah. Eight minutes and thirty seconds came out of that driving sequence.

"The other cuts were in the motel scene. . . . I rambled on maybe another two or three minutes. And those road shots at the end were about another minute leading up to the closing sequence, and then I cut out the end, which was three and a half or four minutes. That's what I cut. There's no tightening or tweaking anywhere else."

Now about the motel scene. That's where the hero imagines a reunion with his onetime lover and she performs oral sex in a graphic scene that gained even greater notoriety after a soft-focus shot of it appeared on a Sunset Strip billboard for three or four days before it was abruptly removed.

"I wanted to show what people do every day all over the world," Gallo said. "In sexualized behavior, your mind fills up with the intimacy of sexual thoughts, but in my character it stays locked in resentment, fear, anger, guilt. When you juxtapose that against images you're used to seeing for the purpose of enhancing pleasure, I felt it could create a disturbing effect. It's metaphysical. You're seeing how he visualizes his own sexuality.

"Never in my life have I had sexual or violent images as components in any of my work and this was not the inspiration of a provocateur; that was not the goal. Some people respond to it deeply in the way that it was intended."

I know what he means. But to explain why the scene works that way, you have to know something it would be unfair to reveal at this point—something about how the scene enters the realm of the character's disturbed mind.

We talked a lot longer. Gallo grew confessional: "When I modeled for some ads, people started saying, oh, you've done modeling. I mean, I know what I look like. My mother knows what I look like, and when you call a person like me a model, I'm aware of people sort of snickering at that comment, so it embarrasses me."

Apart from the news that he is a Republican, that was the most astonishing revelation he made: He doesn't like the way he looks. I disagree; I find him a striking screen presence. His comment provided me with an insight into his character in *The Brown Bunny,* a lonely, solitary wanderer whose life traverses a great emptiness punctuated by unsuccessful, incomplete, or imaginary respites with women.

That's related to something else he said:

"The inspiration for the film was, I was at a discotheque once and I noticed a pretty gal, but it was during a period in my life where I could never talk to a girl that I thought was smart or pretty or interesting in any way. I would just stare at them. And I stared at her and at 11 p.m. she was having fun, she was drinking a little. Three in the morning she was hammered. She was on the floor and the guys in the room were sort of moving around her. They noticed this sort of broken-winged bird or wounded animal. They were like hyenas. It was one of the ugliest things I've ever seen. I saw them eventually leave with her. And it upset me conceptually. I felt the ugliness of mankind's basic nature can be avoided. That's what *The Brown Bunny* is about."

The Brown Bunny

(DIRECTED BY VINCENT GALLO; STARRING VINCENT GALLO, CHLOË SEVIGNY; 2004)
In May of 2003, I walked out of the press screening of Vincent Gallo's *The Brown Bunny* at the Cannes Film Festival and was asked by a camera crew what I thought of the film. I said I thought it was the worst film in the history of the festival. That was hyperbole—I hadn't seen every film in the history of the festival—but I was still vibrating from one of the most disastrous screenings I had ever attended.

The audience was loud and scornful in its dislike for the movie; hundreds walked out, and many of those who remained stayed only because they wanted to boo. Imagine, I wrote, a film so unendurably boring that when the hero changes into a clean shirt, there is applause. The panel of critics convened by *Screen International,* the British trade paper, gave the movie the lowest rating in the history of their annual voting.

But then a funny thing happened. Gallo went back into the editing room and cut 26 minutes of his 118-minute film, or almost a fourth of the running time. And in the process he transformed it. The film's form and purpose now emerge from the miasma of the original cut, and are quietly, sadly effective. It is said that editing is the soul of the cinema; in the case of *The Brown Bunny,* it is its salvation.

Critics who saw the film last autumn at the Venice and Toronto festivals walked in expecting the disaster they'd read about from Cannes. Here is Bill Chambers of Film Freak Central, writing from Toronto: "Ebert catalogued his mainstream biases (unbroken takes: bad; nonclassical structure: bad; name actresses being aggressively sexual: bad) . . . and then had a bigger delusion of grandeur than *The Brown Bunny*'s Gallo-centric credit assignations: 'I will one day be thin, but Vincent Gallo will always be the director of *The Brown Bunny.*'"

Faithful readers will know that I admire long takes, especially by Ozu, that I hunger for nonclassical structure, and that I have absolutely nothing against sex in the cinema. In quoting my line about one day being thin, Chambers might in fairness have explained that I was responding to Gallo calling me a "fat pig"—and, for that matter, since I made that statement I have lost eighty-six pounds and Gallo is indeed still the director of *The Brown Bunny.*

But he is not the director of the same *Brown Bunny* I saw at Cannes, and the film now plays so differently that I suggest the original Cannes cut be included as part of the eventual DVD, so that viewers can see for themselves how twenty-six minutes of aggressively pointless and empty footage can sink a potentially successful film. To cite but one cut: From Cannes, I wrote: "Imagine a long shot on the Bonneville Salt Flats where he races his motorcycle until it disappears as a speck in the distance, followed by another long shot in which a speck in the distance becomes his motorcycle." In the new version we see the motorcycle disappear, but the second half of the shot has been completely cut. That helps in two ways: (1) It saves the scene from an unintended laugh, and (2) it provides an emotional purpose, since to disappear into the distance is a much different thing than to ride away and then ride back again.

The movie stars Gallo as Bud Clay, a professional motorcycle racer who loses a race on the East Coast and then drives his van cross-country. (The race in the original film lasted 270 seconds longer than in the current version, and was all in one shot, of cycles going around and around a track.) Bud is a lonely, inward, needy man, who thinks much about a former lover whose name in American literature has come to embody idealized, inaccessible love: Daisy.

Gallo allows himself to be defenseless and unprotected in front of the camera, and that is a strength. Consider an early scene where he asks a girl behind the counter at a convenience store to join him on the trip to California. When she declines, he says "please" in a pleading tone of voice not one actor in a hundred would have the nerve to imitate. There's another scene not long after that has a sorrowful poetry. In a town somewhere in the middle of America, at a table in a park, a woman (Cheryl Tiegs) sits by herself. Bud Clay parks his van, walks over to her, senses her despair, asks her some questions, and wordlessly hugs and kisses her. She never says a word. After a time he leaves again. There is a kind of communication going on here that is complete and heartbreaking, and needs not one word of explanation, and gets none.

In the original version, there was an endless, pointless sequence of Bud driving through Western states and collecting bug splats on his windshield; the eight and a half minutes Gallo has taken out of that sequence were as exciting as watching paint after it has already dried. Now he arrives sooner in California, and there is the now-famous scene in a motel room involving Daisy (Chloë Sevigny). Yes, it is explicit, and no, it is not gratuitous.

But to reveal how it works on a level more complex than the physical would be to undermine the way the scene pays off. The scene, and its dialogue, and a flashback to the Daisy character at a party, work together to illuminate complex things about Bud's sexuality, his guilt, and his feelings about women. Even at Cannes, even after unendurably superfluous footage, that scene worked, and I wrote: "It must be said that [Sevigny] brings a truth and vulnerability to her scene that exists on a level far above the movie it is in." Gallo takes the materials of pornography and repurposes them into a scene about control and need, fantasy, and perhaps even madness. That scene is many things, but erotic is not one of them. (A female friend of mine observed that Bud Clay, like many men, has a way of asking a woman questions just when she is least prepared to answer them.)

When movies were cut on Movieolas, there was a saying that they could be "saved on the green machine." Make no mistake: The Cannes version was a bad film, but now Gallo's editing has set free the good film inside. *The Brown Bunny* is still not a complete success—it is odd and off-putting when it doesn't want to be—but as a study of loneliness and need, it evokes a tender sadness. I will always be grateful I saw the movie at Cannes; you can't understand where Gallo has arrived unless you know where he started.

A

· · · · · · · · ·

Alex & Emma

(DIRECTED BY ROB REINER; STARRING KATE HUDSON, LUKE WILSON; 2003)

Alex & Emma is a movie about a guy who has to write a novel in thirty days in order to collect the money from his publisher to pay two gamblers who will otherwise kill him. So he hires a stenographer to take dictation, and they fall in love. But the thing is, it's a bad novel. Very bad. Every time the author started dictating, I was struck anew by how bad it was—so bad it's not even good romance fiction.

I guess I didn't expect him to write *The Gambler* by Dostoyevsky—although, come to think of it, Dostoyevsky dictated *The Gambler* in thirty days to pay off a gambling debt, and fell in love with his stenographer. I just expected him to write something presentable. You might reasonably ask why we even need to know what he's writing in the first place, since the story involves the writer and the girl. But, alas, it involves much more: There are cutaways to the story he's writing, and its characters are played by Kate Hudson and Luke Wilson, the same two actors who star in the present-day story.

This other story takes place in 1924 and involves people who dress and act like the characters in *The Great Gatsby.* Not the central characters, but the characters who attend Gatsby's parties and are in those long lists of funny names. It might have been a funny idea for the novelist to actually steal *The Great Gatsby,* confident that neither the gamblers nor his publisher would recognize it, but funny ideas are not easy to come by in *Alex & Emma.*

Alex is played by Luke Wilson. Emma is played by Kate Hudson. He also plays Adam, the young hero of the story within the story, and she plays four different nannies (Swedish, German, Latino, and American) who are employed by a rich French divorcée (Sophie Marceau) who plans to marry a rich guy (David Paymer) for his money, but is tempted by the handsome young Adam, who is a tutor to her children, who remain thoroughly untutored.

So the story is a bore. The act of writing the story is also a bore, because it consists mostly of trying out variations on the 1924 plot and then seeing how they look in the parallel story. Of course chemistry develops between Alex and Emma, who fall in love, and just as well: There is a Hollywood law requiring fictional characters in such a situation to fall in love, and the penalty for violating it is death at the box office. A lot of people don't know that.

Curious, the ease with which Alex is able to dictate his novel. Words flow in an uninterrupted stream, all perfectly punctuated. No false starts, wrong word choices, or despair. Emma writes everything down and then offers helpful suggestions, although she fails to supply the most useful observation of all, which would be to observe that the entire novel is complete crap.

Despite the deadly deadline, which looms ever closer, the young couple finds time to get out of the apartment and enjoy a Semi-Obligatory Lyrical Interlude, that old standby where they walk through the park, eat hot dogs, etc., in a montage about a great day together. I do not remember if they literally walk through the park or eat hot dogs, but if they don't, then they engage in park-like and hot dog–like activities.

Now about his apartment. It's at the top of a classic brownstone, with balconies and tall windows, and in Manhattan would cost thousands of dollars a month, but he's flat broke, see, and just to prove it, there's a place where the plaster has fallen off the wall and you can see the bare slats underneath. He has art hanging all over his apartment, except in front of those slats. All Alex has to do is sublet, and his financial worries are over.

The movie has been directed by Rob Reiner and is not as bad as *The Story of Us* (1999), but this is a movie they'll want to hurry past during the AFI tribute. Reiner has made wonderful movies in the past (*Misery, The Princess Bride, Stand by Me*) and even wonderful romantic comedies (*The Sure Thing, When Harry Met Sally*). He will make wonderful movies in the future. He has not, however, made a wonderful movie in the present.

All the Queen's Men

(DIRECTED BY STEFAN RUZOWITZKY; STARRING MATT LEBLANC, EDDIE IZZARD; 2002)
All the Queen's Men is a perfectly good idea for a comedy, but it just plain doesn't work. It's dead in the water. I can imagine it working well in a different time, with a different cast, in black-and-white instead of color—but I can't imagine it working like this.

The movie tells the story of the "Poof Platoon," a group of four Allied soldiers who parachute into Berlin in drag to infiltrate the all-woman factory where the Enigma machine is being manufactured. This story is said to be based on fact. If it is, I am amazed that such promising material would yield such pitiful results. To impersonate a woman and a German at the same time would have been so difficult and dangerous that it's amazing how the movie turns it into a goofy lark.

The film stars Matt LeBlanc, from *Friends,* who is criminally miscast as Steven O'Rourke, a U.S. officer famous for never quite completing heroic missions. He is teamed with a drag artist named Tony (Eddie Izzard), an ancient major named Archie (James Cosmo), and a scholar named Johnno (David Birkin). After brief lessons in hair, makeup, undergarments, and espionage, they're dropped into Berlin during an air raid and try to make contact with a resistance leader.

This underground hero turns out to be the lovely and fragrant Romy (Nicolette Krebitz), a librarian who, for the convenience of the plot, lives in a loft under the roof of the library, so that (during one of many unbelievable scenes) the spies are able to lift a skylight window in order to eavesdrop on an interrogation.

The plot requires them to infiltrate the factory, steal an Enigma machine, and return to England with it. Anyone who has seen *Enigma, U-571,* or the various TV documentaries about the Enigma machine will be aware that by the time of this movie, the British already had possession of an Enigma machine, but to follow that line of inquiry too far in this movie is not wise. The movie has an answer to it, but it comes so late in the film that although it makes sense technically, the damage has already been done.

The four misfit transvestites totter about Berlin looking like (very bad) Andrews Sisters imitators, and O'Rourke falls in love with the librarian

Romy. How it becomes clear that he is not a woman is not nearly as interesting as how anyone could possibly have thought he was a woman in the first place. He plays a woman as if determined, in every scene, to signal to the audience that he's absolutely straight and only kidding. His voice, with its uncanny similarity to Sylvester Stallone's, doesn't help.

The action in the movie would be ludicrous anyway, but is even more peculiar in a cross-dressing comedy. There's a long sequence in which Tony, the Izzard character, does a marked-down Marlene Dietrich before a wildly enthusiastic audience of Nazis. Surely they know he is, if not a spy, at least a drag queen? I'm not so sure. I fear the movie makes it appear the Nazis think he is a sexy woman, something that will come as a surprise to anyone who is familiar with Eddie Izzard, including Eddie Izzard.

Watching the movie, it occurred to me that Tony Curtis and Jack Lemmon were not any more convincing as women in *Some Like It Hot.* And yet we bought them in that comedy, and it remains a classic. Why did they work, while the Queen's Men manifestly do not? Apart from the inescapable difference in actual talent, could it have anything to do with the use of color?

Black-and-white is better suited to many kinds of comedy because it underlines the dialogue and movement while diminishing the importance of fashions and eliminating the emotional content of various colors. Billy Wilder fought for black-and-white on *Some Like It Hot* because he thought his drag queens would never be accepted by the audience in color, and he was right.

The casting is also a problem. Matt LeBlanc does not belong in this movie in any role other than, possibly, that of a Nazi who believes Eddie Izzard is a woman. He is all wrong for the lead, with no lightness, no humor, no sympathy for his fellow spies, and no comic timing. I can imagine this movie as a black-and-white British comedy, circa 1960, with Peter Sellers, Kenneth Williams, et al., but at this time, with this cast, this movie is hopeless.

Almost Salinas

(DIRECTED BY TERRY GREEN; STARRING JOHN MAHONEY, LINDA EMOND; 2003)

Almost Salinas is a sweet and good-hearted portrait of an isolated cross-roads and the people who live there or are drawn into their lives. Shame about the plot. The people are real, but the story devices are clunkers from Fiction 101; the movie generates goodwill in its setup, but in the last act it goes haywire with revelations and secrets and dramatic gestures. The movie takes place in Cholame, the California town where James Dean died in 1955, and maybe the only way to save it would have been to leave out everything involving James Dean.

John Mahoney stars as Max Harris, the proprietor of a diner in a sparsely populated backwater. He's thinking of reopening the old gas station. Virginia Madsen is Clare, his waitress, and other locals include Nate Davis, as an old-timer who peddles James Dean souvenirs from a roadside table, and Ian Gomez, as the salt-of-the-earth cook.

The town experiences an unusual flurry of activity. A film crew arrives to shoot a movie about the death of James Dean. Max's ex-wife, Allie (Lindsay Crouse), turns up. And a magazine writer named Nina Ellington (Linda Emond) arrives to do a feature about the reopening of the gas station. If this seems like an unlikely subject for a story, reflect that she stays so long she could do the reporting on the reopening of a refinery. She gradually falls in love with Max, while one of the young members of the film crew falls for Clare's young assistant behind the counter.

The place and the people are sound. Mahoney has the gift of bringing quiet believability to a character; his Max seems dependable, kind, and loyal. Virginia Madsen is the spark of the place, not a stereotyped, gum-chewing hash slinger, but a woman who takes an interest in the people who come her way. If Emond is not very convincing as the visiting reporter, perhaps it's because her job is so unlikely. Better, perhaps, to make her a woman with no reason at all to be in Cholame. Let her stay because she has no place better to go, and then let her fall in love.

From the movie's opening moments, there are quick black-and-white shots of Dean's 1955 Porsche Spyder, racing along a rural highway toward its rendezvous with death. The arrival of the film crew, with its own model of the same car, introduces a series of parallels between past and present that it would be unfair to reveal.

Spoiler warning! Without spelling everything out, let us observe, however, that it is unlikely that a character who was locally famous in 1955 could stay in the same area and become anonymous just by changing his name. It is also unlikely that he would be moved, so many years later, to the actions he takes in the film. And cosmically unlikely that they would have the results that they do. Not to mention how pissed off the film company would be.

As the movie's great revelations started to slide into view, I slipped down in my seat, fearful that the simple and engaging story of these nice people would be upstaged by the grinding mechanics of plot contrivance. My fears were well grounded. *Almost Salinas* generates enormous goodwill and then loses it by betraying its characters to the needs of a plot that wants to inspire pathos and sympathy, but inspires instead, alas, groans and the rolling of eyes.

The Amati Girls

(DIRECTED BY ANNE DE SALVO; STARRING CLORIS LEACHMAN, MERCEDES RUEHL; 2001)

A lot of saints are mentioned in *The Amati Girls,* including Christopher, Lucy, Cecelia, Theresa (the Little Flower), and the BVM herself, but the movie should be praying to St. Jude, patron saint of lost causes. Maybe he could perform a miracle and turn this into a cable offering, so no one has to pay to see it.

The movie's a tour of timeworn clichés about family life, performed with desperation by a talented cast. Alone among them, Mercedes Ruehl somehow salvages her dignity while all about her are losing theirs. She even manages to avoid appearing in the shameless last shot, where the ladies dance around the kitchen singing "Doo-wah-diddy, diddy-dum, diddy-dum."

The movie is about a large Italian-American family in Philadelphia. Too large, considering that every character has a crisis, and the story races from one to another like the guy on TV who kept all the plates spinning on top of the poles. This family not only has a matriarch (Cloris Leachman) but her superfluous sister (Lee Grant) and their even more superfluous sister (Edith Field). There are also four grown daughters, two husbands, two hopeful fiancés, at least three kids, and probably some dogs, although we never see them because they are probably hiding under the table to avoid being stepped on.

The adult sisters are Grace (Ruehl), who is married to macho-man Paul Sorvino ("No Padrone male will ever step foot on a ballet stage except as a teamster."); Denise (Dinah Manoff), who is engaged to Lawrence (Mark Harmon) but dreams of show biz (she sings "Kiss of Fire" to demonstrate her own need for St. Jude); Christine (Sean Young), whose husband, Paul (Jamey Sheridan), is a workaholic; and poor Dolores (Lily Knight), who is retarded. Denise and Christine think Grace is ruining her life with guilt because when she was a little girl she ran away and her mother chased her and fell, which of course caused Dolores to be retarded.

Sample subplot: Dolores decides she wants a boyfriend. At the church bingo night, she sits opposite Armand (Doug Spinuzza), who, we are told "has a head full of steel" after the Gulf War. This has not resulted in Armand being a once-normal person with brain damage, but, miraculously, in his being exactly like Dolores. At the movies, after they kiss, he shyly puts his hand on her breast, and she shyly puts her hand on his.

You know the obligatory scene where the reluctant parent turns up at the last moment for the child's big moment onstage? No less than two fathers do it in this movie. Both Joe (Sorvino) and Paul have daughters in a ballet recital, and not only does Joe overcome his loathing for ballet and even attend rehearsals, but Paul overcomes his workaholism and arrives backstage in time to appear with his daughter.

The movie has one unexpected death, of course. That inspires a crisis of faith, and Dolores breaks loose from the funeral home, enters the church, and uses a candlestick to demolish several saints, although she is stopped before she gets to the BVM. There are also many meals in which everyone sits around long tables and talks at once. There is the obligatory debate about who is better, Frank Sinatra or Tony Bennett. And an irritating editing twitch: We are shown the outside of every location before we cut inside. There is also one priceless conversation, in which Lee Grant explains to Cloris Leachman that her hair is tinted "copper bamboo bronze." For Cloris, she suggests "toasted desert sunrise." The Little Flower had the right idea. She cut off her hair and became a Carmelite.

American Outlaws

(DIRECTED BY LES MAYFIELD; STARRING COLIN FARRELL, SCOTT CAAN; 2001)

For years there have been reports of the death of the Western. Now comes *American Outlaws,* proof that even the B Western is dead. It only wants to be a bad movie, and fails. Imagine the cast of *American Pie* given a camera, lots of money, costumes, and horses, and told to act serious and pretend to be cowboys, and this is what you might get.

The movie tells the story of the gang formed by Jesse James and Cole Younger after the Civil War—a gang which, in this movie, curiously embodies the politics of the antiglobalization demonstrators in Seattle, Sweden, and Genoa. A railroad is a-comin' through, and they don't want it. When the railroad hires Pinkertons to blow up farms, and Jesse and Frank's mother is blowed up real good, the boys vow revenge. They will steal the railroad's payroll from banks, and blow up tracks.

It is curious that they are against the railroad. In much better movies like *The Claim,* the coming of the railroad is seen by everybody as an economic windfall, and it creates fortunes by where it decides to lay its tracks. For farmers, it was a lifeblood—a fast and cheap way to get livestock and crops to market. But the James farm is one of those movie farms where nothing much is done. There are no visible herds or crops, just some chickens scratching in the dirt, and Ma James (Kathy Bates) apparently works it by herself while the boys are off to war. Her hardest labor during the whole movie is her death scene.

Jesse James is played by Colin Farrell, who turned on instant star quality in the Vietnam War picture *Tigerland* (2001) and turns it off here. That this movie got a theatrical push and *Tigerland* didn't is proof that

American distribution resembles a crapshoot. Scott Caan plays Jesse's partner, Cole Younger; Gabriel Macht is Frank James; and Jim and Bob Younger are played by Gregory Smith and Will McCormack. Farrell here seems less like the leader of a gang than the lead singer in a boy band, and indeed he and the boys spend time arguing about their billing. Should it be the James Gang? The James-Younger Gang? The Younger-James Gang? (Naw, that sounds like there's an Older James Gang.) There was a great American film about the James-Younger Gang, Philip Kaufman's *The Great Northfield, Minnesota, Raid* (1972), and this movie crouches in its shadow like the Nickelodeon version.

According to *American Outlaws*, Jesse James was motivated not by money but by righteous anger (and publicity—all the boys liked being famous). After getting his revenge and knocking over countless banks, what he basically wants to do is retire from the gang and get himself a farm and settle down with pretty Zee Mimms (Ali Larter). His delusion that the most famous bank robber in America—the perpetrator, indeed, of "the first daylight bank robbery in American history"—could peacefully return to the farm is an indication of his grasp of reality, which is limited.

While we are musing about how many nighttime robberies there had been in American history, we meet the villains. The railroad is owned by Thaddeus Raines (Harris Yulin), who lectures about "the righteousness of progress," and the hired goons are led by Allan Pinkerton (Timothy Dalton), who spends most of the movie looking as if he knows a great deal more than he is saying, some of it about Jesse James, the rest about this screenplay.

There is some truth to the story; the James home really was bombed by the Pinkertons, although Ma didn't die, she only lost an arm. But there's little truth in the movie, which makes the James-Younger Gang seem less like desperadoes than ornery cutups. The shoot-outs follow the timeless movie rule that the villains can't aim and the heroes can't miss. Dozens of extras are killed and countless stuntmen topple forward off buildings, but the stars are treated with the greatest economy, their deaths doled out parsimoniously according to the needs of the formula screenplay.

Should cruel mischance lead you to see this movie, do me a favor and rent Kaufman's *The Great Northfield, Minnesota, Raid* and then meditate on the fact that giants once walked the land in Hollywood. The style, class, and intelligence of a Western like that (in an era which also gave us *The Wild Bunch*) is like a rebuke to *American Outlaws*. What happened to the rough-hewn American intelligence that gave us the Westerns of Ford, Hawks, and Peckinpah? When did cowboys become teen pop idols?

Anatomy of Hell

(DIRECTED BY CATHERINE BREILLAT; STARRING AMIRA CASAR, ROCCO SIFFREDI; 2004) She is the only woman in a gay nightclub. She goes into the toilet and cuts her wrist. He follows her in, sees what she has done, and takes her to a drugstore, where the wound is bandaged. If you cut your wrist and there's time to go to the drugstore, maybe you weren't really trying. He asks her why she did it. "Because I'm a woman," she says, although she might more accurately have replied, "Because I'm a woman in a Catherine Breillat movie."

Breillat is the bold French director whose specialty is female sexuality. Sometimes she is wise about it, as in *36 Fillette* (1989), the story of a troubled teenager who begins a series of risky flirtations with older men. Or in *Fat Girl* (2001), about the seething resentment of a pudgy twelve-year-old toward her sexpot older sister. Sometimes she is provocative about it, as in *Romance* (1999), which is about a frustrated woman's dogged search for orgasm. But sometimes she is just plain goofy, as in *Anatomy of Hell*, which plays like porn dubbed by bitter deconstructionist theoreticians.

The Woman makes an offer to The Man. She will pay him good money to watch her, simply watch her, for four nights. He keeps his end of the bargain, but there were times when I would have paid good money to not watch them, simply not watch them. I remember when hardcore first became commonplace, and there were discussions about what it would be like if a serious director ever made a porn movie. The answer, judging by *Anatomy of Hell*, is that the audience would decide they did not require such a serious director after all.

The Woman believes men hate women, and that gay men hate them even more than straight men, who, however, hate them quite enough.

Men fear women, fear their menstrual secrets, fear their gynecological mysteries, fear that during sex they might disappear entirely within the woman and be imprisoned again by the womb. To demonstrate her beliefs, The Woman disrobes completely and displays herself on a bed, while The Man sits in a chair and watches her, occasionally rousing himself for a shot of Jack on the rocks.

They talk. They speak as only the French can speak, as if it is not enough for a concept to be difficult, it must be impenetrable. No two real people in the history of mankind have ever spoken like this, save perhaps for some of Catherine Breillat's friends that even she gets bored by. "Your words are inept reproaches, they say, and I bless the day I was made immune to you and all your kind." After a few days of epigrams, they suddenly and sullenly have sex, and make a mess of the sheets.

Some events in this movie cannot be hinted at in a family newspaper. Objects emerge to the light of day that would distinguish target practice in a Bangkok sex show. There are moments when you wish they'd lighten up a little by bringing in the guy who bites off chicken heads.

Of course we are expected to respond on a visceral level to the movie's dirge about the crimes of men against women, which, it must be said, are hard to keep in mind given the crimes of The Woman against The Man, and the transgressions committed by The Director against Us. The poor guy is just as much a prop here as men usually are in porn films. He is played by Rocco Siffredi, an Italian porn star. The Woman is played by Amira Casar, who is completely nude most of the time, although the opening titles inform us that a body double will be playing her close-ups in the more action-packed scenes. "It's not her body," the titles explain, "it's an extension of a fictional character." Tell that to the double.

No doubt the truth can be unpleasant, but I am not sure that unpleasantness is the same as the truth. There are scenes here where Breillat deliberately disgusts us, not because we are disgusted by the natural life functions of women, as she implies, but simply because The Woman does things that would make any reasonable Man, or Woman, for that matter, throw up.

Annapolis

(DIRECTED BY JUSTIN LIN; STARRING JAMES FRANCO, TYRESE GIBSON; 2006)

Here I am at Sundance 2006. Four years ago I sat in the Park City Library and saw a film named *Better Luck Tomorrow* by a young man named Justin Lin, and I joined in the cheers. This was a risky, original film by a brilliant new director, who told the story of a group of Asian kids from affluent families in Orange County, who backed into a life of crime with their eyes wide open.

Now it is Sundance again, but I must pause to review *Annapolis,* which is opening in the nation's multiplexes. Let the young directors at Sundance 2006 set aside their glowing reviews and gaze with sad eyes upon this movie, for it is a cautionary lesson. It is the anti-Sundance film, an exhausted wheeze of bankrupt clichés and cardboard characters, the kind of film that has no visible reason for existing, except that everybody got paid.

The movie stars James Franco as Jake Huard, a working-class kid who works as a riveter in a Chesapeake Bay shipyard and gazes in yearning across the waters to the U.S. Naval Academy, which his dead mother always wanted him to attend. His father, Bill (Brian Goodman), opposes the idea: He thinks his kid is too hotheaded to stick it out. But Jake is accepted for an unlikely last-minute opening, and the movie is the story of his plebe year.

That year is the present time, I guess, since Jake is referred to as a member of the class that will graduate in 2008. That means that the Navy is presumably fighting a war somewhere or other in this old world of ours, although there is not a single word about it in the movie. The plebes seem mostly engaged in memorizing the longitude and latitude of Annapolis to avoid doing push-ups.

There is a subplot involving Jake's fat African-American roommate, nicknamed Twins (Vicellous Shannon). There is much suspense over whether Twins can complete the obstacle course in less than five minutes by the end of the year. If I had a year to train under a brutal Marine drill sergeant with his boot up my butt, I could complete the goddamn obstacle course in under five minutes, and so could Queen Latifah.

The drill sergeant is Lt. Cole (Tyrese Gibson), who is a combat-veteran Marine on loan to the academy. Where he saw combat is never mentioned, even when he returns to it at the end of the movie. I've got my money on Iraq. But this movie is not about war. It is about boxing.

Yes, *Annapolis* takes the subject of a young man training to be a Navy officer in a time of war, and focuses its entire plot on whether he can win the "Brigades," which is the academy-wide boxing championship held every spring. It switches from one set of clichés to another in the middle of the film, without missing a single misstep. Because Jake has an attitude and because Cole doubts his ability to lead men, they become enemies, and everything points toward the big match where Jake and Cole will be able to hammer each other in the ring.

I forgot to mention that Jake was an amateur fighter before he entered the academy. His father thought he was a loser at that, too. He tells the old man he's boxing in the finals, but of course the old man doesn't attend. Or could it possibly be that the father, let's say, does attend, but arrives late, and sees the fight, and then his eyes meet the eyes of his son, who is able to spot him immediately in that vast crowd? And does the father give him that curt little nod that means "I was wrong, son, and you have the right stuff?" Surely a movie made in 2006 would not recycle the Parent Arriving Late and Giving Little Nod of Recognition Scene? Surely a director who made *Better Luck Tomorrow* would have nothing to do with such an ancient wheeze, which is not only off the shelf, but off the shelf at the resale store?

Yes, the Navy is at war, and it all comes down to a boxing match. Oh, and a big romance with another of Jake's commanding officers, the cute Ali (Jordana Brewster), who is twenty-five in real life and looks about nineteen in the movie. I have not been to Annapolis, but I think plebes and officers are not supposed to fraternize, kiss, and/or dance and do who knows what else with each other, in spite of the fact that they Meet Cute after he thinks she is a hooker (ho, ho). Ali and the academy's boxing coach (Chi McBride) help train Jake for his big bout.

Here is a movie with dialogue such as:

"You just don't get it, do you, Huard?"

"I don't need advice from you."

Or . . .

"You aren't good enough."

"I've heard that all my life."

Is there a little store in Westwood that sells dialogue like this on rubber stamps? There is only one character in the movie who comes alive and whose dialogue is worth being heard. That is the fat kid, Twins. His story is infinitely more touching than Jake's; he comes from a small Southern town that gave him a parade before he went off to the academy, and if he flunks out, he can't face the folks at home. When Jake's other roommates move out because they don't want to bunk with a loser, Twins stays. Why? His reason may not make audiences in Arkansas and Mississippi very happy, but at least it has the quality of sounding as if a human being might say it out loud.

Baise-Moi

(DIRECTED BY VIRGINIE DESPENTES AND CORALIE TRIN THI; STARRING RAFFAELA ANDERSON, KAREN BACH; 2001)

Baise-Moi is (a) a violent and pornographic film from France about two women, one a rape victim, the other a prostitute, who prowl the countryside murdering men. Or, *Baise-Moi* is (b) an attempt to subvert sexism in the movies by turning the tables and allowing the women to do more or less what men have been doing for years—while making a direct connection between sex and guns, rather than the sublimated connection in most violent movies.

I ask this question because I do not know the answer. Certainly most ordinary moviegoers will despise this movie—or would, if they went to see it, which is unlikely. It alternates between graphic, explicit sex scenes, and murder scenes of brutal cruelty. You recoil from what's on the screen. Later, you ask what the filmmakers had in mind. They are French, and so we know some kind of ideology and rationalization must lurk beneath the blood and semen.

The film has been written and directed by Virginie Despentes, based on her novel; she enlisted Coralie Trin Thi, a porno actress, as her codirector (whether to help with the visual strategy or because of her understanding of the mechanical requirements of onscreen sex, it is hard to say). The movie's central characters, Manu and Nadine, are played by Raffaela Anderson and Karen Bach, who act in hardcore films, and some of the men are also from the porno industry. This is, in fact, the kind of film the director in *Boogie Nights* wanted to make—"porn, but artistic"—although he would have questioned the box office appeal of the praying mantis approach to sex, in which the male is killed immediately after copulation.

As it happens, I saw a Japanese-American coproduction named *Brother* not long after seeing *Baise-Moi.* It was written and directed by Takeshi Kitano, who starred under his acting name, Beat Takeshi. Kitano under any name is the Japanese master of lean, violent, heartless action pictures, and in this one the plot is punctuated every five minutes or so by a bloodbath in which enemies are shot dead. Many, many enemies. We're talking dozens. The killings are separated in *Brother* by about the same length of time as those in *Baise-Moi,* or the sex acts in a porno film. Obviously all three kinds of film are providing payoffs by the clock. Would *Brother* be as depressing as *Baise-Moi* if all the victims had sex before they were gunned down? I don't know, but I'm sure *Baise-Moi* would be perfectly acceptable if the women simply killed men, and no sex was involved. At some level it seems so . . . cruel . . . to shoot a man at his moment of success.

A case can be made that *Baise-Moi* wants to attack sexism in the movies at the same time it raises the stakes. I'm not interested in making that argument. Manu and Nadine are man haters and clinically insane, and not every man is to blame for their unhappiness—no, not even if he sleeps with them. An equally controversial new American movie named *Bully* is also about stupid, senseless murder, but it has the wit to know what it thinks about its characters. *Baise-Moi* is more of a bluff. The directors know their film is so extreme that most will be repelled, but some will devise intellectual defenses and interpretations for it, saving them the trouble of making it clear what they want to say. I can't buy it. Ernest Hemingway, who was no doubt a sexist pig, said it is moral if you feel good after it, and immoral if you feel bad after it. Manu and Nadine do not feel bad, and that is immoral.

Ballistic: Ecks vs. Sever

(Directed by Wych Kaosayananda; starring Antonio Banderas, Lucy Liu; 2002) There is nothing wrong with the title *Ballistic: Ecks vs. Sever* that renaming it *Ballistic* would not have solved. Strange that they would choose such an ungainly title when, in fact, the movie is not about Ecks *versus* Sever but about Ecks *and* Sever working together against a common enemy— although Ecks, Sever, and the audience take a long time to figure that out.

The movie is a chaotic mess, overloaded with special effects and explosions, light on continuity, sanity, and coherence. So short is its memory span that although Sever kills, I dunno, maybe forty Vancouver police officers in an opening battle, by the end, when someone says, "She's a killer," Ecks replies, "She's a mother."

The movie stars Lucy Liu as Sever, a former agent for the Defense Intelligence Agency, which according to www.dia.mil/ is a branch of the U.S. government. Antonio Banderas is Ecks, a former ace FBI agent who is coaxed back into service. Sever has lost her child in an attack and Ecks believes he has lost his wife, so they have something in common, you see, even though . . .

But I'll not reveal that plot secret and will instead discuss the curious fact that both of these U.S. agencies wage what amounts to warfare in Vancouver, which is actually in a nation named Canada that has agencies and bureaus of its own and takes a dim view of machine guns, rocket launchers, plastic explosives, and the other weapons the American agents and their enemies use to litter the streets of the city with the dead.

Both Sever and Ecks, once they discover this, have the same enemy in common: Gant (Gregg Henry), a DIA agent who is married to Talisa Sota and raising her child, although Sever kidnaps the child, who is in fact . . . but never mind, I want to discuss Gant's secret weapon. He has obtained a miniaturized robot so small it can float in the bloodstream and cause strokes and heart attacks.

At one point in the movie a man who will remain nameless is injected with one of these devices by a dart gun, and it kills him. All very well, but consider for a moment the problem of cost overruns in these times of economic uncertainty. A miniaturized assassination robot small enough to slip through the bloodstream would cost how much? Millions? And it is delivered by dart? How's this for an idea: Use a poison dart and spend the surplus on school lunches.

Ballistic: Ecks vs. Sever is an ungainly mess, submerged in mayhem, occasionally surfacing for clichés. When the FBI goes looking for Ecks, for example, they find him sitting morosely on a bar stool, drinking and smoking. That is, of course, where sad former agents always are found, but the strange thing is, after years of drinking he is still in great shape, has all his karate moves, and goes directly into violent action without even a tiny tremor of DTs.

The movie ends in a stock movie location I thought had been retired: a steam and flame factory where the combatants stalk each other on catwalks and from behind steel pillars, while the otherwise deserted factory supplies vast quantities of flame and steam. Vancouver itself, for that matter, is mostly deserted, and no wonder, if word has gotten around that two U.S. agencies and a freelance killer are holding war games. *Ballistic: Ecks vs. Sever* was directed by Wych Kaosayananda of Thailand, whose pseudonym, you may not be surprised to learn, is Kaos.

Basic

<small>(DIRECTED BY JOHN MCTIERNAN; STARRING JOHN TRAVOLTA, SAMUEL L. JACKSON; 2003)</small>

I embarked on *Basic* with optimism and goodwill, confident that a military thriller starring John Travolta and Samuel L. Jackson, and directed by John McTiernan (*Die Hard*), might be entertaining action and maybe more. As the plot unfolded, and unfolded, and unfolded, and unfolded, I leaned forward earnestly in my seat, trying to remember where we had been and what we had learned.

Reader, I gave it my best shot. But with a sinking heart I realized that my efforts were not going to be enough, because this was not a film that *could* be understood. With style and energy from the actors, with every sign of self-confidence from the director, with pictures that were in focus and dialogue that you could hear, the movie descended into a morass of narrative quicksand. By the end, I wanted to do cruel and vicious things to the screenplay.

There's a genre that we could call the Jerk-Around Movie, because what it does is jerk you around. It sets up a situation and then does a bait and switch. You never know which walnut the truth is under. You invest your trust and are betrayed.

I don't mind being jerked around if it's done well, as in *Memento*. I felt *The Usual Suspects* was a long ride for a short day at the beach, but at least as I traced back through it, I could see how it held together. But as nearly as I can tell, *Basic* exists with no respect for objective reality. It is all smoke and no mirrors. If I were to see it again and again, I might be able to extract an underlying logic from it, but the problem is, when a movie's not worth seeing twice, it had better get the job done the first time through.

The film is set in a rainy jungle in Panama. I suspect it rains so much as an irritant, to make everything harder to see and hear. Maybe it's intended as atmosphere. Or maybe the sky gods are angry at the film.

We are introduced to the hard-assed Sgt. Nathan West (Jackson), a sadistic perfectionist who is roundly hated by his unit. When various characters are killed during the confusion of the storm, there is the feeling the deaths may not have been accidental, may indeed have involved drug dealing. A former DEA agent named Tom Hardy (Travolta) is hauled back from alcoholism to join the investigation, teaming with Lt. Julia Osborne (Connie Nielsen).

The murders and the investigation are both told in untrustworthy flashbacks. We get versions of events from such differing points of view, indeed, that we yearn for a good old-fashioned omnipotent POV to come in and slap everybody around. There are so many different views of the same happenings that, hell, why not throw in a musical version?

Of course, there are moments that are engaging in themselves. With such actors (Giovanni Ribisi, Taye Diggs, Brian Van Holt, Roselyn Sanchez, and even Harry Connick Jr.), how could there not be? We listen and follow and take notes, and think we're getting somewhere, and then the next scene knocks down our theories and makes us start again. Finally we arrive at an ending that gives a final jerk to our chain and we realize we never had a chance.

What is the point of a movie like *Basic*? To make us feel cleverly deceived? To do that, the film would have to convince us of one reality and then give us another, equally valid (classics like *Laura* did that). This movie gives no indication even at the end that we have finally gotten to the bottom of things. There is a feeling that *Basic II* could carry right on, undoing the final shots, bringing a few characters back to life and sending the whole crowd off on another tango of gratuitous deception.

Battlefield Earth

(DIRECTED BY ROGER CHRISTIAN; STARRING JOHN TRAVOLTA, BARRY PEPPER; 2000)
Battlefield Earth is like taking a bus trip with someone who has needed a bath for a long time. It's not merely bad; it's unpleasant in a hostile way. The visuals are grubby and drab. The characters are unkempt and have rotten teeth. Breathing tubes hang from their noses like ropes of snot. The sound track sounds like the boom mike is being slammed against the inside of a fifty-five-gallon drum. The plot . . .

But let me catch my breath. This movie is awful in so many different ways. Even the opening titles are cheesy. Sci-fi epics usually begin with a stab at impressive titles, but this one just displays green letters on the screen in a type font that came with my Macintosh. Then the movie's subtitle unscrolls from left to right in the kind of "effect" you see in home movies.

It is the year 3000. The race of Psychlos have conquered Earth. Humans survive in scattered bands, living like actors auditioning for the sequel to *Quest for Fire*. Soon a few leave the wilderness and prowl through the ruins of theme parks and the city of Denver. The ruins have held up well after one thousand years. (The books in the library are dusty but readable, and a flight simulator still works, although where it gets the electricity is a mystery.)

The hero, named Jonnie Goodboy Tyler, is played by Barry Pepper as a smart human who gets smarter thanks to a Psychlo gizmo that zaps his eyeballs with knowledge. He learns Euclidean geometry and how to fly a jet, and otherwise proves to be a quick learner for a caveman. The villains are two Psychlos named Terl (John Travolta) and Ker (Forest Whitaker).

Terl is head of security for the Psychlos, and has a secret scheme to use the humans as slaves to mine gold for him. He can't be reported to his superiors because (I am not making this up), he can blackmail his enemies with secret recordings that, in the event of his death, "would go straight to the home office!" Letterman fans laugh at that line; did the filmmakers know it was funny?

Jonnie Goodboy figures out a way to avoid slave labor in the gold mines. He and his men simply go to Fort Knox, break in, and steal it. Of course it's been waiting there for one thousand years. What Terl says when his slaves hand him smelted bars of gold is beyond explanation. For stunning displays of stupidity, Terl takes the cake; as chief of security for the conquering aliens, he doesn't even know what humans eat, and devises an experiment: "Let it think it has escaped! We can sit back and watch it choose its food." Bad luck for the starving humans that they capture a rat. An experiment like that, you pray for a chicken.

Hiring Travolta and Whitaker was a waste of money, since we can't recognize them behind pounds of matted hair and gnarly makeup. Their costumes look purchased from the Goodwill store on Tatoine. Travolta can be charming, funny, touching, and brave in his best roles; why disguise him as a smelly alien creep? The Psychlos can fly between galaxies, but look at their nails: Their civilization has mastered the hyperdrive but not the manicure.

I am not against unclean characters on principle—at least now that the threat of Smell-O-Vision no longer hangs over our heads. Lots of great movies have squalid heroes. But when the characters seem noxious on principle, we wonder if the art and costume departments were allowed to run wild.

Battlefield Earth was written in 1980 by L. Ron Hubbard, the founder of Scientology. The film contains no evidence of Scientology or any other system of thought; it is shapeless and senseless, without a compelling plot or characters we care for in the slightest. The director, Roger Christian, has learned from better films that directors sometimes tilt their cameras, but he has not learned why.

Some movies run off the rails. This one is like the train crash in *The Fugitive.* I watched it in mounting gloom, realizing I was witnessing something historic, a film that for decades to come will be the punch line of jokes about bad movies. There is a moment here when the Psychlos' entire planet (home office and all) is blown to smithereens, without the slightest impact on any member of the audience (or, for that matter, the cast). If the film had been destroyed in a similar cataclysm, there might have been a standing ovation.

Beautiful

(Directed by Sally Field; starring Minnie Driver, Joey Lauren Adams; 2000)

Beautiful should have gone through lots and lots more rewrites before it was imposed on audiences. It's a movie with so many inconsistencies, improbabilities, unanswered questions, and unfinished characters that we have to suspend not only disbelief but intelligence.

The movie tells the story of Mona, a girl who dreams of becoming a beauty queen and grows up to become obsessed with her dream. Her life is not without difficulties. As a child from Naperville, Illinois, she is graceless, wears braces, chooses costumes Miss Clarabell would not be seen in, cheats, and is insufferably self-centered. As an adult, played by Minnie Driver, she gets rid of the braces but keeps right on cheating, until by the time she becomes Miss Illinois she has survived her third scandal.

Sample scandal. A competitor in a pageant plans to twirl a fire baton. Mona paints the baton with glue so the girl's hand gets stuck to it, and then dramatically races onstage to save the girl with a fire extinguisher. Don't they press criminal charges when you do things like that?

As a girl, Mona is best pals with Ruby, a girl who for no good reason adores her. As an adult, Ruby (now played by Joey Lauren Adams) works as a nurse but inexplicably devotes her life to Mona's career. Mona has had a child out of wedlock, but because beauty contestants aren't supposed to have kids, Ruby even agrees to pose as the little girl's mom.

Why? Why does Ruby devote her entire life to Mona and become a surrogate mother? Search me. Because the plot makes her, I guess. Mona has parents of her own, a mother and a stepfather who are sullen, unhelpful, drink too much, and spend most of their time being seen in unhelpful reaction shots. The screenplay is no help in explaining their personalities or histories. They're props.

Mona's daughter, Vanessa (Hallie Kate Eisenberg), is at least a life source within the dead film, screaming defiantly in frustration because Mona keeps forgetting to take her to her soccer games. She suspects Mona is her real mom and seems fed up being used as a pawn (at one point she gets on the phone to order some foster parents).

And what about Joyce Parkins (Leslie Stefanson), a TV reporter who hates Mona? She knows Mona has a child and is planning to break the story, but no one who has watched television for as long as a day could conceivably believe her character or what she does. Consider the big Miss American Miss pageant, where Joyce keeps telling her viewers she's about to break a big scandal. She is obviously not on the same channel as the pageant, so she must be on another channel. What are that channel's viewers watching when Joyce is not talking? Joyce, I guess, since she addresses them in real time whenever she feels like it. The staging is so inept she is actually seen *eavesdropping* on the pageant by placing her ear near to a wall. No press gallery? Not even a portable TV for her to watch?

As for Mona herself, Minnie Driver finds herself in an acting triathlon. Mona changes personalities, strategies, and IQ levels from scene to scene. There is no way that the Mona of the heartrending conclusion could develop from the Mona of the beginning and middle of the film, but never mind: Those Monas aren't possible, either. They're made of disconnected pieces, held together with labored plot furniture. (I was amazed at one point when people told Mona what the matter with her was, and then she went home and lay down on the sofa and we got flashback voice-overs as memories of the accusing voices echoed in her head. That device was dated in 1950.)

Driver would have been miscast even if the screenplay had been competent. She doesn't come across like the kind of person who could take beauty pageants seriously. Oddly enough, Joey Lauren Adams (the husky-voiced would-be girlfriend from *Chasing Amy*) could have played the beauty queen—and Driver could have played the pal.

And what about Ruby, the nurse played by Adams? She can't be at the big pageant because she's in jail accused of deliberately killing an elderly patient at a nursing home by giving her an overdose of pills. This would be too gruesome for a comedy if anything were done with it, but the death exists only as a plot gimmick—to explain why Ruby can't be there. The filmmakers have no sense of proportion; Ruby could just as easily have been stuck in a gas station with a flat tire and provided the same reaction shots (watching TV) in the climax. Why kill the sweet old lady?

Now consider. Mona has been involved in three scandals. She scarred one of her competitors for life. Her roommate and manager is in jail charged as an Angel of Death. A TV newswoman knows she has a secret child. What are the odds *any* beauty pageant would let that contestant on stage? With this movie, you can't ask questions like that. In fact, you can't ask any questions. This is Sally Field's first film as a director. The executives who green-lighted it did her no favors. You can't send a kid up in a crate like this.

Beautiful Creatures

(DIRECTED BY BILL EAGLES; STARRING RACHEL WEISZ, SUSAN LYNCH; 2001)

I spent last week at the Conference on World Affairs at the University of Colorado, Boulder, where one of my fellow panelists created a stir by standing up and shouting that the women on his panel were "man haters," and he was fed up and wasn't going to take it anymore.

He would have had apoplexy if he'd seen *Beautiful Creatures*, from Scotland. Here is a movie about two of the most loathsome women in recent cinema, and the movie thinks the male characters are the villains. It gets away with this only because we have been taught that women are to be presumed good and men are to be presumed evil. Flip the genders in this screenplay, and there would not be the slightest doubt that the characters named Petula and Dorothy are monsters.

Consider, for example, the setup. Dorothy (Susan Lynch) has been unwise enough to shack up with a boyfriend who is not only a junkie but also a golfer. This makes her a two-time loser. She pawns his golf clubs. He gets revenge by throwing her brassiere in boiling water, dyeing her dog pink, and stealing her money, which is from the pawned golf clubs. Any golfer (or junkie) will tell you that at this point, they are approximately morally even.

Dorothy leaves the house and comes upon a disturbance in the street. Petula (Rachel Weisz) is being beaten by Brian (Tom Mannion). Why is he doing this? Because the movie requires this demonstration of typical male behavior. Dorothy is already mad, and now she loses it. She slams Brian with a pipe to the back of the head, and the two women, instantly bonding, carry his unconscious body to Dorothy's flat, where they share a joint while Brian dies in the bathtub. "You just get sick listening to all that 'gonna (bleeping) kill you' stuff," Dorothy explains.

Imagine a scene where a man slams a woman with a pipe, and then joins her boyfriend in dragging the body into the bathtub and sharing a joint while she dies. Difficult. Even more difficult in a comedy, which, I neglected to mention, *Beautiful Creatures* intends to be. But I don't want to get mired in male outrage. Men are more violent than women, yes, and guilty of abuse, yes, although the percentage of male monsters is incalculably higher in the movies than in life. Like Thelma and Louise, Dorothy and Petula commit crimes that are morally justifiable because of their gender. We even like them for it. They have to conceal the death, for example, because "no one would believe" they had not committed murder. My own theory is that any jury in Scotland would believe their story that the man was violent and Dorothy had come to the defense of a sister.

The movie, set in Glasgow and one of the many offspring of *Trainspotting,* uses local color for a lot of its gags. Instead of picketing *The Sopranos,* Italian-Americans should protest the new wave of films from Scotland, which indicate Scots make funnier, more violent, more eccentric, and more verbal gangsters than they do. Films and TV shows that portray ethnic groups as interesting and colorful are generally a plus, since those viewers dumb enough to think every story is an accurate portrait are beyond our help anyway.

The plot. The dead man has a brother who is a rich bad guy. The women cut off the corpse's finger and send it with a ransom demand. A detective (Alex Norton) comes to investigate, gets in on the scheme, and alters it with designs of his own. Meanwhile, the junkie boyfriend turns up again, and one thing leads to another. You know how it is.

There is some dark humor in the movie, of the kind where you laugh that you may not gag. And the kind of convoluted plotting that seems obligatory in crime films from Scotland (consider *Shallow Grave*). I am not really offended by the movie's gender politics, since I am accustomed to the universal assumption in pop (and academic) culture that women are in possession of truth and goodness and men can only benefit from learning from them. In fact, if the movie had been able to make me laugh, I might have forgiven it almost anything.

Be Cool

(DIRECTED BY F. GARY GRAY; STARRING JOHN TRAVOLTA, UMA THURMAN; 2005)
John Travolta became a movie star by playing a Brooklyn kid who wins a dance contest in *Saturday Night Fever* (1977). He revived his career by dancing with Uma Thurman in *Pulp Fiction* (1994). In *Be Cool,* Uma

Thurman asks if he dances. "I'm from Brooklyn," he says, and then they dance. So we get it: "Brooklyn" connects with *Fever*, Thurman connects with *Pulp*. That's the easy part. The hard part is, what do we do with it?

Be Cool is a movie that knows it is a movie. It knows it is a sequel and contains disparaging references to sequels. All very cute at the screenplay stage, where everybody can sit around at story conferences and assume that a scene will work because the scene it refers to worked. But that's the case only when the new scene is also good as itself, apart from what it refers to.

Quentin Tarantino's *Pulp Fiction* knew that Travolta won the disco contest in *Saturday Night Fever*. But Tarantino's scene didn't depend on that; it built from it. Travolta was graceful beyond compare in *Fever*, but in *Pulp Fiction* he's dancing with a gangster's girlfriend on orders from the gangster, and part of the point of the scene is that both Travolta and Thurman look like they're dancing not out of joy, but out of duty. So we remember *Fever* and then we forget it, because the new scene is working on its own.

Now look at the dance scene in *Be Cool*. Travolta and Thurman dance in a perfectly competent way that is neither good nor bad. Emotionally they are neither happy nor sad. The scene is not necessary to the story. The filmmakers have put them on the dance floor without a safety net. And so we watch them dancing and we think, yeah, *Saturday Night Fever* and *Pulp Fiction*, and when that thought has been exhausted, they're still dancing.

The whole movie has the same problem. It is a sequel to *Get Shorty* (1995), which was based on a novel by Elmore Leonard just as this is based on a sequel to that novel. Travolta once again plays Chili Palmer, onetime Miami loan shark, who in the first novel traveled to Los Angeles to collect a debt from a movie producer and ended up pitching him on a movie based on the story of why he was in the producer's living room in the middle of the night threatening his life.

This time Chili has moved into the music business, which is less convincing because, while Chili was plausibly a fan of the producer's sleazy movies, he cannot be expected, ten years down the road, to know or care much about music. Funnier if he had advanced to the front ranks of movie producers and was making a movie with A-list stars when his past catches up with him.

Instead, he tries to take over the contract of a singer named Linda Moon (Christina Milian), whose agent (Vince Vaughn) acts as if he is black. He is not black, and that's the joke, I guess. But where do you go with it? Maybe by sinking him so deeply into dialect that he cannot make himself understood, and has to write notes. Chili also ventures into the hip-hop culture; he runs up against a Suge Knight type named Sin LaSalle (Cedric the Entertainer), who has a bodyguard named Elliot Wilhelm, played by The Rock.

I pause here long enough to note that Elliot Wilhelm is the name of a friend of mine who runs the Detroit Film Theater, and that Elmore Leonard undoubtedly knows this because he also lives in Detroit. It's the kind of in-joke that doesn't hurt a movie unless you happen to know Elliot Wilhelm, in which case you can think of nothing else every second The Rock is on the screen.

The deal with The Rock's character is that he is manifestly gay, although he doesn't seem to realize it. He makes dire threats against Chili Palmer, who disarms him with flattery, telling him in the middle of a confrontation that he has all the right elements to be a movie star. Just as the sleazy producer in *Get Shorty* saved his own life by listening to Chili's pitch, now Chili saves his life by pitching The Rock.

There are other casting decisions that are intended to be hilarious. Sin LaSalle has a chief of staff played by Andre 3000, who is a famous music type, although I did not know that and neither, in my opinion, would Chili. There is also a gag involving Steven Tyler turning up as himself.

Be Cool becomes a classic species of bore: a self-referential movie with no self to refer to. One character after another, one scene after another, one cute line of dialogue after another, refers to another movie, a similar character, a contrasting image or whatever. The movie is like a bureaucrat who keeps sending you to another office.

It doesn't take the in-joke satire to an additional level that might skew it funny. To have The Rock play a gay narcissist is not funny because all we can think about is that The Rock is not a gay narcissist. But if they had cast someone who was *also* not The Rock, but someone removed from The Rock at right angles, like Steve Buscemi or John Malkovich, then that might have worked, and The Rock could have played another character at right angles to himself—for example, the character played here by Harvey Keitel as your basic Harvey Keitel character. Think what The Rock could do with a Harvey Keitel character.

In other words: (1) Come up with an actual story, and (2) if you must have satire and self-reference, rotate it 90 degrees off the horizontal instead of making it ground level. Also (3) go easy on the material that requires a familiarity with the earlier movie, as in the scenes with Danny DeVito, who can be the funniest man in a movie, but not when it has to be a movie other than the one he is appearing in.

Behind Enemy Lines

(DIRECTED BY JOHN MOORE; STARRING OWEN WILSON, GENE HACKMAN; 2001)

The premiere of *Behind Enemy Lines* was held aboard the aircraft carrier USS *Carl Vinson*. I wonder if it played as a comedy. Its hero is so reckless and its villains so incompetent that it's a showdown between a man begging to be shot, and an enemy that can't hit the side of a Bosnian barn. This is not the story of a fugitive trying to sneak through enemy terrain and be rescued but of a movie character magically transported from one photo opportunity to another.

Owen Wilson stars as Burnett, a hotshot Navy flier who "signed up to be a fighter pilot—not a cop on a beat no one cares about." On a recon mission over Bosnia, he and his partner, Stackhouse (Gabriel Macht), venture off mission and get digital photos of a mass grave and illegal troop movements. It's a Serbian operation in violation of a fresh peace treaty, and the Serbs fire two missiles to bring the plane down. The plane's attempts to elude the missiles supply the movie's high point.

The pilots eject. Stackhouse is found by Tracker (Vladimir Mashkov), who tells his commander, Lokar (Olek Krupa), to forget about a big pursuit and simply allow him to track Burnett. That sets up the cat-and-mouse game in which Burnett wanders through open fields, stands on the tops of ridges, and stupidly makes himself a target, while Tracker is caught in one of those nightmares where he runs and runs but just can't seem to catch up.

Back on the USS *Vinson*, Admiral Reigart (Gene Hackman) is biting his lower lip. He wants to fly in and rescue Burnett, but is blocked by his NATO superior, Admiral Piquet (Joaquim de Almeida)—who is so devious he substitutes NATO troops for Americans in a phony rescue mission and calls them off just when Burnett is desperately waving from a pickup area. Admiral Piquet, who sounds French, is played by a Portuguese actor.

The first-time director is John Moore, who has made lots of TV commercials, something we intuit in a scene where Reigart orders Burnett to proceed to another pickup area, and Burnett visualizes fast-motion whooshing tracking shots up and down mountains and through valleys before deciding, uh-uh, he ain't gonna do that.

What Burnett does do is stroll through Bosnia like a bird-watcher, exposing himself in open areas and making himself a silhouette against the skyline. He's only spotted in the first place because when his buddy is cornered, he's hiding safely but utters a loud involuntary yell and then starts to run up an exposed hillside. First rule of not getting caught: No loud involuntary yells within the hearing of the enemy.

This guy is a piece of work. Consider the scene where Burnett substitutes uniforms with a Serbian fighter. He even wears a black ski mask covering his entire face. He walks past a truck of enemy troops, and then what does he do? Why, he *removes the ski mask,* revealing his distinctive blond hair, and then he *turns back toward the truck* so we can see his face, in case we didn't know who he was. How did this guy get through combat training? Must have been a social promotion to keep him with his age group.

At times Burnett is pursued by the entire Serbian army, which fires at him with machine guns, rifles, and tanks, of course never hitting him. The movie recycles the old howler where hundreds of rounds of ammo miss the hero, but all he has to do is aim and fire, and—pow! another bad guy jerks back, dead. I smiled during the scene where Admiral Reigart is able to use heat-sensitive satellite imagery to look at high-res silhouettes of Burnett stretched out within feet of the enemy. Maybe this is possible. What I do not believe is that the enemies in this scene could not spot the American uniform in a pile of enemy corpses.

Do I need to tell you that the ending involves a montage of rueful grins, broad smiles, and meaningful little victorious nods, scored with upbeat rock music? No, probably not. And of course we get shots of the characters and are told what happened to them after the story was over—as if this is based on real events. It may have been inspired by the adventures of Air Force pilot Scott O'Grady, who was rescued after being shot down over Bosnia in 1995, but based on real life, it's not.

Blade: Trinity

(DIRECTED BY DAVID GOYER; STARRING WESLEY SNIPES, KRIS KRISTOFFERSON; 2004) I liked the first two Blade movies, although my description of *Blade II* as a "really rather brilliant vomitorium of viscera" might have sounded like faint praise. The second film was directed by Guillermo del Toro, a gifted horror director with a sure feel for quease inducing, and was even better, I thought, than the first. Now comes *Blade: Trinity,* which is a mess. It lacks the sharp narrative line and crisp comic-book clarity of the earlier films, and descends too easily into shapeless fight scenes that are chopped into so many cuts that they lack all form or rhythm.

The setup is a continuation of the earlier films. Vampires are waging a war to infect humanity, and the most potent fighter against them is the half-human, half-vampire Blade (Wesley Snipes). He has been raised from childhood by Whistler (Kris Kristofferson), who recognized his unique ability to move between two worlds, and is a fearsome warrior, but, despite some teammates, is seriously outnumbered.

As *Trinity* opens, the Vampire Nation and its leader, Danica (played by Parker Posey—yes, Parker Posey), convince the FBI that Blade is responsible for, if I heard correctly, 1,182 murders. "They're waging a goddamned publicity campaign," Whistler grumbles, in that great Kris Kristofferson seen-it-all voice.

Agents surround Blade headquarters, which is your basic action movie space combining the ambience of a warehouse with lots of catwalks and high places to fall from and stuff that blows up good. Whistler goes down fighting (although a shotgun seems retro given the sci-fi weapons elsewhere in the movie), and Blade is recruited by the Night Stalkers, who reach him through Whistler's daughter, Abigail (Jessica Biel). It would have been too much, I suppose, to hope for Whistler's mother.

The Night Stalkers have information that the Vampire Nation is seeking the original Dracula because, to spread the vampire virus, "they need better DNA; they need Dracula's blood." Dracula's superior DNA means he can operate by day, unlike his descendants, who must operate by night. The notion that DNA degrades or is somehow diluted over the centuries flies in the face of what we know about the double helix, but who needs science when you know what's right? "They found Dracula in Iraq about six months ago," we learn, and if that's not a straight line, I'm not Jon Stewart.

Dracula is some kinduva guy. Played by Dominic Purcell, he isn't your usual vampire in evening dress with overdeveloped canines, but a creature whose DNA seems to have been infected with the virus of Hollywood monster effects. His mouth and lower face unfold into a series of ever more horrifying fangs and suchlike, until he looks like a mug shot of the original *Alien*. He doesn't suck blood; he vacuums it.

Parker Posey is an actress I have always had affection for, and now it is mixed with increased admiration for the way she soldiers through an impossible role, sneering like the good sport she is. Jessica Biel becomes the first heroine of a vampire movie to listen to her iPod during slayings. That's an excuse to get the sound track by Ramin Djawadi and RZA into the movie, I guess, although I hope she downloaded it from the iTunes Store and isn't a pirate on top of being a vampire.

Vampires in this movie look about as easy to kill as the ghouls in *Dawn of the Dead*. They have a way of suddenly fizzing up into electric sparks, and then collapsing in a pile of ash. One of the weapons used against them by the Night Stalkers is a light-saber device that is, and I'm sure I have this right, "half as hot as the sun." Switch on one of those babies and you'd zap not only the vampires but British Columbia and large parts of Alberta and Washington State.

Jessica Biel is the resident babe, wearing fetishistic costumes to match Blade's, and teaming up with Hannibal King (Ryan Reynolds), no relation to Hannibal Lecter, a former vampire who has come over to the good side. The vampire killers and their fellow Night Stalkers engage in an increasingly murky series of battles with the vampires, leading you to ask this simple strategic question: Why, since the whole world is theirs for the taking, do the vampires have to turn up and fight the Night Stalkers in the first place? Why not just figure out that since the Stalkers are in Vancouver, the vampires should concentrate on, say, Montreal?

Boat Trip

(DIRECTED BY MORT NATHAN; STARRING CUBA GOODING JR, HORATIO SANZ; 2003)
Boat Trip arrives preceded by publicity saying many homosexuals have been outraged by the film. Now that it's in theaters, everybody else has a chance to join them. Not that the film is outrageous. That would be asking too much. It is dimwitted, unfunny, too shallow to be offensive, and way too conventional to use all of those people standing around in the background wearing leather and chains and waiting hopefully for their cues. This is a movie made for nobody, about nothing.

The premise: Jerry (Cuba Gooding Jr.) is depressed after being dumped by his girl (Vivica A. Fox). His best buddy Nick (Horatio Sanz) cheers him up: They'll take a cruise together. Nick has heard that the ships are jammed with lonely women. But they offend a travel agent, who books them on a cruise of gay men, ho ho.

Well, it could be funny. Different characters in a different story with more wit and insight might have done the trick. But *Boat Trip* requires its heroes to be so unobservant that it takes them hours to even figure out it's a gay cruise. And then they go into heterosexual panic mode, until the profoundly conventional screenplay supplies the only possible outcome:

The sidekick discovers that he's gay, and the hero discovers a sexy woman on board and falls in love with her.

Her name is Gabriella (Roselyn Sanchez), and despite the fact that she's the choreographer on a gay cruise, she knows so little about gay men that she falls for Jerry's strategy: He will pretend to be gay, so that he can get close to her and then dramatically unveil his identity, or something. Uh, huh. Even Hector, the cross-dressing queen in the next stateroom, knows a straight when he sees one: "You want to convince people you are gay, and you don't know the words to 'I Will Survive'?"

The gays protesting the movie say it deals in stereotypes. So it does, but then again, so does the annual gay parade, and so do many gay nightclubs, where role-playing is part of the scene. Yes, there are transvestites and leather guys and muscle boys on the cruise, but there are also more conventional types, like Nick's poker-playing buddies. The one ray of wit in the entire film is provided by Roger Moore, as a homosexual man who calmly wanders through the plot dispensing sanity, as when, at the bar, he listens to the music and sighs, "Why do they always play Liza?"

One of the movie's problems is a disconnect between various levels of reality. Some of the scenes play as if they are intended to be realistic. Then Jerry or Nick goes into hysterics of overacting. Then Jerry attempts to signal a helicopter to rescue him, and shoots it down with a flare gun. Then it turns out to be carrying the Swedish Sun-Tanning Team on its way to the Hawaiian Tropic finals. Then Jerry asks Gabriela to describe her oral sex technique, which she does with the accuracy and detail of a porn film, and then Jerry—but that pathetic moment you will have to witness for yourself. Or maybe you will not.

Note: The credit cookies weren't very funny, either, but at least they kept me in the theater long enough to notice the credits for the film's Greek Support Team.

Bootmen

(DIRECTED BY DEIN PERRY; STARRING ADAM GARCIA, SAM WORTHINGTON; 2000)

Bootmen is the story of a young dancer and his friends who revisit the clichés of countless other dance movies in order to bring forth a dance performance of clanging unloveliness. Screwing metal plates to the soles of their work boots, they stomp in unison on flat steel surfaces while banging on things. Imagine Fred Astaire as a punch-press operator.

The movie has been adapted by director Dein Perry from his own performance piece, which he might have been better advised to make into a concert film. It takes place in Australia, where Sean (Adam Garcia) dreams of becoming a dancer. His salt-of-the earth father, a steelworker, opposes the plan. Sean cannot face life without dance in Newcastle, a steel town, despite the charms of the fragrant Linda (Sophie Lee), a hairdresser who has given him to understand that he might someday, but not yet, enjoy her favors. He flees to Sydney to pursue his career, leaving behind his brother Mitchell, who basks in the old man's favor by adopting a reasonable occupation and stealing cars for their parts.

In Sydney, Sean encounters a hard-nosed choreographer (William Zappa), a staple of dance movies, who is not easy to impress. Sean is too talented to be dismissed, but at rehearsals he angers the star (Dein Perry himself) because the star's girlfriend likes his looks, and Sean gets fired. It is one of the oddities of this movie about dance that almost everyone in it is not merely straight but ferociously macho; it's as if the Village People really did work eight hours a day as linemen, Indian chiefs, etc. I am not suggesting that all, or most, or many dancers are gay, but surely one has heard that some are?

Sean returns disillusioned but undefeated to Newcastle, where Mitchell meanwhile has gotten the lonely Linda drunk, plied her with morose theories about Sean's long absence, and bedded her during an alcoholic lapse of judgment on her part (Mitchell has no judgment). Sean arrives in the morning, discovers that Mitchell and Linda have sailed into waters that Linda had assured him would remain uncharted pending their own maiden voyage, and becomes so depressed that we realize we have reached the Preliminary Crisis as defined in elementary screenwriting outlines.

Now what? It remains only for the steel mills to close so that Sean can realize that the millworkers should be retrained as computer experts. But there are no computers. Why not have a benefit? Sean gathers his friends and says, in other words, "Say, gang! Let's rent the old steel mill, and put on a show!" He trains his buddies in the art of synchronized stomping so that the town can turn out to watch them clang and bang. Judging by the crowd they attract, and estimating $10 a ticket, they raise enough money for approximately two computers, but never mind; cruel fate will quickly turn these recycled steelworkers into unemployed dot-com workers, so the fewer, the better.

Is there a scene near the end of the performance where the once-bitter dad enters, sees that his son is indeed talented, and forgives all? Is Linda pardoned for her lapse of faithfulness? Do Mitchell and Sean realize that even though Mitchell may have slept with the woman Sean loves it was because Mitchell had too much to drink, something that could happen in any family? Do the townspeople of Newcastle give a lusty ovation to the performance? Is there an encore? Veteran moviegoers will walk into the theater already possessing the answers to these and many other questions.

Bride of the Wind

(DIRECTED BY BRUCE BERESFORD; STARRING SARAH WYNTER, JONATHAN PRYCE; 2001)
I'm not just any widow! I'm Mahler's widow!   —ALMA MAHLER

She must have been a monster. The Alma Mahler depicted in *Bride of the Wind* is a woman who prowls restlessly through the beds of the famous, making them miserable while displaying no charm of her own. Whether this was the case with the real woman I do not know. But if she was anything like the woman in this movie, then Gustav Mahler, Gustav Klimt, Oskar Kokoschka, Walter Gropius, and Frank Werfel should have fled from her on sight.

Bride of the Wind, which tells her story, is one of the worst biopics I have ever seen, a leaden march through a chronology of Alma's affairs, clicking them off with the passion of an encyclopedia entry. The movie has three tones: overwrought, boring, laughable. Sarah Wynter, who plays Alma, does not perform the dialogue but recites it. She lacks any conviction as a seductress, seems stiff and awkward, and should have been told that great women in turn-of-the-century Vienna didn't slouch.

We first meet her going to a ball her father has forbidden her to attend. He is stern with her when she returns. So much for her adolescence. We move on to a dinner party where she flirts with the artist Klimt (August Schmolzer), who labors over one-liners like, "Mahler's music is much better than it sounds." She insults Mahler (Jonathan Pryce) at dinner, offending and fascinating him, and soon the older man marries her.

She has affairs throughout their marriage. She cheats with the architect Gropius (Simon Verhoeven), who unwisely writes a love letter to Alma but absentmindedly addresses it to Gustav—or so he says. "You drove me to him," she pouts to her husband. Mahler is always going on about his music, you see, and thinks himself a genius. Well, so does Gropius. The screenplay shows the egos of the men by putting big, clanging chunks of information in the dialogue. Sample:

"You've been very kind, Herr Gropius."

"Dancing is one of the two things I do well."

"And what is the other?"

"I am an architect."

Since Alma already knows this, the movie misses a bet by not having her ask, winsomely, "Is there a . . . third . . . thing you at least do not do badly?"

There is. Another affair is with the sculptor and painter Oskar Kokoschka (Vincent Perez), who goes off to fight the war and is shot through the head and bayoneted after falling wounded. In what the movie presents as a dying vision, he imagines Alma walking toward him. Since his head is flat on the ground, she walks toward him sideways, rotated ninety degrees from upright. But, of course, a vision stands upright no matter what position one's head is in, or dreams would take place on the ceiling.

Oskar's mother posts herself outside Alma's house with a pistol, seeking revenge for her son's death. "I was never popular with mothers," Alma sighs. She becomes involved with the writer Werfel. Just when we are wondering if Oskar's mother is still lying in ambush outside the gates, Kokoschka himself returns a year later—alive!—and surprises her in her drawing room. "It's not every man who is shot in the head, bayoneted, and lives to tell about it," he observes. Then he sees she is pregnant and rejoices that she decided to have his baby after all, instead of an abortion. "But it has been a year," Alma tells him. "Think, Oskar! A year."

The penny falls. He stalks away, disgusted either at the fact that she is bearing another man's child or that he cannot count. I meanwhile am thinking that when one is reported dead in action, it is only common good manners to wire ahead before turning up unexpectedly at a lover's house. Ben Affleck makes the same mistake in *Pearl Harbor.*

Bride of the Wind was directed by Bruce Beresford, who has made wonderful films (*Tender Mercies, Crimes of the Heart, The Fringe Dwellers, Driving Miss Daisy*). At a loss to explain this lapse, I can only observe that another of his filmed biographies, *King David* (1985), was also very bad. Maybe there is something about a real-life subject that paralyzes him.

If Sarah Wynter is not good as Alma Mahler, the other actors seem equally uneasy—even the usually assured Pryce and Perez. Something must have been going wrong on this production. Even that doesn't explain the lack of Bad Laugh Control. Filmmakers need a sixth sense for lines that might play the wrong way. For example:

After Alma has slept with as many Viennese artists as she can manage without actually double booking, she quarrels with the latest. Her winsome little daughter, Maria (Francesca Becker), whines, "Is he going to leave us? Are you going to send him away?" Alma replies, "What made you think that?" Wrong answer. At the end of the movie there are titles telling us what happened to everyone; Gropius moved to America and went on to become a famous architect, etc. We are not surprised to learn that little Maria went on to be married five times.

Cabin Fever

(Directed by Eli Roth; starring Rider Strong, Jordan Ladd; 2003)

Unsure of whether it wants to be a horror film, a comedy, an homage, a satire or a parable, *Cabin Fever* tries to cover every base; it jumps around like kids on those arcade games where the target lights up and you have to stomp on it. It assembles the standard package of horror heroes and heroines (sexy girl, nice girl, stalwart guy, uncertain guy, drunk guy) and takes them off for a post-exam holiday in the woods where things get off to a bad start when a man covered with blood comes staggering out of the trees.

What they eventually figure out is that the man has some kind of disease—for which we could, I suppose, read AIDS or SARS—and it may be catching. When the nice girl (Jordan Ladd) comes down with the symptoms, they lock her in a shed, but before long they're all threatened, and there is a scene where the sexy girl (Cerina Vincent) is shaving her legs in the bathtub and finds, eek, that she's shaving a scab.

The film could develop its plague story in a serious way, like a George Romero picture or *28 Days Later*, but it keeps breaking the mood with weird humor involving the locals. Everyone at the corner general store seems seriously demented, and the bearded old coot behind the counter seems like a racist (when at the end we discover that he isn't, the payoff is more offensive than his original offense). There's a deputy sheriff named Winston (Giuseppe Andrews) who is a seriously counterproductive character; the movie grinds to an incredulous halt every time he's onscreen.

The drama mostly involves the characters locking the door against dogs, the locals, and each other; running into the woods in search of escape or help; trying to start the truck (which, like all vehicles in horror films, runs only when the plot requires it to) and having sex, lots of sex. The nature of the disease is inexplicable; it seems to involve enormous quantities of blood appearing on the surface of the skin without visible wounds, and then spreading in wholesale amounts to every nearby surface.

If some of this material had been harnessed and channeled into a disciplined screenplay with a goal in mind, the movie might have worked. But the director and coauthor, Eli Roth, is too clever for his own good, and impatiently switches between genres, tones, and intentions. There are truly horrible scenes (guy finds corpse in reservoir, falls onto it), over-the-top horrible scenes (dogs have eaten skin off good girl's face, but she is still alive), and just plain inexplicable scenes (Dennis, the little boy at the general store, bites people). By the end, we've lost all interest. The movie adds up to a few good ideas and a lot of bad ones, wandering around in search of an organizing principle.

Catwoman

(Directed by Pitof; starring Halle Berry, Benjamin Bratt; 2004)

Catwoman is a movie about Halle Berry's beauty, sex appeal, figure, eyes, lips, and costume design. It gets those right. Everything else is secondary, except for the plot, which is tertiary. What a letdown. The filmmakers have given great thought to photographing Berry, who looks fabulous, and little thought to providing her with a strong character, story, supporting characters, or action sequences. In a summer when *Spider-Man 2* represents the state of the art, *Catwoman* is tired and dated.

Although the movie's faults are many, the crucial one is that we never get any sense of what it feels like to turn into a catwoman. The strength of *Spider-Man 2* is in the ambivalence that Peter Parker has about being part nerdy student, part superhero. In *Catwoman,* where are the scenes where a woman comes to grips with the fact that her entire nature and even her species seems to have changed?

Berry plays Patience Philips, a designer for an ad agency, who dies and is reborn after Midnight, a cat with ties to ancient Egypt, breathes new life into her. She becomes Catwoman, but what is a catwoman? She can leap like a cat, strut around on top of her furniture, survive great falls, and hiss. Halle Berry looks great doing these things and spends a lot of time on all fours, inspiring our almost unseemly gratitude for her cleavage.

She gobbles down tuna and sushi. Her eyes have vertical pupils instead of horizontal ones. She sleeps on a shelf. The movie doesn't get into the litter box situation. What does she *think* about all of this? Why isn't she more astonished that it has happened to her? How does it affect her relationship with that cute cop, Tom Lone (Benjamin Bratt)?

The movie makes it clear that they make love at least once, but we don't see that happening because *Catwoman,* a film that was born to be rated R, has been squeezed into the PG-13 category to rake in every last teenage dollar. From what we know about Catwoman, her style in bed has probably changed along with everything else, and sure enough the next day he notices a claw mark on his shoulder. Given the MPAA's preference for violence over sex, this might have been one sex scene that could have sneaked in under the PG-13.

Catwoman dresses like a dominatrix, with the high heels and the leather skirt, brassiere, mask, and whip. But why? Because the costume sketches looked great, is my opinion. The film gives her a plot that could have been phoned in from the 1960s: She works for a corporation that's introducing a new beauty product that gives women eternal youth, unless they stop taking it, in which case they look like burn victims. When Patience stumbles over this unfortunate side effect, she is attacked by security guards, flushed out of a waste pipe, and is dead when Midnight finds her.

Soon she has a dual identity: Patience by day, Catwoman by night. She already knows Tom Lone. They met when she crawled out of her window and balanced on an air conditioner to rescue Midnight, and Tom thought she was committing suicide and saved her after she slipped. Uh, huh. That meeting begins a romance between Patience and Tom that is remarkable for its complete lack of energy, passion, and chemistry. If the movie had been ten minutes longer it would have needed a scene where they sigh and sadly agree their relationship is just not working out. One of those things. Not meant to be.

The villains are Laurel and George Hedare (Sharon Stone and Lambert Wilson). He runs the cosmetics company and fires his wife as its model when she turns forty. She is not to be trifled with, especially not in a movie where the big fight scene is a real catfight, so to speak, between the two women. Stone's character is laughably one-dimensional, but then that's a good fit for this movie, in which none of the characters suggest any human dimensions and seem to be posing more than relating. Take George, for example, whose obnoxious mannerisms are so grotesque he's like the *Saturday Night Live* version of Vincent Price.

Among many silly scenes, the silliest has to be the Ferris wheel sequence, which isn't even as thrilling as the one in *The Notebook*. Wouldn't you just know that after the wheel stalls, the operator would recklessly strip the gears, and the little boy riding alone would be in a chair where the guard rail falls off, and then the seat comes loose, and then the wheel tries to shake him loose and no doubt would try to electrocute him if it could.

The score by Klaus Badelt is particularly annoying; it faithfully mirrors every action with what occasionally sounds like a karaoke rhythm section. The director, whose name is Pitof, was probably issued with two names at birth and would be wise to use the other one on his next project.

Cecil B. Demented

(DIRECTED BY JOHN WATERS; STARRING MELANIE GRIFFITH, STEPHEN DORFF; 2000)
My best guess is that John Waters produced the talent shows in his high school. There's always been something cheerfully amateurish about his more personal films—a feeling that he and his friends have dreamed up a series of skits while hanging out together. *Cecil B. Demented* takes this tendency to an almost unwatchable extreme, in a home movie that's like a bunch of kids goofing off.

To be sure, he has real stars in the picture; Melanie Griffith stars as a Hollywood star, and Stephen Dorff plays the cult leader who kidnaps her as part of his guerrilla assault on mainstream cinema. But they're used more as exhibits than performers (Look! It's Melanie Griffith!). The movie has a radical premise, as Weathermen-type movie lovers try to destroy dumb commercial films, but it is pitched at the level of a very bad sketch on *Saturday Night Live.*

Cinema guerrilla Cecil B. Demented (Dorff) and his cult group kidnap Griffith, who will be forced to star in their own film. Their targets include the Maryland Film Commission, the big shots who produced Griffith's own new film, and *Gump Two,* a sequel to *Forrest Gump,* which is being shot in Baltimore. Some of this stuff is funny in concept (when they attack the director's cut of *Patch Adams,* that's good for a laugh, although the scene itself isn't).

And Griffith, as a spoiled star named Honey Whitlock, gets into the spirit. She makes the life of her assistant (Ricki Lake) miserable, she makes impossible demands, she sends back a limousine that's the wrong color (not fiction; I once actually saw Ginger Rogers do this), and she is not a good sport when it comes to eating Maryland seafood. ("I'm not interested in some kind of meal you have to beat with a mallet while wearing some stupid little bib, while families of mutants gawk in your face.")

But the story and dialogue are genuinely amateur night, and there are times when you can almost catch the actors giggling, like kids in a senior class sketch. It's been like that in a lot of Waters's movies, from the raunchy early sleazoids like *Pink Flamingos,* through his transitional phase (*Polyester*) to his studio productions (*Hairspray, Cry-Baby, Serial Mom*). Now he seems to have returned to his middle period again, if such a thing is possible.

Cecil B. Demented got its title, Waters says, because that's what he was called in an early review. Like Ed Wood (but inevitably at a higher level of artistry), he seems to enjoy the actual process of making films: He likes to go to the set, have actors, say "Action!" and see everyone have a good time. Sometimes, in this film, that geniality works against him; the actors are having a better time than we are.

Too much of the movie feels like the kind of film where you're supposed to say, "Look! There's . . ." and fill in the name of a faded TV personality. Patricia Hearst, who appeared in Waters's funny *Cry-Baby,* is back, for example, to add ironic weight to a story about a kidnap victim who identifies with her captors. How entertaining is that really supposed to be?

Waters has always embraced a tacky design look in his films, and here a lot of the sets seem decorated by stuff everybody brought from home. Old movie posters are plastered on the walls, the cult hangs around in what looks like a rec room, and there are movie in-jokes everywhere. (Cult members have the names of their favorite directors tattooed on their arms.)

Cecil also tells us, "I don't believe in phony life-affirming endings." He sure doesn't. The ending of *Cecil B. Demented* may be phony, but it's not life affirming. One wonders if the script simply says, "Everyone runs around like crazy."

There will however always be a (small) corner of my heart filled with admiration for John Waters. He is an anarchist in an age of the cautious, an independent in an age of studio creatures, a man whose films are homemade and contain no chemicals or preservatives. Even with *Cecil B. Demented*, which fails on just about every level, you've got to hand it to him: The idea for the film is kind of inspired. When this kid gets out of high school he's going to amount to something. You wait and see.

Charlie's Angels

(Directed by McG; starring Cameron Diaz, Drew Barrymore, Lucy Liu; 2000)

Charlie's Angels is eye candy for the blind. It's a movie without a brain in its three pretty little heads, which belong to Cameron Diaz, Drew Barrymore, and Lucy Liu. This movie is a dead zone in their lives, and mine.

What is it? A satire? Of what? Of satires, I guess. It makes fun of movies that want to make fun of movies like this. It's an all-girl series of mindless action scenes. Its basic shot consists of Natalie, Dylan, and Alex, the angels, running desperately toward the camera before a huge explosion lifts them off their feet and hurls them through the air and smashes them against windshields and things—but they survive with injuries only to their makeup.

Why, I am asking, is this funny? I am thinking hard. So much money and effort was spent on these explosions that somebody must have been convinced they had a purpose, but I, try as I might, cannot see them as anything other than action without mind, purpose, humor, excitement, or entertainment.

The movie's premise will be familiar to anyone who ever watched the original TV show. I never watched the show, and the plot was familiar even to me. A disembodied voice (John Forsythe) issues commands to the three babes who work for his detective agency, and they perform his missions while wearing clothes possibly found at the thrift shop across the street from Coyote Ugly.

Barrymore, Diaz, and Liu represent redhead, blonde, and brunette respectively (or, as my colleague David Poland has pointed out, T, A, and Hair). Sad, isn't it, that three such intelligent, charming, and talented actresses could be reduced to their most prominent component parts? And voluntarily, too. At the tops of their careers, they *chose* to make this movie (Barrymore even produced it). They volunteered for what lesser talents are reduced to doing.

The cast also contains Bill Murray, who likes to appear unbilled in a lot of his movies and picked the wrong one to shelve that policy. He is winsome, cherubic, and loopy, as usual, but the movie gives him nothing to push against. There's the curious feeling he's playing to himself. Sam Rockwell plays a kidnapped millionaire, Tim Curry plays a villain, and . . . why go on?

In the months to come there will be several movies based on popular video games, including one about *Tomb Raiders* and its digital babe, Lara Croft. *Charlie's Angels* is like the trailer for a video game movie, lacking only the video game and the movie.

Christmas with the Kranks

(DIRECTED BY JOE ROTH; STARRING TIM ALLEN, JAMIE LEE CURTIS; 2004)

Christmas with the Kranks doesn't have anything wrong with it that couldn't be fixed by adding Ebenezer Scrooge and Bad Santa to the cast. It's a holiday movie of stunning awfulness that gets even worse when it turns gooey at the end. And what is it finally so happy about? Why, that the Kranks' neighbors succeed in enforcing their lockstep conformity upon them. They form a herd mentality, without the mentality.

The movie is not funny, ever, in any way, beginning to end. It's a colossal miscalculation. Tim Allen and Jamie Lee Curtis star as Luther and Nora Krank, who live in a Chicago suburb with their daughter, Blair (Julie Gonzalo). Julie is going to Peru in the Peace Corps, so this will be their first Christmas without her, and Luther suggests that instead of spending $6,000 on Christmas, he and Nora spend $3,000 on a Caribbean cruise.

Sounds reasonable to me. But perhaps you're wondering how a couple with one child and no other apparent relatives on either side of the family spends $6,000 on Christmas. The answer is, they decorate. Their street coordinates a Christmas display every year in which neighbors compete to hang the most lights from their eaves and clutter the lawn with secular symbolism. Everyone has Frosty on their rooftop.

When the word gets around that the Kranks are taking a year off, the neighborhood posse gets alarmed. Their leader is Vic Frohmeyer (Dan Aykroyd), who leads a delegation to berate them. Before long, pickets are on the front lawn, chanting "Free Frosty!" and the local paper writes a story about "The only house on the block that's keeping Frosty in the basement."

As a satire against neighborhood conformity, *Christmas with the Kranks* might have found a way to be entertaining. But no. The reasonable Kranks are pounded down by the neighbors, and then their daughter decides, after having been away only about two weeks, to fly home for Christmas with her new Peruvian fiancé. So the Kranks of course must have their traditional Christmas Eve party after all, and the third act consists of all the neighbors pitching in to decorate the house, prepare the food and decorations, etc., in a display of self-righteous cooperation that is supposed to be merry but frankly is a little scary. Here's an idea: Why don't the Kranks meet Blair and her fiancé in Miami and go on the cruise together?

The movie's complete lack of a sense of humor is proven by its inability to see that the Kranks are reasonable people and their neighbors are monstrous. What it affirms is not the Christmas spirit but the Kranks caving in. What is the movie really about? I think it may play as a veiled threat against nonconformists who don't want to go along with the majority opinion in their community. What used to be known as American individualism is now interpreted as ominous. We're supposed to think there's something wrong with the Kranks. The buried message is: Go along, and follow the lead of the most obnoxious loudmouth on the block.

Christmas, some of my older readers may recall, was once a religious holiday. Not in this movie. Not a single crucifix, not a single creche, not a single mention of the J-name. It's not that I want *Christmas with the Kranks* to get all religious, but that I think it's secular as a cop-out, to avoid any implication of religious intolerance. No matter what your beliefs or lack of them, you can celebrate Christmas in this neighborhood, because it's not about beliefs; it's about a shopping season.

So distant are the spiritual origins of the holiday, indeed, that on Christmas Eve one of the guests at the Kranks' big party is the local priest (Tom Poston), who hangs around gratefully with a benevolent smile. You don't have to be raised Catholic to know that priests do not have time off on Christmas Eve. Why isn't he preparing for Midnight Mass? Apparently because no one in the Kranks' neighborhood is going to attend—they're too busy falling off ladders while stringing decorations on rooftops.

There is, however, one supernatural creature in the movie, and I hope I'm not giving away any secrets by revealing that it is Santa Claus. The beauty of this approach is that Santa is a nonsectarian saint, a supernatural being who exists free of theology. Frosty, on the other hand, is apparently only a snowman.

A Cinderella Story

(DIRECTED BY MARK ROSMAN; STARRING HILARY DUFF, JENNIFER COOLIDGE; 2004)
"*Ernest Madison says he swore off movie critics when they panned* Dragonslayer, *one of the favorites of his childhood. 'I stopped paying attention to critics because they kept giving bad reviews to good movies,' says Madison, now thirty-five.*

"*Fourteen-year-old Byron Turner feels the same way. He turns to the Web for movie information and trailers, then shares what he's discovered with his friends, his sister, Jasmine, even his mother, Toni.*

"'*I used to watch Roger Ebert, but now I get most of my information from Byron,' Toni Turner says. 'I don't really pay attention to critics anymore.'*"
—STORY BY BOB CURTRIGHT IN THE *WICHITA EAGLE*

Dear Byron,

I know what your mother means because when I was fourteen I was also pummeling my parents with information about new movies and singing stars. I didn't have the Internet, but I grabbed information anywhere I could— mostly from other kids, Hollywood newspaper columnists, and what disk jockeys said. Of course, that was a more innocent time, when movies slowly crept around the country and there was time to get advance warning of a turkey.

Your task is harder than mine was because the typical multiplex movie is heralded by an ad campaign costing anywhere from $20 million to $50 million. Fast-food restaurants now have tie-ins with everyone from Shrek to Spider-Man; when I was a kid we were lucky to get ketchup with the fries. Enormous pressure is put on the target audience to turn out on opening weekends. And Hollywood's most valued target audience, Byron, is teenage males. In other words, you.

So I am writing you in the hope of saving your friends, your sister, Jasmine, and your mother, Toni, from going to see a truly dismal new movie. It is called A Cinderella Story, *and they may think they'll like it because it stars Hilary Duff. I liked her in* Cheaper by the Dozen, *and said she was beautiful and skilled in* The Lizzie McGuire Movie, *but wrote:*

As a role model, Lizzie functions essentially as a spokeswoman for the teen retail fashion industry, and the most-quoted line in the movie is likely to be when the catty Kate accuses her of being an "outfit repeater." Since many of the kids in the audience will not be millionaires and do indeed wear the same outfit more than once, this is a little cruel, but there you go.

That's probably something your mother might agree with.

In A Cinderella Story, Hilary plays Sam, a Valley Girl whose happy adolescence ends when her dad is killed in an earthquake. That puts her in the clutches of an evil stepmother (Jennifer Coolidge, whom you may remember fondly as Stifler's mom in the American Pie movies, although since they were rated R, of course you haven't seen them). Sam also naturally has two evil step-sisters. Half the girls in school have a crush on Austin (Chad Michael Murray), a handsome football star, but Sam never guesses that Austin is secretly kind of poetic—and is, in fact, her best chat room buddy. She agrees to meet him at the big Halloween dance, wearing a mask to preserve her anonymity; as a disguise, the mask makes her look uncannily like Hilary Duff wearing a mask.

Anyway, this is a lame, stupid movie, but Warner Bros. is spending a fortune, Byron, to convince you to see it and recommend it to your mom and Jasmine. So you must be strong and wise, and do your research. Even though your mother no longer watches my TV show, you use the Internet as a resource and no doubt know about movie review sources like rottentomatoes.com, metacritic.com, and even (pardon me while I wipe away a tear) rogerebert.com. Even when a critic dislikes a movie, if it's a good review, it has enough information so you can figure out whether you'd like it anyway.

For example, this review is a splendid review because it lets you know you'd hate A Cinderella Story, and I am pretty much 100 percent sure that you would. So I offer the following advice. Urgently counsel your mom and sister to forget about going out to the movies this week, and instead mark the calendar for August 24, when Ella Enchanted will be released on video. This is a movie that came out in April and sank without a trace, despite the fact that it was magical, funny, intelligent, romantic, and charming. It stars the beautiful Anne Hathaway (from The Princess Diaries) as a young girl whose fairy godmother

(Vivica A. Fox) puts a spell on her that makes her life extremely complicated. She has the usual evil stepmother and two jealous stepsisters. Will she win the love of Prince Charmont (Hugh Dancy)? A Cinderella Story is a terrible movie, sappy and dead in the water, but Ella Enchanted is a wonderful movie, and if Jasmine and your mom insist on Cinderella you can casually point out what Ella is short for.

As for that guy Ernest Madison, he was about eleven when Dragonslayer came out. He must have been a child prodigy, to swear off movie critics at an age when most kids don't even know they exist. If he still feels the same way, I hope he goes to see A Cinderella Story. That'll teach him.

Your fellow critic,
Roger

Cold Creek Manor

(DIRECTED BY MIKE FIGGIS; STARRING DENNIS QUAID, SHARON STONE; 2003)

Cold Creek Manor is another one of those movies where a demented fiend devotes an extraordinary amount of energy to setting up scenes for the camera. Think of the trouble it would be for one man, working alone, to kill a horse and dump it into a swimming pool. The movie is an anthology of clichés, not neglecting both the Talking Killer, who talks when he should be at work, and the reliable climax where both the villain and his victims go to a great deal of inconvenience to climb to a high place so that one of them can fall off.

The movie stars Dennis Quaid and Sharon Stone as Cooper and Leah Tilson, who get fed up with the city and move to the country, purchasing a property that looks like *The House of the Seven Gables* crossed with *The Amityville Horror.* This house is going to need a lot of work. In *Under the Tuscan Sun,* another new movie, Diane Lane is able to find some cheerful Polish workers to rehab her Tuscan villa, but the Tilsons have the extraordinarily bad judgment to hire the former owner of the house, Dale Massie (Stephen Dorff), an ex-con with a missing family. "Do you know what you're getting yourselves into?" asks a helpful local. No, but everybody in the audience does.

The movie, of course, issues two small children to the Tilsons, so that their little screams can pipe up on cue, as when the beloved horse is found in the pool. And both Cooper and Leah are tinged with the suggestion of adultery, because in American movies, as we all know, sexual misconduct leads to bad real estate choices.

In all movies involving city people who move to the country, there is an unwritten rule that everybody down at the diner knows all about the history of the new property and the secrets of its former owners. The locals act as a kind of Greek chorus, living permanently at the diner and prepared on a moment's notice to issue portentous warnings or gratuitous insults. The key player this time is Ruby (Juliette Lewis), Dale's battered girlfriend, whose sister is Sheriff Annie Ferguson (Dana Eskelson). Ruby smokes a lot, always an ominous sign, and is ambiguous about Dale—she loves the lug, but gee, does he always have to be pounding on her? The scene where she claims she wasn't hit, she only fell, is the most perfunctory demonstration possible of the battered woman in denial.

No one in this movie has a shred of common sense. The Tilsons are always leaving doors open even though they know terrible dangers lurk outside, and they are agonizingly slow to realize that Dale Massie is not only the wrong person to rehab their house, but the wrong person to be in the same state with.

Various clues, accompanied by portentous music, ominous winds, gathering clouds, etc., lead to the possibility that clues to Dale's crimes can be found at the bottom of an old well, and we are not disappointed in our expectation that Sharon Stone will sooner or later find herself at the bottom of that well. But answer me this: If you were a vicious mad-dog killer and wanted to get rid of the Tilsons and had just pushed Leah down the well, and Cooper was all alone in the woods leaning over the well and trying to pull his wife back to the surface, would you just go ahead and push him in? Or what?

But no. The audience has to undergo an extended scene in which Cooper is not pushed down the well, in order for everyone to hurry back to the house, climb up to the roof, fall off, etc. Dale Massie is not a villain in this movie, but an enabler, a character who doesn't want to kill but exists only to expedite the plot. Everything he does is after a look at the script, so that he appears, disappears, threatens, seems nice, looms, fades, pushes, doesn't push, all so that we in the audience can be frightened or, in my case, amused.

Cold Creek Manor was directed by Mike Figgis, a superb director of drama (*Leaving Las Vegas*), digital experimentation (*Timecode*), adaptations of the classics (*Miss Julie*), and atmospheric film noir (*Stormy Monday*). But he has made a thriller that thrills us only if we abandon all common sense. Of course, preposterous things happen in all thrillers, but there must be at least a gesture in the direction of plausibility, or we lose patience. When evil Dale Massie just stands there in the woods and doesn't push Cooper Tilson down the well, he stops being a killer and becomes an excuse for the movie to toy with us—and it's always better when a thriller toys with the victims instead of the audience.

Company Man

(Directed by Peter Askin and Douglas McGrath; starring Douglas McGrath, Sigourney Weaver; 2001)

Company Man is the kind of movie that seems to be wearing a strained smile, as if it's not sure we're getting the jokes. If it could, it would laugh for us. It's an arch, awkward, ill-timed, forced political comedy set in 1959 and seemingly stranded there.

Astonishing, that a movie could be this bad and star Sigourney Weaver, John Turturro, Anthony LaPaglia, Denis Leary, Woody Allen, Alan Cumming, and Ryan Phillippe. I am reminded of Gene Siskel's classic question, "Is this movie better than a documentary of the same actors having lunch?" In this case, it is not even better than a documentary of the same actors ordering room service while fighting the stomach flu.

In addition to the cast members listed above, the movie stars Douglas McGrath, its author and codirector, who is a low-rent cross between Jack Lemmon and Wally Cox and comes across without any apparent comic effect. He plays Allen Quimp, rhymes with wimp, a grammar teacher from Connecticut whose wife (Weaver) frets that he needs a better job. To get her and his own family off his back, he claims to be a CIA agent, and that leads, through a series of events as improbable as they are uninteresting, to his involvement in the defection of a Russia ballet star (Phillippe) and his assignment to Cuba on the eve of Castro's revolution.

His contact agent there is Fry, played by Denis Leary, who looks appalled at some of the scenes he's in. Example: As Fry denies that a revolutionary fever is sweeping the island, a man with a bottle full of gasoline approaches them and borrows a light from Quimp. Soon after, the man runs past in the opposite direction and they pass (without noticing—ho, ho) a burning auto. And not any burning auto, but an ancient, rusty, abandoned hulk filled with phony gas flames obviously rigged and turned on for the movie. How does it help the revolution to restage ancient auto fires?

But never mind. Fry introduces Quimp to Lowther (Woody Allen), the CIA's man in charge, who also denies a revolution is under way, while turning aside to light his cigarette from a burning effigy of Batista (ho, ho). The mystery of what Woody Allen is doing in this movie is solved in a two-name search on the Internet Movie Database, which reveals that McGrath cowrote the screenplay for Allen's *Bullets Over Broadway*. Now Allen is returning the favor, I guess.

Well, that was a funny movie, and the same search identifies McGrath as the writer-director of *Emma* (1996), a nice little comedy with Gwyneth Paltrow. So he is obviously not without talent—except in this movie. Maybe the mistake was to star himself. He doesn't have the presence to anchor a comedy; all those jokes about Quimp the nonentity ring true, instead of funny.

As bad movies go, *Company Man* falls less in the category of Affront to the Audience and more in the category of Nonevent. It didn't work me up into a frenzy of dislike, but dialed me down into sullen indifference. It was screened twice for the Chicago press, and I sat through the first thirty minutes of the second screening, thinking to check it against a different crowd. I heard no laughter. Just an occasional cough, or the shuffling of feet, or a yawn, or a sigh, like in a waiting room.

Connie and Carla

(DIRECTED BY MICHAEL LEMBECK; STARRING NIA VARDALOS, TONI COLLETTE; 2004)
Connie and Carla plays like a genial amateur theatrical, the kind of production where you'd like it more if you were friends with the cast. The plot is creaky, the jokes are laborious, and total implausibility is not considered the slightest problem. Written by and starring Nia Vardalos, it's a disappointment after her hilarious *My Big Fat Greek Wedding.*

This time, in a retread of *Some Like It Hot,* Vardalos and Toni Collette play Connie and Carla, two friends who have been a singing duo since schooldays. Now they're in their thirties, stardom has definitively passed them by, and they perform a medley of musical comedy hits in an airport lounge that resembles no airport lounge in history, but does look a lot like somebody's rec room with some tables and chairs and a cheesy stage.

The guys they date beg them to face facts: They'll never really be any good. But they still dream the dream, and then, in a direct lift from *Some Like It Hot,* they witness a mob murder and have to go on the lam. The way this scene is handled is typical of the film's ham-handed approach: They're hiding in a parking garage when their boss is rubbed out, so what do they do? Stay hidden? Nope, they both stand up, scream, and wave their hands. They have to: Otherwise, there wouldn't be any movie.

Connie and Carla hit the road, head for Los Angeles, happen into a drag bar, and inspiration strikes: They can pretend to be female impersonators! That way no one will find them, or even know where to look. One of the running gags in *Some Like It Hot* was that Jack Lemmon and Tony Curtis did not make very plausible women, but the movie handled that by surrounding them with dim bulbs like the characters played by Marilyn Monroe and Joe E. Brown. *Connie and Carla* is set in today's Los Angeles gay community, where the other characters are supposed to be real, I guess, and where never in a million years could they pass as boys passing as girls.

Their danger from the mob is put on hold as the movie switches to another reliable formula, the showbiz rags-to-riches epic. Their act, of course, is an immediate hit, they make lots of buddies among the other drag queens, and there are many close calls as they're almost discovered out of drag, or would that be not out of drag? The time scheme of the movie is sufficiently forgiving for them to suggest that their little club remodel itself and double in size; and there is actually a scene where the show goes on while plastic sheeting separates the old club from the new addition. Next scene, the construction work is finished. Forget the drag queens, get the names of those contractors.

Nia Vardalos was of course wonderful in *My Big Fat Greek Wedding*, and Toni Collette has proven she can do about anything—but she can't do this. The movie masks desperation with frenzied slapstick and forced laughs. And when Connie meets a straight guy she likes (David Duchovny), we groan as the plot manufactures Meet Cutes by having them repeatedly run into each other and knock each other down. Uh, huh. I think maybe the point in *Some Like It Hot* was that Joe E. Brown fell in love with Jack Lemmon, not Marilyn Monroe. I'm not saying *Connie and Carla* would have been better if Connie had attracted a gay guy, or maybe a lesbian who saw through the drag, but at least that would have supplied a comic problem, not a romantic one.

My Big Fat Greek Wedding was such a huge success that it gave Vardalos a free ticket for her next movie. Someone should have advised her this wasn't the right screenplay to cash in the pass. Nor does director Michael Lembeck save the day. He's done a lot of TV sitcoms, including many episodes of *Friends,* and his only other feature film, *The Santa Clause 2,* was funny enough, but here he took on an unfilmable premise and goes down with it. By the end, as the gangsters, the Midwestern boyfriends, Duchovny, various drag queens, and Debbie Reynolds (herself) all descend on the finale, we're not watching a comedy, we're watching a traffic jam.

Constantine

(DIRECTED BY FRANCIS LAWRENCE; STARRING KEANU REEVES, RACHEL WEISZ; 2005)
No, *Constantine* is not part of a trilogy including *Troy* and *Alexander.* It's not about the emperor at all, but about a man who can see the world behind the world, and is waging war against the scavengers of the

damned. There was a nice documentary about emperor penguins, however, at Sundance this year. The males sit on the eggs all winter long in, like, sixty degrees below zero.

Keanu Reeves plays Constantine as a chain-smoking, depressed demon hunter who lives above a bowling alley in Los Angeles. Since he was a child, he has been able to see that not all who walk among us are human. Some are penguins. Sorry about that. Some are half-angels and half-devils. Constantine knows he is doomed to hell because he once tried to kill himself, and is trying to rack up enough frames against the demons to earn his way into heaven.

There is a scene early in the movie where Constantine and his doctor look at his X-rays, never a good sign in a superhero movie. He has lung cancer. The angel Gabriel (Tilda Swinton) tells him, "You are going to die young because you've smoked thirty cigarettes a day since you were thirteen." Gabriel has made more interesting announcements. Constantine has already spent some time in hell, which looks like a post-nuclear Los Angeles created by animators with a hangover. No doubt it is filled with carcinogens.

The half-angels and half-devils are earthly proxies in the war between God and Satan. You would think that God would be the New England Patriots of this contest, but apparently there is a chance that Satan could win. Constantine's lonely mission is to track down half-demons and cast them back to the fires below. Like Blade, the vampire killer, he is surprisingly optimistic, considering he is one guy in one city dealing on a case-by-case basis, and the enemy is global.

Constantine has a technical adviser named Beeman (Max Baker), who lives in the ceiling of the bowling alley among the pin-spotting machines, and functions like Q in the James Bond movies. Here he is loading Constantine with the latest weaponry: "Bullet shavings from the assassination attempt on the pope, holy water from the river of Jordan, and, you'll love this, screech beetles." The screech beetles come in a little matchbox. "To the fallen," Beeman explains, "the sound is like nails on a blackboard." Later there is a scene where Constantine is inundated by the creatures of hell, and desperately tries to reach the matchbox and *get* those beetles to *screeching*.

Rachel Weisz plays Angela Dodson, an L.A. police detective whose twin sister, Isabel, has apparently committed suicide. Isabel reported seeing demons, so Angela consults Constantine, who nods wisely and wonders if Isabel jumped, or was metaphysically pushed. Later in the film, to show Angela that she also has the gift of seeing the world behind the world, Constantine holds her underwater in a bathtub until she passes out and sees the torments of hell. No bright white corridors and old friends and Yanni for her. You wonder what kind of an L.A. cop would allow herself to be experimentally drowned in a bathtub by a guy who lives over a bowling alley.

Together, they prowl the nighttime streets. At one point, Constantine needs to consult Midnite (Djimon Hounsou), a former witch doctor who runs a private nightclub where half-angels and half-demons can get half-loaded and talk shop. There is a doorman. To gain admittance, you have to read his mind and tell him what's on the other side of the card he's holding up. "Two frogs on a bench," Constantine says. Could have been a lucky guess.

There is a priest in the film, the alcoholic Father Hennessy (Pruitt Taylor Vince), whose name, I guess, is product placement. Strange that there is a priest, since that opens the door to Catholicism and therefore to the news that Constantine is not doomed unless he wages a lifelong war against demons, but needs merely go to confession; three Our Fathers, three Hail Marys, and he's outta there. Strange that movies about Satan always require Catholics. You never see your Presbyterians or Episcopalians hurling down demons.

The forces of hell manifest themselves in many ways. One victim is eaten by flies. A young girl is possessed by a devil, and Constantine shouts, "I need a mirror! Now! At least three feet high!" He can capture the demon in the mirror and throw it out the window, see, although you wonder why supernatural beings would have such low-tech security holes.

Keanu Reeves has a deliberately morose energy level in the movie, as befits one who has seen hell, walks among half-demons, and is dying. He keeps on smoking. Eventually he confronts Satan (Peter Stormare), who wears a white suit. (Satan to tailor: "I want a suit just like God's.")

Oh, and the plot also involves the Spear of Destiny, which is the spear that killed Christ, and which has been missing since World War II, which seems to open a window to the possibility of Nazi villains, but no.

Corky Romano

(DIRECTED BY ROB PRITTS; STARRING CHRIS KATTAN, PETER FALK; 2001)

Corky Romano continues the *Saturday Night Live* jinx, which in recent years has frustrated the talented members of the TV program in their efforts to make watchable movies. It's a desperately unfunny gangster spoof, starring Chris Kattan as the kid brother in a Mafia family, so trusting and naive he really does believe his father is in the landscaping business.

This is the third time the jinx has claimed Kattan as a victim, after *A Night at the Roxbury* (1998) and this year's *Monkeybone,* two films that will be among the first to go when Blockbuster destroys 25 percent of its VHS tape inventory, and will not be leading the chain's list of DVD replacement titles.

Now when I use the words *desperately unfunny,* what do I mean? Consider one of Corky's earlier scenes, where we see him as an assistant veterinarian. Clumsy beyond belief, he knocks over everything in a room full of ailing animals, and a snake crawls up his pants and eventually, inevitably, emerges from his fly.

I submit as a general principle that it is not funny when a clumsy person knocks over *everything* in a room. The choreography makes it obvious that the character, in one way or another, is deliberately careening from one collision to another. It always looks deliberate. Indeed, it looks like a deliberate attempt to force laughs instead of building them. One movie where it does work is *The Mummy,* where Rachel Weisz knocks over a bookcase and a whole library tumbles over domino-style. But there an original accident builds and builds beyond her control; *Corky Romano's* approach would be to reel around the room knocking over every bookcase individually.

In the movie, Corky's father is played by Peter Falk. True, Falk is one of the first guys you'd think of for the role, but they should have kept thinking. He has played similar roles so many times that he can sleepwalk through his dialogue; a completely unexpected casting choice might have been funnier. Corky has two very tough brothers (Peter Berg and Chris Penn) who doubt their father's plan, which is that the youngest son should infiltrate the FBI in order to destroy the evidence against the old man.

That brings Corky into contact with Howard Schuster (Richard Roundtree), the local FBI chief, who is given the thankless comic task of never knowing more than he needs to know in order to make the wrong decision. There's also Vinessa Shaw as an FBI agent who goes undercover as a sexy nurse. Or maybe she's a sexy agent who goes undercover as a nurse. Such a thin line separates the two concepts.

Corky Romano is like a dead zone of comedy. The concept is exhausted, the ideas are tired, the physical gags are routine, the story is labored, and the actors look like they can barely contain their doubts about the project.

The Crew

(DIRECTED BY MICHAEL DINNER; STARRING RICHARD DREYFUSS, BURT REYNOLDS; 2000)
Hot on the heels of *Space Cowboys*, which was about four astro-codgers, here comes *The Crew,* about four mobster-codgers. Go with the cowboys. One difference between the two movies is that *Space Cowboys* develops quirky characters and tells a story that makes it necessary for the old friends to have a reunion, while *The Crew* is all contrivance and we don't believe a minute of it.

Of course, *The Crew* wants only to be a comedy, not a bittersweet coda to *Wise Guys*. But even at that it fails, because we don't buy the opening premise, which is that four onetime heavy-duty mobsters would all retire to the same seedy residential hotel on South Beach in Miami, there to tick down their days lined up in wicker chairs on the porch, watching the dollies go by. This is a situation that shouts out Plot, not Life, and everything that happens to them seems generated from overconfident chuckles in the screenwriting process.

The retired mobsters are Bobby Bartellemeo, Joey "Bats" Pistella, Mike "The Brick" Donatelli, and Tony "Mouth" Donato (Bobby violently rejected a nickname in his youth and never got another). In the same order, they're played by Richard Dreyfuss, Burt Reynolds, Dan Hedaya, and Seymour Cassel. After this movie and *Mad Dog Time* (1996), which reached a kind of grandeur as one of the worst films of all time, Dreyfuss and Reynolds should instruct their agents to reject all further mob "comedies" on sight. The later stages of their careers cannot withstand another one.

The plot has to do with plans to upgrade their fleabag hotel into yet another art-retro South Beach yuppie playpen. The old guys like where they live and want to preserve it, so they dream up a cockamamie scheme in which they steal a corpse from the morgue (Hedaya has a part-time job among the stiffs) and bring it back to the hotel, where they plan to shoot it and make it look like a murder, except that, as Bats complains, the old guy "looks like the pope." And so he does—Pope Pius XII, who was several popes ago, back when young Bats was no doubt taking a livelier interest in the church.

One thing leads to another. Turns out the corpse is in fact the ancient father of a current Miami crime lord. The old guy had Alzheimer's, wandered away from the nursing home, died anonymously, and it was just their bad luck to make the wrong choice at the morgue. Their pseudo-whack of the old dead guy is imprudently revealed by Mouth to a nightclub stripper named Ferris (Jennifer Tilly), whose stepmother turns out to be Pepper Lowenstein (Lainie Kazan), known to the Mafia-codgers from the deli she used to run in New York, back in their carefree youth when they were blowing up trucks. Into the mix come two local detectives (Carrie-Anne Moss and Jeremy Piven), and one of them has an unexpected link to the past, too.

And so on. Somehow it all needs to be more desperate, or more slapstick, or have more edge, or turn up the heat in some other way. Lainie Kazan's presence suggests one obvious idea: Why not a comedy about four Mafia widows in Miami Beach? *The Crew* unfolds as a construction, not a series of surprises and delights. Occasionally a line of dialogue or two will float into view, providing a hint of the edge the whole movie might have had. (My favorite: A gun dealer, happily selling them a shotgun with no background check, adds, "Don't thank me—thank the Republicans.")

Comparing this to *Space Cowboys,* I realize how much more heft and dimension the cowboys had. Attention was paid to making them individuals, instead of just rattling off attributes and body types. And Clint Eastwood, who directed that movie, is a better filmmaker than Michael Dinner, who seems too content and not hungry enough—too complacent that his material will sell itself. There is also the fact that Eastwood, James Garner, Tommy Lee Jones, and Donald Sutherland have built up goodwill and screen authority by avoiding movies like *The Crew* instead of making them.

Crossroads

(DIRECTED BY TAMRA DAVIS; STARRING BRITNEY SPEARS, ZOE SALDANA; 2002)

I went to *Crossroads* expecting a glitzy bimbo fest and got the bimbos but not the fest. Britney Spears's feature debut is curiously low-key and even sad. Yes, it pulls itself together occasionally for a musical number, but even those are so locked into the "reality" of the story that they don't break loose into fun.

The movie opens with three eighth-graders burying a box filled with symbols of their dreams of the future. Four years later, on high school graduation day, the girls are hardly on speaking terms, but they meet to dig up the box, tentatively renew their friendship, and find themselves driving to California in a convertible piloted by a hunk.

Lucy (Spears) hopes to find her long-indifferent mother in Arizona. Kit (Zoe Saldana) wants to find her fiancé in Los Angeles; he has become ominously vague about wedding plans. Mimi (Taryn Manning) is pregnant, but wants to compete in a record company's open audition. Spoiler warning! Stop reading now unless you want to learn the dismal outcome of their trip, as Lucy's mom informs her she was a "mistake," Kit's fiancé turns out to have another woman *and* to be guilty of date-rape, and Mimi, who was the rape victim, has a miscarriage.

I'm not kidding. *Crossroads,* which is being promoted with ads show-ing Britney bouncing on the bed while lip-synching a song, is a downer that would be even more depressing if the plot wasn't such a lame soap opera.

This is the kind of movie where the travelers stop by the roadside to yell "Hello!" and keep on yelling, unaware that there is no echo. Where Britney is a virgin at eighteen and enlists her lab partner to deflower her. Where when that doesn't work out she finds herself attracted to Ben (Anson Mount), the guy who's giving them the ride, even though he is alleged to have killed a man. Where the apparent age difference between Spears and Mount makes it look like he's robbing the cradle. (In real life, he's twenty-nine and she's twenty, but he's an experienced twenty-nine and she's playing a naive eighteen-year-old.)

Of the three girls, Mimi has the most to do. She teaches Kit how to land a punch, tells the others why she doesn't drink, and deals almost casually with her miscarriage. Kit is a slow study who takes forever to fig-ure out her fiancé has dumped her. And Spears, as Lucy, seems to think maybe she's in a serious Winona Ryder role, but with songs.

"What are you writing in that book?" Ben asks her. "Poems," she says. He wants her to read one for him. She does. "Promise not to laugh," she says. He doesn't, but the audience does. It's the lyrics for her song "I'm Not a Girl, Not Yet a Woman." Didn't anyone warn her you can't introduce famous material as if it's new without risking a bad laugh? Later, Ben com-poses music for the words, and he plays the piano while she riffs endlessly to prove she has never once thought about singing those words before.

The movie cuts away from the payoffs of the big scenes. We get the foreplay for both of Britney's sex scenes, but never see what happens. Her big meeting with her mother lacks the showdown. We can be grateful, I suppose, that after Mimi falls down some stairs after learning that Kit's fiancé is the man who raped her, we are spared the details of her miscar-riage and cut to her later in the hospital. Perhaps study of the live child-birth scene in the Spice Girls movie warned the filmmakers away from obstetric adventures in this one.

Like *Coyote Ugly,* a movie it resembles in the wardrobe department, *Crossroads* is rated PG-13 but is going on seventeen. Caution, kids: It can be more dangerous to get a ride in a convertible with a cute but ominous guy than you might think. (See *Kalifornia*.)

And you can't always support yourself by tips on Karaoke Night. When the girls sing in a karaoke contest, a three-gallon jug is filled with bills, which, after they're piled in stacks on the bar, are enough to pay for car repairs and the rest of the trip. Uh, huh. Curious about that karaoke bar. It has a position on the stage with an underlight and one of those poles that strippers twine around. You don't see those much in karaoke clubs.

Daddy Day Care

(DIRECTED BY STEVE CARR; STARRING EDDIE MURPHY, JEFF GARLIN; 2003)

Daddy Day Care is a woeful miscalculation, a film so wrongheaded audiences will be more appalled than amused. It imagines Eddie Murphy and sidekick Jeff Garlin in charge of a day-care center that could only terrify parents in the audience, although it may look like fun for their children. The center's philosophy apparently consists of letting kids do whatever they feel like, while the amateur staff delivers one-liners.

I realize that the movie is not intended as a serious work about day-care centers. It is a comedy (in genre, not in effect). But at some point we might expect it to benefit from real life, real experiences, real kids. Not a chance. It's all simply a prop for the Eddie Murphy character. Aggressively simpleminded, it's fueled by the delusion that it has a brilliant premise: Eddie Murphy plus cute kids equals success. But a premise should be the starting point for a screenplay, not its finish line.

In the film, Murphy plays Charlie Hinton, an advertising executive assigned to the account of a breakfast cereal based on vegetables. This leads eventually to desperate scenes involving Murphy dressed in a broccoli suit, maybe on the grounds that once, long ago, he was funny in a Gumby suit. The cereal fails, and he's fired along with his best pal Phil (Garlin). Charlie's wife, Kim (Regina King), goes to work as a lawyer, leaving her husband at home to take care of their son, Ben (Khamani Griffin). Next thing you know, Charlie has the idea of opening a day-care center.

Enter the villainess, Miss Haridan (Anjelica Huston), whose own day-care center is so expensive that Charlie can no longer afford to send Ben there. Huston plays the role as your standard dominatrix, ruling her school with an iron hand, but you know what? It looks to me like a pretty good school, with the kids speaking foreign languages and discussing advanced science projects. Obviously, in the terms of this movie, any school where the kids have to study is bad, just as a school where the kids can run around and raise hell is good. This bias is disguised as Charlie's insight into child psychology.

The new school is successful almost from the outset, and empty seats begin to turn up in Miss Harridan's school as parents switch their kids to the cheaper alternative. No sane parent would trust a child to Charlie and Phil's chaotic operation, but never mind. Soon the partners hire an assistant, Marvin, played by Steve Zahn as a case of arrested development. Miss Harridan, facing the failure of her school, mounts a counterattack and of course is vanquished. She appears in the movie's final shot in a pathetically unfunny attempt to force humor long after the cause has been lost.

What the movie lacks is any attempt to place Murphy and his costars in a world of real kids and real day care. This entire world looks like it exists only on a studio lot. A few kids are given identifiable attributes (one won't take off his superhero costume), but basically they're just a crowd of rug-rats in the background of the desperately forced comedy. Even the movie's poop joke fails, and if you can't make a poop joke work in a movie about kids, you're in trouble.

The movie's miscalculation, I suspect, is the same one that has misled Murphy in such other recent bombs as *I Spy* and *The Adventures of Pluto Nash* (which was unseen by me and most of the rest of the world). That's the delusion that Murphy's presence will somehow lend magic to an undistinguished screenplay. A film should begin with a story and characters, not with a concept and a star package.

Dear Wendy

(DIRECTED BY THOMAS VINTERBERG; STARRING JAMIE BELL, BILL PULLMAN; 2005)

Thomas Vinterberg's *Dear Wendy* is a tedious exercise in style, intended as a meditation on guns and violence in America but more of a meditation on itself, the kind of meditation that invites the mind to stray. Mine strayed to the fact that the screenplay is by Vinterberg's Danish mentor Lars von Trier, and the movie, although filmed on three-dimensional sets, feels as artificial and staged as his *Dogville* (2003). Once again a small group of people inhabit a small space, can all see each other out the window, and live in each other's pockets.

The movie is set in Electric Park, a set in which two rows of buildings face each other and a third row supplies the end of the street. Towering overhead is the elevator for the mine shaft; the locals were mostly miners, but the mines are nearly played out. Dick (Jamie Bell), the orphaned son of a miner, lives with his protective black housekeeper, Clarabelle (Novella Nelson), and his life lacks purpose until he goes into a store to buy a toy gun.

The weapon, as it happens, is real. Dick is a pacifist, but falls in love with the gun, which he names Wendy. Much of the movie consists of a letter he writes to Wendy, about how he loved her and lost her, and how everything went wrong. He descends into an abandoned mine for target practice, finds he has a psychic bond with Wendy (he can hit a bulls-eye blindfolded), and soon enlists other people his age into a secret society named the Dandies.

They meet in the mine, which they redecorate as the "Temple," and begin to dress in oddments of haberdashery, like fools or clowns. They have the obligatory unlimited supply of candles. They take a vow of nonviolence. Then Clarabelle's grandson Sebastian (Danso Gordon) appears on the scene, fresh from jail. The local sheriff (Bill Pullman) suggests that Dick "could be like Sebastian's friend, and keep an eye on him."

Sebastian is black because he is Clarabelle's grandson, of course, but also because as the only young black man in the film he is made into the catalyst for violence. This is the Vinterberg/von Trier version of insight into America, roughly as profound as the scene in *Dirty Love* where Carmen Electra holds a gun to a man's head simply because she likes to act black and thinks that will help. To call such reasoning racist is tempting, and yet I suspect in both movies the real reasons for it are stupidity and cluelessness.

Right away there is trouble. A romantic triangle forms, as Sebastian holds Wendy tenderly and Dick gets jealous. Sebastian helpfully supplies all of the Dandies with guns, and then a challenge emerges: Clarabelle visits her granddaughter at the end of the street every year, and has become afraid to leave the house. The Dandies devise an ingenious scheme to protect her from danger during her one-block walk, despite the fact that the town seems to contain no danger. I am reminded of a guy I knew who said he carried a gun because he lived in a dangerous neighborhood, and another guy told him, "It would be a lot safer if you moved."

What happens during Clarabelle's progress down the street I will leave for you to experience if you are unwise enough to see the film. As the Dandies plan their operation, Dick draws a diagram of the town that looks uncannily like an aerial view of the chalk outlines on a sound stage floor that von Trier used to create Dogville. Odd, that the Dogma movement from Denmark, which originally seemed to call for the use of actual locations exactly as they were, has become more stylized and artificial than German Expressionism.

It is true that America has problems, and that many of them are caused by a culture of guns and violence. It is also true that a movie like David Cronenberg's *A History of Violence* (or I could name countless others) is wiser and more useful on the subject than the dim conceit of *Dear Wendy*.

Apart from what the movie says, which is shallow and questionable, there is the problem of how it says it. The style is so labored and obvious that with all the goodwill in the world you cannot care what happens next. It is all just going through the motions, silly and pointless motions, with no depth, humor, edge, or timing. Vinterberg has made wonderful films like *The Celebration* (1998), filled with life and emotion. Here he seems drained of energy, plodding listlessly on the treadmill of style, racking up minutes on the clock but not getting anywhere.

Death to Smoochy

(DIRECTED BY DANNY DE VITO; STARRING ROBIN WILLIAMS, EDWARD NORTON; 2002)
Only enormously talented people could have made *Death to Smoochy*. Those with lesser gifts would have lacked the nerve to make a film so bad, so miscalculated, so lacking any connection with any possible audience. To make a film this awful, you have to have enormous ambition and confidence, and dream big dreams.

The movie, directed by Danny DeVito (!), is about two clowns. That violates a cardinal rule of modern mass entertainment, which is that everyone hates clowns almost as much as they hate mimes. (*Big Fat Liar,* a much better recent showbiz comedy, got this right. When the clown arrived at a birthday party, the kids joyfully shouted, "Hey, it's the clown! Let's hurt him!") Most clowns are simply tiresome (I exempt Bozo). There are, however, two dread categories of clowns: clowns who are secretly vile and evil, and clowns who are guileless and good. *Death to Smoochy* takes no half-measures, and provides us with one of each.

We begin with Rainbow Randolph, played by Robin Williams, an actor who should never, ever play a clown of any description, because the role writes a license for him to indulge in those very mannerisms he should be striving to purge from his repertoire. Rainbow is a corrupt drunk who takes bribes to put kids on his show. The show itself is what kiddie TV would look like if kids wanted to see an Ann Miller musical starring midgets.

The good clown is Smoochy (Edward Norton), a soul so cheerful, earnest, honest, and uncomplicated you want to slap him and bring him back to his senses. Sample helpful Smoochy song for kids: "My Stepdad's Not Bad, He's Just Adjusting." Both of these clowns wear the kinds of costumes seen at the openings of used car lots in states that doubt the possibility of evolution. Rainbow is convoluted, but Smoochy is so boring that the film explains why, on a long bus ride, you should always choose to sit next to Mrs. Robinson, for example, rather than Benjamin.

Enter the film's most engaging character, a TV producer named Nora (Catherine Keener), who, like Rachel Griffiths, cannot play dumb and is smart enough never to try. She's taking instructions from the network boss (Jon Stewart, who might have been interesting as one of the clowns). They're trapped in an inane subplot involving two bad guys, Burke (De Vito) and Merv Green (played by the gravel-voiced Harvey Fierstein, who, as he puts on weight, is becoming boulder-voiced). There is also Vincent Schiavelli as a former child star, now a crackhead.

The drama of the two clowns and their battle for the time slot is complicated by Rainbow Randolph's attempts to smear Smoochy by tricking him into appearing at a neo-Nazi rally. One wonders idly: Are there enough neo-Nazis to fill a thundering convention center? Do they usually book clowns? The answer to the second question may be yes.

The movie ends by crossing an ice show with elements of *The Manchurian Candidate*. It involves an odd sexual predilection: Nora has a fetish for kiddie show hosts. It has a lesbian hit-squad leader with a thick Irish brogue. It uses four-letter language as if being paid by the word. In all the annals of the movies, few films have been this odd, inexplicable, and unpleasant.

D.E.B.S.

(DIRECTED BY ANGELA ROBINSON; STARRING SARA FOSTER, MEAGAN GOOD; 2005)

At some point during the pitch meetings for *D.E.B.S.* someone must certainly have used the words *Charlie's Lesbians*. The formula is perfectly obvious: Four sexy young women work for a secret agency as a team that is gifted at lying, cheating, stealing, and killing. How do we know they have these gifts? Because of the movie's funniest moment, during the opening narration, when we learn that trick questions on SAT exams allow an agency to select high school graduates who can and will lie, cheat, steal, kill.

Amy (Sara Foster), the leader of the group, is a latent lesbian. Lucy Diamond (Jordana Brewster), a thief and master criminal, goes on a blind date with a semiretired Russian assassin named Ninotchka (Jessica Cauffiel). When the D.E.B.S. monitor the date on a surveillance assignment, Amy is attracted to the smiling, seductive Lucy, which causes security complications. Pause for a moment to ask with me, would this movie be as interesting if the blind date had been with a guy? I submit it would not, because the lesbian material is all that separates D.E.B.S. from the standard teenage Insta-flick.

The character traits of the D.E.B.S. are only slightly more useful than the color-coded uniforms of the Teenage Mutant Ninja Turtles. In such movies, taxonomy is personality; once you've got the label straight, you know all you're ever going to know about the character. In addition to Amy, who is a lesbian, we meet Max (Meagan Good), who is black, Janet (Jill Ritchie), who is white, and Dominique (Devon Aoki), who corners the market on character attributes by being an Asian with a French accent who smokes all the time. I would not identify the characters by race, but the movie leaves us with no other way to differentiate them.

Dominique's smoking fascinates me. She never lights a cigarette, extinguishes one or taps an ash. She simply exists with a freshly lit filter tip in her mouth, occasionally removing it to emit a perky little puff of uninhaled smoke. I wish I had stayed through the credits to see if there was a cigarette wrangler. Dominique's very presence on the screen inspires me to imagine an excited pitch meeting during which the writer-director, Angela Robinson, said with enthusiasm: "And Dominique, the Asian chick, smokes all the time!" At which the studio executives no doubt thanked the gods for blessing them with such richness and originality in character formation.

I have mentioned the pitch more than once because this movie is all pitch. It began as a popular short subject at Sundance, where audiences were reportedly amused by a send-up of the *Charlie's Angels* formula in which the angels were teenagers and one was a lesbian. The problem is, a short subject need only delight while a feature must deliver.

At one point in D.E.B.S. a team member uses the term *supervillain*, not ironically but descriptively, leading to a new rule for *Ebert's Little Movie*

Glossary: "Movies that refer to supervillains not ironically but descriptively reveal an insufficient disconnect between the pitch and the story." The rule has countless subsets, such as characters referring to themselves or others as heroes. Best friends who say, "I'm only comic relief" are given a provisional pass.

The Charlie figure in the movie is the president of the D.E.B.S. Academy, played by Michael Clarke Duncan, who looks spiffy in a tailored suit and rimless glasses. He gives them their orders, while never asking himself, I guess, how goes the homeland security when bimbos are minding the front lines. For that matter, Lucy Diamond, whose middle name I hope is Intheskywith, would rather make love than war, which leads to some PG-13 smooching.

Mrs. Peatree (Holland Taylor), headmistress of the D.E.B.S. academy, asks Amy to turn the situation to her advantage by using herself as bait ("like Jodie did in that movie—you know the one, what was its name?"). I confess at this point I was less interested in Jodie's filmography than in the news that the D.E.B.S. academy has a headmistress. I found myself wanting to know more about the academy's school song, lunchroom menu, student council, and parents' day. ("Janet has perfect scores in lying and cheating, but needs work on her stealing, and is flunking murder.") The uniform is cute little plaid skirts and white blouses, with matching plaid ties.

Other notes: I think I heard correctly, but may not have, that one character's "Freudian analysis" is that she suffers from a "dangerous Jungian symbiosis." Now there's a Freudian analysis you don't hear every day. I know I heard correctly when two of the girls share their dream: "Let's pretend we're in Barcelona, and you're at art school and I'm renting boats to tourists." The young people today, send them on junior year abroad, they go nuts. I note in passing that the movie quotes accurately from the famous shot in *Citizen Kane* where the camera moves straight up past the catwalks, drops, ropes, and pulleys above a stage. For me, that shot was like the toy in a box of Cracker-Jack: not worth much, but you're glad they put it in there.

Dirty Love

(DIRECTED BY JOHN MALLORY ASHER; STARRING JENNY MCCARTHY, CARMEN ELECTRA; 2005)

Dirty Love wasn't written and directed; it was committed. Here is a film so pitiful it doesn't rise to the level of badness. It is hopelessly incompetent. It stars and was scripted by Jenny McCarthy, the cheerfully sexy model who, judging by this film, is fearless, plucky, and completely lacking in common sense or any instinct for self-preservation.

Yes, it takes nerve to star in a scene where you plop down in a supermarket aisle surrounded by a lake of your own menstrual blood. But to expect an audience to find that funny verges on dementia. McCarthy follows it with a scene where the cops strip-search her and she's wearing a maxi pad that would be adequate for an elephant. She doesn't need to do this. It's painful to see a pretty girl, who seems nice enough, humiliating herself on the screen. I feel sorry for her.

The film basically consists of McCarthy and her half-dressed friends Carmen Electra and Kam Heskin grouped awkwardly on the screen like high school girls in that last heedless showoff stage before a designated driver straps them in and takes them home. At times they literally seem to be letting the camera roll while they try to think up something goofy to do. There is also a lot of crude four-letter dialogue, pronounced as if they know the words but not the music.

The plot: McCarthy plays Rebecca, who seems well dressed and with great wheels for someone with no apparent income. She is cheated on by her boyfriend, Richard (Victor Webster), aka Dick, who looks like the model on the cover of a drugstore romance novel about a girl who doesn't know that guys who look like that spend all of their time looking like that. When she discovers his treachery, Rebecca has a grotesque emotional spasm. She weeps, wails, staggers about Hollywood Boulevard flailing her arms and screaming, crawls on the pavement, and waves her butt at strangers while begging them to ravage her because she is simultaneously worthless and wants to teach Dick a lesson. Then, to teach Dick a lesson, she dates scummy losers.

These events are directed by McCarthy's former partner John Mallory Asher and photographed by Eric Wycoff so incompetently that Todd McCarthy, the esteemed film critic of *Variety*, should have won the Jean Hersholt Humanitarian Award for generosity after writing the "whole package has a cheesy look." This movie is an affront to cheese. Also to breasts. Jenny McCarthy has a technologically splendid bosom that should, in my opinion, be put to a better use than being vomited upon.

The Carmen Electra character meanwhile struts around like a ho in a bad music video, speaking black street talk as if she learned it phonetically, and pulling out a gun and holding it to a man's head because she thinks, obviously, that pulling guns on guys is expected of any authentic black woman. A scene like that would be insulting in any other movie; here it possibly distracts her from doing something even more debasing.

I would like to say more, but—no, I wouldn't. I would not like to say more. I would like to say less. On the basis of *Dirty Love,* I am not certain that anyone involved has ever seen a movie, or knows what one is. I would like to invite poor Jenny McCarthy up here to the Toronto Film Festival, where I am writing this review while wonderful films are playing all over town, and get her a pass, and require her to go to four movies a day until she gets the idea.

A Dirty Shame

(Directed by John Waters; starring Tracey Ullman, Johnny Knoxville; 2004)
There is in showbiz something known as *a bad laugh.* That's the laugh you don't want to get, because it indicates not amusement but incredulity, nervousness, or disapproval. John Waters's *A Dirty Shame* is the only comedy I can think of that gets more bad laughs than good ones.

Waters is the poet of bad taste and labors mightily here to be in the worst taste he can manage. That's not the problem—no, not even when Tracey Ullman picks up a water bottle using a method usually employed only in Bangkok sex shows. We go to a Waters film expecting bad taste, but we also expect to laugh, and *A Dirty Shame* is monotonous, repetitive, and sometimes wildly wrong in what it hopes is funny.

The movie takes place in Baltimore, as most Waters films do. Stockholm got Bergman, Rome got Fellini, and Baltimore—well, it also has Barry Levinson. Ullman plays Sylvia Stickles, the owner of a 7-Eleven type store. Chris Isaak plays Vaughn, her husband. Locked in an upstairs room is their daughter, Caprice (Selma Blair), who was a legend at the local go-go bar until her parents grounded and padlocked her. She worked under the name of Ursula Udders, a name inspired by breasts so large they are obviously produced by technology, not surgery.

Sylvia has no interest in sex until a strange thing happens. She suffers a concussion in a car crash, and it turns her into a sex maniac. Not only can't she get enough of it, she doesn't even pause to inquire what it is before she tries to get it. This attracts the attention of a local auto mechanic named Ray-Ray Perkins, played by Johnny Knoxville, who no longer has to consider *Jackass* his worst movie. Ray-Ray has a following of sex addicts who joyfully proclaim their special tastes and gourmet leanings.

A digression. In 1996, David Cronenberg made a movie named *Crash,* about a group of people who had a sexual fetish for car crashes, wounds, broken bones, crutches, and so on. It was a good movie, but as I wrote at the time, it's about "a sexual fetish that, in fact, no one has." I didn't get a lot of letters disagreeing with me.

John Waters also goes fetish-shopping in *A Dirty Shame,* treating us to such specialties as infantilism (a cop who likes to wear diapers), bear lovers (those who lust after fat, hairy men), and Mr. Pay Day, whose fetish does not involve the candy bar of the same name. We also learn about such curious pastimes as shelf humping, mallet whacking, and tickling. As the movie introduced one sex addiction after another, I sensed a curious current running through the screening room. How can I describe it? Not disgust, not horror, not shock, but more of a sincere wish that Waters had found a way to make his movie without being quite so encyclopedic.

The plot, such as it is, centers on Sylvia and other characters zapping in and out of sex addiction every time they hit their heads, which they do with a frequency approaching the kill rate in *Crash.* This is not really very funny the first time and grows steadily less funny until it becomes a form of monomania.

I think the problem is fundamental: Waters hopes to get laughs because of what the characters are, not because of what they do. He works at the level of preadolescent fart jokes, hoping, as the French say, to *epater les bourgeois*. The problem may be that Waters has grown more bourgeois than his audience, which is *epatered* that he actually thinks he is being shocking.

To truly deal with a strange sexual fetish can indeed be shocking, as *Kissed* (1996) demonstrated with its quiet, observant portrait of Molly Parker playing a necrophiliac. It can also be funny, as James Spader and Maggie Gyllenhaal demonstrated in *Secretary* (2002). Tracey Ullman is a great comic actress, but for her to make this movie funny would have required not just a performance but a rewrite and a miracle.

Fetishes are neither funny nor shocking simply because they exist. You have to do more with them than have characters gleefully celebrate them on the screen. Waters's weakness is to expect laughs because the *idea* of a moment is funny. But the idea of a moment exists only for the pitch; the movie has to develop it into a reality, a process, a payoff. An illustration of this is his persisting conviction that it is funny by definition to have Patty Hearst in his movies. It is only funny when he gives Ms. Hearst, who is a good sport, something amusing to do. She won't find it in this movie.

Divine Secrets of the Ya-Ya Sisterhood

(DIRECTED BY CALLIE KHOURI; STARRING SANDRA BULLOCK, ELLEN BURSTYN; 2002)
Divine Secrets of the Ya-Ya Sisterhood has a title suggesting that the movie will be cute and about colorful, irrepressible, eccentric originals. Heavens deliver us. The Ya-Ya Sisterhood is rubber-stamped from the same mold that has produced an inexhaustible supply of fictional Southern belles who drink too much, talk too much, think about themselves too much, try too hard to be the most unforgettable character you've ever met, and are, in general, insufferable. There must be a reason these stories are never

set in Minnesota. Maybe it's because if you have to deal with the winter it makes you too realistic to become such a silly goose.

There is not a character in the movie with a shred of plausibility, not an event that is believable, not a confrontation that is not staged, not a moment that is not false. For their sins the sisterhood should be forced to spend the rest of their lives locked in a Winnebago camper. The only character in the movie who is bearable is the heroine as a young woman, played by Ashley Judd, who suggests that there was a time before the story's main events when this creature was palatable.

The heroine is Vivi, played by Ellen Burstyn in her sixties, Judd in her thirties, and, as a child, by a moppet whose name I knoweth not. Yes, this is one of those movies that whisks around in time, as childhood vows echo down through the years before we whiplash back to the revelations of ancient secrets. If life were as simple as this movie, we would all have time to get in shape and learn Chinese.

As the film opens, four little girls gather around a campfire in the woods and create the Ya-Ya Sisterhood, exchanging drops of their blood, no doubt while sheriff's deputies and hounds are searching for them. Flash forward to the present. Vivi's daughter Sidda (Sandra Bullock) is a famous New York playwright, who tells an interviewer from *Time* magazine that she had a difficult childhood, mostly because of her mother. Whisk down to Louisiana, where Vivi reads the article and writes the daughter forever out of her life—less of a banishment than you might think, since they have not seen each other for seven years and Vivi doesn't even know of the existence of Sidda's Scottish fiancé, Connor (Angus MacFadyen).

Connor seems cut from the same mold as Shep Walker (James Garner), Vivi's husband. Both men stand around sheepishly while portraying superfluous males. No doubt their women notice them occasionally and are reminded that they exist and are a handy supply of sperm. Shep's role for decades has apparently been to beam approvingly as his wife gets drunk, pops pills, and stars in her own mind. Both men are illustrations of the impatience this genre has for men as a gender; they have the presence of souvenirs left on the mantel after a forgotten vacation.

Anyway. We meet the other adult survivors of the Ya-Ya Sisterhood: Teensy (Fionnula Flanagan), Necie (Shirley Knight), and Caro (Maggie Smith). Why do they all have names like pet animals? Perhaps because real names, like Martha, Florence, or Esther, would be an unseemly burden for such featherweights. Summoned by Vivi so that she can complain about Sidda, Teensy, Necie, and Caro fly north and kidnap Sidda, bringing her back to Louisiana so that they can show her that if she really knew the secrets of her mother's past, she would forgive her all shortcomings, real and imagined. Since the central great mystery of Vivi's past is how she has evaded rehab for so long, this quest is as pointless as the rest of the film.

Why do gifted actresses appear in such slop? Possibly because good roles for women are rare, for those over sixty precious. Possibly, too, because for all the other shortcomings of the film, no expense has been spared by the hair, makeup, and wardrobe departments, so that all of the women look just terrific all of the time, and when Vivi is distraught and emotional, she looks even more terrific. It's the kind of movie where the actresses must love watching the dailies as long as they don't listen to the dialogue.

The movie is a first-time directing job by Callie Khouri, author of *Thelma and Louise*. She seems uncertain what the film is about, where it is going, what it hopes to prove apart from the most crashingly obvious clichés of light women's fiction. So inattentive is the screenplay that it goes to the trouble of providing Vivi with two other children in addition to Sidda, only to never mention them again. A fellow critic, Victoria Alexander, speculates that the secret in Vivi's past may have been that she drowned the kids, but that's too much to hope for.

Domestic Disturbance

(DIRECTED BY HAROLD BECKER; STARRING JOHN TRAVOLTA, VINCE VAUGHN; 2001)
John Travolta plays a nice guy better than just about anybody else, which is why it's hard to figure out why his seemingly intelligent wife would divorce him, in *Domestic Disturbance,* to marry Vince Vaughn, who plays a creep better than just about anybody else. Maybe that's because it's not

until the wedding day that her new husband's best friend turns up, and it's Steve Buscemi, who plays the creep's best friend absolutely better than anybody else.

All of this is a setup for a child-in-terror movie, in which a child is the eyewitness to a brutal murder and the incineration of the body. Then the kid sees his father hammered to within an inch of his life, his mother beaten until she has a miscarriage, and himself as the unwitting cause of an electrocution. I mention these details as a way of explaining why the flywheels at the MPAA Ratings Board gave the movie a PG-13 rating. Certainly it doesn't deserve an R, like *Amelie* or *Waking Life*.

The movie is a paid holiday for its director, Harold Becker. I say this because I know what Becker is capable of. This is the same director who made *The Onion Field, The Boost,* and *Sea of Love.* If this is the best screenplay he could find to work on, and it probably was, all I can do is quote Norman Jewison at this year's Toronto Film Festival: "You wouldn't believe the —— the studios want you to make these days."

Sad, because there are scenes here showing what the film could have been, if it hadn't abandoned ambition and taken the low road. Travolta plays Frank Morrison, a boat builder and all-around nice guy—so nice he's even optimistic about the approaching marriage of his ex-wife, Susan (Teri Polo). Frank's son, Danny (Matthew O'Leary), is a little dubious about this new guy, so Frank even takes the three of them on a fishing trip together. But Danny is still upset, and has a habit of lying, running away, and not turning up for basketball games. He's Trying to Tell Them Something.

The fiancé is Rick Barnes (Vaughn), new in town, who has made a lot of money and is about to be honored by the Chamber of Commerce. But when his old buddy Ray (Buscemi) turns up uninvited at the wedding, Rick's eyes narrow and his pulse quickens and it is only a matter of time until the domestic drama turns into a domestic monster movie. You know it's a bad sign when you're Frank, the understanding ex-husband, standing around at the reception, and Ray tells you your ex-wife "must know some pretty good tricks to make old Rick settle down."

Suspense builds, not exactly slowly, in scenes involving an ominous game of catch. Then there's a scene that flies in the face of all logic, in the way the child is made to be an eyewitness to murder. The physical details are so unlikely they seem contrived even in a thriller. All leads up to a final confrontation so badly choreographed that I was not the least bit surprised when the studio called to say the Chicago critics had seen "the wrong last reel," and would we like to see the correct reel on Monday? I agreed eagerly, expecting revised footage—but, no, the only problem was the earlier reel was lacking the final music mix.

Music is the last thing wrong with that reel. Apparently the filmmakers saw no problem with the way a key character enters on cue, at a dead run, without any way of knowing (from outside) where to run to, or why. No problem with a fight scene so incomprehensibly choreographed it seems to consist mostly of a chair. And no problem with a spectacularly inappropriate speech at a crucial moment (it's the one beginning, "Too bad . . ."). This speech provides additional information that is desperately unwanted, in a way that inspires only bad laughs from the audience, just when you want to end the movie without any more stumbles.

Doom

(DIRECTED BY ANDRZEJ BARTKOWIAK; STARRING KARL URBAN, ROSAMUND PIKE; 2005)

Doom has one great shot. It comes right at the beginning. It's the Universal logo. Instead of a spinning Earth with the letters U-N-I-V-E-R-S-A-L rising in the east and centering themselves over Lebanon, Kansas, we see the red planet Mars. Then we fly closer to Mars until we see surface details and finally the Olduvai Research Station, helpfully described on the movie's Web site as "a remote scientific facility on Mars"—where, if you give it but a moment's thought, all of the scientific facilities are remote.

Anyway, that's the last we see of the surface of Mars. A lot of readers thought I was crazy for liking *Ghosts of Mars* (2001) and *Red Planet* (2000) and *Total Recall* (1990), but blast it all, at least in those movies *you get to see Mars.* I'm a science fiction fan from way back. I go to Mars, I expect to see it. Watching *Doom* is like visiting Vegas and never leaving your hotel room.

The movie has been "inspired by" the famous video game. No, I haven't played it, and I never will, but I know how it feels *not* to play it, because I've seen the movie. *Doom* is like some kid came over and is using your computer and won't let you play.

The movie involves a group of marines named the Rapid Response Tactical Squad, which if they would take only the slightest trouble could be renamed the Rapid Action Tactical Squad, which would acronym into RATS. The year is 2046. In the middle of an American desert has been discovered a portal to an ancient city on Mars. The Olduvai facility has been established to study it, and now there is a "breech of level five security," and the RRTS are sent to Mars through the portal to take care of business. Their leader is Sarge (The Rock), and their members include Reaper (Karl Urban), Destroyer (Deobia Oparei), Mac (Yao Chin), Goat (Ben Daniels), Duke (Raz Adoti), Portman (Richard Brake), and The Kid (Al Weaver). Now you know everything you need to know about them.

On Mars, we see terrified humans running from an unseen threat. Dr. Carmack (Robert Russell) closes an automatic steel door on a young woman whose arm is onscreen longer than she is, if you get my drift, and then he spends a lot of time huddled in the corner vibrating and whimpering. We meet Samantha Grimm (Rosamund Pike), sister of Reaper (aka John Grimm). She is an anthropologist at the station, and has reconstructed a complete skeleton of a humanoid Martian woman huddled protectively over her child. If you know your anthropology, you gotta say those are bones that have survived a lot of geological activity.

The original Martians were not merely humanoid, Dr. Grimm speculates, but superhuman: They bioengineered a twenty-fourth chromosome. We have twenty-three. The extra chromosome made them super smart, super strong, super fast, and super quick to heal. But it turned some of them into monsters, which is presumably why the others built the portal to Earth, where—what? They became us, but left the twenty-fourth chromosome behind? Is that the kind of Intelligent Design we want our kids studying?

Despite all of her chromosome counting, Dr. Grimm says at another point: "Ten percent of the human genome has not yet been mapped. Some say it's the soul." Whoa! The Human Genome Project was completed in 2003, something you would think a scientist like Dr. Grimm should know. I am reminded of the astronauts in *Stealth* reminding each other what a prime number is.

The monsters are still there on Mars. They are big mothers and must have awesome daily caloric requirements. How they survive, how they breathe Earth atmosphere in the station, and what, as carnivores, they eat and drink—I think we can all agree these are questions deserving serious scientific study. Meanwhile their pastime is chasing humans, grabbing them, smashing them, eviscerating and disemboweling them, pulling them through grates, and in general doing anything that can take place obscurely in shadows and not require a lot of special effects.

Toward the end of the movie, there is a lengthy point-of-view shot looking forward over the barrel of a large weapon as it tracks the corridors of the research station. Monsters jump out from behind things and are blasted to death, in a sequence that abandons all attempts at character and dialogue and uncannily resembles a video game. Later, when the names of the actors appear on the screen, they are also blasted into little pieces. I forget whether the director, Andrzej Bartkowiak, had his name shot to smithereens, but for the DVD I recommend that a monster grab it and eat it.

Double Take

(DIRECTED BY GEORGE GALLO; STARRING ORLANDO JONES, EDDIE GRIFFIN; 2001)

Double Take is the kind of double-triple-reverse movie that can drive you nuts because you can't count on *anything* in the plot. Characters, motivations, and true identities change from scene to scene at the whim of the screenplay. Finally, you weary of trying to follow the story. You can get the rug jerked out from under you only so many times before you realize the movie has the attention span of a gnat, and thinks you do, too.

Orlando Jones stars as Daryl Chase, a businessman who becomes the dupe of a street hustler named Freddy Tiffany (Eddie Griffin). The movie opens with Daryl as the victim of a complicated briefcase-theft scam, which turns out not to be what it seems, and to involve more people than it appears to involve. Freddy is at the center of it, and Daryl soon learns that Freddy will be at the center of everything in his life for the rest of the movie.

Who is this guy? He seems to have an almost supernatural ability to materialize anywhere, to know Daryl's secret plans, to pop up like a genie, and to embarrass him with a jive-talking routine that seems recycled out of the black exploitation pictures of the 1970s. The movie's attitudes seem so dated, indeed, that when I saw a computer screen, it came as a shock: The movie's period feels as much pre-desktop as it does pre-taste.

Freddy embarrasses Daryl a few more times, including during a fashion show, where he appears on the runway and shoulders aside the models. Meanwhile, Daryl discovers he is under attack by mysterious forces, for reasons he cannot understand, and to his surprise Freddy turns out to be an ally. The obnoxious little sprite even helps him out of a dangerous spot in a train station by changing clothes with him, after which the two men find themselves in the dining car of a train headed for Mexico. The switch in wardrobe of course inspires a switch in personalities; Freddy orders from the menu in a gourmet-snob accent, while Daryl is magically transformed into a ghetto caricature who embarrasses the waiter by demanding Schlitz Malt Liquor.

And so on. Wardrobes, identities, motivations, and rationales are exchanged in a dizzying series of laboriously devised "surprises," until we find out that nothing is as it seems, and that isn't as it seems, either. It's not that we expect a movie like this to be consistent or make sense. It's that when the double-reverse plotting kicks in, we want it to be funny or entertaining or anything but dreary and arbitrary and frustrating.

The movie was directed by George Gallo, who wrote the much better *Midnight Run* and here again has latched onto the idea of a nice guy and an obnoxious one involved in a road trip together. One of his problems is with Eddie Griffin. Here is a fast-thinking, fast-talking, nimble actor who no doubt has good performances in him, but his Freddy Tiffany is unbearable—so obnoxious he approaches the fingernails-on-a-blackboard category. You know you're in trouble when your heart sinks every time a movie's live-wire appears on the screen. I realized there was no hope for the movie, because the plot and characters had alienated me beyond repair. If an audience is going to be entertained by a film, first they have to be able to stand it.

Down to Earth

(DIRECTED BY CHRIS WEITZ AND PAUL WEITZ; STARRING CHRIS ROCK, REGINA KING; 2001)

Down to Earth is an astonishingly bad movie, and the most astonishing thing about it comes in the credits: "Written by Elaine May, Warren Beatty, Chris Rock, Lance Crouther, Ali LeRoi, and Louis C.K." These are credits that deserve a place in the Writer's Hall of Fame, right next to the 1929 version of *The Taming of the Shrew* ("screenplay by William Shakespeare, with additional dialogue by Sam Taylor").

Yes, Chris Rock and his writing partners have adapted Elaine May's Oscar-nominated 1978 screenplay for *Heaven Can Wait* (Warren Beatty falls more in the Sam Taylor category). It wasn't broke, but boy, do they fix it.

The premise: Lance Barton (Rock) is a lousy stand-up comic, booed off the stage during an amateur night at the Apollo Theater. Even his faithful manager, Whitney (Frankie Faison), despairs for him. Disaster strikes. Lance is flattened by a truck, goes to heaven, and discovers from his attending angel (Eugene Levy) that an error has been made. He was taken before his time. There is a meeting with God, aka "Mr. King" (Chazz Palminteri), who agrees to send him back to Earth for the unexpired portion of his stay.

The catch is, only one body is available: Mr. Wellington, an old white millionaire. Lance takes what he can get and returns to Earth, where he finds a sticky situation: His sexpot wife (Jennifer Coolidge) is having an affair with his assistant, who is stealing his money. Meanwhile, Lance, from his vantage point inside Mr. Wellington, falls in love with a young African-American beauty named Suntee (Regina King).

Let's draw to a halt and consider the situation as it now stands. The world sees an old white millionaire. So does Suntee, who has disliked him up until the point where Lance occupies the body. But we in the audience see Chris Rock. Of course, Rock and Regina King make an agreeable couple, but we have to keep reminding ourselves he's a geezer, and so does she, I guess, since soon they are holding hands and other parts.

The essential comic element here, I think, is the disparity between the two lovers, and the underlying truth that they are actually a good match. Wouldn't that be funnier if Mr. Wellington looked like . . . Mr. Wellington? He could be played by Martin Landau, although, come to think of it, Martin Landau played an old white millionaire who gets involved with Halle Berry and Troy Beyer in *B.A.P.S.* (1997), and don't run out to Blockbuster for *that* one.

The real problem with Mr. Wellington being played by an old white guy, even though he is an old white guy, is that the movie stars Chris Rock, who is getting the big bucks, and Chris Rock fans do not want to watch Martin Landau oscillating with Regina King no matter *who* is inside him. That means that in the world of the movie everyone sees an old white guy, but we have, like, these magic glasses, I guess, that allow us to see Chris Rock. Well, once or twice we sort of catch a glimpse of the millionaire, in reflections and things, but nothing is done with this promising possibility.

The story then involves plots against and by Mr. Wellington, plus Lance's scheming to get a better replacement body, plus Suntee being required to fly in the face of emotional logic and then fly back again, having been issued an emotional round-trip ticket. If I were an actor, I would make a resolution to turn down all parts in which I fall in and out of love at a moment's notice, without logical reason, purely for the convenience of the plot.

Chris Rock is funny and talented, and so I have said several times. I even proposed him as emcee for the Academy Awards (they went for an old white millionaire). This project must have looked promising, since the directors are the Weitz brothers, Chris and Paul Weitz, fresh from *American Pie*. But the movie is dead in the water.

Dreamcatcher

(DIRECTED BY LAWRENCE KASDAN; STARRING MORGAN FREEMAN, THOMAS JANE; 2003)

Dreamcatcher begins as the intriguing story of friends who share a telepathic gift and ends as a monster movie of stunning awfulness. What went wrong? How could director Lawrence Kasdan and writer William Goldman be responsible for a film that goes so awesomely wrong? How could even Morgan Freeman, an actor all but impervious to bad material, be brought down by the awfulness? Goldman, who has written insightfully about the screenwriter's trade, may get a long, sad book out of this one.

The movie is based on a novel by Stephen King, unread by me, apparently much altered for the screen version, especially in the appalling closing sequences. I have just finished the audiobook of King's *From a Buick 8*, was a fan of his *Hearts in Atlantis,* and like the way his heart tugs him away from horror ingredients and into the human element in his stories.

Here the story begins so promisingly that I hoped, or assumed, it would continue on the same track: Childhood friends, united in a form of telepathy by a mentally retarded kid they protect, grow up to share psychic gifts and to deal with the consequences. The problem of *really* being telepathic is a favorite science-fiction theme. If you could read minds, would you be undone by the despair and anguish being broadcast all around you? This is unfortunately not the problem explored by *Dreamcatcher.*

The movie does have a visualization of the memory process that is brilliant filmmaking; after the character Gary "Jonesy" Jones (Damian Lewis) has his mind occupied by an alien intelligence, he is able to survive hidden within it by concealing his presence inside a vast memory warehouse, visualized by Kasdan as an infinitely unfolding series of rooms containing Jonesy's memories. This idea is like a smaller, personal version of Jorge Luis Borges's *The Library of Babel,* the imaginary library that contains all possible editions of all possible books. I can imagine many scenes set in the warehouse—it's such a good idea it could support an entire movie—but the film proceeds relentlessly to abandon this earlier inspiration in its quest for the barfable.

But let me back up. We meet at the outset childhood friends: Henry Devlin, Joe "Beaver" Clarendon, Jonesy Jones, and Pete Moore. They happen upon Douglas "Duddits" Cavell, a retarded boy being bullied by older kids, and they defend him with wit and imagination. He's grateful, and in some way he serves as a nexus for all of them to form a precognitive, psychic network. It isn't high-level or controllable, but it's there.

Then we meet them as adults, played by (in order) Thomas Jane, Jason Lee, Lewis, and Timothy Olyphant (Duddits is now Donnie Wahlberg). When Jonesy has an accident of startling suddenness, that serves as the catalyst for a trip to the woods, where the hunters turn into the hunted as alien beings attack.

It would be well not to linger on plot details, since if you are going to see the movie, you will want them to be surprises. Let me just say that the aliens, who look like a cross between the creature in *Alien* and the things that crawled out of the drains in that David Cronenberg movie, exhibit the same problem I often have with such beings: How can an alien that consists primarily of teeth and an appetite, that apparently has no limbs, tools, or language, travel to Earth in the first place? Are they little clone creatures for a superior race? Perhaps; an alien nicknamed Mr. Gray turns up, who looks and behaves quite differently, for a while.

For these aliens, space travel is a prologue for trips taking them where few have gone before; they explode from the business end of the intestinal tract, through that orifice we would be least willing to lend them for their activities. The movie, perhaps as a result, has as many farts as the worst teenage comedy—which is to say, too many farts for a movie that keeps insisting, with mounting implausibility, that it is intended to be good. These creatures are given a name by the characters that translates in a family newspaper as Crap Weasels.

When Morgan Freeman turns up belatedly in a movie, that is usually a good sign, because no matter what has gone before, he is likely to import more wit and interest. Not this time. He plays Col. Abraham Curtis, a hard-line military man dedicated to doing what the military always does in alien movies, which is to blast the aliens to pieces and ask questions later. This is infinitely less interesting than a scene in King's *Buick 8* where a curious state trooper dissects a batlike thing that seems to have popped through a portal from another world. King's description of the autopsy of weird alien organs is scarier than all the gnashings and disembowelments in *Dreamcatcher.*

When the filmmakers are capable of the first half of *Dreamcatcher,* what came over them in the second half? What inspired their descent into the absurd? On the evidence here, we can say what we already knew: Lawrence Kasdan is a wonderful director of personal dramas (*Grand Canyon, The Accidental Tourist, Mumford*). When it comes to Crap Weasels, his heart just doesn't seem to be in it.

The Dukes of Hazzard

(Directed by Jay Chandrasekhar; starring Seann William Scott, Johnny Knoxville; 2005)

The Dukes of Hazzard is a comedy about two cousins who are closer'n brothers, and their car, which is smarter'n they are. It's a retread of a sitcom that ran from about 1979 to 1985, years during which I was able to find better ways to pass my time. Yes, it is still another TV program I have never ever seen. As this list grows, it provides more and more clues about why I am so smart and cheerful.

The movie stars Johnny Knoxville, from *Jackass,* Seann William Scott, from *American Wedding,* and Jessica Simpson, from Mars. Judging by her recent conversation on TV with Dean Richards, Simpson is so remarkably uninformed that she should sue the public schools of Abilene, Texas, or maybe they should sue her. On the day he won his seventh Tour de France, not many people could say, as she did, that they had no idea who Lance Armstrong was.

Of course, you don't have to be smart to get into *The Dukes of Hazzard.* But people like Willie Nelson and Burt Reynolds should have been smart enough to stay out of it. Here is a lamebrained, outdated wheeze about a couple of good ol' boys who roar around the back roads of the South in the General Lee, their beloved 1969 Dodge Charger. As it happens, I also drove a 1969 Dodge Charger. You could have told them apart because mine did not have a Confederate flag painted on the roof.

Scott and Knoxville play Bo Duke and Luke Duke; the absence of a Puke Duke is a sadly missed opportunity. They deliver moonshine manufactured by their Uncle Jesse (Willie Nelson), and depend on the General to outrun the forces of Sheriff Roscoe P. Coltrane (M. C. Gainey). The movie even has one of those obligatory scenes where the car is racing along when there's a quick cut to a gigantic Mack truck, its horn blasting as it bears down on them. They steer out of the way at the last possible moment. That giant Mack truck keeps busy in the movies, turning up again and again during chase scenes and always just barely missing the car containing the heroes, but this is the first time I have seen it making 60 mph down a single-lane dirt track.

Jessica Simpson plays Daisy Duke, whose short shorts became so famous on TV that they were known as "Daisy Dukes." She models them to a certain effect in a few brief scenes, but is missing from most of the movie. Maybe she isn't even smart enough to wear shorts. I learn from the Internet that Simpson has a dog named Daisy, but have been unable to learn if she named it before or after being signed for the role, and whether the dog is named after the character, the shorts, the flower, or perhaps (a long shot), Daisy Duck.

The local ruler is Boss Jefferson Davis Hogg (Burt Reynolds), "the meanest man in Hazzard County," who issues orders to the sheriff and everybody else, and has a secret plan to strip-mine the county and turn it into a wasteland. I wonder if there were moments when Reynolds reflected that, karma-wise, this movie was the second half of what *Smokey and the Bandit* was the first half of.

There are a lot of scenes in the movie where the General is racing down back roads at high speeds and becomes airborne, leaping across ditches, rivers, and suchlike, miraculously without breaking the moonshine bottles. Surely if you have seen, say, twelve scenes of a car flying through the air, you are not consumed by a need to see twelve more.

There is a NASCAR race in the film, and some amusing dialogue about car sponsorship. You know the film is set in modern times because along with Castrol and Coke, one of the car sponsors is Yahoo! I noted one immortal passage of dialogue, about a charity that is raising money "for one of the bifidas." I was also amused by mention of *The Al Unser Jr. Story,* "an audiobook narrated by Laurence Fishburne."

The movie has one offensive scene, alas, that doesn't belong in a contemporary comedy. Bo and Luke are involved in a mishap that causes their faces to be blackened with soot, and then, wouldn't you know, they drive into an African-American neighborhood, where their car is surrounded by ominous young men who are not amused by blackface or by the Confederate flag painted on the car. I was hoping maybe the boyz n the hood would carjack the General, which would provide a fresh twist to the story, but no, the scene sinks into the mire of its own despond.

Elektra

(DIRECTED BY ROB BOWMAN; STARRING JENNIFER GARNER, GORAN VISNJIC; 2005)

Elektra plays like a collision between leftover bits and pieces of Marvel superhero stories. It can't decide what tone to strike. It goes for satire by giving its heroine an agent who suggests mutual funds for her murder-for-hire fees, and sends her a fruit basket before her next killing. And then it goes for melancholy, by making Elektra a lonely, unfulfilled overachiever who was bullied as a child and suffers from obsessive-compulsive disorder. It goes for cheap sentiment by having her bond with a thirteen-year-old girl, and then . . . but see for yourself. The movie's a muddle in search of a rationale.

Elektra, you may recall, first appeared onscreen in *Daredevil* (2003), the Marvel saga starring Ben Affleck as a blind superhero. Jennifer Garner, she of the wonderful lips, returns in the role as a killer for hire, which seems kind of sad, considering that in the earlier movie she figured in the beautiful scene where he imagines her face by listening to raindrops falling on it.

Now someone has offered her $2 million for her next assassination, requiring only that she turn up two days early for the job—on Christmas Eve, as it works out. She arrives in a luxurious lakeside vacation home and soon meets the young girl named Abby (Kirsten Prout), who lives next door. Abby's father is played by Goran Visnjic with a three-day beard, which tells you all you need to know: Powerful sexual attraction will compel them to share two PG-13-rated kisses.

The back story, which makes absolutely no mention of Daredevil, involves Elektra's training under the stern blind martial arts master Stick (Terence Stamp), who can restore people to life and apparently materialize at will, yet is reduced to martial arts when he does battle. Her enemies are assassins hired by the Order of the Hand, which is a secret Japanese society that seeks the Treasure, and the Treasure is . . . well, see for yourself.

As for the troops of the Hand, they have contracted Movie Zombie's Syndrome, which means that they are fearsome and deadly until killed, at which point they dissolve into a cloud of yellow powder. I don't have a clue whether they're real or imaginary. Neither do they, I'll bet. Eagles and wolves and snakes can materialize out of their tattoos and attack people, but they, too, disappear in clouds. Maybe this is simply to save Elektra the inconvenience of stepping over her victims in the middle of a fight.

The Order of the Hand is not very well defined. Its office is a pagoda on top of a Tokyo skyscraper, which is promising, but inside all we get is the standard scene of a bunch of suits sitting around a conference table giving orders to paid killers. Their instructions: Kill Elektra, grab the Treasure, etc. Who are they and what is their master plan? Maybe you have to study up on the comic books.

As for Elektra, she's a case study. Flashbacks show her tortured youth, in which her father made her tread water in the family's luxury indoor pool until she was afraid she'd drown. (Her mother, on balcony overlooking pool: "She's only a girl!" Her father, at poolside: "Only using your legs! Not your hands!" Elektra: "Glub.")

Whether this caused her OCD or not, I cannot say. It manifests itself not as an extreme case, like poor Howard Hughes, but fairly mildly: She counts her steps in groups of five. This has absolutely nothing to do with anything else. A superheroine with a bad case of OCD could be interesting, perhaps; maybe she would be compelled to leap tall buildings with bound after bound after bound.

The movie's fight scenes suffer from another condition, attention deficit disorder. None of their shots are more than a few seconds long, saving the actors from doing much in the way of stunts and the director from having to worry overmuch about choreography. There's one showdown between Elektra and the head killer of the Hand that involves a lot of white sheets, but all they do is flap around; we're expecting maybe an elegant Zhang Yimou sequence, and it's more like they're fighting with the laundry.

Jennifer Garner is understandably unable to make a lot of sense out of this. We get a lot of close-ups in which we would identify with what she was thinking, if we had any clue what that might be. Does she wonder why she became a paid killer instead of a virtuous superheroine? Does she wonder why her agent is a bozo? Does she clearly understand that the Order of the Hand is the group trying to kill her? At the end of the movie, having reduced her enemies to yellow poofs, she tells Goran Visnjic to "take good care" of his daughter. Does she even know those guys in suits are still up there in the pagoda, sitting around the table?

Enough

(DIRECTED BY MICHAEL APTED; STARRING JENNIFER LOPEZ, BILLY CAMPBELL; 2002)

Enough is a nasty item masquerading as a feminist revenge picture. It's a step or two above *I Spit on Your Grave,* but uses the same structure, in which a man victimizes a woman for the first half of the film, and then the woman turns the tables in an extended sequence of graphic violence. It's surprising to see a director like Michael Apted and an actress like Jennifer Lopez associated with such tacky material.

It is possible to imagine this story being told in a good film, but that would involve a different screenplay. Nicholas Kazan's script makes the evil husband (Billy Campbell) such an unlikely caricature of hard-breathing, sadistic testosterone that he cannot possibly be a real human being. Of course there are men who beat their wives and torture them with cruel mind games, but do they satirize themselves as the heavy in a B movie? The husband's swings of personality and mood are so sudden, and his motivation makes so little sense, that he has no existence beyond the stereotyped Evil Rich White Male. The fact that he preys on a poor Latino waitress is just one more cynical cliché.

The story: Jennifer Lopez plays Slim, a waitress in a diner where she shares obligatory sisterhood and bonding with Ginny (Juliette Lewis), another waitress. A male customer tries to get her to go on a date, and almost succeeds before another customer named Mitch (Billy Campbell) blows the whistle and reveals the first man was only trying to win a bet. In the movie's headlong rush of events, Slim and Mitch are soon married, buy a big house, have a cute child, and then Slim discovers Mitch is having affairs, and he growls at her: "I am, and always will be, a person who gets what he wants." He starts slapping her around.

Although their child is now three or four, this is a Mitch she has not seen before in their marriage. Where did this Mitch come from? How did he restrain himself from pounding and strangling her during all of the early years? Why did she think herself happy until now? The answer, of course, is that Mitch turns on a dime when the screenplay requires him to. He even starts talking differently.

The plot (spoiler warning) now involves Slim's attempts to hide herself and the child from Mitch. She flees to Michigan and hooks up with a battered-wife group, but Mitch, like the hero of a mad slasher movie, is always able to track her down. Along the way Slim appeals for help to the father (Fred Ward) who has never acknowledged her, and the father's dialogue is so hilariously over the top in its cruelty that the scene abandons all hope of working seriously and simply functions as haywire dramaturgy.

Slim gets discouraging advice from a lawyer ("There is nothing you can do. He will win."). And then she gets training in self-defense from a martial arts instructor. Both of these characters are African-American, following the movie's simplistic moral color-coding. The day when the evil husband is black and the self-defense instructor is white will not arrive in our lifetimes.

The last act of the movie consists of Slim outsmarting her husband with a series of clever ploys in which she stage-manages an escape route, sets a booby trap for his SUV, and then lures him into a confrontation where she beats the shinola out of him, at length, with much blood, lots of stunt work, breakaway furniture, etc. The movie, in time-honored horror movie tradition, doesn't allow Mitch to really be dead the first time. There is a plot twist showing that Slim can't really kill him—she's the heroine, after all—and then he lurches back into action like the slasher in many an exploitation movie, and is destroyed more or less by accident. During this action scene Slim finds time for plenty of dialogue explaining that any court will find she was acting in self-defense.

All of this would be bad enough without the performance of Tessa Allen as Gracie, the young daughter. She has one of those squeaky, itsy-bitsy piped-up voices that combines with babyish dialogue to make her more or less insufferable; after the ninth or tenth scream of "Mommy! Mommy!" we hope that she will be shipped off to an excellent day-care center for the rest of the story.

Jennifer Lopez is one of my favorite actresses, but not here, where the dialogue requires her to be passionate and overwrought in a way that is simply not believable, maybe because no one could take this cartoon of a story seriously. No doubt she saw *Enough* as an opportunity to play a heavy, dramatic role, but there is nothing more dangerous than a heavy role in a lightweight screenplay, and this material is such a melodramatic soap opera that the slick production values seem like a waste of effort.

Everybody's Famous

(DIRECTED BY DOMINIQUE DERUDDERE; STARRING JOSSE DE PAUW, WERNER DE SMEDT; 2001)

Everybody's Famous opens at a dreary talent contest at which the plump, desperate Marva demonstrates that she cannot sing, and could not deliver a song if she could. The judges, including the local mayor, hold up Olympic-style paddles scoring her with twos and threes, and we feel they're generous. But Jean, Marva's father, remains fanatically convinced that his daughter is talented and has a future—this despite the thankless girl's rudeness toward her old man.

Poor Jean (Josse De Pauw) is a good man, endured by his patient wife, Chantal (Gert Portael), treasured by his best friend, Willy (Werner De Smedt), and chained to the night shift at a factory where he has to inspect endless lines of bottles for hours at a time. At home, he joins his family in admiring the concerts of a pop singer named only Debbie (Thekla Reuten), who wears an incandescent blue polyester wig.

One day a bolt of coincidence joins Debbie and Jean. He finds an opportunity to kidnap her, and does, enlisting Willy to help him. His ransom demand: Debbie's manager (Victor Low) must record and release a song that Jean has written and that Marva (Eva van der Gucht) must sing.

This sets into motion a plot that begins with the same basic situation as *The King of Comedy,* where the Robert De Niro character kidnapped a TV host played by Jerry Lewis, but the difference here is that *Everybody's Famous* is cheerful and optimistic, and if by the end everybody is not famous at least everybody has gotten what they want in life.

Three of the characters—the mother, the best friend, and the pop star—are so bland they're essentially placeholders. Josse De Pauw does what he can with the lead role, as a simple, goodhearted man who can't even get a goodnight kiss from the daughter he has sacrificed everything for. Victor Low seems like a very low-rent pop impresario, especially considering he can get a song scored, recorded, and on the charts in about twenty-four hours. But Eva van der Gucht brings some pouting humor to the role of the untalented daughter, whose costumes look like somebody's idea of a cruel joke and who is bluntly told that she sings with a complete absence of emotion.

The big scene at the end involves one of those TV news situations that never happen in real life, where a reporter and camera materialize at a crucial point and are seemingly at the pleasure of the plot. And there's a surprise during a televised talent show, which will not come as that much of a surprise, however, to any sentient being.

The movie, from the Flemish community of Belgium, was one of this year's Oscar nominees for best foreign film, leading one to wonder what films were passed over to make room for it. It is as pleasant as all get-out, sunny and serendipitous, and never even bothers to create much of a possibility that it will be otherwise. By the time the police spontaneously applaud a man they have every reason to believe is holding a hostage, the movie has given up any shred of plausibility and is simply trying to be a nice comedy. It's nice, but it's not much of a comedy.

Failure to Launch

(Directed by Tom Dey; starring Matthew McConaughey, Sarah Jessica Parker; 2006)

During the course of *Failure to Launch,* characters are bitten by a chipmunk, a dolphin, a lizard, and a mockingbird. I am thinking my hardest why this is considered funny, and I confess defeat. Would the movie be twice as funny if the characters had also been bitten by a Chihuahua, a naked mole rat, and a donkey?

I was bitten by a donkey once. It was during a visit to Stanley Kubrick's farm outside London. I was the guest of the gracious Christiane Kubrick, who took me on a stroll and showed me the field where she cares for playground donkeys after their retirement. I rested my hand on the fence, and a donkey bit me. "Stop that!" I said, and the donkey did. If I had lost a finger, it would have been a great consolation to explain that it had been bitten off by one of Mrs. Stanley Kubrick's retired donkeys.

But I digress. *Failure to Launch* is about a thirty-five-year-old man named Tripp (Matthew McConaughey) who still lives at home with his parents. They dream of being empty nesters, and hire a woman named Paula (Sarah Jessica Parker), who is a specialist at getting grown men to move out of their parents' homes. Her method is simple: You look nice, you find out what they like, and you pretend to like it, too. You encourage them to share a sad experience with you. And you ask them to teach you something. In this case, he likes paintball, her dog has to be put to sleep, and he teaches her to sail. Actually, it's not her dog and it's not really put to sleep, but never mind.

Sue and Al (Kathy Bates and Terry Bradshaw) are Tripp's parents. "I never sleep with my clients," Paula tells them. What she does is take hardened bachelors, force them to fall in love with her, and use that leverage to get them to move out of the parental home, after which she breaks up with them and they're fine. If this sounds to you like a cross between pathological cruelty and actionable fraud, I could not agree more. On the other hand, Tripp is no more benign. His strategy is to date a girl until she begins to like him, and then take her home to bed, not telling her it is his parents' home. "The only reason he brings girls to dinner is because he's breaking up with them!" Sue warns Paula.

Oh, what stupid people these are. Stupid to do what they do, say what they say, think what they think, and get bitten by a chipmunk, a dolphin, a lizard, and a mockingbird. Actually, it's Tripp's friend Ace (Justin Bartha) who is bitten by the mockingbird. He is dating Paula's surly roommate, Kit (Zooey Deschanel). She hates the mockingbird because it keeps her awake at nights. They hunt it with a BB gun, only intending to wound it, but alas the bird is peppered with BBs and seems to be dead, and . . . no, I'm not even going to go there. "You can't kill a mockingbird!" a gun salesman tells her. "Why not?" she asks. "You know!" he says. "That book, *To Kill a Mockingbird!*" No, she doesn't know. "I can't believe you don't know that," the guy says. Not know what? It's not titled *To Kill a Mocking-bird Would Be Wrong.*

Ace gives the bird the kiss of life and they pump its furry little chest, and it recovers and bites Ace. Kit meanwhile has fallen in love with Ace. Which is my cue to tell you that Zooey Deschanel on this same weekend is opening in two movies; in this one she plays an airhead who saves the life of a mockingbird, and in the other one, *Winter Passing,* she plays an alcoholic actress who drowns her cat, which is dying from leukemia. It's an impressive stretch, like simultaneously playing Lady Macbeth and judging *American Idol.* Deschanel is actually very good in *Winter Passing* and fairly good in *Failure to Launch.* You know the joke about how polite Canadians are. If a movie is great they say it's "very good," and if a movie is terrible, they say it's "fairly good."

I cannot bring myself to describe how Tripp's friend Ace kidnaps him, locks him in a closet, and tricks Paula into being locked in the room with him, so that they will be forced to confess their love to each other while Tripp remains tied to a chair and Ace uses hidden iSight cameras to telecast this event, live and with sound, for the entertainment of complete strangers in a restaurant, who watch it on a wall-sized video screen.

Now to get technical. The editing of the film is strangely fragmented. I first noticed this during a backyard conversation between the parents. There's unusually jerky cutting on lines of dialogue, back and forth, as if the film is unwilling to hold the characters in the same shot while they talk to one another. This turbulence continues throughout the film. Back and forth we go, as if the camera's watching a tennis match. I would question the editor, Steven Rosenblum, but he's the same man who edited *Braveheart, Glory,* and *The Last Samurai,* so I know this isn't his style. Did the director, Tom Dey, favor quick cutting for some reason? Perhaps because he couldn't stand to look at any one shot for very long? That's the way I felt.

Fantastic Four

(DIRECTED BY TIM STORY; STARRING IOAN GRUFFUDD, JESSICA ALBA; 2005)

So you get in a spaceship and you venture into orbit to research a mysterious star storm hurtling toward Earth. There's a theory it may involve properties of use to man. The ship is equipped with a shield to protect its passengers from harmful effects, but the storm arrives ahead of schedule and saturates everybody on board with unexplained but powerful energy that creates radical molecular changes in their bodies.

They return safely to Earth, only to discover that Reed Richards (Ioan Gruffudd), the leader of the group, has a body that can take any form or stretch to unimaginable lengths. Call him Mr. Fantastic. Ben Grimm (Michael Chiklis) develops superhuman powers in a vast and bulky body that seems made of stone. Call him Thing. Susan Storm (Jessica Alba) can become invisible at will, and generate force fields that can contain propane explosions, in case you have a propane explosion that needs containing but want the option of being invisible. Call her Invisible Woman. And her brother, Johnny Storm (Chris Evans), has a body that can burn at supernova temperatures. Call him the Human Torch. I almost forgot the villain, Victor Von Doom (Julian McMahon), who becomes Doctor Doom and wants to use the properties of the star storm and the powers of the Fantastic Four for his own purposes. He eventually becomes metallic.

By this point in the review, are you growing a little restless? What am I gonna do, list names and actors and superpowers and nicknames forever? That's how the movie feels. It's all setup and demonstration and naming and discussing and demonstrating, and it never digests the complications of the Fantastic Four and gets on to telling a compelling story. Sure, there's a nice sequence where Thing keeps a fire truck from falling off a bridge, but you see one fire truck saved from falling off a bridge, you've seen them all.

The Fantastic Four are, in short, underwhelming. The edges kind of blur between them and other superhero teams. That's understandable. How many people could pass a test right now on who the X-Men are and what *their* powers are? Or would want to? I wasn't watching *Fantastic*

Four to study it, but to be entertained by it, but how could I be amazed by a movie that makes its own characters so indifferent about themselves? The Human Torch, to repeat, *can burn at supernova temperatures!* He can become so hot, indeed, that he could *threaten the very existence of the Earth itself!* This is absolutely stupendously amazing, wouldn't you agree? If you could burn at supernova temperatures, would you be able to stop talking about it? I know people who won't shut up about winning fifty bucks in the lottery.

But after Johnny Storm finds out he has become the Human Torch, he takes it pretty much in stride, showing off a little by setting his thumb on fire. Later he saves the Earth, while Invisible Woman simultaneously contains his supernova so he doesn't destroy it. That means Invisible Woman could maybe create a force field to contain the sun, which would be a big deal, but she's too distracted to explore the possibilities; she gets uptight because she will have to be naked to be invisible, because otherwise people could see her empty clothes; it is no consolation to her that invisible nudity is more of a metaphysical concept than a condition.

Are these people complete idiots? The entire nature of their existence has radically changed, and they're about as excited as if they got a makeover on *Oprah*. The exception is Ben Grimm, as Thing, who gets depressed when he looks in the mirror. Unlike the others, who look normal except when actually exhibiting superpowers, he looks like—well, he looks like his suits would fit The Hulk, just as the Human Torch looks like The Flash, and the Invisible Woman reminds me of Storm in *X-Men*. Is this the road company? Thing clomps around on his size eighteen boulders and feels like an outcast until he meets a blind woman named Alicia (Kerry Washington) who loves him, in part because she can't see him. But Thing looks like Don Rickles crossed with Mount Rushmore; he has a body that feels like a driveway and a face with crevices you could hide a toothbrush in. Alicia tenderly feels his face with her fingers, like blind people often do while falling in love in the movies, and I guess she likes what she feels. Maybe she's extrapolating.

The story involves Dr. Doom's plot to . . . but perhaps we need not concern ourselves with the plot of the movie, since it is undermined at every moment by the unwieldy need to involve a screenful of characters who, despite the most astonishing powers, have not been made exciting or even interesting. The X-Men are major league compared to them. And the really good superhero movies, like *Superman, Spiderman II,* and *Batman Begins,* leave *Fantastic Four* so far behind that the movie should almost be ashamed to show itself in some of the same theaters.

Fast Food, Fast Women

(DIRECTED BY AMOS KOLLEK; STARRING ANNA THOMSON, JAMIE HARRIS; 2001)

There's nothing wrong with *Fast Food, Fast Women* that a casting director and a rewrite couldn't have fixed. The rewrite would have realized that the movie's real story involves a sweet, touching romance between two supporting characters. The casting director would have questioned the sanity of using Anna Thomson in the lead role.

The sweet love story stars Louise Lasser in her best performance, as Emily, a widow who finds Paul (Robert Modica) through a personals ad. Their courtship is complicated by pride and misunderstanding, and by way too many plot contrivances. The lead role involves Thomson as Bella, a waitress who is said to be thirty-five.

A gentleman does not question a lady about her age, but Thomson was playing adult roles twenty years ago, has obviously had plastic surgery, and always dresses to emphasize her extreme thinness and prominent chest, so that we can't help thinking she's had a boob job.

Faithful readers will know I rarely criticize the physical appearance of actors. I would have given Thomson a pass, but the movie seems to be inviting my thoughts about her character, since Lasser's character has one big scene where she confesses she's not really as young as she claims, and another where she wonders if she should have her breasts enlarged—and then Thomson's character asks the taxi driver, "Aren't I voluptuous enough?" It's unwise to have one character being honest about issues when we're supposed to overlook the same questions raised by another character.

The movie takes place in one of those movie diners where everybody hangs out all day long and gets involved in each other's business. Bella rules the roost, pouring coffee for Paul and his pal Seymour (Victor Argo). The diner has so many regulars, it even has a regular hooker, Vitka (Angelica Torn), who stutters, so that guys can't tell she's asking them if they feel like having a good time. We learn that for years Bella has been having an affair with the married George (Austin Pendleton), who claims to be a Broadway producer, but whose shows sound like hallucinations. He spends most of their time together looking away from her and grinning at a private joke.

Bella meets a cab driver named Bruno (Jamie Harris), who has become the custodian of two children, leading to more misunderstandings that threaten to derail their future together. And then Bruno meets Emily, Seymour falls for Wanda, a stripper in a peep show, and there comes a point when you want to ask Amos Kollek, the writer-director, why the zany plot overkill when your real story is staring you in the face? (You want to ask him that even before the zebras and the camels turn up, and long before the unforgivable "happy ending.")

Lasser and Modica, as Emily and Paul, are two nice, good, lovable people who deserve each other, and whenever the movie involves their story, we care (even despite some desperate plot contrivances). Lasser's vulnerability, her courage, and the light in her eyes all bring those scenes to life, as does Paul's instinctive courtesy and the way he responds to her warmth. There's the movie. If it has to pretend to be about Bella, Kollek as the director should at least have been able to see the character more clearly—clearly enough to know the audience cannot believe she is thirty-five, and thinks of her whenever anyone else mentions plastic surgery.

Final Destination 2

(DIRECTED BY DAVID ELLIS; STARRING ALI LARTER, A. J. COOK; 2003)
Look, we drove a long way to get here, so if you know how to beat death, we'd like to know.

So say pending victims to a morgue attendant in *Final Destination 2,* which takes a good idea from the first film and pounds it into the ground, not to mention decapitating, electrocuting, skewering, blowing up, incinerating, drowning, and gassing it. Perhaps movies are like history and repeat themselves, first as tragedy, then as farce.

The earlier film involved a group of friends who got off an airplane after one of them had a vivid precognition of disaster. The plane crashes on takeoff. But then, one by one, most of the survivors die, as if fate has to balance its books.

That movie depends on all the horror clichés of the Dead Teenager Movie (formula: Teenagers are alive at beginning, dead at end). But it is well made and thoughtful. As I wrote in my review: "The film in its own way is biblical in its dilemma, although the students use the code word 'fate' when what they are really talking about is God. In their own terms, in their own way, using teenage vernacular, the students have existential discussions."

That was then; this is now. Faithful to its genre, *Final Destination 2* allows one of its original characters, Clear Rivers (Ali Larter), to survive, so she can be a link to the earlier film. In the new film, Clear is called upon by Kimberly Corman (A. J. Cook), a twenty-something, who is driving three friends in her SUV when she suddenly has a vision of a horrendous traffic accident. Kimberly blocks the on-ramp, saving the drivers behind her when logs roll off a timber truck, gas tanks explode, etc.

But is it the same old scenario? Are the people she saved all doomed to die? "There is a sort of force—an unseen malevolent presence around us every day," a character muses. "I prefer to call it death."

The malevolent presence doesn't remain unseen for long. Soon bad things are happening to good people, in a series of accidents that Rube Goldberg would have considered implausible. In one ingenious sequence, we see a character who almost trips over a lot of toys while carrying a big Macintosh iMac box. In his house, he starts the microwave and lights a fire under a frying pan, then drops his ring down the garbage disposal, then gets his hand trapped in the disposal while the microwave explodes and the frying pan starts a fire, then gets his hand loose, breaks a window that mysteriously slams shut, climbs down a fire escape, falls to the ground, and finally, when it seems he is safe . . . well, everything that could possibly go wrong does, except that he didn't get a Windows machine.

Other characters die in equally improbable ways. One is ironically killed by an air bag, another almost chokes in a dentist's chair, a third is severed from his respirator, and so on, although strange things do happen in real life. I came home from seeing this movie to read the story about the teenager who was thrown twenty-five feet in the air after a car crash, only to save himself by grabbing some telephone lines. If that had happened in *Final Destination 2,* his car would have exploded, blowing him off the lines with a flying cow.

There is a kind of dumb level on which a movie like this works, once we understand the premise. People will insist on dying oddly. Remember the story of the woman whose husband left her, so she jumped out the window and landed on him as he was leaving the building?

The thing about *FD2* is that the characters make the mistake of trying to figure things out. Their reasoning? If you were meant to die, then you owe death a life. But a new life can cancel out an old one. So if the woman in the white van can safely deliver her baby, then that means that someone else will be saved, or will have to die, I forget which. This is the kind of bookkeeping that makes you wish Arthur Andersen were still around.

Note: The first *Final Destination* (2000) had characters named after famous horror-film figures, including Browning, Horton, Lewton, Weine, Schreck, Hitchcock, and Chaney. The sequel has just two that I can identify: Corman and Carpenter.

Finding Home

(DIRECTED BY LAWRENCE D. FOLDES; STARRING LISA BRENNER, GENEVIEVE BUJOLD; 2005)

The end credits for *Finding Home* thank no less than six experts on false memory. If only they had consulted even one expert on flashbacks involving false memories, or memories of any kind, or flashbacks of any kind. Here is a movie in which the present functions mostly as a launching pad for the past, which is a hotbed of half-remembered out-of-focus screams, knives, secrets, blood, and piano lessons.

As the story opens, Amanda (Lisa Brenner) is planning her first visit to her grandmother, Esther (Louise Fletcher), when she gets a message that Esther has died. Esther's death doesn't deprive Fletcher of screen time, however, since she's present in so many flashbacks that the timeline could have just been flipped, with the story taking place in the past with flashforwards. To be sure, the flashbacks are confused and fragmented, but the present-day scenes don't make any more sense, even though we can see and hear them, which you might think would be an advantage.

Amanda's grandmother owned and operated an inn on a Maine island. The inn is one of those New England clapboard jobs with a dock and cozy public rooms and two or three floors of guest rooms. Hold that thought. We'll need it. Because of whatever happened more than ten years ago, Amanda has been forbidden to ever mention the grandmother or the inn to her mother, Grace (Jeannetta Arnette). When Amanda is ferried to the island in a boat piloted by Dave (Misha Collins), she focuses on his knife with such intensity we're reminded of the zoom-lens eye belonging to Alastor ("Mad-Eye") Moody in the new Harry Potter picture. Admittedly, a character who toys with a knife all the time in a movie makes you think.

Dave is a nice young man, ostensibly, although he spends an alarming amount of time in his work shed, carving large blocks of wood into measurably smaller ones. "Who is that going to be?" Amanda asks him of one block that already looks so much like Amanda it might as well be wearing a name tag. "I don't know who is inside it yet," he says, a dead giveaway that he has read *The Agony and the Ecstasy* and knows that with Amanda he can safely steal anything Michelangelo ever said.

"You and Dave were inseparable," Amanda is told by Katie (Genevieve Bujold), her grandmother's best friend, who has managed the inn for years. Then what happened to make Amanda fear him so, and dislike him so, and stare so at his knife? I personally think Katie knows the whole story: "Something happened between your mother and grandmother that summer," she also tells Amanda. And, "Can you really believe what she tells you about that summer?"

Before we can answer these questions, Amanda's mother Grace herself arrives on the island, along with, let's see, thumbing through my notes here, the family lawyer (Jason Miller), Amanda's boss and boyfriend, Nick (Johnny Messner), Amanda's best friend, Candace (Sherri Saum), *her* boyfriend, C.J. (Andrew Lukich), and the accountant Prescott (Justin Henry), who after all the trouble that nice Dustin Hoffman went to on his behalf in *Kramer vs. Kramer* has grown up to be a bad accountant. There is room for all these visitors because not a single guest is ever seen at the inn.

But hold on, how do I know Prescott is incompetent? Have you kept the inn fixed in your memory as I requested? The dock, the cozy public rooms, the clapboard siding, several acres of forested grounds? The hardwood floors, the pewter, the quilts, the Arts & Crafts furniture, the canned preserves? The smell of apple pies in the oven? Well, Amanda discovers that she has inherited the inn from her grandmother, who cut off Grace with a lousy brooch. Prescott the accountant then estimates that the inn could sell for, oh, about $400,000. It is unspeakably rude for a movie critic to talk aloud during a screening, but at the screening I attended, someone cried out, "I'll buy it!" I shamefully admit that person was me.

Are Dave and Katie the caretaker depressed that Amanda might sell her grandmother's inn? Not as much as you might think. Does this have anything to do with the flashbacks, the screams, the blood, the knife, and the piano lessons? Not as much as you might think. Did Dave sexually assault Amanda ten years ago? Not as much as you might think. Why does another character choose this moment to announce she is pregnant? Who could the father be? Given the Law of Economy of Characters, it has to be someone on the island. Or maybe it was someone in one of the flashbacks, who flash-forwarded in a savage act of phallic time travel and then slunk back to the past, the beast.

The solution to the mysteries, when it comes, is not so much anti-climactic as not climactic at all. I think it is wrong to bring a false memory on board only to discover that it is really false. After what this movie puts us through, the false memory should at least have a real false memory concealed beneath it. What were all those experts for?

First Descent

(Directed by Kemp Curly and Kevin Harrison; starring Shawn Farmer, Terje Haakonsen; 2005)

First Descent is boring, repetitive, and maddening about a subject you'd think would be fairly interesting: Snowboarding down a mountain. And not just any mountain. This isn't about snowboarders at Aspen or Park City. It's about experts who are helicoptered to the tops of virgin peaks in Alaska, and snowboard down what look like almost vertical slopes.

I know nothing about snowboarding. A question occurs to me. If it occurs to me, it will occur to other viewers. The question is this: How do the snowboarders know where they are going? In shot after shot, they hurtle off snow ledges into thin air, and then land dozens or hundreds of feet lower on another slope. Here's my question: As they approach the edge of the ledge, how can they know for sure what awaits them over the edge? Wouldn't they eventually be surprised, not to say dismayed, to learn that they were about to drop half a mile? Or land on rocks? Or fall into a chasm? Shouldn't the mountains of Alaska be littered with the broken bodies of extreme snowboarders?

I search the Internet and find that indeed snowboarders die not infrequently. "All I heard was Gore-Tex on ice," one survivor recalls after two of his companions disappeared. The movie vaguely talks about scouting a mountain from the air and picking out likely descent paths, but does the mountain look the same when you're descending it at forty-five degrees and high speed? Can rocks be hidden just beneath the surface? Can crevices be hidden from the eye?

The film features five famous names in the sport: Veterans Shawn Farmer, Terje Haakonsen, and Nick Perata, and teenage superstars Hannah Teter and Shaun White. For at least twenty minutes at the top of the movie, they talk and talk about the "old days," the "new techniques," the "gradual acceptance" of snowboarding, the way ski resorts first banned snowboarders but now welcome them. "As the decade progressed, so did snowboarding," we learn at one point, leading me to reflect that as the decade progressed, so did time itself.

There are a lot of shots of snowboarders in the movie, mostly doing the same things again and again, often with the camera at such an angle that we cannot get a clear idea of the relationship between where they start and where they land. To be sure, if it's hard to ski down a virgin mountainside, it must be even harder to film someone doing it. (When I saw the IMAX documentary about climbing Everest, it occurred to me that a more interesting doc would have been about the people who carried the camera.) In this case, the action footage is repetitive and underwhelming, no match for the best docs about surfing, for example. The powerful surfing film *Riding Giants* (2004), directed by Stacy Perata, does everything right that *First Descent* does wrong.

The movie's fundamental problem, I think, is journalistic. It doesn't cover its real subject. The movie endlessly repeats how exciting, or thrilling, or awesome it is to snowboard down a mountain. I would have preferred more detail about how dangerous it is, and how one prepares to do it, and what precautions are taken, and how you can anticipate avalanches on virgin snow above where anybody has ever snowboarded before.

The kicker on the trailer says: "Unless you're fully prepared to be in a situation of life and death, you shouldn't be up here." So, OK, how can you possibly be fully prepared in a situation no one has been in before, and which by definition can contain fatal surprises? Since the five stars of the movie are all still alive as I write this review, they must have answers for those questions. Maybe interesting ones. Maybe more interesting than what a thrill it is.

The Flintstones in Viva Rock Vegas

(DIRECTED BY BRIAN LEVANT; STARRING MARK ADDY, STEPHEN BALDWIN; 2000)

The Flintstones in Viva Rock Vegas has dinosaurs that lumber along crushing everything in their path. The movie's screenplay works sort of the same way. Think of every possible pun involving stones, rocks, and prehistoric times, and link them to a pea-brained story that creaks and groans on its laborious march through unspeakably obvious, labored, and idiotic humor.

This is an ideal first movie for infants, who can enjoy the bright colors on the screen and wave their tiny hands to the music. Children may like it because they just plain like going to the movies. But it's not delightful or funny or exciting, and for long stretches it looks exactly like hapless actors standing in front of big rocks and reciting sitcom dialogue.

The story isn't a sequel to *The Flintstones* (1994) but a prequel, recalling those youthful days when Fred and Wilma Flintstone first met and fell in love. Fred is portrayed this time by Mark Addy, the beefiest of the guys in *The Full Monty.* His best pal, Barney Rubble, is played by Stephen Baldwin, who recites his lines as if he hopes Fred will ask him to come out and play, but is afraid he won't. As the movie opens, Fred and Barney have gotten jobs at the rock quarry, and have settled down to a lifetime of quarrying rocks, which their world does not seem to need any more of, but never mind.

Meanwhile, in a parallel plot, Wilma Slaghoople (Kristen Johnston) resists the schemes of her mother (Joan Collins) to get her to marry the millionaire Chip Rockefeller (get it?). Fleeing the rich neighborhood, she ends up working in a drive-in restaurant ("Bronto King") with Betty O'Shale (Jane Krakowski), and soon the two of them have met Fred and Barney. There's instant chemistry, and the two couples grind off to a weekend in Rock Vegas. The jealous Chip (Thomas Gibson) is waiting there to foil romance and get his hands on the Slaghoople fortune. His conspirator is a chorus line beauty named Roxie (Second City grad Alex Meneses), whose boulders are second to none. The Vegas sequence is livened by a sound-track rendition of "Viva Las (and/or Rock) Vegas" by Ann-Margret.

Another story line involves Gazoo (Alan Cumming), an alien who arrives in a flying saucer. He looks exactly like a desperate measure to flesh out an uninteresting plot with an uninteresting character. The movie would be no better and no worse without Gazoo, which is a commentary on both Gazoo and the movie, I think.

The pun, it has been theorized, is the lowest form of humor. This movie proves that theory wrong. There is a lower form of humor: jokes about dinosaur farts. The pun is the second lowest form of humor. The third lowest form is laborious plays on words, as when we learn that the Rock Vegas headliners include Mick Jagged and the Stones.

Minute by weary minute the movie wends its weary way toward its joyless conclusion, as if everyone in it is wearing concrete overshoes, which, come to think of it, they may be. The first film was no masterpiece, but it was a lot better than this. Its slot for an aging but glamorous beauty queen was filled by Elizabeth Taylor. This time it is Joan Collins. As Joan Collins is to Elizabeth Taylor, so *The Flintstones in Viva Rock Vegas* is to *The Flintstones*.

Formula 51

(DIRECTED BY RONNY YU; STARRING SAMUEL L. JACKSON, ROBERT CARLYLE; 2002)

Pulp Fiction and *Trainspotting* were two of the most influential movies of the past ten years, but unfortunately their greatest influence has been on rip-offs of each other—movies like *Formula 51,* which is like a fourth-rate *Pulp Fiction* with accents you can't understand. Here, instead of the descent into the filthiest toilet in Scotland, we get a trip through the most bilious intestinal tract in Liverpool; instead of a debate about Cheese Royales, we get a debate about the semantics of the word *bollocks*; the F-word occupies 50 percent of all sentences, and in the opening scenes Samuel L. Jackson wears another one of those Afro wigs.

Jackson plays Elmo McElroy, a reminder that only eight of the seventy-four movies with characters named Elmo have been any good. In the prologue, he graduates from college with a pharmaceutical degree, is busted for pot, loses his license, and thirty years later is the world's most brilliant inventor of illegal drugs.

Now he has a product named "P.O.S. Formula 51," which he says is fifty-one times stronger than crack, heroin, you name it. Instead of selling it to a drug lord named The Lizard (Meat Loaf), he stages a spectacular surprise for Mr. Lizard and his friends and flies to Liverpool, trailed by Dakota Phillips (Emily Mortimer), a skilled hit woman hired by The Lizard to kill him or maybe keep him alive, depending on The Lizard's latest information.

In Liverpool, we meet Felix DeSouza (Robert Carlyle), a reminder that only six of the two hundred movies with a character named Felix have been any good. (The stats for "Dakota" are also discouraging, but this is a line of inquiry with limited dividends.) Felix has been dispatched by the Liverpudlian drug king Leopold Durant (Ricky Tomlinson), whose hemorrhoids require that a flunky follow him around with an inner tube that makes whoopee-type whistles whenever the screenplay requires.

The movie is not a comedy so much as a farce, grabbing desperately for funny details wherever possible. The Jackson character, for example, wears a kilt for most of the movie. My online correspondent Ian Waldron-Mantgani, a critic who lives in Liverpool but doesn't give the home team a break, points out that the movie closes with the words "No one ever found out why he wore a kilt," and then explains why he wore the kilt. "You get the idea how much thought went into this movie," Waldron-Mantgani writes, with admirable restraint.

Many of the jokes involve Felix's fanatic support of the Liverpool football club, and a final confrontation takes place in an executive box of the stadium. Devices like this almost always play as a desperate attempt to inject local color, especially when the movie shows almost nothing of the game, so that Americans will not be baffled by what they call football. There are lots of violent shoot-outs and explosions, a kinduva love affair between Felix and Dakota, and an ending that crosses a red herring, a Maguffin, and a shaggy dog.

Freddy Got Fingered

(DIRECTED BY TOM GREEN; STARRING TOM GREEN, RIP TORN; 2001)

It's been leading up to this all spring. When David Spade got buried in crap in *Joe Dirt,* and when three supermodels got buried in crap in *Head Over Heels,* and when human organs fell from a hot air balloon in *Monkeybone* and were eaten by dogs, and when David Arquette rolled around in dog crap and a gangster had his testicles bitten off in *See Spot Run,* and when a testicle was eaten in *Tomcats,* well, somehow the handwriting was on the wall. There had to be a movie like *Freddy Got Fingered* coming along.

This movie doesn't scrape the bottom of the barrel. This movie isn't the bottom of the barrel. This movie isn't below the bottom of the barrel. This movie doesn't deserve to be mentioned in the same sentence with barrels.

Many years ago, when surrealism was new, Luis Bunuel and Salvador Dali made a film so shocking that Bunuel filled his pockets with stones to throw at the audience if it attacked him. Green, whose film is in the surrealist tradition, may want to consider the same tactic. The day may come when *Freddy Got Fingered* is seen as a milestone of neosurrealism. The day may never come when it is seen as funny.

The film is a vomitorium consisting of ninety-three minutes of Tom Green doing things that a geek in a carnival sideshow would turn down. Six minutes into the film, his character leaps from his car to wag a horse penis. This is, we discover, a framing device—to be matched by a scene late in the film where he sprays his father with elephant semen, straight from the source.

Green plays Gord Brody, a twenty-eight-year-old who lives at home with his father (Rip Torn), who despises him, and his mother (Julie Hagerty), who wrings her hands a lot. He lives in a basement room still stocked with his high school stuff, draws cartoons, and dreams of becoming an animator. Gord would exhaust a psychiatrist's list of diagnoses. He is unsocialized, hostile, manic, and apparently retarded. Retarded? How else to explain a sequence where a Hollywood animator tells him to "get inside his animals," and he skins a stag and prances around dressed in the coat, covered with blood?

His romantic interest in the movie is Betty (Marisa Coughlan), who is disabled and dreams of rocket-powered wheelchairs and oral sex. A different kind of sexual behavior enters the life of his brother, Freddy, who gets the movie named after him just because, I suppose, Tom Green thought the title was funny. His character also thinks it is funny to falsely accuse his father of molesting Freddy.

Tom Green's sense of humor may not resemble yours. Consider, for example, a scene where Gord's best friend busts his knee open while skateboarding. Gord licks the open wound. Then he visits his friend in the hospital. A woman in the next bed goes into labor. Gord rips the baby from her womb and, when it appears to be dead, brings it to life by swinging it around his head by its umbilical cord, spraying the walls with blood. If you wanted that to be a surprise, then I'm sorry I spoiled it for you.

Full Frontal

(DIRECTED BY STEVEN SODERBERGH; STARRING BLAIR UNDERWOOD, JULIA ROBERTS; 2002)

Every once in a while, perhaps as an exercise in humility, Steven Soderbergh makes a truly inexplicable film. There was the Cannes secret screening of his *Schizopolis* in 1996, which had audiences filing out with sad, thoughtful faces, and now here is *Full Frontal*, a film so amateurish that only the professionalism of some of the actors makes it watchable.

This is the sort of work we expect from a film school student with his first digital camera, not from the gifted director of *Traffic* and *Out of Sight*. Soderbergh directs at far below his usual level, and his cinematography is also wretched; known as one of the few directors who shoots some of his own films, he is usually a skilled craftsman, but here, using a digital camera and available light, he produces only a demonstration of his inability to handle the style. Many shots consist of indistinct dark blobs in front of blinding backlighting.

The plot involves a film within a film, on top of a documentary about some of the people in the outside film. The idea apparently is to provide a view of a day in the life of the Los Angeles entertainment industry and its satellites. The movie within the movie stars Julia Roberts as a journalist interviewing Blair Underwoood; shots that are supposed to be this movie are filmed in lush 35 mm, and only serve to make us yearn for the format as we see the other scenes in digital.

The doc is not quite, or entirely, a doc; there are voice-overs describing and analyzing some of the characters, but other scenes play as dramatic fiction, and there's no use trying to unsort it all, because Soderbergh hasn't made it sortable. If this movie is a satire of the sorts of incomprehensible, earnest "personal" films that would-be directors hand out on cassettes at film festivals, then I understand it. It's the kind of film where you need the director telling you what he meant to do and what went wrong and how the actors screwed up and how there was no money for retakes, etc.

The other characters include Catherine Keener and David Hyde Pierce, as an unhappily married couple. She leaves him a goodbye note in the morning, then goes off to work as a personnel director, spending the day in a series of bizarre humiliations of employees (forcing them, for example, to stand on a chair while she throws an inflated world globe at them). In these scenes she is clearly deranged, and yet there is a "serious" lunch with her sister Linda (Mary McCormack), a masseuse who has never met Mr. Right.

Linda does, however, meet Gus (David Duchovny), a producer who is having a birthday party in a big hotel, hires her for a massage, and then offers her $500 to "release his tension." She needs the money because she is flying off the next day to see a guy she met on the Internet. She thinks he's twenty-two, but in fact he's about forty, and is not an artist as he says, but a director whose new play features Hitler as a guy who, he tells Eva Braun, has "so many responsibilities I can't think of a relationship right now."

Meanwhile, Pierce is fired at work ("He said I have confused my personality quirks with standards") and returns home to find his beloved dog has overdosed on hash brownies, after which he has a heart-to-heart with the veterinarian's assistant. All of these scenes feel like improvs that have been imperfectly joined, with no through-line. The scenes that work (notably McCormack's) are perhaps a tribute to the professionalism of the actor, not the director. Among the false alarms are little details like this: A love note that Underwood's character thinks came from Roberts's character is written on the same kind of red stationery as Keener's note to her husband. Is there a connection? Short answer: No.

Just yesterday I saw *Sex and Lucia,* also shot on digital, also involving a story within a story, with double roles for some of the characters. With it, too, I was annoyed by the digital photography (both films have more contrast between shadow and bright sunlight than their equipment seems able to handle). *Sex and Lucia* was even more confusing when it came to who was who (*Full Frontal* is fairly easy to figure out). But at least *Sex and Lucia* was made by a director who had a good idea of what he wanted to accomplish and established a tone that gave the material weight and emotional resonance. There is a scene in *Full Frontal* where a character comes to a tragic end while masturbating. That could symbolize the method and fate of this film.

The Game of Their Lives

(DIRECTED BY DAVID ANSPAUGH; STARRING GERARD BUTLER, WES BENTLEY; 2005)

The Game of their Lives tells the story of an astonishing soccer match in 1950, when an unsung team of Americans went to Brazil to compete in the World Cup, and defeated England, the best team in the world. So extraordinary was the upset, I learn on the Internet Movie Database, "that London bookmakers offered odds of 500 to 1 against such an preposterous event, and the *New York Times* refused to run the score when it was first reported, deeming it a hoax."

So it was a hell of an upset. Pity about the movie. Obviously made with all of the best will in the world, its heart in the right place, this is a sluggish and dutiful film that plays more like a eulogy than an adventure. Strange, how it follows the form of a sports movie but has the feeling of an educational film. And all the stranger because the director, David Anspaugh, has made two exhilarating movies about underdogs in sports, *Hoosiers* (1986) and *Rudy* (1993).

In those films he knew how to crank up the suspense and dramatize the supporting characters. Here it feels more like a group of Calvin Klein models have gathered to pose as soccer players from St. Louis. Shouldn't there be at least one player not favored by nature with improbably good looks? And at least a couple who look like they're around twenty, instead of thirty-five? And a goalie who doesn't look exactly like Gerard Butler, who played *The Phantom of the Opera*? True, Frank Borghi, the goalie, is played by Gerard Butler, but that's no excuse: In *Dear Frankie*, Butler played a perfectly believable character who didn't look like he was posing for publicity photos.

The one personal subplot involves a player who thinks he can't go to Brazil because it's a conflict with his wedding day. Instead of milking this for personal conflict, Anspaugh solves it all in one perfunctory scene: The coach talks to the future father-in-law, the father-in-law talks to his daughter, she agrees to move up the wedding, and so no problem-o.

This team is so lackluster, when they go out to get drunk, they don't get drunk. It's 1950, but there's only one cigarette and three cigars in the whole movie. The sound track could have used big band hits from the period, but William Ross's score is so inspirational it belongs on a commercial.

As the movie opens, we see a St. Louis soccer club from a mostly Italian-American neighborhood, and hear a narration that sounds uncannily like an audiobook. Word comes that soccer players from New York will travel to Missouri, an American team will be chosen, and they'll travel to Brazil. The players get this information from their coach, Bill Jeffrey (John Rhys-Davis), who is so uncoachlike that at no point during the entire movie does he give them one single word of advice about the game of soccer. Both Rhys-Davis and the general manager, Walter Giesler (Craig Hawksley), are perfectly convincing in their roles, but the screenplay gives them no dialogue to suggest their characters know much about soccer.

As for the big game itself, the game was allegedly shot on location in Brazil, but never do we get a sense that the fans in the long shots are actually watching the match. The tempo of the game is monotonous, coming down to one would-be British goal after another, all of them blocked by Borghi. This was obviously an amazing athletic feat, but you don't get that sense in the movie. You don't get the sense of soccer much at all; *Bend It Like Beckham* had better soccer—*lots* better soccer, and you could follow it and get involved.

At the end of the film, before a big modern soccer match, the surviving members of that 1950 team are called out onto the field and introduced. That should provide us with a big emotional boost, as we see the real men next to insets of their characters in the movie. But it doesn't, because we never got to know the characters in the movie. *The Game of Their Lives* covers its story like an assignment, not like a mission.

The Girl Next Door

(DIRECTED BY LUKE GREENFIELD; STARRING EMILE HIRSCH, ELISHA CUTHBERT; 2004)

The studio should be ashamed of itself for advertising *The Girl Next Door* as a teenage comedy. It's a nasty piece of business, involving a romance between a teenage porn actress and a high school senior. A good movie could presumably be made from this premise—a good movie can be made from anything, in the right hands and way—but this is a dishonest, quease-inducing "comedy" that had me feeling uneasy and then unclean. Who in the world read this script and thought it was acceptable?

The film stars Emile Hirsch as Matthew Kidman. (Please tell me the *Kidman* is not an oblique reference to Nicole Kidman and therefore to Tom Cruise and therefore to *Risky Business,* the film this one so desperately wants to resemble.) One day he sees a sexy girl moving in next door, and soon he's watching through his bedroom window as she undresses as girls undress only in his dreams. Then she sees him, snaps off the light, and a few minutes later rings the doorbell.

Has she come to complain? No, she says nothing about the incident and introduces herself to Matthew's parents: Her aunt is on vacation, and she is house-sitting. Soon they're in her car together and Danielle is coming on to Matthew: "Did you like what you saw?" He did. She says now it's her turn to see him naked, and makes him strip and stand in the middle of the road while she shines the headlights on him. Then she scoops up his underpants and drives away, leaving him to walk home naked, ho, ho. (It is not easy to reach out of a car and scoop up underpants from the pavement while continuing to drive. Try it sometime.)

Danielle (Elisha Cuthbert) has two personalities: In one, she's a sweet, misunderstood kid who has never been loved, and in the other she's a twisted emotional sadist who amuses herself by toying with the feelings of the naive Matthew. The movie alternates between these personalities at its convenience, making her quite the most unpleasant character I have seen in some time.

They have a romance going before one of Matthew's buddies identifies her, correctly, as a porn star. The movie seems to think, along with Matthew's friends, that this information is in her favor. Matthew goes through the standard formula: First he's angry with her, then she gets through his defenses, then he believes she really loves him and that she wants to leave the life she's been leading. Problem is, her producer is angry because he wants her to keep working. This character, named Kelly, is played by Timothy Olyphant with a skill that would have distinguished a better movie, but it doesn't work here, because the movie never levels with us. When a guy his age (thirty-six, according to IMDB) "used to be the boyfriend" of a girl her age (nineteen, according to the plot description) and she is already, at nineteen, a famous porn star, there is a good chance the creep corrupted her at an early age; think Traci Lords. That he is now her "producer" under an "exclusive contract" is an elevated form of pimping. To act in porn as a teenager is not a decision freely taken by most teenage girls, and not a life to envy.

There's worse. The movie produces a basically nice guy, named Hugo Posh (James Remar), also a porn king, who is Kelly's rival. That a porn king saves the day gives you an idea of the movie's limited moral horizons. Oh, and not to forget Matthew's best friends, named Eli and Klitz (Chris Marquette and Paul Dano). Klitz? "Spelled with a K," he explains.

Kelly steals the money that Matthew has raised to bring a foreign exchange student from Cambodia, and to replace the funds, the resourceful Danielle flies in two porn star friends (played by Amanda Swisten and Sung Hi Lee), so that Matthew, Eli, and Klitz can produce a sex film during the senior prom. The nature of their film is yet another bait-and-switch, in a movie that wants to seem dirtier than it is. Like a strip show at a carnival, it lures you in with promises of sleaze, and after you have committed yourself for the filthy-minded punter you are, it professes innocence.

Risky Business (1983) you will recall, starred Tom Cruise as a young man left home alone by his parents, who wrecks the family Porsche and ends up enlisting a call girl (Rebecca De Mornay) to run a brothel out of his house to raise money to replace the car. The movie is the obvious model for *The Girl Next Door*, but it completely misses the tone and wit of the earlier film, which proved you can get away with that plot, but you have to know what you're doing and how to do it, two pieces of knowledge conspicuously absent here.

One necessary element is to distance the heroine from the seamier side of her life. *The Girl Next Door* does the opposite, actually taking Danielle and her "producer" Kelly to an adult film convention in Las Vegas, and even into a dimly lit room where adult stars apparently pleasure the clients. (There is another scene where Kelly, pretending to be Matthew's friend, takes him to a lap dance emporium and treats him.) We can deal with porn stars, lap dances, and whatever else, in a movie that declares itself and plays fair, but to insert this material into something with the look and feel of a teen comedy makes it unsettling. The TV ads will attract audiences expecting something like *American Pie*; they'll be shocked by the squalid content of this film.

Gods and Generals

(DIRECTED BY RONALD F. MAXWELL; STARRING JEFF DANIELS, STEPHEN LANG; 2003)

Here is a Civil War movie that Trent Lott might enjoy. Less enlightened than *Gone with the Wind*, obsessed with military strategy, impartial between South and North, religiously devout, it waits seventy minutes before introducing the first of its two speaking roles for African-Americans; Stonewall Jackson assures his black cook that the South will free him, and the cook looks cautiously optimistic. If World War II were handled this way, there'd be hell to pay.

The movie is essentially about brave men on both sides who fought and died so that . . . well, so that they could fight and die. They are led by generals of blinding brilliance and nobility, although one Northern general makes a stupid error and the movie shows hundreds of his men being slaughtered at great length as the result of it.

The Northerners, one Southerner explains, are mostly Republican profiteers who can go home to their businesses and families if they're voted out of office after the conflict, while the Southerners are fighting for their homes. Slavery is not the issue, in this view, because it would have withered away anyway, although a liberal professor from Maine (Jeff Daniels) makes a speech explaining it is wrong. So we get that cleared up right there, or for sure at Strom Thurmond's birthday party.

The conflict is handled with solemnity worthy of a memorial service. The music, when it is not funereal, sounds like the band playing during the commencement exercises at a sad university. Countless extras line up, march forward, and shoot at each other. They die like flies. That part is accurate, although the stench, the blood, and the cries of pain are tastefully held to the PG-13 standard. What we know about the war from the photographs of Mathew Brady, the poems of Walt Whitman, and the documentaries of Ken Burns is not duplicated here.

Oh, it is a competently made film. Civil War buffs may love it. Every group of fighting men is identified by subtitles, to such a degree that I wondered, fleetingly, if they were being played by Civil War reenactment hobbyists who would want to nudge their friends when their group appeared on the screen. Much is made of the film's total and obsessive historical accuracy; the costumes, flags, battle plans, and ordnance are all doubtless flawless, although there could have been no Sgt. "Buster" Kilrain in the 20th Maine, for the unavoidable reason that "Buster" was never used as a name until Buster Keaton used it.

The actors do what they can, although you can sense them winding up to deliver pithy quotations. Robert Duvall, playing Gen. Robert E. Lee, learns of Stonewall Jackson's battlefield amputation and reflects sadly, "He has lost his left arm, and I have lost my right." His eyes almost twinkle as he envisions that one ending up in Bartlett's. Stephen Lang, playing Jackson, has a deathbed scene so wordy, as he issues commands to imaginary subordinates and then prepares himself to cross over the river, that he seems to be stalling. Except for Lee, a nonbeliever, both sides trust in God, just like at the Super Bowl.

Donzaleigh Abernathy plays the other African-American speaking role, that of a maid named Martha who attempts to jump the gun on Reconstruction by staying behind when her white employers evacuate, and telling the arriving Union troops it is her own house. Later, when they commandeer it as a hospital, she looks a little resentful. This episode, like many others, is kept so resolutely at the cameo level that we realize material of such scope and breadth can be shoehorned into 3½ hours only by sacrificing depth.

Gods and Generals is the kind of movie beloved by people who never go to the movies, because they are primarily interested in something else—the Civil War, for example—and think historical accuracy is a virtue instead of an attribute. The film plays like a special issue of *American Heritage*. Ted Turner is one of its prime movers, and gives himself an instantly recognizable cameo appearance. Since sneak previews must already have informed him that his sudden appearance draws a laugh, apparently he can live with that.

Note: The same director, Ron Maxwell, made the much superior *Gettysburg* (1993) and at the end informs us that the third title in the trilogy will be *The Last Full Measure.* Another line from the same source may serve as a warning: "The world will little note, nor long remember, what we say here."

Godzilla

(DIRECTED BY ISHIRO HONDA; STARRING TAKASHI SHIMURA, MOMOKO KOCHI; 2004)

Regaled for fifty years by the stupendous idiocy of the American version of *Godzilla,* audiences can now see the original 1954 Japanese version, which is equally idiotic, but, properly decoded, was the *Fahrenheit 9/11* of its time. Both films come after fearsome attacks on their nations, embody urgent warnings, and even incorporate similar dialogue, such as, "The report is of such dire importance it must not be made public." Is that from 1954 Tokyo or 2004 Washington?

The first *Godzilla* set box-office records in Japan and inspired countless sequels, remakes, and rip-offs. It was made shortly after an American H-bomb test in the Pacific contaminated a large area of ocean and gave radiation sickness to a boatload of Japanese fishermen. It refers repeatedly to Nagasaki, H-bombs, and civilian casualties, and obviously embodies Japanese fears about American nuclear tests.

But that is not the movie you have seen. For one thing, it doesn't star Raymond Burr as Steve Martin, intrepid American journalist, who helpfully explains, "I was headed for an assignment in Cairo when I dropped off for a social call in Tokyo." The American producer Joseph E. Levine bought the Japanese film, cut it by forty minutes, removed all of the political content, and awkwardly inserted Burr into scenes where he clearly did not fit. The hapless actor gives us reaction shots where he's looking in the wrong direction, listens to Japanese actors dubbed into the American idiom (they always call him "Steve Martin" or even "the famous Steve Martin"), and provides a reassuring conclusion in which Godzilla is seen as some kind of public health problem, or maybe just a malcontent.

The Japanese version, now in general U.S. release to mark the film's fiftieth anniversary, is a bad film, but with an undeniable urgency. I learn from helpful notes by Mike Flores of the Psychotronic Film Society that the opening scenes, showing fishing boats disappearing as the sea boils up, would have been read by Japanese audiences as a coded version of U.S. underwater H-bomb tests. Much is made of a scientist named Dr. Serizawa (Akihiko Hirata), who could destroy Godzilla with his secret weapon, the Oxygen Destroyer, but hesitates because he is afraid the weapon might fall into the wrong hands, just as H-bombs might, and have. The film's ending warns that atomic tests may lead to more Godzillas. All cut from the U.S. version.

In these days of flawless special effects, Godzilla and the city he destroys are equally crude. Godzilla at times looks uncannily like a man in a lizard suit, stomping on cardboard sets, as indeed he was, and did. Other scenes show him as a stiff, awkward animatronic model. This was not state-of-the-art even at the time; *King Kong* (1933) was much more convincing.

When Dr. Serizawa demonstrates the Oxygen Destroyer to the fiancée of his son, the superweapon is somewhat anticlimactic. He drops a pill into a tank of tropical fish, the tank lights up, he shouts "Stand back!" The fiancée screams, and the fish go belly-up. Yeah, that'll stop Godzilla in his tracks.

Reporters covering Godzilla's advance are rarely seen in the same shot with the monster. Instead, they look offscreen with horror; a TV reporter, broadcasting for some reason from his station's tower, sees Godzilla looming nearby and signs off, "Sayonara, everyone!" Meanwhile, searchlights sweep the sky, in case Godzilla learns to fly.

The movie's original Japanese dialogue, subtitled, is as harebrained as Burr's dubbed lines. When the Japanese Parliament meets (in what looks like a high school home room), the dialogue is portentous but circular:

"The professor raises an interesting question! We need scientific research!"

"Yes, but at what cost?"

"Yes, that's the question!"

Is there a reason to see the original *Godzilla*? Not because of its artistic stature, but perhaps because of the feeling we can sense in its parable about the monstrous threats unleashed by the atomic age. There are shots of Godzilla's victims in hospitals, and they reminded me of documentaries of Japanese A-bomb victims. The incompetence of scientists, politicians, and the military will ring a bell. This is a bad movie, but it has earned its place in history, and the enduring popularity of Godzilla and other monsters shows that it struck a chord. Can it be a coincidence, in these years of trauma after 9/11, that in a 2005 remake, King Kong will march once again on New York?

Good Boy!

(DIRECTED BY JOHN ROBERT HOFFMAN; STARRING LIAM AIKEN, KEVIN NEALON; 2003)

Millions of Dog Owners Demand to Know: "Who's a Good Boy?"

— HEADLINE IN THE *ONION*

If a child and a dog love each other, the relationship is one of mutual wonder. Making the dog an alien from outer space is not an improvement. Giving it the ability to speak is a disaster. My dog Blackie used his eyes to say things so eloquent that Churchill would have been stuck for a comeback. Among my favorite recent movie dogs are Skip, in *My Dog Skip*, who teaches a boy how to be a boy, and Shiloh, in *Shiloh*, who teaches a boy that life is filled with hard choices. Hubble, the dog in *Good Boy!* teaches that dogs will be pulled off Earth and returned to their home planet in a "global recall."

I've told you all you really need to know about the movie's plot. Owen Baker (Liam Aiken), the young hero, adopts a terrier who turns out to have arrived in a flying saucer to investigate why dogs on Earth are our pets, instead of the other way around. This will be a no-brainer for anyone who has watched a dog operating a pooper-scooper, nor do dogs look like the master race when they go after your pants leg. But I am willing to accept this premise if anything clever is done with it. Nothing is.

Having seen talking and/or audible dogs in many movies (how the years hurry by!), I have arrived at the conclusion that the best way to present animal speech is by letting us hear their thoughts in voice-over. Sometimes it works to show their lips moving (it certainly did in *Babe*), but in *Good Boy!* the jaw movements are so mechanical it doesn't look like speech, it looks like a film loop. Look at *Babe* again and you'll appreciate the superior way in which the head movements and body language of the animals supplement their speech.

But speech is not the real problem with *Good Boy!* What they talk about is. The movie asks us to consider a race of superior beings who are built a few feet off the ground, lack opposable thumbs, and walk around nude all the time. Compared to them, the aliens in *Signs* are a model of plausibility. The dogs live within a few blocks of one another in Vancouver, and we meet their owners. I kept hoping maybe Jim Belushi had moved to the neighborhood with Jerry Lee from *K-9*, or that I'd spot Jack Nicholson walking Jill. (Jack and Jill: I just got it.)

But no. The humans are along the lines of Kevin Nealon and Molly Shannon, as Owen's parents. The dogs are voiced by Matthew Broderick (as Hubble), Brittany Moldowan, Brittany Murphy, Donald Faison, Carl Reiner, and Delta Burke. Voicing one of the dogs in this movie is the career move of people who like to keep working no matter what. At least when you do the voice of an *animated* animal, they make it look a little like you, and your character can be the star. But when you voice a real dog, do you have to stand around all day between shots talking to the trainer about what a good dog it is?

The Grudge

(DIRECTED BY TAKASHI SHIMIZU; STARRING SARAH MICHELLE GELLAR, JASON BEHR; 2004)

The Grudge has a great opening scene, I'll grant you that. Bill Pullman wakes up next to his wife, greets the day from the balcony of their bedroom, and then—well, I, for one, was gob-smacked. I'm not sure how this scene fits into the rest of the movie, but then I'm not sure how most of the scenes fit into the movie. I do, however, understand the underlying premise: There is a haunted house, and everybody who enters it will have unspeakable things happen to them.

These are not just any old unspeakable things. They rigidly follow the age-old formula of horror movies, in which characters who hear alarming sounds go to investigate, unwisely sticking their heads/hands/body parts into places where they quickly become forensic evidence. Something attacks them in a shot so brief and murky it could be a fearsome beast, a savage ghost—or, of course, Only a Cat.

The movie, set in Japan but starring mostly American actors, has been remade by Takashi Shimizu from his original Japanese version. It loses intriguing opportunities to contrast American and Japanese cultures, alas, by allowing everyone to speak English; I was hoping it would exploit its locations and become *Lost, Eviscerated, and Devoured in Translation.*

An opening title informs us that when an event causes violent rage, a curse is born that inhabits that place and is visited on others who come there. We are eventually given a murky, black-and-white, tilt-shot flashback glimpse of the original violent rage, during which we can indistinctly spot some of the presences who haunt the house, including a small child with a big mouth and a catlike scream.

The house shelters, at various times, the mother of one of the characters, who spends most of her time in bed or staring vacantly into space, and a young couple who move in, and a real estate agent who sees that the bathtub is filled up and sticks his hand into the water to pull the plug, and is attacked by a woman with long hair who leaps out of the water. This woman's hair, which sometimes looks like seaweed, appears in many scenes, hanging down into the frame as if it dreams of becoming a boom mike.

Various cops and social workers enter the house, some never to emerge, but the news of its malevolence doesn't get around. You'd think that after a house has been associated with gruesome calamities on a daily basis, the neighbors could at least post an old-timer outside to opine that some mighty strange things have been a-happening in there.

I eventually lost all patience. The movie may have some subterranean level on which the story strands connect and make sense, but it eluded me. The fragmented time structure is a nuisance, not a style. The house is not particularly creepy from an architectural point of view, and if it didn't have a crawl space under the eaves, the ghosts would have to jump out from behind sofas.

Sarah Michelle Gellar, the nominal star, has been in her share of horror movies, and all by herself could have written and directed a better one than this. As for Bill Pullman, the more I think about his opening scene, the more I think it represents his state of mind after he signed up for the movie, flew all the way to Japan, and read the screenplay.

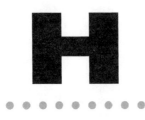

Half Past Dead

(DIRECTED BY DON MICHAEL PAUL; STARRING STEVEN SEAGAL, MORRIS CHESTNUT; 2002)
Half Past Dead is like an alarm that goes off while nobody is in the room. It does its job and stops, and nobody cares. It goes through the motions of an action thriller, but there is a deadness at its center, a feeling that no one connected with it loved what they were doing. There are moments, to be sure, when Ja Rule and Morris Chestnut seem to hear the music, but they're dancing by themselves.

The plot is preposterous, but that's acceptable with a thriller. The action is preposterous, too: Various characters leap from high places while firing guns, and the movie doesn't think to show us how, or if, they land. A room is filled with tear gas, but what exactly happens then? The movie takes the form of a buddy movie, but is stopped in its tracks because its hero, played by Steven Seagal, doesn't have a buddy gene in his body. (I know, he takes seven bullets for his partner Nick, but I don't think he planned it: "I'll take seven bullets for Nick!")

Seagal's great contribution to the movie is to look very serious, even menacing, in close-ups carefully framed to hide his double chin. I do not object to the fact that he's put on weight. Look who's talking. I object to the fact that he thinks he can conceal it from us with knee-length coats and tricky camera angles. I would rather see a movie about a pudgy karate fighter than a movie about a guy you never get a good look at.

The film has little dialogue and much action. It places its trust so firmly in action that it opens with a scene where the characters have one of those urban chase scenes where the car barely misses trailer trucks, squeals through 180-degree turns, etc., *and they're not even being chased.* It's kind of a warm-up, like a musician practicing the scales.

Do not read further if you think the plot may have the slightest importance to the movie. Seagal plays an undercover FBI guy who has teamed up with the crook Nick Frazier (Ja Rule), who vouched for him with the master criminal Sonny Ekvall (Richard Bremmer), who runs, if I have this correct, "the biggest crime syndicate between Eastern Europe and the Pacific Rim." He doesn't say whether the syndicate extends easterly or westerly between those demarcations, which would affect the rim he has in mind. Maybe easterly, since Seagal's character is named Sascha Petrosevitch. "You're Russian, right?" he asks Seagal, who agrees. Seagal's answer to this question is the only time in the entire movie he has a Russian accent.

Nick gets thrown into New Alcatraz. Sascha Petrosevitch gets thrown in, too. Later, after his cover is blown, he explains to Nick that the FBI thought if he did time with Nick, it would help him get inside the criminal organization. The sentence is five years. What a guy.

Then, let's see, the prison contains an old man who is about to go to the chair with the secret of $200 million in gold bars. Bad guys want his secret and cooperate with an insider (Morris Chestnut) to break into the prison, taking hostage a female U.S. Supreme Court justice who is on a tour of death row (she's one of those liberals). They want to escape with the old guy and get the gold. Among their demands: a fully fueled jet plane to an "undisclosed location." My advice: At least disclose the location to the pilot.

Nick and Sascha Petrosevitch team up to risk their lives in a non-stop series of shoot-outs, explosions, martial arts fights, and shoulder-launched rocket battles in order to save the Supreme Court justice. We know why Sascha Petrosevitch is doing this. But why is Nick? Apparently he is another example of that mysterious subset of the law of gravitation that attracts the black actor with second billing in an action movie to the side of the hero.

At the end of *Half Past Dead* there is a scene where Nick looks significantly at Sascha Petrosevitch and nods and smiles a little, as if to say, you some kinda white guy. Of course, Sascha Petrosevitch has just promised to spring him from New Alcatraz, which can easily inspire a nod and a little smile.

Meanwhile, I started wondering about that $200 million in gold. At the end of the movie, we see a chest being winched to the surface and some gold bars spilling out. If gold sells at, say, $321 per troy ounce, then $200 million in gold bars would represent 623,052 troy ounces, or 42,720 pounds, and would not fit in that chest. You would expect the FBI guys would know this. Maybe not these FBI guys.

Note: I imagine the flywheels at the MPAA congratulating each other on a good day's work as they rated *Half Past Dead* PG-13, after giving the anti-gun movie *Bowling for Columbine* an R.

Head Over Heels

(DIRECTED BY MARK S. WATERS; STARRING MONICA POTTER, FREDDIE PRINZE JR; 2001)

Head Over Heels opens with fifteen funny minutes and then goes dead in the water. It's like they sent home the first team of screenwriters and brought in Beavis and Butthead. The movie starts out with sharp wit and edgy zingers, switches them off, and turns to bathroom humor. And not funny bathroom humor, but painfully phony gas-passing noises, followed by a plumbing emergency that buries three supermodels in a putrid delivery from where the sun don't shine. It's as if the production was a fight to the death between bright people with a sense of humor and cretins who think the audience is as stupid as they are.

Monica Potter and Freddie Prinze Jr. star, in another one of those stories where it's love at first sight and then she gets the notion that he's clubbed someone to death. The two characters were doing perfectly well being funny as *themselves*, and then the movie muzzles them and brings in this pea-brained autopilot plot involving mistaken identities, dead bodies, and the Russian Mafia.

Why? I wanted to ask the filmmakers. Why? You have a terrific cast and the wit to start out well. Why surrender and sell out? Isn't it a better bet, and even better for your careers, to make a whole movie that's smart and funny, instead of showing off for fifteen minutes and then descending into cynicism and stupidity? Why not make a movie you can show to the friends you admire, instead of to a test audience scraped from the bottom of the IQ barrel?

Monica Potter is radiant as Amanda, an art restorer at the Museum of Modern Art. She has been betrayed by a boyfriend, and vows to focus on her job. "I love art better than real life," she says, because the people in paintings "stay in love forever." True of the Grecian urn, perhaps, if not of Bosch, but never mind; her latest challenge is to restore a priceless Titian, which the curator hauls into the room with his fingers all over the paint, banging it against the doorway.

Moving out from her faithless boyfriend, she finds a $500-a-month room (i.e., closet) in a vast luxury apartment occupied by "the last four nonsmoking models in Manhattan" (Shalom Harlow, Ivana Milicevic, Sarah O'Hare, and Tomiko Fraser). And then she falls head over heels in love with a neighbor, Jim (Prinze), who walks a big dog that knocks her over and sets up a conversation in which she says all of the wrong things. That's the dialogue I thought was so funny.

In a film with more confidence, the comedy would continue to be based on their relationship. This one prefers to recycle aged clichés. She thinks she sees him club someone to death. We know he didn't, because— well, because (a) it happens in silhouette, so the movie is hiding something, and (b) Freddie Prinze is not going to play a *real* club-murderer, not in a movie with a cute dog. Idiot Plot devices prevent either one of them from saying the two or three words that would clear up the misunderstanding. Meanwhile, the exhausted screenwriters haul in the Russian Mafia and other sinister characters in order to make this movie as similar as possible to countless other brain-dead productions.

As my smile faded and I realized the first fifteen minutes were bait-and-switch, my restless mind sought elsewhere for employment. I focused on Amanda's job, art restoration. Her challenge: An entire face is missing from a grouping by Titian. She "restores" it by filling the gap with, yes, Freddie Prinze's face and head, complete with a haircut that doesn't exactly match the Renaissance period.

But never mind. Give the movie the benefit of the doubt. Maybe one of those Renaissance geniuses like Michelangelo invented Supercuts clippers at the same time he invented bicycles and submarines. What's really odd is that the face is not in the style of Titian, but in the style of Norman Rockwell. Obviously it was only with the greatest restraint that Amanda was able to prevent herself from adding a soda fountain to the background.

Now what about that eruption of unspeakable brown stuff that coats the supermodels as they hide behind a shower curtain in a bathroom? Why was that supposed to be funny? The scene betrays a basic ignorance of a fundamental principle of humor: It isn't funny when innocent bystanders are humiliated. It's funny when they humiliate themselves. For example, *Head Over Heels* would be funny if it were about the people making this movie.

High Tension

(DIRECTED BY ALEXANDRE AJA; STARRING CECILE DE FRANCE, MAIWENN LE BESCO; 2005)

The philosopher Thomas Hobbes tells us life can be "poor, nasty, brutish, and short." So is this movie. Alexandre Aja's *High Tension* is a slasher film about a madman prowling a rural area of France, chopping, slicing, and crunching his way through, let's see, a body count of five or six people, including a small child that the film does not neglect to show crumpled and dead in a cornfield. That's what it's about, anyway, until we discover it actually consists of something else altogether, something I think is not possible, given our current understanding of the laws of physics.

The movie premiered at Toronto 2003 in a version that would clearly have received an NC-17 rating. It has been edited down to an R, perhaps the hardest R for violence the MPAA has ever awarded, and into the bargain Lions Gate has dubbed great parts of it into English. Not all: There are inexplicable sections where the characters swear in French, which is helpfully subtitled.

I had forgotten how much I hate dubbing, especially when it's done as badly as in *High Tension*. It's lip-flap on parade. The movie was originally shot in French, but for purposes of dubbing, one of the characters, Alex (Maiween Le Besco), has been given an American accent. As she and her friend Marie (Cecile De France) arrive at the country home of Alex's family, Alex warns her: "Their French is even worse than mine." Since the parents hardly speak except to scream bilingually, this is not a problem.

The story: Alex and Marie are driving out to a country weekend with Alex's parents. Alex seems normal, but Marie is one of those goofy sorts who wanders into a cornfield for no better reason than for Alex to follow her, shouting "Marie! Marie!" while the wind sighs on the sound track—a track that beavers away with Ominous Noises throughout the movie; is there a technical term like Ominoise?

The girls are followed into the deep, dark woods by a large man in blood-soaked coveralls, who drives a battered old truck that must have been purchased used from a 1940s French crime movie. We know he's up to no good the first time we see him. We know this because he drops a woman's severed head out the window of his truck.

At the isolated country home, Marie gets the guest room in the attic and goes out into the Ominoise night to have a smoke. There is a swing hanging from a tree limb, and she sways back and forth on it while she smokes, so that later we can get the standard thriller shot of the swing seat still swinging, but now suddenly empty. This is not because Marie has been shortened by the decapitator, but because she has gone back into the house. Soon it's lights out, although there is enough in the way of moon-glow and night lights for us to see Marie masturbate, perhaps so that we can see if it makes her lose her mind or anything.

The killer (Philippe Nahon) breaks into the house, stomps around heavily, and slaughters everyone except Alex, whom he takes prisoner, and Marie, who hides under the bed—yes, *hides under the bed.* The killer lifts up the mattress to check, but looks under the wrong end. Uh, huh. Marie should then remain still as a church mouse until the killer leaves, but no, she follows him downstairs and eventually ends up locked in the back of the truck with the kidnapped and chained Alex.

From the point when Marie crawls out from under the bed and follows the killer downstairs, she persists in making one wrong decision after another and ignoring obvious opportunities to escape. Perhaps she feels her presence is needed for the movie to continue, a likely possibility as the list of living characters shrinks steadily. She does have wit enough to pick up a big kitchen knife, so that we can enjoy the slasher movie cliché where such knives make the noise of steel-against-steel all by themselves, just by existing, and without having to scrape against anything.

After the truck leaves the deserted house and stops at a gas station, Marie has another opportunity to get help, but blows it. Reader, take my advice and never hang up on a 911 operator just because you get mad at him because he's so stupid he wants to know where you're calling from, especially not if the slasher has picked up an ax.

The rest of the movie you will have to see for yourself—or not, which would be my recommendation. I am tempted at this point to issue a Spoiler Warning and engage in discussion of several crucial events in the movie that would seem to be physically, logically, and dramatically impossible, but clever viewers will be able to see for themselves that the movie's plot has a hole that is not only large enough to drive a truck through, but in fact does have a truck driven right through it.

Note: The film's British title is *Switchblade Romance,* which, if you see the film, will seem curiouser and curiouser.

The Hills Have Eyes

(DIRECTED BY ALEXANDRE AJA; STARRING AARON STANFORD, KATHLEEN QUINLAN; 2006)

It always begins with the Wrong Gas Station. In real life, as I pointed out in my review of a previous Wrong Gas Station movie, most gas stations are clean, well-lighted places, where you can buy not only gasoline but also groceries, clothes, electronic devices, Jeff Foxworthy CDs, and a full line of Harley merchandise. In horror movies, however, the only gas station in the world is located on a desolate road in a godforsaken backwater. It is staffed by a degenerate who shuffles out in his coveralls and runs through a disgusting repertory of scratchings, spittings, chewings, twitchings, and leerings, while thoughtfully shifting mucus up and down his throat.

The clean-cut heroes of the movie, be they a family on vacation, newlyweds, college students, or backpackers, all have one thing in common. They believe everything this man tells them, especially when he suggests they turn left on the unpaved road for a shortcut. Does it ever occur to them that in this desolate wasteland with only one main road, it *must* be the road to stay on if they ever again want to use their cell phones?

No. It does not. They take the fatal detour, and find themselves the prey of demented mutant incestuous cannibalistic gnashing slobberers, who carry pickaxes the way other people carry umbrellas. They occupy junkyards, towns made entirely of wax, nuclear waste zones and Motel Hell ("It takes all kinds of critters to make Farmer Vincent's fritters"). That is the destiny that befalls a vacationing family in *The Hills Have Eyes,* which is a very loose remake of the 1977 movie of the same name.

The Carter family is on vacation. Dad (Ted Levine) is a retired detective who plans to become a security guard. Mom is sane, lovable Kathleen Quinlan. A daughter and son-in-law (Vinessa Shaw and Aaron Stanford) have a newborn babe. There are also two other Carter children (Dan Byrd and Emilie de Ravin), and two dogs named Beauty and Beast. They have hitched up an Airstream and are on a jolly family vacation through the test zones where 331 atmospheric nuclear tests took place in the 1950s and 1960s.

After the Carters turn down the wrong road, they're fair game for the people who are the eyes of the hills. These are descendants of miners who refused to leave their homes when the government ordered them away from the testing grounds. They hid in mines, drank radioactive water, reproduced with their damaged DNA, and brought forth mutants who live by eating trapped tourists.

There is an old bomb crater filled with the abandoned cars and trucks of their countless victims. It is curiously touching, in the middle of this polluted wasteland, to see a car that was towing a boat that still has its outboard motor attached. No one has explained what the boat was seeking at that altitude.

The plot is easily guessed. Ominous events occur. The family makes the fatal mistake of splitting up; Dad walks back to the Wrong Gas Station, while the dogs bark like crazy and run away, and young Bobby chases them into the hills. Meanwhile, the mutants entertain themselves by passing in front of the camera so quickly you can't really see them, while we hear a loud sound, halfway between a swatch and a swootch, on the sound track. Just as a knife in a slasher movie can make a sharpening sound just because it exists, so do mutants make swatches and swootches when they run in front of cameras.

I received some appalled feedback when I praised Rob Zombie's *The Devil's Rejects* (2005), but I admired two things about it: (1) It desired to entertain and not merely to sicken, and (2) its depraved killers were individuals with personalities, histories, and motives. *The Hills Have Eyes* finds an intriguing setting in "typical" fake towns built by the government, populated by mannequins, and intended to be destroyed by nuclear blasts. But its mutants are simply engines of destruction. There is a misshapen creature who coordinates attacks with a walkie-talkie; I would have liked to know more about him, but no luck.

Nobody in this movie has ever seen a Dead Teenager Movie, and so they don't know (1) you never go off alone, (2) you especially never go off alone at night, and (3) you never follow your dog when it races off barking insanely, because you have more sense than the dog. It is also possibly not a good idea to walk back to the Wrong Gas Station to get help from the degenerate who sent you on the detour in the first place.

It is not faulty logic that derails *The Hills Have Eyes,* however, but faulty drama. The movie is a one-trick pony. We have the eaters and the eatees, and they will follow their destinies until some kind of desperate denouement, possibly followed by a final shot showing that It's Not Really Over, and there will be a *The Hills Have Eyes II.* Of course, there was already a *The Hills Have Eyes Part II* (1985), but then again there was a *The Hills Have Eyes* (1977) and that didn't stop them. Maybe this will. Isn't it pretty to think so.

Hoot

(DIRECTED BY WIL SHRINER; STARRING LOGAN LERMAN, LUKE WILSON; 2006)

Hoot has its heart in the right place, but I have been unable to locate its brain. Here is a movie about three kids who begin by disliking or fearing one another, and end up as urban guerrillas, sabotaging the construction of a pancake house that will destroy a nesting ground for burrowing owls. Yes, there are such birds, who sublet burrows originally dug by squirrels and prairie dogs and such, or occasionally dig their own dream burrows. They seem wide-eyed with astonishment at their lifestyle, but actually that is just the way they look.

The hero of the movie is Roy Eberhardt (Logan Lerman), whom we meet on horseback in Montana, complaining that his family is moving again—this time to Florida. His dad has moved something like five times in eight years, which in the white-collar world means you are either incompetent or the CEO. In his new school, he's picked on by a bully and breaks the bully's nose to create a subplot utterly unnecessary to the story.

His school career takes an upturn when he meets two extraordinary (not to say unbelievable) students his own age. Beatrice the Bear (Brie Larson) is a soccer player with a fearsome reputation, which the movie half-heartedly establishes in a perfunctory manner before revealing her as a true-blue best pal who befriends Roy Eberhardt (he is often referred to by both names). Meanwhile, Roy Eberhardt is fascinated by a kid he sees running barefoot through the town. He tries to chase him, fails, finally catches up with him, is scared off by a sack of cottonmouth snakes, and eventually makes friends with him. This is Mullet Fingers (Cody Linley), a cross between Tarzan and Huckleberry Finn.

Mullet lives in hiding on a houseboat, doesn't go to school, and devotes his life to sabotaging the efforts by Curly (Tim Blake Nelson) to build the hated pancake house. He pulls up the surveying stakes, steals the seat from the bulldozer, and otherwise generates trouble for the local Keystone Kop, named Officer Delinko (Luke Wilson). Delinko is so incompetent that one night he stakes out the construction site and oversleeps because Mullet Fingers has painted all the windows of his prowler black.

The movie's climax involves one of those situations where everyone in the town arrives at the same time in the same place to hear incriminating evidence that forces the dastardly villains to abandon their plans. Oops, I gave away the ending, if you were expecting that the film would conclude with the death of the owls.

Hoot is based on a Newbery Honor novel by Carl Hiaasen, the Florida novelist. That gives it a provenance, but not a pedigree. (Having written the preceding sentence, I do not know what it means, but I like the way it reads.) I suspect the movie's target audience will think it plays suspiciously like an after-school special, and lacks the punch and artistry of such superior family films as *Millions* and *Shiloh*. The villains are sitcom caricatures, the kids (especially Mullet Fingers) are likable but not remotely believable, and it is never quite explained why anyone would build a pancake house in a wilderness area that seems to be far from any major road.

The Hot Chick

(DIRECTED BY TOM BRADY; STARRING ROB SCHNEIDER, ANNA FARIS; 2002)

The Hot Chick is about a woman who is magically transported into a man's body, and takes several days to learn how to urinate correctly with her new equipment. This despite getting a how-to lecture from a helpful washroom attendant. Luckily, she finds that passing gas is a skill that ports easily between the genders. Meanwhile, the former occupant of her male body has been magically transported into her former female body, and immediately becomes a hooker and a stripper.

How is this switch possible? It happens because of a pair of magic earrings. Their history is shown in an introductory scene helpfully subtitled "Abyssinia, 50 B.C." The scene is clearly inspired by *The Arabian Nights*; the screenplay is by the director, Tom Brady, and the star, Rob Schneider, who have confused Africa with the Middle East, but the prologue is over before we can grow depressed by its geographical and ethnographic ignorance.

In modern times, we are introduced to a cadre of hot chicks who all go to the same high school. The Rob Schneider character, named Clive, no doubt after Clive of India, who would have been a much more interesting character, mugs one of the hot chicks and gets one of her earrings. When Clive and the chick put on the earrings, they are wondrously transported into each other's bodies. Jessica (Rachel McAdams) occupies Clive.

Clive also occupies Jessica, but only gets a couple of scenes, in which he quickly masters feminine skills, starting with buying tampons and progressing quickly to stripping. The movie's conviction that we would rather see the outside of Rob Schneider's body than the outside of Rachel McAdams's body is not the least of its miscalculations. Rob Schneider's outside has most of its scenes with Jessica's best friend, played by Anna Faris, whose resemblance to Britney Spears in the hair and makeup departments is a complete coincidence.

The way the movie handles the switch is that Rob Schneider, visually appearing as himself, has Jessica trapped inside. He/she convinces his/her best girlfriends of this transformation. This is one of the most astonishing events in the history of mankind, incredible and miraculous, and so what inflames the curiosity of the three girlfriends? His penis.

That they are stupid goes without saying. That the filmmakers could think of nothing more creative to do with their premise is a cause for despair. Body-switch movies had a brief vogue in the 1980s, when there were some cute ones (*Big, Vice Versa*), but Hollywood has so downgraded its respect for the audience that *The Hot Chick* is now considered acceptable.

The movie resolutely avoids all the comic possibilities of its situation, and becomes one more dumb high school comedy about sex gags and prom dates. Jessica, as Clive, becomes the best boy/girl friend a girl could want, during a week in which the female Jessica's parents absentmindedly observe that she has been missing for days. (That a girl looking exactly like the most popular girl in high school is stripping and hooking escapes the attention of the local slackwits.)

Lessons are learned, Jessica sees things from a different point of view, sweetness triumphs, and the movie ends with one of those "deleted" scenes over the final credits. This particular credit cookie is notable for being even more boring and pointless than the movie. Through superhuman effort of the will, I did not walk out of *The Hot Chick*, but reader, I confess I could not sit through the credits.

(The MPAA rates this PG-13. It is too vulgar for anyone under thirteen, and too dumb for anyone over thirteen.)

House of D

(Directed by David Duchovny; starring Anton Yelchin, Tea Leoni; 2005)

Yes, I take notes during the movies. I can't always read them, but I persist in hoping that I can. During a movie like *House of D,* I jot down words I think might be useful in the review. Peering now at my three-by-five cards, I read "sappy, inane, cornball, shameless," and, my favorite, "doofusoid." I sigh. The film has not even inspired interesting adjectives, except for the one I made up myself. I have been reading Dr. Johnson's invaluable *Dictionary of the English Language,* and propose for the next edition:

> doofusoid, *adj.,* possessing the qualities of a doofus; sappy, inane, cornball, shameless. "The plot is composed of *doofusoid* elements."

You know a movie is not working for you when you sit in the dark inventing new words. *House of D* is the kind of movie that particularly makes me cringe, because it has such a shameless desire to please; like Uriah Heep, it bows and scrapes and wipes its sweaty palm on its trouser leg, and also like Uriah Heep it privately thinks it is superior.

I make free with a reference to Uriah Heep because I assume if you got past Dr. Johnson and did not turn back, Uriah Heep will be like an old friend. You may be asking yourself, however, why I am engaging in wordplay, and the answer is: I am trying to entertain myself before I must get down to the dreary business of this review. Think of me as switching off my iPod just before going into traffic court.

So. *House of D*. Written and directed by David Duchovny, who I am quite sure created it with all of the sincerity at his command, and believed in it so earnestly that it did not occur to him that no one else would believe in it at all. It opens in Paris with an artist (Duchovny) who feels he must return to the Greenwich Village of his youth, there to revisit the scenes and people who were responsible, I guess, for him becoming an artist in Paris, so maybe a thank-you card would have done.

But, no, we return to Greenwich Village in 1973, soon concluding Duchovny would more wisely have returned to the Greenwich Village of 1873, in which the clichés of Victorian fiction, while just as agonizing, would at least not have been dated. We meet the hero's younger self, Tommy (Anton Yelchin). Tommy lives with his mother, Mrs. Warshaw (Tea Leoni), who sits at the kitchen table smoking and agonizing and smoking and agonizing. (Spoiler warning!) She seems deeply depressed, and although Tommy carefully counts the remaining pills in her medicine cabinet to be sure his mother is still alive, she nevertheless takes an overdose and, so help me, goes into what the doctor tells Tommy is a "persistent vegetative state." How could Duchovny have guessed when he was writing his movie that such a line, of all lines, would get a laugh?

Tommy's best friend is Pappass, played by Robin Williams. Pappass is retarded. He is retarded in 1973, that is; when Tommy returns many years later, Pappass is proud to report that he has been upgraded to "challenged." In either case, he is one of those characters whose shortcomings do not prevent him from being clever like a fox as he (oops!) blurts out the truth, underlines sentiments, says things that are more significant than he realizes, is insightful in the guise of innocence, and always appears exactly when and where the plot requires.

Tommy has another confidant, named Lady Bernadette (Erykah Badu), who is an inmate in the Women's House of Detention. She is on an upper floor with a high window in her cell, but by using a mirror she can see Tommy below, and they have many conversations, in which their speaking voices easily carry through the Village traffic noise and can be heard across, oh, fifty yards. Lady Bernadette is a repository of ancient female wisdom, and advises Tommy on his career path and the feelings of

Pappass, who "can't go where you're going"—no, not even though he steals Tommy's bicycle.

The whole business of the bicycle being stolen and returned, and Pappass and Tommy trading responsibility for the theft, and the cross-examination by the headmaster of Tommy's private school (Frank Langella) is tendentious beyond all reason. (Tendentious, adj. Tending toward the dentious, as in having one's teeth drilled.) The bicycle is actually an innocent bystander, merely serving the purpose of creating an artificial crisis that can cause a misunderstanding so that the crisis can be resolved and the misunderstanding healed. What a relief it is that Pappass and Tommy can hug at the end of the movie.

Damn! I didn't even get to the part about Tommy's girlfriend, and my case is being called.

How to Lose a Guy in 10 Days

(Directed by Donald Petrie; starring Kate Hudson, Matthew McConaughey; 2003) I am just about ready to write off movies in which people make bets about whether they will, or will not, fall in love. The premise is fundamentally unsound, since it subverts every love scene with a lying subtext. Characters are nice when they want to be mean or mean when they want to be nice. The easiest thing at the movies is to sympathize with two people who are falling in love. The hardest thing is to sympathize with two people who are denying their feelings, misleading each other, and causing pain to a trusting heart. This is comedy only by dictionary definition. In life, it is unpleasant and makes the audience sad.

Unless, of course, the characters are thoroughgoing rotters in the first place, as in *Dirty Rotten Scoundrels* (1988), in which Steve Martin and Michael Caine make a $50,000 bet on who will be the first to con the rich American Glenne Headly. They deserve their comeuppance, and we enjoy it. *How to Lose a Guy in 10 Days* is not, alas, pitched at that modest level of sophistication, and provides us with two young people who are like pawns in a sex game for the developmentally shortchanged.

He works at an ad agency. She works for a magazine that is *Cosmopolitan,* spelled a different way. She pitches her editor on an article about how to seduce a guy and then drive him away in ten days. He pitches his boss on an idea that involves him being able to get a woman to fall in love with him in ten days. They don't even Meet Cute, but are shuffled together by a treacherous conspirator.

Now, of course, they will fall in love. That goes without saying. They will fall in love even though she deliberately creates scenes no man could abide, such as nicknaming his penis Princess Sophia. She allows her disgusting miniature dog to pee on his pool table. She even puts a plate of sandwiches down on top of the pot in their poker game, something Nancy would be too sophisticated to do to Sluggo.

He puts up with this mistreatment because he has his own bet to win, and also because, doggone it, he has fallen in love with this vaporous fluffball of narcissistic cluelessness. That leaves only one big scene for us to anticipate, or dread: the inevitable moment when they both find out the other made a bet. At a moment like that, a reasonably intelligent couple would take a beat, start laughing, and head for the nearest hot-sheets haven. But no. These characters descend from the moribund fictional ideas of earlier decades and must react in horror, run away in grief, prepare to leave town, etc., while we in the audience make our own bets about their IQs.

Matthew McConaughey and Kate Hudson star. I neglected to mention that, maybe because I was trying to place them in this review's version of the Witness Protection Program. If I were taken off the movie beat and assigned to cover the interior design of bowling alleys, I would have some idea of how they must have felt as they made this film.

● ● ● ● ● ● ● ● ● ●

I Am David

(DIRECTED BY PAUL FEIG; STARRING BEN TIBBER, JAMES CAVIEZEL; 2004)

I Am David tells the story of a twelve-year-old orphan boy who escapes from a Bulgarian forced labor camp and travels alone through Greece, Italy, and Switzerland to his eventual destiny in Denmark. He has awfully good luck: Along the way, he meets mostly nice people who do what they can to help him, and there's an enormous coincidence just when it's most needed. Benji encounters more hazards on his travels than this kid.

I know, I know, I'm supposed to get sentimental about this heartwarming tale. But I couldn't believe a moment of it, and never identified with little David, who is played by young Ben Tibber as if he was lectured to mind his manners. In an era with one effective child performance after another, here is a bad one.

The premise: In the Cold War, enemies of the Bulgarian state are sent to forced labor camps, where they break up rocks into gravel under the merciless prodding of sadistic guards. I am sure the movie explains how David became an enemy of the state at his tender age, but the detail escaped me; maybe he inherited his status from his dead parents. Certainly he's lucky in his choice of friends, starting with Johannes (James Caviezel), a fellow inmate who gives him encouragement and dreams before—well, see for yourself.

A mysterious voice on the sound track advises David to escape. He is supplied with a bar of soap, half a loaf of bread, a compass, and an envelope not to be opened until he gets to Denmark, or finds Carmen Sandiego, whichever comes first. Sorry about that. The power is conveniently turned off for thirty seconds on the camp's electrified fences so that David can run across an open field and begin his long odyssey.

How, you may wonder, will the lad communicate in the many lands he must traverse? "You've picked up many languages from the others in the camp," the voice reminds him, and indeed David apparently speaks Bulgarian, Greek, Italian, and English, all with a wee perfect British accent. He lucks into rides on trucks, gets over the border to Greece through an unlikely series of events, stows away on a ship for Italy with astonishing ease, and fetches up in an Italian bakery where, please, sir, may I have a loaf? When the baker calls the cops, the kid is able to escape, although not with any bread.

Then something happens that would seem far-fetched even in a silent melodrama. He comes upon a burning cabin, hears screams, breaks in, and rescues a young girl who is tied to a chair. This girl, as it happens, is the victim of a prank by her younger siblings, who didn't mean to set the fire. The girl's rich parents embrace the lad and feed him, but ask too many questions, so he moves on to Switzerland and happens into friendship with a grandmotherly painter (Joan Plowright), who brings his story to a happy ending through a spectacularly unlikely coincidence.

As it turns out, the papers in his envelope could probably have been read by anyone in Greece or Italy and solved David's dilemma, and the advice to travel all the way to Denmark was not necessarily sound. But we forget that when we discover the secret of the mysterious voice that advised David—a secret I found distinctly underwhelming, although the movie makes much of it. The lesson, I guess, is that if you are a twelve-year-old orphan in a Bulgarian forced labor camp, you need not despair, because the world is filled with good luck and helpful people, and besides, you speak all those languages.

Note: In stark contrast to the fairy-tale events of *I Am David,* the 2003 film *In This World,* by Michael Winterbottom, tells the story of a sixteen-year-old Afghan boy who journeys to London from a refugee camp in Pakistan. The film follows a real boy on a real journey, and includes scenes of documentary reality; it helps underline the unreal storytelling of *David.*

Invisible Circus

(Directed by Adam Brooks; starring Jordana Brewster, Christopher Eccleston; 2001)

Adam Brooks's *Invisible Circus* finds the solution to searing personal questions through a tricky flashback structure. There are two stories here, involving an older sister's disappearance and a younger sister's quest, and either one would be better told as a straightforward narrative. When flashbacks tease us with bits of information, it has to be done well, or we feel toyed with. Here the mystery is solved by stomping in thick-soled narrative boots through the squishy marsh of contrivance.

Jordana Brewster stars as Phoebe, eighteen years old in 1976. In the summer of 1969, she tells us in her narration, her sister Faith went to Europe and never came back. The story was that Faith (Cameron Diaz) killed herself in Portugal. Phoebe doesn't buy it. After a heart-to-heart with her mother (Blythe Danner), Phoebe sets off on a quest to solve the mystery, message, meaning, method, etc., of Faith's disappearance.

The search begins with Wolf (Christopher Eccleston), Faith's old boyfriend, now engaged and living in Paris. Since Wolf knows all the answers, and that's pretty clear to us (if not to Phoebe), he is required to be oblique to a tiresome degree. And there is another problem. In any movie where a lithesome eighteen-year-old confronts her older sister's lover, there is the inescapable possibility that she will sleep with him. This danger, which increases alarmingly when the character is named Wolf, is to be avoided, since the resulting sex scene will usually play as gratuitous, introducing problems the screenplay is not really interested in exploring. I cringe when a man and a woman pretend to be on a disinterested quest, and their unspoken sexual agenda makes everything they say sound coy.

Wolf and Faith, we learn, were involved in radical 1960s politics. Faith was driven by the death of her father, who died of leukemia caused by giant corporations (the science is a little murky here). Phoebe feels her dad always liked Faith more than herself. What was Dad's reason? My theory: Filial tension is required to motivate the younger sister's quest, so he was just helping out.

The movie follows Faith, sometimes with Wolf, sometimes without, as she joins the radical Red Army, becomes an anarchist, is allowed to help out on protest raids, fails one test, passes another, and grows guilt-ridden when one demonstration has an unexpected result. Phoebe traces Faith's activities during an odyssey/travelogue through Paris, Berlin, and Portugal, until we arrive at the very parapet Faith jumped or fell from, and all is revealed.

I can understand the purpose of the film, and even sense the depth of feeling in the underlying story, based on a novel by Jennifer Egan. But the clunky flashback structure grinds along, doling out bits of information, and it doesn't help that Wolf, as played by Eccleston, is less interested in truth than in Phoebe. He is a rat, which would be all right if he were a charming one.

There is a better movie about a young woman who drops out of sight of those who love her and commits to radical politics. That movie is *Waking the Dead* (2000). It has its problems, too, but at least it is unclouded by extraneous sex and doesn't have a character who withholds information simply for the convenience of the screenplay. And its Jennifer Connelly is much more persuasive than Cameron Diaz as a young woman who becomes a radical; she enters a kind of solemn holy trance, unlike Diaz, who seems more like a political tourist.

Isn't She Great

(DIRECTED BY ANDREW BERGMAN; STARRING BETTE MIDLER, NATHAN LANE; 2000)

Perhaps it's appropriate that Jacqueline Susann's biopic has been written by Paul Rudnick, whose alter ego, Libby Gelman-Waxner, waxes witty and bitchy in her *Premiere* magazine column every month. It was Truman Capote who said on a talk show that Jackie Susann "looks like a truck driver in drag," but whenever that image swims into view, it somehow seems to have the Gelman-Waxner byline attached.

Susann became famous writing potboilers about the sex and drug lives of the stars. Identifying the real-life models for her thinly veiled characters grew into a parlor game, and her *Valley of the Dolls* became the best-selling novel of all time. She also became famous for revolutionizing book retailing; Susann and her agent husband, Irving Mansfield, turned the book tour into a whistle-stop of America, and there was scarcely a bookseller, interviewer, or indeed shipping dock worker who didn't get the Susann treatment.

So tireless was her publicity that she even talked to me, at a time when I was twenty-three years old and had been on the *Sun-Times* for ten minutes. Jackie, Irving, and I had lunch at Eli's the Place for Steak, although all I can recall of the conversation is that she said, "I'm like Will Rogers. I never met a dog I didn't like." Full disclosure: Three years later I wrote the screenplay for the parody *Beyond the Valley of the Dolls,* and a few years after that, the Fox studio was sued by Mansfield on the grounds that the film diminished his wife's literary reputation. (Had I been called to testify, I would have expressed quiet pride in whatever small part I had played in that process.)

Susann's life would seem to be the perfect target for the Libby Gelman-Waxner sensibility; who better to write about the woman whose prose one reader described as "like overhearing a conversation in the ladies' room." My hopes soared when I learned that Andrew Bergman, who made the wacky comedies *Honeymoon in Vegas* and *Soapdish,* would be directing—and that John Cleese would play her publisher. I was hoping for satire, but they've made a flat and peculiar film that in its visual look and dramatic style might be described as the final movie of the 1950s.

Maybe that was the purpose. Maybe the whole look, feel, and sensibility of *Isn't She Great* is part of the joke. It's a movie that seems to possess the same color scheme and style sense as *Valley of the Dolls,* but, alas, without Jackie's dirty mind. So devout is this story that when Irving (Nathan Lane) walks out on Jackie (Bette Midler), we don't even find out why he really left. Jackie would have given us the scoopola.

And when they get back together again, is it with tearful recriminations and shocking accusations? Not at all. There is a tree in Central Park that they hold precious, because to them it represents God, and one day when Jackie visits the tree Irving is there already talking to God. To prove how much he loves her, on this and another occasion, he even wades into the Central Park lagoon. I think, although the movie isn't clear, that Irving left her not because of another person, but because the diamond brooch he bought for Jackie at the height of her success was upstaged by the diamond necklace given by her publisher. As her agent, shouldn't his gift be only 10 percent as expensive as her publisher's?

Money brings up another point: their lifestyle. Once Jackie makes it big time, they have a lot of money. But even before then, they live in Mansfield's lavishly expensive Manhattan apartment, reproduced on one of those spacious Hollywood sets where people make dramatic entrances and exits and the interior decorators have taste as vague as their budgets. Where did Mansfield get the money to live like this? When they first meet, he drops names like Perry Como and Frank Sinatra, but it turns out he represents their distant relatives.

Never mind. Factual accuracy is not what we're looking for anyway. What we want, I think, is the portrait of a funny trash talker, not a secular saint who bravely bore the birth of an autistic son (visited on weekends in a luxury care center) and later battled cancer. Bette Midler would seem to be the right casting choice for Jackie, but not for this Jackie, who is not bright enough, vicious enough, ambitious enough, and complicated enough to be the woman who became world-famous through sheer exercise of will. Stockard Channing, who plays Jackie's boozy best friend, does a better job of suggesting the Susann spirit.

Jackie Susann deserved better than *Isn't She Great*. A woman who writes *Valley of the Dolls* shouldn't be punished with a biopic that makes her look only a little naughtier than Catherine Cookson. There's a scene here where Jackie and Irving visit with Jackie and Aristotle on the Onassis yacht. Consider for a moment what Susann could have done with that. Then look at the tepid moment where Ari sighs fondly, "Perhaps I married the wrong Jackie." Uh, huh. Here is a movie that needed great trash, great sex, and great gossip, and at all the crucial moments Susann is talking to a tree.

Jason X

(DIRECTED BY JAMES ISAAC; STARRING KANE HODDER, LEXA DOIG; 2002)
This sucks on so many levels.

—DIALOGUE FROM *JASON X*

Rare for a movie to so frankly describe itself. *Jason X* sucks on the levels of storytelling, character development, suspense, special effects, originality, punctuation, neatness, and aptness of thought. Only its title works.

Jason X is technically *Friday the 13th, Part 10.* It takes place centuries in the future, when Earth is a wasteland and a spaceship from Earth II has returned to the Camp Crystal Lake Research Facility and discovered two cryogenically frozen bodies, one of them holding a machete and wearing a hockey mask.

The other body belongs to Rowan (Lexa Doig), a researcher who is thawed out and told it is now the year 2455: "That's 455 years in the future!" Assuming that the opening scenes take place now, you've done the math and come up with 453 years in the future. The missing two years are easily explained: I learn from the Classic Horror Web site that the movie was originally scheduled to be released on Halloween 2000, and was then bumped to March 2001, summer 2001 and Halloween 2001 before finally opening on the 16th anniversary of Chernobyl, another famous meltdown.

The movie is a low-rent retread of the *Alien* pictures, with a monster attacking a spaceship crew; one of the characters, Dallas, is even named in homage to the earlier series. The movie's premise: Jason, who has a "unique ability to regenerate lost and damaged tissue," comes back to life and goes on a rampage, killing the ship's plentiful supply of sex-crazed students and staff members. Once you know that the ship contains many dark corners and that the crew members wander off alone as stupidly as the campers at Camp Crystal Lake did summer after summer, you know as much about the plot as the writers do.

There's been a lot of talk lately about how good computer-generated special effects have become. On the basis of the effects in *Jason X* and the (much more entertaining) *Scorpion King*, we could also chat about how bad they are getting. Perhaps audiences do not require realistic illusions, but simply the illusion of realistic illusions. Shabby special effects can have their own charm.

Consider a scene where the spaceship is about to dock with Solaris, a gigantic mother ship, or a city in space, or whatever. Various controls go haywire because Jason has thrown people through them, and the ship fails to find its landing slot and instead crashes into Solaris, slicing off the top of a geodesic dome and crunching the sides of skyscrapers (why Solaris has a city-style skyline in outer space I do not presume to ask).

This sequence is hilariously unconvincing. But never mind. Consider this optimistic dialogue by Professor Lowe (Jonathan Potts), the greedy top scientist who wants to cash in on Jason: "Everyone OK? We just overshot it. We'll turn around." Uh, huh. We're waiting for the reaction from Solaris Air Traffic Control when a dull thud echoes through the ship and the characters realize Solaris has just exploded. Fine, but how could they hear it? Students of *Alien* will know that in space, no one can hear you blow up.

The characters follow the usual rules from Camp Crystal Lake, which require the crew members to split up, go down dark corridors by themselves, and call out each other's names with the sickening certainty that they will get no reply. Characters are skewered on giant screws, cut in half, punctured by swords, get their heads torn off and worse. A veteran pilot remains calm: "You weren't alive during the Microsoft conflict. We were beating each other with our own severed limbs."

There is one good effects shot, in which a scientist's face is held in super-cooled liquid until it freezes, and then smashed into smithereens against a wall. There is also an interesting transformation, as the onboard regenerator restores Jason and even supplies him with superhero armor and a new face to replace his hockey mask and ratty Army surplus duds. I left the movie knowing one thing for sure: There will be a *Jason XI*—or, given the IQ level of the series, *Jason X, Part 2*.

Jeepers Creepers 2

(DIRECTED BY VICTOR SALVA; STARRING RAY WISE, JONATHAN BRECK; 2003)
Every 23rd spring, for 23 days, it gets to eat.

—OPENING TITLE OF *JEEPERS CREEPERS 2*

The next shot is ominously subtitled : *Day 22*. A young boy is installing scarecrows in a field when he notices that one of them looks—not right. He approaches, sees the claws, and then becomes the first of many characters in this movie to fortify the Creeper for his next twenty-three-year hibernation. Cut to a school bus filled with a team returning from an out-of-town game along a highway where there is not one single other vehicle. The team and cheerleaders are singing a song, which is more or less required, I think, on buses where the passengers will soon be faced with unspeakable horrors.

Victor Salva's *Jeepers Creepers 2* supplies us with a first-class creature, a fourth-rate story, and dialogue possibly created by feeding the screenplay into a pasta maker. The movie basically consists of a half-man, half-bat that whooshes down out of the sky and snatches its prey. Sometimes it rips the tops off of old Rambler station wagons, and it opens up a pretty good hole in the top of the school bus. Meanwhile local farmer Jack Taggart (Ray Wise) tears himself away from his post-hole puncher, narrows his eyes, and stares intently at the edge of the screen while remembering that this all happened twenty-three years ago (maybe) or that the creature has eaten his youngest son (certainly).

The most notable character on the bus is Scott Braddock (Eric Nenninger), a virulent homophobe who doth, I think, protest too much as he accuses fellow team members of being gay. Later he tries to clear the bus of everyone the Creeper looked at, because then the ones who aren't his targets will be safe. This sidesteps the fact that the Creeper looked at Scott. One of the pom-pom girls has a hallucination or vision or something, and is able to explain that the creature chooses his victims according to body parts he requires, both as nutrition and as replacements. (Think through the lyrics of the song *Jeepers Creepers,* and you'll get the idea.)

To call the characters on the bus paper thin would be a kindness. Too bad, then, that we spend so much time on the bus, listening to their wretched dialogue and watching as they race from one window to another to see what foul deeds are occurring outside. Speaking of outside, Scott is the obligatory obstreperous jerk who is forever speculating that the creature has gone and won't return; he keeps suggesting they leave the bus to trek to a hypothetical nearby farmhouse. He's a direct throwback to the standard character in Dead Teenager Movies who's always saying, "Hmmm . . . all of the other campers have been found dead and eviscerated, Mimsy, so this would be an ideal time to walk out into the dark woods and go skinny-dipping in the pond where dozens of kids have died in the previous movies in this series."

Despite Scott's homophobia, the movie has a healthy interest in the male physique, and it's amazing how many of the guys walk around barechested. The critic John Fallon writes, "At a certain point, I thought I was watching soft gay erotica," and observes that when four of the guys go outside to pee, they line up shoulder to shoulder, which strikes him as unlikely since they are in a very large field. True in another movie, but in a film where the Creeper is likely to swoop down at any second and carry someone away, I would pick the tallest guy and stand next to him, on the theory that lightning will strike the tree and not you.

It is futile to bring logic to a film like this, but here goes: At one point, we hear local newscasters discussing the shocking discovery of three hundred corpses knit together into a tapestry in the basement of an old church—all of them with one body part missing. So obviously the Creeper has been operating in the area for years. Would anyone notice three hundred disappearances in a county so small that the main road has no traffic? Maybe that's what Jack Taggart is thinking about as he studies the side of the screen: "Hmmm . . . wonder if the disappearance of my son is connected to the carnage that occurs every twenty-three years hereabouts?"

The movie wants to work at the level of scaring us every so often with unexpected sudden attacks of the Creeper, although in this genre you expect sudden unexpected attacks, so you end up evaluating the craftsmanship instead of being scared. On that level, praise for the makeup and costume departments, including Richard Redlefsen, credited for "Creeper makeup and lead suit." Why the creature is called the Creeper when he leaps and flies, I am not sure. Why Francis Ford Coppola decided to produce this movie, I am also not sure.

Jiminy Glick in La La Wood

(DIRECTED BY VADIM JEAN; STARRING MARTIN SHORT, JAN HOOKS; 2005)

The problem with Jiminy Glick is that he doesn't know who he is. Or, more precisely, Martin Short doesn't know who he is. Jiminy is allegedly a chubby TV news entertainment reporter from Butte, Montana, who alternates between fawning over celebrities, insulting them, and not quite knowing who they are. I can sympathize. When I ran into Jiminy at the Toronto Film Festival, I didn't know he was Martin Short; the makeup job was masterful, and I hadn't seen the character in his earlier TV manifestations. One of the side effects of seeing five hundred movies a year is that you miss a lot of TV.

Martin Short himself is one of the funniest men alive, or can be, and has been. But Jiminy Glick needs definition if he's to work as a character. We have to sense a consistent comic personality, and we don't; Short changes gears and redefines the character whenever he needs a laugh. That means Jiminy is sometimes clueless, sometimes uses knowledgeable in-jokes, sometimes is a closeted gay, sometimes merely neuter, sometimes an inane talk-show host, and at other times essentially just Martin Short having fun with his celebrity friends.

Jiminy Glick in La La Wood takes the character to the Toronto Film Festival, where he confronts celebrities in situations that are sometimes spontaneous, sometimes scripted. He stays in a hotel from hell with his wife, Dixie (Jan Hooks), and their twin sons, Matthew and Modine. He is obsessed with getting an interview with the reclusive Ben DiCarlo (Corey Pearson), director of *Growing Up Gandhi,* in which the young Mahatma is seen as a prizefighter. He is also entranced by the presence of the legendary star Miranda Coolidge (Elizabeth Perkins).

The movie combines two story lines: Jiminy interviewing celebs, and Jiminy trapped in a nightmarish murder scenario narrated by David Lynch (played by Short himself, uncannily well). Lynch lights his already-lit cigarette and intones ominous insights about the lonely highway of doom, and Miranda's blood-drenched handkerchief turns up in Jiminy's possession; perhaps he did not merely dream that he murdered her.

The murder plot is a nonstarter (not funny, not necessary), and although Short does a good David Lynch, he stops at imitation and doesn't go for satire. He's at his best in a couple of sit-down interviews with cooperative movie stars (Kurt Russell and Steve Martin), in what feel like improvised Q&A sessions; he asks Martin, for example, if it's true that the commies still run Hollywood, and Martin refuses to name names—except for Meg Ryan and Tom Hanks. There is also an intriguing discussion of Martin's theory of tabletops and testicles, which put me in mind of his famous magic trick where eggs and lighted cigarettes emerge from his fly.

A comedy could be made about inane celebrity interviewers, yes, but it would have to be more reality oriented. When a real person like Joe Franklin exists, how can Jiminy Glick outflank him? A comedy could be made about the Toronto Film Festival, but it would need to know more about festivals; interviewers from Butte, Montana, do not ordinarily have their own private festival publicity person to knock on the hotel room every morning with a list of the day's interviews, and Glick (or Short) misses a chance to skewer publicists, junkets, and the panic attacks of critics afraid they'll miss a big movie.

Some stand-alone moments are funny. Jiminy thinks Whoopi Goldberg is Oprah Winfrey ("Remember, my name is spelled O-p-e-r-a," she advises him). Rappers in a hotel corridor try to teach an African how to sound like an American hip-hopper, but try as he will, "Y'allknowhaimean" comes out as "Yao Ming." And Jiminy and Kurt Russell begin a discussion about Elvis Presley, whom Russell starred with as a child actor and later, as an adult, played in a movie. Where this discussion eventually leads is hard to believe and impossible to describe. And when David Lynch says, "My name is David Lynch. I'm a director," I like Jiminy's reply: "Well who isn't, dear?"

Joe Dirt
(DIRECTED BY DENNIE GORDON; STARRING DAVID SPADE, BRITTANY DANIEL; 2001)

I wrote the words *Joe Dirt* at the top of my notepad and settled back to watch the new David Spade movie. Here is the first note I took: "Approx. 6 min. until first cow fart set afire." *Joe Dirt* doesn't waste any time letting you know where it stands.

This is the kind of movie where the hero finds two things that have fallen from the skies—a meteor and an atomic bomb—and both turn out to be a case of mistaken identity. Yes, the meteor is actually a large chunk of frozen treasure from an airplane lavatory, and the bomb is actually a large human waste storage unit.

We professional movie critics count it a banner week when only one movie involves eating, falling into, or being covered by excrement (or a cameo appearance by Carson Daly). We are not prudes. We are prepared to laugh. But what these movies, including *Joe Dirt,* often do not understand is that the act of being buried in crap is not in and of *itself* funny.

Third-graders might think so (they're big on fart jokes, too), but trust me: When Joe Dirt thinks he has an atom bomb until the cap gets knocked off and a geyser of brown crud pours out, and he *just stands there* while it covers him—that's not funny. Especially since we know he's only standing there to be sure we get the joke. Otherwise, he would move to avoid being entirely covered. Wouldn't you? (Direct quote from the press release, in connection with a scene where Spade is nearly eaten by an alligator: "David Spade performed his own stunts with the animatronic reptile. Trapped in a tangle of cable while lodged in the beast's mouth, he joked to the crew that he hoped he'd never have to get a job at a zoo." To which I can only add, "What? And leave show business?!")

Spade plays Joe Dirt, who is white trash. The movie uses that expression constantly, even observing at one point that his facial hair has grown in "white trash style" without the need for trimming. Joe's haircut is one of those 1970s mullet jobs; we learn it's not real hair but a wig supplied by his parents to cover a crack in his infant head that exposed his brain. (Note: This is also supposed to be funny.) The wig is a rare gift from his parents, who apparently abandoned him at the Grand Canyon when he was eight and happily playing in a garbage can.

Joe's origins and adventures are related many years later, when he happens into the studio of a talk jock played by Dennis Miller, whose own facial hair makes him look uncannily like the BBC's recent computer reconstruction of historical Jesus. Little Joe has been on his own ever since he was eight, he says, wandering the country as kind of a low-rent Forrest Gump, stumbling into interesting people and strange experiences. Where Forrest might meet a president, however, Joe is more likely to accidentally find himself in the gondola of a hot air balloon in the shape of a tooth.

The movie's production notes further inform us: "Spade says this is the first time he has ever played a character that is likable. 'It's a big switch for me,' he says." I think he may still have his first likable character ahead of him. Joe Dirt is so obviously a construction that it is impossible to find anything human about him; he is a concept, not a person, and although Spade arguably looks better in the mullet wig than he does with his trademark mop-top, he still has the same underlying personality. Here is a man born to play the Peter Lorre role.

The movie has a very funny moment. (Spoiler alert!) It involves Christopher Walken, an actor with so much identity and charisma that his mere appearance on a screen generates interest in any audience (and gratitude and relief from this one). He plays a character named Clem, who has good reasons for not wanting to appear on television. Eventually he reveals that he has gone underground with a new identity and is now Gert B. Frobe.

Note: The movie's PG-13 rating is one more plaque on the Jack Valenti Wall of Shame. The press kit quotes Spade on the movie: "Honestly, I think it's kind of good for kids. I mean, here's a guy that's just trying to be a good guy. He's not mean to people, and he's not sarcastic, and he's not a jerk." That could be an apology for the mean, sarcastic jerks he's played up until now, but probably not.

Joe Somebody

(Directed by John Pasquin; starring Tim Allen, James Belushi; 2001)

Joe Somebody plays like an after-school special with grown-ups cast in the kids' roles. It's a simple, wholesome parable, crashingly obvious, and we sit patiently while the characters and the screenplay slowly arrive at the inevitable conclusion. It needs to take some chances and surprise us. Everybody in the movie is kinda nice (except for the bully), and the principal—I mean, the boss—is patient while they learn their lessons and Joe finds out he really is somebody when the smart girl smiles at him.

Tim Allen is likable as the hero named Joe, but is likable enough? He's a milquetoast video guy at a marketing agency, divorced, lonely, with nothing much to talk about, who makes up stuff to say to the cute Meg (Julie Bowen) when he runs into her in the office, because his real life is too boring to contemplate. The most exciting point in the day is when he staples his sleeve to the wall.

He dotes on his daughter, Natalie (Hayden Panettiere), and takes her along on Bring Your Daughter to Work Day. But in the company parking lot for employees with ten years or more of service, he is cut off by a big SUV driven by the bully (Patrick Warburton), who is not only rude and reckless but also doesn't even have ten years of service. When Joe protests, he is slapped and knocked down in front of his daughter, and decides, thinking it over, that he won't take her to work that day after all.

We feel really bad for him. He seems on the edge of tears. His spirit is crushed, he enters into a depression, and then he decides to get even. Enter Chuck Scarett (James Belushi), a martial arts instructor who is, I think, intended to remind us of Steven Seagal (and who looks rather more sleek and fit than Seagal himself has recently). Chuck has an ancient and obligatory role as the coach who will take the underdog and turn him into a contender. And Joe demands a rematch with the bully.

This pays the unexpected dividend of making his stock rise at the office, although his boss's reasons for promoting him are suitably devious. He even has more to talk about with Meg now, although she looks at his changes with concern, and we are reminded of the schoolmarm in a Western who gets worried when the farmer takes to carrying a rifle.

What happens, and how and why, will be perfectly clear to any sentient moviegoer as soon as the plot lays down its tracks. There are few experiences more disheartening (at the movies, anyway) than a film that suffers from preordination. By the end of *Joe Somebody*, we are faced with the dismal prospect of being denied a climax that, if it occurred, would be just as predictable as its substitute.

Joe Somebody is Tim Allen's third film directed by John Pasquin; they worked together on TV's *Home Improvement*. Their previous movies were *The Santa Clause* (1994) and *Jungle2Jungle* (1997). The first was mediocre, the second was aggressively awful, and now we get this movie, well-meaning but pretty thin soup.

I agree with all the sentiments in *Joe Somebody*, and indeed I can see them being cobbled into a parable of considerable power, especially if Joe were played by somebody who really seemed to have a capacity for violence. But Tim Allen plays Joe as a guy who never really changes, while the screenplay desperately tells us he does. And when the girl seems to turn away—isn't that what the girl always does in these plots, so that later she can turn back again?

Johnny English

(DIRECTED BY PETER HOWITT; STARRING ROWAN ATKINSON, JOHN MALKOVICH; 2003)
Can we all pretty much agree that the spy genre has been spoofed to death? The James Bond movies have supplied the target for more than

forty years, and generations of Bond parodies have come and gone, from Dean Martin's Matt Helm to Mike Myers's Austin Powers. If *Austin Powers* is the funniest of the Bondian parodies, *Johnny English* is the least necessary, a mild-mannered ramble down familiar paths.

The movie stars Rowan Atkinson, best known in America as Mr. Bean, star of *Bean* (1997), and as the star of the PBS reruns of *The Black Adder*, where he played countless medieval schemers and bumblers in "the most gripping sitcom since 1380." He's the master of looking thoughtful after having committed a grievous breach of manners, logic, the law, personal hygiene, or common sense.

In *Johnny English*, he plays a character who became famous in Britain as the star of a long-running series of credit card commercials. Johnny English is a low-level functionary in the British Secret Service pressed into active duty when a bomb destroys all of the other agents. His assignment: Foil a plot to steal the Crown Jewels.

The evil mastermind is Pascal Sauvage (John Malkovich), a French billionaire who believes his family was robbed of the crown two centuries ago. Now the head of a mega-billion-dollar international chain of prisons, he poses as a benefactor who pays to protect the jewels in new theft-proof quarters in the Tower of London—but actually plans to steal them and co-opt the archbishop of Canterbury to crown him king. And how does Queen Elizabeth II feel about this? The film's funniest moment has her signing an abdication form after a gun is pointed at the head of one of her beloved corgis.

The movie is a series of scenes demonstrating how dangerously incompetent Johnny English is, as when he lectures on how the thieves got into the tower without noticing he is standing on the edge of a tunnel opening. He can't even be trusted to drive during a chase scene, and spends most of one in a car suspended from a moving wrecker's crane. Meanwhile the beautiful Lorna Campbell (Natalie Imbruglia) turns up coincidentally wherever he goes, performing a variety of functions, of which the only explicable one is to be the beautiful Lorna Campbell.

John Malkovich does what can be done with Pascal Sauvage, I suppose, including the French accent we assume is deliberately bad, since

Malkovich lives in France and no doubt has a better one. The character is such a stick and a stooge, however, that all Malkovich can do is stand there and be mugged by the script. Funnier work is done by Ben Miller, as Johnny's sidekick Bough (pronounced *Boff*). After Johnny breaks up the wrong funeral, Bough saves the day by passing him off as an escaped lunatic.

And so on. Rowan Atkinson is terrifically popular in Britain, less so here, because as a nation we do not find understatement hilarious. *Johnny English* plays like a tired exercise, a spy spoof with no burning desire to be that or anything else. The thing you have to credit Mike Myers for is that he loves to play Austin Powers and is willing to try anything for a laugh. Atkinson seems to have had Johnny English imposed upon him. And thus upon us.

John Q.

(Directed by Nick Cassavetes; starring Denzel Washington, Robert Duvall; 2002)

John Q. is the kind of movie *Mad* magazine prays for. It is so earnest, so overwrought, and so wildly implausible that it begs to be parodied. I agree with its message—that the richest nation in history should be able to afford national health insurance—but the message is pounded in with such fevered melodrama, it's as slanted and manipulative as your average political commercial.

The film stars Denzel Washington as John Q. Archibald, a Chicago factory worker whose apparently healthy son collapses during a Little League game. John Q. and his wife, Denise (Kimberly Elise), race the kid to an emergency room, where his signs are stabilized, and then a cardiologist (James Woods) explains that young Mike's heart is three times normal size.

There are two options: a heart transplant, or optimizing Mike's "quality of life" during the "months . . . weeks . . . days" left to him. Joining the doctor is appropriately named hospital administrator Rebecca

Payne (Anne Heche), who already knows the Archibalds have no money and argues for the "quality of life" choice.

John Q. thinks he's covered by insurance, but no: His company switched to a new HMO that has a $20,000 ceiling, and since John has been downsized to twenty hours a week, he's lucky to have that much coverage. Payne demands a $75,000 down payment on the $250,000 operation, and explains the harsh realities of life for "cash patients." John Q. considers taking the kid to County Hospital, but is urged by a friendly hospital employee to stay right there at the ominously named Crisis of Hope Memorial Hospital.

The TV ads have already informed you that John Q. exhausts all his options and eventually pulls a gun and takes hostages, demanding that his son be put at the top of the list of eligible recipients. (He wouldn't be jumping the queue because the Heche character explains Mike is so sick he would automatically be the first recipient—if the money were available.)

The hostages are your usual cross section of supporting roles: a gunshot victim, a battered woman and her violent boyfriend, a pregnant mother who has "started to dilate!" and so on. Plus Dr. Turner. The cops surround the building, and veteran negotiator Grimes (Robert Duvall) tries to build a relationship with John Q., while hotshot police chief Monroe (Ray Liotta) grandstands for the TV cameras—displaying sixteen stars on his uniform, four each on both collars and both lapels. Any more and he'd be Tinker Bell.

The underlying situation here is exactly the same as in *Dog Day Afternoon* (1975), an infinitely smarter hostage picture. What *John Q.* lacks is the confidence to allow its characters to act intelligently. Chief Monroe is almost hilariously stupid. Consider this. A local TV station somehow manages to tap the police feed from the hospital's security cameras, and broadcasts live video and sound of John Q. inside the hospital. Monroe smuggles a sniper into the hospital who has John Q. in his sights. John Q. is in the act of having an emotional and heartbreaking telephone conversation with his little boy when Monroe, who is (a) unaware of the TV feed, or (b) too dumb to live, orders the marksman to fire.

Does John Q. die? That's a question you find yourself asking a lot during this film. To avoid spoilers, I won't go into detail, but there is a moment when the movie just plain cheats on the question of John Q.'s status, and I felt conned.

There are passages where the actors transcend the material. John Q.'s farewell to his son is one. Kimberly Elise's relationship with her husband is well handled. But in a sense special honors should go to James Woods and Robert Duvall for achieving what they can with roles so awkwardly written that their behavior whipsaws between good, evil, and hilarious. Anne Heche is deep-sixed by her role, which makes her a penny-pinching shrew and then gives her a cigarette to smoke just in case we missed that she's the villain. The Grim Reaper would flee from this woman.

Josie and the Pussycats

(DIRECTED BY HARRY ELFONT; STARRING RACHAEL LEIGH COOK, TARA REID; 2001)

Josie and the Pussycats are not dumber than the Spice Girls, but they're as dumb as the Spice Girls, which is dumb enough. They're a girl band recruited as they're crossing the street by a promoter who wants to use their songs as a carrier for subliminal messages. The movie is a would-be comedy about prefab bands and commercial sponsorship, which may mean that the movie's own plugs for Coke, Target, Starbucks, Motorola, and Evian are part of the joke.

The product placement for Krispy Kreme doughnuts is, however, an ominous development, since it may trigger a war with Dunkin' Donuts, currently the most visible product placer in the movies. With Krispy and Dunkin' dukin' it out, there may soon be no doughnut-free movies not actually featuring gladiators.

The movie, based on a comic book from the Archie stable, stars Rachel Leigh Cook as Josie McCoy, its lead singer; Tara Reid as Melody Valentine, the bubble-brained blonde; and Rosario Dawson as Valerie Brown. None of these women have families, friends, or employers, apparently, and are free to move randomly through the plot as a unit without ever calling home. After a prologue in which a previous prefab boy band disappears in a plane crash, a nefarious record producer named Wyatt Frame (Alan Cumming, the gay villain du jour) hires them on first sight, without hearing them sing a note, to be his newest promotion.

The prologue has some vaguely *Spinal Tap* overtones. (I liked the detail that its members wear headsets at all times, not just on stage.) But *Josie* ignores bountiful opportunities to be a satire of the Spice Girls and other manufactured groups and gets dragged down by a lame plot involving the scheme to control teen spending with the implanted messages. (The movie calls them "subliminal." Since they're sound waves, they're actually "subaural," but never mind; the Pussycats would probably think subaural was a kind of foreplay.)

One curiosity about the movie is its stiff and sometimes awkward dialogue; the words don't seem to flow, but sound as if the actors are standing there and reciting them. The movie's market on verbal wit is cornered by Cumming, in the Richard E. Grant role, who has one (1) funny moment in which he demonstrates how very well-trained the boy band is. The rest of the time, he has the thankless task of acting as if he is funny in a plot that is not funny.

The music is pretty bad. That's surprising, since Kenneth (Babyface) Edmunds is one of the producers, and knows his way around music. Maybe it's *supposed* to sound like brainless preteen fodder, but it's not good enough at being bad to be funny, and stops merely at the bad stage.

Parker Posey has one of those supporting roles from hell, where she has to make her entrance as a cliché and then never even gets to play with the conventions of her role. She's Cummings's boss, one of the masterminds of the nefarious subaural marketing scheme, and since she is, in fact, a funny and talented actress with wicked timing, her failure to make anything of this role is proof there's nothing for her to work with. Also drifting aimlessly through the plot is a character named Alexandra Cabot (Missi Pyle), who at least has the best explanation for why she's in the movie, as well as the movie's second (2nd) funny line of dialogue. "Why are you here?" she's asked, and replies with serene logic, "I'm here because I was in the comic book."

The Jungle Book 2

(DIRECTED BY STEVE TRENBIRTH; STARRING HALEY JOEL OSMENT, JOHN GOODMAN; 2003)

The Jungle Book 2 is so thin and unsatisfying it seems like a made-for-DVD version, not a theatrical release. Clocking in at seventy-two minutes and repeating the recycled song "The Bare Necessities" three if not four times, it offers a bare-bones plot in which Mowgli wanders off into the jungle, is threatened by a tiger and a snake, is protected by a bear, takes care of his little girlfriend, and sings and dances with Baloo.

There's none of the complexity here, in story or style, we expect in this new golden age of animation. It's a throwback in which cute animals of no depth or nuance play with the hero or threaten him in not very scary ways.

As the film opens, Mowgli (who once, long ago and at another level of literacy, was the hero of stories by Rudyard Kipling) lives in a village and is forbidden to cross the river. But "you can take boy out of the jungle, but you can't take the jungle out of boy," we learn. Whoever wrote that dialogue must have gone home weary after a hard day's work.

Mowgli (voice by Haley Joel Osment) and his little village playmate Shanti (voice by Mae Whitman) do, however, venture into the forest, where Mowgli's old friend Baloo the Bear (John Goodman) is delighted to see him, although a little jealous of all the attention he is paying to Shanti. Maybe Baloo should discuss this problem with a counselor. They dance and sing and peel mangos, and then Mowgli and/or Shanti wander off alone to be threatened by the tiger and the snake (whose coils are cleverly animated), and to be rescued by Baloo, with a reprise or two of "The Bare Necessities."

In a time that has given us Miyazaki's great animated film *Spirited Away* (also a Disney release), parents have some kind of duty to take a close look at the films offered. I got in an argument at Sundance with a Salt Lake City man who sells software that automatically censors DVDs in order to remove offending scenes and language. (Theoretically, there could be a version of *Fight Club* suitable for grade-schoolers, although it would be very short.) By this yardstick, *The Jungle Book 2* is inoffensive and harmless.

But it is not nutritious. A new book argues that the average American child spends twice as much time watching television than interacting with his parents, and movies like *The Jungle Book 2* are dim-witted baby-sitters, not growth experiences. If kids grow up on the movie equivalent of fast food, they will form an addiction to that instant action high and will never develop the attention span they need to love worthwhile fiction.

Disney can do better, will do better, usually does better. To release this film theatrically is a compromise of its traditions and standards. If you have children in the target age range, keep them at home, rent an animated classic or Miyazaki's great *My Neighbor Totoro,* and do them a favor.

Just a Kiss

(DIRECTED BY FISHER STEVENS; STARRING RON ELDARD, KYRA SEDGWICK; 2002)

If only it were clever, *Just a Kiss* would be too clever by half. Here is a movie that was apparently made by working its way through a list of styles, so that we have poignancy jostling against farce, thoughtful dialogue elbowed aside by one-liners, and a visual style that incorporates rotoscope animation for no apparent reason except, maybe, that it looks neat.

Just a Kiss, directed by the actor Fisher Stevens, begins with a kiss between two people who should not be kissing, and ends after those people, and their significant others and assorted insignificant others, undergo sexual and emotional misunderstandings, survive plane crashes, end up in a hospital or comatose, etc., while occasionally appearing to be animated like the characters in *Waking Life.*

Now *Waking Life* was an accomplished movie, in which Richard Linklater took live-action footage of his characters and passed it through a software program that kept their basic appearances and movements while allowing artists to overlay an animated layer. It worked. It does not work in *Just a Kiss,* and I'm about to explain why.

In *Waking Life,* all of the characters are animated. That is what they are and how we accept them, and whatever reality they have is conveyed visually through the animation. But in *Just a Kiss,* the characters are photographed realistically, so that when they suddenly undergo "rotomation," their reality is violently displaced and our attention is jerked up to the surface of the movie. They exist now, not as characters, but as animated displays who used to be characters and may be characters again.

I can imagine a way in which this could work, in a *Roger Rabbit*–type movie that moves in and out of the cartoon dimension. But it doesn't work here, because it is manifestly and distractingly only a stunt. And the whole movie, in various ways, has the same problem: It's all surface, without an entry point into whatever lurks beneath. The characters, dialogue, personal styles, and adventures are all mannerisms. The actors are merely carriers of the director's contrivances.

Consider, for example, a sequence in which one character on an airplane uses his cell phone to tell another that he loves her. His phone emits lethal transmissions that cause the plane to crash. Everyone in first class lives; everyone in tourist class dies. I smile as I write the words. This would be a good scene in *Airplane!* What is it doing here, in a movie where we are possibly expected to care about the characters' romances and infidelities? To admit farce into a drama is to admit that the drama is farce.

But is it a drama? I haven't a clue. The movie seems to reinvent itself from moment to moment, darting between styles like a squirrel with too many nuts. There is one performance that works, sort of, and it is by Marisa Tomei, as a bartender whose psychic gifts allow her to find meaning in the rings left by cold beers. She is a crazy, homicidal maniac, but, hey, at least that means that nothing she does is out of character.

As for the other actors, they know Stevens from the indie films they've made together and were good sports to volunteer for this project. Ron Eldard, Kyra Sedgwick, Patrick Breen (who wrote the screenplay), Marley Shelton, Taye Diggs, Sarita Choudhury, and Bruno Amato do what they can with characters who are reinvented from minute to minute. And Zoe Caldwell, as a choreographer who is the mother of the Shelton character, has moments of stunningly effective acting that are so isolated from the rest of the movie that they appear like the result of channel surfing.

Note: Eldard's character is named "Dag." On the Internet Movie Database, he is listed as "Dag Hammerskjold," but on the movie's official site he is only "named after Dag Hammerskjold." Maybe it's supposed to be ironic

that this Dag survives a plane crash. Whatever. Of course, the movie mis-
spells Hammarskjold's name, so maybe this character is descended from a
person who was constantly having to explain how he was the Dag Hammerskjold who spelled his name with an *e*.

Just Friends
(DIRECTED BY ROGER KUMBLE; STARRING RYAN REYNOLDS, AMY SMART; 2005)
The best scenes in *Just Friends* take place offscreen. If they were in the
movie, they would involve the makeover of Chris, the hero. As the film
opens he is a fat, unpopular nerd in high school. Flash-forward ten years,
and he is thin, fit, rich, handsome, and working in the music industry.
Obviously, during the missing decade he hired Oprah's trainer and studied
the self-help tapes sold by that guy on late-night TV—you know, the guy
who will make you into a person willing to accept success. You have to *be
willing,* that's the trick. The guy's methods are proven because he is a success himself, having been willing to make millions by selling his tapes.

But already we're off the subject of the film. This will be a hard subject to stay on. I am going to the kitchen right now and set the timer on
the stove to go off every sixty seconds as a reminder to stay on the subject.
Now I'm back from the kitchen. You know that late-night TV guy? Basically,
he's offering an updated version of the old classified ad that said, "Send 25
cents to learn how to get hundreds of quarters through the mail." *Ding!*

In *Just Friends,* Ryan Reynolds plays Chris, who looks like he gets his
fat suits from Jiminy Glick's tailor. He wants to hook up with a sexy babe
named Jamie, played by Amy Smart. Jamie likes Chris a whole lot, but only
as a friend. When a girl says she likes you as a friend, what she means is:
"Rather than have sex with you, I would prefer to lose you as a friend."

Chris is crushed. In adventures that will no doubt be included in
the deleted scenes on the DVD, he apparently moves to L.A., loses 150
pounds, becomes a hockey star, opens an account at SuperCuts, and turns
into a babe magnet. His boss wants him to sign up an overnight pop superstar named Samantha, who is called Samantha because screenwriters love

women named Samantha because when you call them *Sam* it sounds like you know them, when in fact their entire backstory may be limited to the fact that their nickname is *Sam. Ding!*

Sam is supposed to make us think of Brittany or Britney or Britannia or whatever her name is. Now I remember: Her name is Paris Hilton. The other night at dinner I met a Motorola executive who told me Paris Hilton is their best customer for cell phones because she has gone through seventy of them. As Oscar Wilde once said, "To lose one cell phone may be regarded as a misfortune; to go through seventy looks like carelessness."

Sam is played by Anna Faris, who in *The Hot Chick* played the best friend of Rachel McAdams, whose character is magically transported into the body of Rob Schneider, causing the audience to urgently desire that he had been transported into her body instead, because then he would look like her. Actually, they do trade bodies, but the plot follows the Rob Schneider body, which is like taking the Gatorland exit on your way to Disney World. The assignment of Anna Faris is to relate to Rob Schneider's body as if it contained Rachel McAdams, a challenge I doubt even Dame Judi Dench would be equal to.

Sam and Chris are on a private jet to Paris Hilton when it makes an emergency landing in Chris's hometown in New Jersey, where he meets up with Jamie again on Christmas Eve. There is not a spark of chemistry between Chris and Jamie, although the plot clearly requires them to fall in love. There is so much chemistry involved with the Anna Faris character, however, that she can set off multiple chain reactions with herself, if you see what I mean. The problem with Chris is that although he's a cool dude in L.A., the moment he finds himself with Jamie again, he reverts to hapless dweebdom.

On the *Just Friends* message board at the Internet Movie Database, *ecbell-1* writes: "I live about a block away from where they filmed this movie." It was Francois Truffaut who said it was impossible to pay attention to a movie filmed in a house where you once lived because you would constantly be distracted by how it looked different and they had changed the wallpaper, etc. Did *ecbell-1* experience this phenomena? "It was pretty cool, he writes, because I watched some of it being filmed, and even got to meet some of the actors." Nothing about the Truffaut theory. The New Jersey house, by the way, is in *ecbell-1's* hometown of Regina, Saskatchewan. *Ding! Ding! Awopbopaloobop, alopbamboom!*

Just Married

(DIRECTED BY SHAWN LEVY; STARRING ASHTON KUTCHER, BRITTANY MURPHY; 2003)

Just Married is an ungainly and witless comedy, made more poignant because its star, Brittany Murphy, made such a strong impression as Eminem's sometime girlfriend in *8 Mile*. With her fraught eyes and husky voice, she has a rare and particular quality (I think of Jennifer Jason Leigh), and yet here she's stuck in a dumb sitcom.

She and Ashton Kutcher play newlyweds in a plot that proves that opposites repel. She's a rich kid named Sarah, expensively raised and educated. He's Tom, an example of the emerging subspecies Sports Bar Man. They have a perfect relationship, spoiled by marriage (I think that may even be one of the lines in the movie). They're too tired for sex on their wedding night, but make up for it on their honeymoon flight to Europe with a quickie in the toilet of the airplane. There is perhaps the potential for a glimmer of comedy there, but not in Sam Harper's overwritten and Shawn Levy's overdirected movie, which underlines and emphasizes like a Power Point presentation for half-wits.

Consider. It may be possible to find humor in a scene involving sex in an airplane restroom, but not by pushing the situation so far that Tom's foot gets caught in the toilet and the bitchy flight attendant suffers a broken nose. Later, in their honeymoon hotel in Venice, it may be possible that energetic sex could break a bed frame—but can it actually destroy the wall to the adjoining room? And it may be possible for an improper electrical device to cause a short in a hotel's electrical system, but need the offending device be a vibrator? And for that matter, isn't it an alarming sign of incipient pessimism to take a vibrator along on your honeymoon?

Europe was not the right choice for this honeymoon. He should have gone to Vegas, and she should have stayed single. Sarah wants to visit every church and museum, but Tom abandons her in the middle of Venice when he finds a bar that's showing an American baseball game. This is as likely as a sports bar in Brooklyn televising *boules* in French.

Sarah and Tom have nothing to talk about. They are a pathetic, stupid couple and deserve each other. What they do not deserve, perhaps, is a screenplay that alternates between motivation and slapstick. Either it's character-driven or it isn't. If it is, then you can't take your plausible characters and dump them into Laurel and Hardy. Their rental car, for example, gets a cheap laugh, but makes them seem silly in the wrong way. And earlier in the film, Tom is responsible for the death of Sarah's dog in a scenario recycled directly from an urban legend everyone has heard.

Would it have been that much more difficult to make a movie in which Tom and Sarah were plausible, reasonably articulate newlyweds with the humor on their honeymoon growing out of situations we could believe? Apparently.

The Ladies Man

(DIRECTED BY REGINALD HUDLIN; STARRING TIM MEADOWS, KARYN PARSONS; 2000)
The Ladies Man is yet another desperately unfunny feature-length spin-off from *Saturday Night Live,* a TV show that would not survive on local access if it were as bad as most of the movies it inspires. There have been good SNL movies, like *Wayne's World, The Blues Brothers,* and *Stuart Saves His Family.* They all have one thing in common: SNL producer Lorne Michaels was not primarily responsible for them.

Michaels had nothing to do with *Stuart* and *Brothers*. Credit for the glories of the *Wayne's World* pictures, which he did produce, should arguably go to their directors and stars. Mike Myers went on to *Austin Powers*. Michaels went on to *Coneheads, Superstar, A Night at the Roxbury,* and now *The Ladies Man.*

If I were a Hollywood executive, I would automatically turn down any Michaels SNL project on the reasonable grounds that apart from the Mike Myers movies he has never made a good one. He doesn't even come close. His average star rating for the last four titles is 1.125. Just to put things in perspective, the last three Pauly Shore movies I reviewed scored 1.5.

The Ladies Man, directed by Reginald (*House Party*) Hudlin, stars Tim Meadows as Leon Phelps, a boundlessly enthusiastic seducer who seems stylistically and ideologically stuck in the sexist early 1970s. The character, with his disco suits and giant Afro, is funny on TV—but then so are most of the reoccurring SNL characters; that's why the show recycles them. At feature length, Leon loses his optimistic charm and slogs through a lamebrained formula story that doesn't understand him.

He plays a radio talk show host in Chicago (i.e., Toronto with CTA buses), who offers late-night advice to the sexually challenged. (To one lonely lady who can't seem to meet the right guy: "Take yo panties off and hang out at the bus station.") In real life he has extraordinary luck picking up girls, for reasons perhaps explained in one scene where he displays his equipment to a girl he's just met. We can't share the sight because he's standing on the other side of the bar, but from the way her face lights up while angelic music swells on the sound track, his pants obviously contain a spotlight and the Mormon Tabernacle Choir.

Leon gets into trouble for what he says on the radio, is fired, and lands briefly at a Christian station, where he tries to sound devout but finds the struggle is too much for him. Following him loyally is his producer Julie (Karyn Parsons), who likes him because she can see he's a nice guy inside. Tiffani Thiessen costars as one of Leon's admirers, Billy Dee Williams is the bartender and narrator, and Julianne Moore has an inexplicable scene as the lustful Bloopie the Clown.

There is a painfully bad sequence involving bets in a bar about who is willing to eat what; it exists *only* (italics mine) to get a merde-eating scene into the movie. Meanwhile, a posse of outraged husbands forms on the Internet and wants to hunt Leon down for seducing their wives. They know they're all looking for the same guy because he has a smiley face tattooed on his butt. At one point the outraged husbands have a song-and-dance scene. The movie makes the mistake of thinking it is funny *that* they sing and dance; next-level thinking would have suggested their song and dance be funny in itself.

All of the outraged husbands but one are white. Leon is black. The movie makes no point of this, for which we can be grateful, since lynch mobs are very hard to make amusing. Spike Lee's *Bamboozled* would have been funnier if this very movie, rather than a blackface minstrel show, had been offered as an example of black stereotypes marketed by white executives. While Lee's fictitious TV show could never conceivably be aired, *The Ladies Man* has been made and distributed and is in theaters as proof that Lee's pessimism is not exaggerated.

La Mujer de Mi Hermano (My Brother's Wife)

(Directed by Ricardo de Montreuil; starring Barbara Mori, Christian Meier; 2006)

I do not, alas, remember every detail of those steamy Isabel Sarli melodramas from Argentina that used to play on Times Square and provide such a diversion from the New York Film Festival. Having now seen the new Argentinean-Mexican-Peruvian-American film *La Mujer de Mi Hermano (My Brother's Wife)*, I suspect I know the reason: There were no details.

Sarli, a former Miss Argentina, was married to her director, Armando Bo, who cast her in films never to be forgotten, such as *Thunder Among the Leaves, Positions of Love, The Hot Days, Naked Temptation, Tropical Ecstasy, Fuego,* and *Fever.* In these films the plot was entirely disposable, except as a device to propel Miss Sarli on an insatiable quest not so much for sex as for admiration. She clearly thought she was the sexiest woman alive, and that itself made her erotic, even in a scene where she attempted suicide by jumping off some rocks and into a pride of sea lions.

I have not thought about Isabel Sarli in years, not since reviewing Theo Angelopoulos's *Ulysses' Gaze* in 1997. It starred Harvey Keitel as a movie director who returns to his roots in Greece and makes love to lots of women. I quote from my review: "I was reminded of Armando Bo's anguished 1960s Argentinean soft-core sex films, which starred his wife, Isabel Sarli, whose agony was terrible to behold and could only be slaked in the arms of a man. [Keitel] and the women make love in this movie as if trying to apply unguent inside each other's clothes."

The Sarli role in *La Mujer de Mi Hermano* is filled (and that is the word) by Barbara Mori, a TV Azteca and Telemundo star who provides persuasive reasons why there are ever so many more plunging necklines on the Spanish-language channels than on their chaste Anglo equivalents. If Oprah were on Telemundo, Tom Cruise would have stayed on the couch.

The movie's title translates as *My Brother's Wife*, although it would be more accurate to call it *My Husband's Brother*, since it is told entirely from the point of view of Zoe (Mori). She has been married for ten years to Ignacio (Christian Meier), who is a businessman. In these movies, "businessman" translates as "doesn't satisfy his wife." Zoe complains to a friend that Ignacio likes to have sex only on Saturdays. We find this hard to believe until a scene where a symbolic unguent application is interrupted by Ignacio: "Remember that today's not Saturday." When she cannot believe her ears (or any other organ), he whines, "Honey, that's the way I am."

What a contrast with his brother Gonzalo (Manolo Cardona), an artist with the kind of five o'clock shadow where the whiskers seem forced out through his skin by testosterone. Zoe attends one of Gonzalo's gallery openings and purchases a painting, which Ignacio throws into the pool of his multimillion-dollar house, an example of modern domestic architecture that looks as if Frank Lloyd Wright's Fallingwater had conceived a child with Donald Trump.

Ignacio begins to suspect something, although not nearly enough and none too quickly, as Zoe and Gonzalo star in *Never on Saturday*. The two brothers, they love each other, and yet dark secrets from their past beg to be revealed. Indeed, by this point secrets from anybody's past would be welcome. The movie is astonishingly simpleminded, depicting characters who obediently perform their assigned roles as adulterers, cuckolds, etc. At least with Isabel Sarli you had the impression she was not only having a good time while she made her movies, but enjoyed hours and hours just looking at them.

The League of Extraordinary Gentlemen

(DIRECTED BY STEPHEN NORRINGTON; STARRING SEAN CONNERY, SHANE WEST; 2003)
The League of Extraordinary Gentlemen assembles a splendid team of heroes to battle a plan for world domination, and then, just when it seems about to become a real corker of an adventure movie, plunges into incomprehensible action, idiotic dialogue, inexplicable motivations, causes without effects, effects without causes, and general lunacy. What a mess.

And yet it all starts so swimmingly. An emissary from Britain arrives at a private club in Kenya, circa 1899, to invite the legendary adventurer Allan Quartermain (Sean Connery) to assist Her Majesty's government in averting a world war. Villains have used a tank to break into the Bank of England and have caused great destruction in Germany, and each country is blaming the other. Quartermain at first refuses to help, but becomes annoyed when armored men with automatic rifles invade the club and try to kill everybody. Quartermain and friends are able to dispatch them with some head-butting, a few rights to the jaw, and a skewering on an animal horn, and then he goes to London to attend a meeting called by a spy master named—well, he's named M, of course.

Also assembled by M are such fabled figures as Captain Nemo (Naseeruddin Shah), who has retired from piracy; Mina Harker (Peta Wilson), who was involved in that messy Dracula business; Rodney Skinner (Tony Curran), who is the Invisible Man; Dorian Gray (Stuart Townsend), who, Quartermain observes, seems to be missing a picture; Tom Sawyer (Shane West), who works as an agent for the U.S. government; and Dr. Henry Jekyll (Jason Flemyng), whose alter ego is Mr. Hyde.

These team members have skills undreamed of by the authors who created them. We are not too surprised to discover that Mina Harker is an immortal vampire, since she had those puncture wounds in her throat the last time we saw her, but I wonder if Oscar Wilde knew that Dorian Gray was also immortal and cannot die (or be killed!) as long as he doesn't see his portrait; at one point, an enemy operative perforates him with bullets, and he comes up smiling. Robert Louis Stevenson's Mr. Hyde was about the same size as Dr. Jekyll, but here Hyde expands into a creature scarcely smaller than the Hulk, and gets his pants from the same tailor, since they expand right along with him while his shirt is torn to shreds. Hyde looks uncannily like the WWF version of Fat Bastard.

Now listen carefully. M informs them that the leaders of Europe are going to meet in Venice, and that the mysterious villains will blow up the city to start a world war. The League must stop them. When is the meeting? In three days, M says. Impossible to get there in time, Quartermain says, apparently in ignorance of railroads. Nemo volunteers his submarine, the Nautilus, which is about ten stories high and as long as an aircraft carrier, and which we soon see cruising the canals of Venice.

It's hard enough for gondolas to negotiate the inner canals of Venice, let alone a sub the size of an ocean liner, but no problem; *The League of Extraordinary Gentlemen* either knows absolutely nothing about Venice, or (more likely) trusts that its audience does not. At one point, the towering Nautilus sails under the tiny Bridge of Sighs and only scrapes it a little. In no time at all there is an action scene involving Nemo's newfangled automobile, which races meaninglessly down streets that do not exist, because there are no streets in Venice and you can't go much more than a block before running into a bridge or a canal. Maybe the filmmakers did their research at the Venetian hotel in Las Vegas, where Sean Connery arrived by gondola for the movie's premiere.

Bombs begin to explode Venice. It is Carnival time, and Piazza San Marco is jammed with merrymakers as the Basilica explodes and topples into ruin. Later there is a scene of this same crowd engaged in lighthearted chatter, as if they have not noticed that half of Venice is missing. Dozens of other buildings sink into the lagoon, which does not prevent Quarter-main from exalting, "Venice still stands!"

Now back to that speeding car. Its driver, Tom Sawyer, has been sent off on an urgent mission. When he finds something—an underwater bomb, I think, although that would be hard to spot from a speeding car—he's supposed to fire off a flare, after which I don't know what's supposed to happen. As the car hurtles down the nonexistent streets of Venice, enemy operatives stand shoulder-to-shoulder on the rooftops and fire at it with machine guns, leading us to hypothesize an enemy meeting at which the leader says, "Just in case they should arrive by submarine with a fast car, which hasn't been invented yet, I want thousands of men to line the rooftops and fire at it, without hitting anything, of course."

Later there is a sinister encounter in a Venetian graveyard, among the crumbling headstones. But hold on: Venice of all cities doesn't *have* graves because the occupants would be underwater. Like New Orleans, another city with a groundwater problem, Venetians find it prudent to bury their dead in above-ground crypts.

But never mind. The action now moves to the frozen lakes of Mongolia, where the enemy leader (whose identity I would not dream of revealing) has constructed a gigantic factory palace to manufacture robot soldiers, apparently an early model of the clones they were manufacturing in *Attack* of the same. This palace was presumably constructed recently at great expense (it's a bitch getting construction materials through those frozen lakes). And yet it includes vast neglected and forgotten rooms.

I don't really mind the movie's lack of believability. Well, I mind a little; to assume audiences will believe cars racing through Venice is as insulting as giving them a gondola chase down the White House lawn. What I do mind is that the movie plays like a big wind came along and blew away the script and they ran down the street after it and grabbed a few pages and shot those. Since Oscar Wilde contributed Dorian Gray to the movie, it may be appropriate to end with his dying words: "Either that wallpaper goes, or I do."

The Legend of Zorro

(DIRECTED BY MARTIN CAMPBELL; STARRING ANTONIO BANDERAS, CATHERINE ZETA-JONES; 2005)

The Legend of Zorro commits a lot of movie sins, but one is mortal: It turns the magnificent Elena into a nag. You will recall *The Mask of Zorro* (1998), which first united Antonio Banderas and Catherine Zeta-Jones as Zorro and Elena, in a resurrection of the character first played by Douglas Fairbanks Sr. and subsequently by Tyrone Power, John Carroll, Guy Williams, and—here's a team for you—George Hamilton and Anthony Hopkins.

Hopkins played the elder Zorro in the 1998 film, and Banderas played a street urchin who grew up to be a bandit but was taken under old Zorro's wing and taught the tricks of the trade, such as swordsmanship, horsemanship, and charm. That was a grand movie, filled with swashes and buckles. Banderas and Zeta-Jones rose to the occasion with performances of joy and unbounded energy, and it was probably the best Zorro movie ever made, although having not seen them all I can only speculate.

Now come Banderas and Zeta-Jones again, with the same director, Martin Campbell, and of all of the possible ideas about how to handle the Elena character, this movie has assembled the worst ones. The sublime adventuress has turned into the kind of wife who wants her husband to quit Zorroing because "you do not know your own son," and besides, Zorro comes home late, she never knows where he is, etc. We are inflicted with such dialogue as:

> *"People still need Zorro!"*
> *"No—you still need Zorro!"*
> *"You're overreacting!"*

Saints preserve us from Mr. and Mrs. Zorro as the Bickersons. And what are we to make of their son, Joaquin (a good little actor named Adrian Alonso), who dresses like Little Lord Fauntleroy but has developed, apparently by osmosis, all of the skills of his father, such as shadowing bad guys, eavesdropping on plots, improvising in emergencies, and exposing a dastardly scheme to overthrow the government.

He's a bright kid, but not bright enough to recognize that Zorro is his own father. To be sure, Zorro wears a mask, but let me pose a hypothetical exercise for my readers. Imagine your own father. That's it. Now place him in a typical setting: pushing back from the dinner table, cutting off some jerk in an intersection, or scratching his dandruff. Now imagine your dad wearing black leather pants, a black linen shirt, a black cloak, a flat black hat, and a black mask that covers his eyes. Got that? Now imagine him pushing back from the table. Still your dad, right? You can almost hear your mom: "Now don't you go getting any ideas about that whip."

To be sure, Zorro's work keeps him away from home a lot, which is one of the things Elena is complaining about. Maybe the son has never seen his father. In that case, Elena has a point. Meanwhile, the villains have a plot to use a superweapon in order to bring about the collapse of the union and protect us from "inferior races," by which they mean Zorro and all of his kind. Strange, how movie characters who hate "inferior races" somehow themselves never look like breeding stock. If they reproduced, they would found a line of dog whisperers and undersecretaries of defense.

The circumstances under which Zorro and the villain fight a duel with polo mallets is unprecedented in the annals of chivalry, but never mind: What's with this secret society named the Knights of Aragon, who have secretly controlled the world for centuries? When you belong to an ancient order that runs the world and you're reduced to dueling with polo mallets, it's like you're running the Scientology office in Thule.

There is a neat scene here where Zorro and his horse race a train, and then the horse leaps from a trestle and lands on top of the train. That Zorro thinks a horse would do this shows that Zorro does not know as much about horses as he should. For that matter, the horse itself is surprisingly uninformed. It must have had the mumps the week the other horses studied about never jumping blind from a high place onto something that, assuming it is there, will be going 40 mph.

I am searching for the correct word to describe the scene where Zorro is served with divorce papers. Ah, I've found it! Shame I can't use it. Four letters. This is a family newspaper. Starts with s. Then Zorro has to attend a fancy dress ball where Elena turns up as the escort of Armand

(Rufus Sewell), a wealthy French vineyard owner. This is like *Supergirl* dating Jughead. For maximum poignancy, we need a scene where little Joaquin approaches Armand and says, "Father?"

Levity

(DIRECTED BY ED SOLOMON; STARRING BILLY BOB THORNTON, MORGAN FREEMAN; 2003)

Levity is an earnest but hopeless attempt to tell a parable about a man's search for redemption. By the end of his journey, we don't care if he finds redemption, if only he finds wakefulness. He's a whiny slug who talks like a victim of overmedication. I was reminded of the Bob and Ray routine about the Slow Talkers of America.

That this unfortunate creature is played by Billy Bob Thornton is evidence, I think, that we have to look beyond the actors in placing blame. His costars are Morgan Freeman, Holly Hunter, and Kirsten Dunst. For a director to assemble such a cast and then maroon them in such a witless enterprise gives him more to redeem than his hero. The hero has merely killed a fictional character. Ed Solomon, who wrote and directed, has stolen two hours from the lives of everyone who sees the film, and weeks from the careers of these valuable actors.

The movie stars Thornton as Manual Jordan, a man recently released from custody after serving twenty-two years of a sentence for murder. That his first name reminds us of Emmanuel and his surname echoes the Jordan River is not, I fear, an accident; he is a Christ figure, and Thornton has gotten into the spirit with long hair that looks copied from a bad holy card. The only twist is that instead of dying for our sins, the hero shot a young convenience store clerk—who died, I guess, for Manual's sins.

Now Manual returns to the same district where the killing took place. This is one of those movie neighborhoods where all the characters live close to one another and meet whenever necessary. Manual soon encounters Adele Easley (Holly Hunter), the sister of the boy he killed. They become friendly and the possibility of romance looms, although he hesitates to confess his crime. She has a teenage son named Abner (Geoffrey Wigdor), named after her late brother.

In this district a preacher named Miles Evans (Freeman) runs a storefront youth center, portrayed so unconvincingly that we suspect Solomon has never seen a store, a front, a youth, or a center. In this room, which looks ever so much like a stage set, an ill-assorted assembly of disadvantaged youths are arrayed about the room in such studied "casual" attitudes that we are reminded of extras told to keep their places. Preacher Evans intermittently harangues them with apocalyptic rantings, which they attend patiently. Into the center walks Sofia Mellinger (Dunst), a lost girl who is tempted by drugs and late-night raves, who wanders this neighborhood with curious impunity.

We know that sooner or later Manual will have to inform Adele that he murdered her brother. But meanwhile the current Abner has fallen in with bad companions, and a silly grudge threatens to escalate into murder. This generates a scene of amazing coincidence, during which in a lonely alley late at night, all of the necessary characters coincidentally appear as they are needed, right on cue, for fraught action and dialogue that the actors must have studied for sad, painful hours, while keeping their thoughts to themselves.

Whether Manual finds forgiveness, whether Sofia finds herself, whether Abner is saved, whether the preacher has a secret, whether Adele can forgive, whether Manual finds a new mission in life, and whether the youths ever tire of sermons, I will leave to your speculation. All I can observe is that there is not a moment of authentic observation in the film; the director has assembled his characters out of stock melodrama. A bad Victorian novelist would find nothing to surprise him here, and a good one nothing to interest him. When this film premiered to thunderous silence at Sundance 2003, Solomon said he had been working on the screenplay for twenty years. Not long enough.

Life or Something Like It

(DIRECTED BY STEPHEN HEREK; STARRING ANGELINA JOLIE, STOCKARD CHANNING; 2002)
Someone once said, live every day as if it will be your last.

Not just someone once said that. Everyone once said it, over and over again, although *Life or Something Like It* thinks it's a fresh insight. This is an ungainly movie, ill-fitting, with its elbows sticking out where the knees should be. To quote another ancient proverb, "A camel is a horse designed by a committee." *Life or Something Like It* is the movie designed by the camel.

The movie stars Angelina Jolie as Lanie Kerigan, a bubbly blond Seattle TV reporter whose ignorance of TV is equaled only by the movie's. I don't know how the filmmakers got their start, but they obviously didn't come up through television. Even a *viewer* knows more than this.

Example. Sexy Pete the cameraman (Edward Burns) wants to play a trick on Lanie, so he fiddles with her microphone during a stand-up report from the street, and her voice comes out like Mickey Mouse's squeak—like when you talk with helium in your mouth. Everybody laughs at her. Except, see, your voice comes out of your *body,* and when it goes through the air it sounds like your voice to the people standing around. When it goes into the microphone, it kind of *stays* inside there, and is recorded on videotape, which is not simultaneously played back live to a street crowd.

Lanie dreams of going to New York to work on *AM USA,* the network show. She gets her big invitation after attracting "national attention" by covering a strike and leading the workers in singing "Can't Get No Satisfaction" while she dances in front of them, during a tiny lapse in journalistic objectivity. Meanwhile, she is afraid she will die, because a mad street person named Prophet Jack has predicted the Seattle Mariners will win, there will be a hailstorm tomorrow morning, and Lanie will die next Thursday. They win, it hails, Lanie believes she will die.

This leads to a romantic crisis. She is engaged to Cal Cooper (Christian Kane), a pitcher with the Mariners. He's on the mound, he looks lovingly at her, she smiles encouragingly, he throws a pitch, the batter hits a home run, and she jumps up and applauds. If he sees that, she may not last until Thursday. Meanwhile, she apparently hates Pete the sexy cameraman, although when Cal is out of town and she thinks she's going to die, they make love, and *then* we find out, belatedly, they've made love before. The screenplay keeps doubling back to add overlooked info.

Cal comes back to town and she wants a heart-to-heart, but instead he takes her to the ballpark, where the friendly groundskeeper (who hangs around all night in every baseball movie for just such an opportunity) turns on the lights so Cal can throw her a few pitches. Is she moved by this loving gesture? Nope: "Your cure for my emotional crisis is batting practice?" This is the only turning-on-the-lights-in-the-empty-ballpark scene in history that ends unhappily.

Lanie and Pete the sexy cameraman become lovers, until Pete whipsaws overnight into an insulted, wounded man who is hurt because she wants to go to New York instead of stay in Seattle with him and his young son. This about-face exists *only* so they can break up so they can get back together again later. It also inspires a scene in the station's equipment room, where Jolie tests the theoretical limits of hysterical overacting.

Lanie's *AM USA* debut involves interviewing the network's biggest star, a Barbara Walters–type (Stockard Channing), on the star's twenty-fifth anniversary. So earthshaking is this interview, the *AM USA* anchor breathlessly announces, "We welcome our viewers on the West Coast for this special live edition!" It's 7 a.m. in New York. That makes it 4 a.m. on the West Coast. If you lived in Seattle, would you set your alarm to 4 a.m. to see Barbara Walters plugging her network special?

Lanie begins the interview, pauses, and is silent for thirty seconds while deeply thinking. She finally asks, "Was it worth everything?" What? "Giving up marriage and children for a career?" Tears roll down Channing's cheeks. Pandemonium. Great interview. Network president wants to hire Lanie on the spot. Has never before heard anyone ask, "Was it worth it?" The question of whether a woman can have both a career and a family is controversial in *Life or Something Like It*—even when posed by Ms. Jolie, who successfully combines tomb raiding with Billy Bob Thornton.

I want to close with the mystery of Lanie's father, who is always found stationed in an easy chair in his living room, where he receives visits from his daughters, who feel guilty because since Mom died they have not been able to communicate with Dad, who, apparently as a result, just sits there waiting for his daughters to come back and feel guilty some more. Eventually there's an uptick in his mood, and he admits he has always been proud of Lanie and will "call in sick" so he can watch Lanie on *AM USA*. Until then I thought he *was* sick. Maybe he's just tired because he's on the night shift, which is why he would be at work at 4 a.m.

London

(Directed by Hunter Richards; starring Chris Evans, Jessica Biel; 2006)

At one point in *London*, a Japanese experiment is described. Scientists place containers of white rice in two different rooms. One container is praised. Nice rice. Beautiful rice. The other container is insulted. Ugly rice. Bad rice. At the end of a month, the rice in the first container is fresh and fragrant. The rice in the other room is decayed and moldy. If there is any validity to this experiment, I expect *London* to start decaying any day now. Bad movie. Ugly movie.

Another experiment is described. Baby bunnies. They are removed from their mother. Every time one is killed, the mother's vital signs show a sudden spike. *London* was given birth by the writer and director Hunter Richards, and if there is anything to the bunny theory, he's going to get jumpy when the reviews of his movie appear. There may be perspiration and trembling. Maybe anxiety attacks.

The rice and bunny experiments are two of many topics discussed by Syd (Chris Evans) and Bateman (Jason Statham) as they pace the floor of an upstairs bathroom at a Manhattan party, inhaling untold amounts of cocaine. Syd also guzzles tequila from a bottle. He met Bateman in a bar and insisted the older man, a Brit, accompany him to the party. He needed someone along for moral support because it was a going-away party for his girlfriend, London (Jessica Biel), and Syd wasn't invited. After I got to know Syd, I was not surprised that he wasn't invited, and I was not surprised that she was going away.

Let's track back a little. When first we see Syd, he has just treated himself to cocaine and the remains of a beer and has passed out in his apartment. The phone rings, he learns about the party, uses the f-word for the first of, oh, several hundred times, and smashes up the place, including a big aquarium. Curious that when the aquarium shatters, there are no shots of desperate fish gasping on the floor. Maybe Nemo has already led them to freedom.

At the party, Syd and Bateman get relentlessly stoned while discussing the kinds of tiresome subjects that seem important in the middle of the night in a bar when two drunks are analyzing the meaning of it all. Bartenders have been known to drink in order to endure these conversations. They usually consist of the two drunks exchanging monologues. During the parts when sober people would be listening, drunks are waiting until they get to talk again. Syd and Bateman are powerless over dialogue and their scenarios have become unmanageable.

There are personal confessions. Syd relates his unhappy romance with London, and we get flashbacks of them fighting, loving, talking, weeping, and running through all the other exercises in Acting 101. Bateman was married once, but it didn't work out. What a surprise. Now he pays good money to have S&M mistresses humiliate him. He describes their procedures in clinical detail, and we get flashbacks of those, too. Ugly. Bad. Syd is amazed that Bateman pays $200 to be treated in such a way, although I am not sure if he is amazed that it is so much, or so little.

Occasionally one of the women from downstairs drifts into the bathroom. We meet Mallory (Joy Bryant) and Maya (Kelli Garner). Beautiful. Nice. They could do better. One of them says she heard Syd tried to commit suicide. That's a lie, says Syd, explaining a misunderstanding that occurred involving the drugs his dog takes for epilepsy. There is also a great deal of talk about God and faith, and whether Syd or Bateman feels the most pain. This discussion is theoretical, since neither one is feeling anything. "With all the drugs on the market, you'd think they'd have a pill to take the edge off of leaving a chick," Syd observes. Of course, he didn't leave her; she left him. But the treatment would probably be the same.

Chris Evans and Jason Statham have verbal facility and energy, which enables them to propel this dreck from one end of ninety-two minutes to the other, and the women in the movie are all perfectly adequate at playing bimbo cokeheads. I have seen all of these actors on better days in better movies, and I may have a novena said for them.

Two things mystify me. (1) How can you use that much cocaine and drink that much booze and remain standing and keep speaking, especially in the case of Syd, who was already stoned when he started? (2) Where is the camera? At least half of the movie is shot in the bathroom, which has a mirror along one wall. The mirror should be reflecting a camera, but I didn't see one. Well, of course, it's the job of the professionals to keep the camera hidden, and maybe cinematographer Jo Willems was trying to hide it in another movie.

The Lost Skeleton of Cadavra

(DIRECTED BY LARRY BLAMIRE; STARRING LARRY BLAMIRE, FAY MASTERSON; 2004)
It is a curious attribute of camp that it can only be found, not made.

So observes Dave Kehr, in his *New York Times* review of *The Lost Skeleton of Cadavra*. I did not read the rest of the review, because (1) I had to write my own, and (2), well, his first sentence says it all, doesn't it? True camp sincerely wants to be itself. In this category I include the works of Ed Wood and the infinitely more talented Russ Meyer. False camp keeps digging you in the ribs with a bony elbow. In this category falls *The Lost Skeleton of Cadavra*. Movies like the Austin Powers series are in a different category altogether, using the framework of satire for the purpose of comedy.

The Lost Skeleton of Cadavra, which is a loving tribute to the worst science fiction movies ever made, is about a three-way struggle for possession of the rare element atmosphereum. The contestants include an American scientist and his wife, a married (I think) couple from outer space, and a mad scientist and his sidekick, which is, of course, the lost skeleton of cadavra. There is also a creature that seems to have been created by an explosion at a sofa factory, and a sexy girl named Animala, whose role is to appear in the movie and be a sexy girl. More about her later.

The photography, the dialogue, the acting, the script, the special effects, and especially the props (such as a space ship that looks like it would get a D in shop class) are all deliberately bad in the way that such films were bad when they were *really* being made. The locations remind me of the old *Captain Video* TV series, in which the same fake rocks were always being moved around to indicate we were in a new place on the alien planet. The writer and director, Larry Blamire, who also plays the saner of the scientists, has the look so well mastered that if the movie had only been made in total ignorance fifty years ago, it might be recalled today as a classic. A minor, perhaps even minuscule, classic.

A funny thing happened while I was watching it. I began to flash back to *Trog* (1970). This is an example of camp that was made, not found. That it was directed by the great cinematographer Freddie Francis I have absolutely no explanation for. That it starred Joan Crawford, in almost her final movie role, I think I understand. Even though she was already enshrined as a Hollywood goddess, she was totally unable to stop accepting roles, and took this one against all reason.

The plot of *Trog*, which I will abbreviate, involves a hairy monster. When it goes on a killing spree and is captured, Joan Crawford, an anthropologist, realizes it is a priceless scientific find: the Missing Link between ape and man. Then Trog kidnaps a small girl and crawls into a cave, and reader, although many years have passed since I saw the movie, I have never forgotten the sight of Joan Crawford in her designer pants suit and all the makeup, crawling on her hands and knees into the cave and calling out, "Trog! Trog!" As if Trog knew the abbreviation of its scientific name.

But never mind; you see the point. *Trog* is perfect camp because Freddie Francis and Joan Crawford would never have allied themselves with a movie that was deliberately bad. (I am not so sure about Joe Cornelius, who played Trog.) It is bad all on its own. *The Lost Skeleton of Cadavra* has been made by people who are trying to be bad, which by definition reveals that they are playing beneath their ability. Poor Ed Wood, on the other hand, always and sincerely made the very best film he possibly could. How rare is a director like Russ Meyer, whose work satirizes material that doesn't even exist except in his satire of it, and who is also very funny; no coincidence that the Austin Powers movies are always careful to quote him.

But what have I neglected to tell you about *The Lost Skeleton of Cadavra*? Reading my notes, I find that "there is enough atmosphereum in one teaspoon to go to the moon and back six times," which is not quite the statement it seems to be. Oh, and the sexy girl named Animala is described as: "part human, part four different forest animals, and she can dance! Oh, how she can dance! Like I've never seen a woman dance before!" A possible mate for Trog?

A Lot Like Love

(DIRECTED BY NIGEL COLE; STARRING ASHTON KUTCHER, AMANDA PEET; 2005)

A Lot Like Love is a romance between two of the dimmer bulbs of their generation. Judging by their dialogue, Oliver and Emily have never read a book or a newspaper, seen a movie, watched TV, had an idea, carried on an interesting conversation, or ever thought much about anything. The movie thinks they are cute and funny, which is embarrassing, like your uncle who won't stop with the golf jokes. This is not the fault of the stars, Ashton Kutcher and Amanda Peet, who are actors forced to walk around in Stupid Suits.

Last week I was at Boulder for a conference at the University of Colorado, and I found myself walking across campus with a kid who confessed he was studying philosophy.

"What do you plan to do with it?" I asked.

He said he wasn't sure. All of his friends were on career tracks, "but I dunno. I just find this stuff interesting."

"Yes!" I said. "Yes! Don't treat education as if it's only a trade school. Take some electives just because they're interesting. You have long years to get through, and you must guard against the possibility of becoming a bore to yourself."

A *Lot Like Love*, written by Colin Patrick Lynch and directed by Nigel Cole, is about two people who have arrived at adulthood unequipped for the struggle. The lives of Oliver and Emily are Idiot Plots, in which every misunderstanding could be solved by a single word they are vigilant never to utter. They Meet Cute, over and over again. They keep finding themselves alone because their lovers keep walking out on them. Well, no wonder. "I'm going," one of her lovers says, and goes. Any more of an explanation and she might have had to take notes.

He has an Internet start-up selling diapers over the Web. She's dumped by a rock musician in the opening scene, where she seems to be a tough Goth chick, but that's just the costume. Later Ollie gives her a camera and she becomes a photographer, and even has a gallery exhibit of her works, which look like photos taken on vacation with cell phone cameras and e-mailed to you by the children of friends.

The movie is ninety-five minutes long, and neither character says a single memorable thing. You've heard of being too clever by half? Ollie and Emily are not clever enough by three-quarters. During a dinner date they start spitting water at each other. Then she crawls under the table, not for what you're thinking, but so they can trade sides and spit in the opposite direction. Then it seems like she's choking on her food, but he refuses to give her the Heimlich Maneuver, and even tells the waitress not to bother. So take a guess: Is she really choking, or not? If she's playing a trick, she's a doofus, and if she isn't, he's a doofus. They shouldn't be allowed to leave the house without a parent or adult guardian.

They continue to Meet Cute over many long years, which are spelled out in titles: "Three Years Later," "Six Months Later," and so on. I was reminded of the little blue thermometers telling you the software will finish downloading in nineteen hours. Their first Meet Cute is a doozy: On a flight to New York, she enlists him in the Mile-High Club before they even know each other's names. But that's Strike One against him, she says, because she had to make the first move. Yeah, like a guy on an airplane should push into the restroom for sex with a woman he doesn't know. That's how you get to wear the little plastic cuffs.

Later they Meet Cute again, walk into a bar, drink four shots of Jack Daniels in one minute, and order a pitcher of beer. No, they're not alcoholics. This is just Movie Behavior; for example, at first she smokes and then she stops and then she starts again. That supplies her with a Personality Characteristic. Still later, they sing together, surprisingly badly. The movie is filled with a lot of other pop music. These songs tend toward plaintive dirges complaining, "My life can be described by this stupid song." At one point he flies to New York to pitch his dot-com diapers to some venture capitalists, and is so inarticulate and clueless he could be a character in this movie. To call the movie dead in the water is an insult to water.

● ● ● ● ● ● ● ● ●

The Man

(DIRECTED BY LES MAYFIELD; STARRING SAMUEL L. JACKSON, EUGENE LEVY; 2005)

The Man is another one of those movies, like *Lethal Weapon 2*, where the outsider finds himself in the dangerous world of cops and robbers. The cop this time is Derrick Vann, a hard-boiled Detroit ATF agent played by Samuel L. Jackson, and the outsider is Andy Fidler (Eugene Levy), a dental supplies salesman from Wisconsin. Fidler loves his product so much he chats up strangers about the glories of flossing.

The plot: Agent Vann's partner, who is on the take, has died in connection with a heist of guns from the ATF lock-room. A crook named Booty (Anthony Mackie) may be the key to the killing. Vann, an honest agent, mistakes Fidler for an underworld contact working with Booty. When he finds out how very wrong he is, he still needs Fidler to pretend to be a black market arms dealer if the sting is going to work.

Whether the sting and the movie work are two different questions. Jackson and Levy are in full sail as their most familiar character types: Jackson hard as nails, Levy oblivious to the world outside his own blissfully limited existence. They could play these characters in their sleep. Their differences provide the setup for the whole movie: these two guys linked together in an unlikely partnership during which their personalities (and Fidler's problems with intestinal gas) will make it difficult for them to share the front seat of Vann's customized Caddy.

The Man is very minor. The running time of seventy-nine minutes indicates (a) thin material, and (b) mercy toward the audience by not stretching it any further than what is already the breaking point. You know a movie like this is stalling for time when it supplies Agent Vann with a family so that his wife can call him in the middle of the action: "Your daughter wants to know if you'll be at her recital tonight." Yes, it's the ancient and sometimes reliable Dad Too Busy for Child's Big Moment formula. Does Vann wrap up the case in time to walk into the room just as the recital is beginning? Do he and his daughter exchange a quiet little nod to show family does, after all, come first? I would not dream of giving away such a plot detail.

Levy has funny moments as the fussy dental supplies fetishist, but never goes into full obnoxious mode as Joe Pesci did in *Lethal Weapon 2*. He plays the character like a conventioneer trying to be nice to an alarming taxi driver. Jackson plays the cop like a man who has found a bug in the front seat of his car. What's interesting, however, is that they don't get locked into a lot of black-white shtick; their differences are defined through occupation, not race, except for the odd ethnic in-joke involving hot sauce.

The inescapable fact about *The Man* is that this movie is completely unnecessary. Nobody needed to make it, nobody needs to see it, Jackson and Levy are too successful to waste time with it. It plays less like a film than like a deal.

At Telluride over the weekend I was talking to James Mangold, the director of *Walk the Line* and other ambitious pictures, and he said an interesting thing: Hollywood executives are reluctant to green-light a project that depends on the filmmakers being able to pull it off. They want familiar formulas in safe packages. An original movie idea involves faith that the script will work, the director knows what he's doing, and the actors are right for the story. Too risky. Better to make a movie where when you hear the pitch you can already envision the TV commercial, because the movie will essentially be the long form of the thirty-second spot.

Go online, look at the trailer for *The Man,* and you will know everything you could possibly need to know about this movie except how it would feel if the trailer were eighty minutes long.

Masked and Anonymous

(DIRECTED BY LARRY CHARLES; STARRING JEFF BRIDGES, PENELOPE CRUZ; 2003)

Bob Dylan idolatry is one of the enduring secular religions of our day. Those who worship him are inexhaustible in their fervor, and every enigmatic syllable of the great poet is cherished and analyzed as if somehow he conceals profound truths in his lyrics, and if we could only decrypt them, they would be the solution to—I dunno, maybe everything.

In *Masked and Anonymous,* where he plays a legendary troubadour named (I fear) Jack Fate, a religious fanatic played by Penelope Cruz says: "I love his songs because they are not precise—they are completely open to interpretation." She makes this statement to characters dressed as Gandhi and the pope, but lacks the courtesy to add, "But hey, guys, what do *you* think?"

I have always felt it ungenerous to have the answer but wrap it in enigmas. When Woody Guthrie, the great man's inspiration, sings a song, you know what it is about. Perhaps Dylan's genius was to take simple ideas and make them impenetrable. Since he cannot really sing, there is the assumption that he cannot be performing to entertain us, and that therefore, there must be a deeper purpose. The instructive documentary *The Ballad of Ramblin' Jack* suggests that it was Ramblin' Jack Elliott who was the true follower of Woody, and that after he introduced Dylan to Guthrie he was dropped from the picture as Dylan studiously repackaged the Guthrie genius in 1960s trappings.

That Dylan still exerts a mystical appeal there can be no doubt. When *Masked and Anonymous* premiered at Sundance 2003, there was a standing ovation when the poet entered the room. People continued to stand during the film, in order to leave, and the auditorium was half-empty when the closing credits played to thoughtful silence. One of the more poignant moments in Sundance history then followed, as director Larry Charles stood on the stage with various cast members, asking for questions and then asking, "Aren't there any questions?"

The movie's cast is a tribute to Dylan's charisma. Here are the credits which, after Dylan, proceed alphabetically: Bob Dylan, Jeff Bridges, Penelope Cruz, John Goodman, Jessica Lange, Luke Wilson. Also Angela Bassett, Steven Bauer, Paul Michael Chan, Bruce Dern, Ed Harris, Val Kilmer, Cheech Marin, Chris Penn, Giovanni Ribisi, Mickey Rourke, Richard Sarafian, Christian Slater, Fred Ward, Robert Wisdom. In a film where salaries must have been laughable, these people must have thought it would be cool to be in a Dylan movie. Some of them exude the aw-shucks gratitude of a visiting singer beckoned onstage at the Grand Ole Opry. Ironically, the credits do not name the one performer in the movie whose performance actually was applauded; that was a young black girl named Tinashe Kachingwe, who sang "The Times They Are a-Changin'" with such sweetness and conviction that she was like a master class.

The plot involves a nation in the throes of postrevolutionary chaos. This is "a ravaged Latin American country" (*Variety*) or perhaps "a sideways allegory about an alternative America" (*Salon*). It was filmed in run-down areas of Los Angeles, nudge, nudge. A venal rock promoter named Uncle Sweetheart (John Goodman) and his brassy partner Nina Veronica (Jessica Lange) decide to spring Jack Fate from prison to give a benefit concert to raise funds for poverty relief (maybe) and Uncle and Nina (certainly). That provides the pretense for Dylan to sing several songs, although the one I liked best, "Dixie," seemed a strange choice for a concert in a republic that, wherever it is, looks in little sympathy with the land of cotton.

The enormous cast wanders bewildered through shapeless scenes. Some seem to be improvising, and Goodman and Jeff Bridges (as a rock journalist) at least have high energy and make a game try. Others look like people who were asked to choose their clothing earlier in the day at the costume department; the happenings of the 1960s come to mind.

Dylan occupies this scenario wearing a couple of costumes borrowed from the Tinhorn Dictator rack. Alarmingly thin, he sprawls in chairs in postures that a merciful cinematographer would have talked him out of. While all about him are acting their heads off, he never speaks more than one sentence at a time, and his remarks uncannily evoke the language and philosophy of Chinese fortune cookies.

Masked and Anonymous is a vanity production beyond all reason. I am not sure, however, that the vanity is Dylan's. I don't have any idea what to think about him. He has so long since disappeared into his persona that there is little received sense of the person there. The vanity belongs perhaps to those who flattered their own by working with him, by assuming (in the face of all they had learned during hard days of honest labor on a multitude of pictures) that his genius would somehow redeem a screenplay that could never have seemed other than what it was—incoherent, raving, juvenile meanderings. If I had been asked to serve as consultant on this picture, my advice would have amounted to three words: More Tinashe Kachingwe.

The Master of Disguise

(Directed by Perry Andelin Blake; starring Dana Carvey, Jennifer Esposito; 2002)
The Master of Disguise pants and wheezes and hurls itself exhausted across the finish line after barely sixty-five minutes of movie, and then follows it with fifteen minutes of end credits in an attempt to clock in as a feature film. We get outtakes, deleted scenes, flubbed lines, and all the other versions of the "credit cookie," which was once a cute idea but is getting to be a bore.

The credits go on and on and on. The movie is like a party guest who thinks he is funny and is wrong. The end credits are like the same guest taking too long to leave. At one point they at last mercifully seemed to be over, and the projectionist even closed the curtains, but no: There was Dana Carvey, still visible against the red velvet, asking us what we were still doing in the theater. That is a dangerous question to ask after a movie like *The Master of Disguise*.

The movie is a desperate miscalculation. It gives poor Dana Carvey nothing to do that is really funny, and then expects us to laugh because he acts so goofy all the time. But *acting* funny is not funny. Acting in a situation that's funny—that's funny.

The plot: Carvey plays an Italian waiter named Pistachio Disguisey, who is unfamiliar with the First Law of Funny Names, which is that funny names in movies are rarely funny. Pistachio comes from a long line of masters of disguise. His father Fabbrizio (James Brolin), having capped his career by successfully impersonating Bo Derek, retires and opens a New York restaurant. He doesn't tell his son about the family trade, but then, when he's kidnapped by his old enemy Bowman (Brent Spiner), Pistachio is told the family secret by his grandfather (Harold Gould).

Grandfather also gives him a crash course in disguise-craft, after locating Fabbrizio's hidden workshop in the attic (a Disguisey's workshop, we learn, is known as a nest). There is now a scene representative of much of the movie, in which Pistachio puts on an inflatable suit, and it suddenly balloons so that he flies around the room and knocks over Granddad. That scene may seem funny to kids. Real, real little, little kids.

Carvey, of course, is himself a skilled impersonator, and during the film we see him as a human turtle, Al Pacino from *Scarface,* Robert Shaw from *Jaws,* a man in a cherry suit, a man with a cow pie for a face, George W. Bush, and many other guises. In some cases the disguises are handled by using a double and then employing digital technology to make it appear as if the double's face is a latex mask that can be removed. In other cases, such as Bush, Carvey simply impersonates him.

The plot helpfully supplies Pistachio with a girl named Jennifer (Jennifer Esposito) who becomes his sidekick in the search for Fabbrizio, and they visit a great many colorful locations. One of them is a secret headquarters where Bowman keeps his priceless trove of treasures, including the lunar landing module, which is used for one of those fight scenes where the hero dangles by one hand. The movie's director, Perry

Andelin Blake, has been a production designer on fourteen movies, including most of Adam Sandler's, and, to be sure, *The Master of Disguise* has an excellent production design. It is less successful at disguising itself as a comedy.

Me, Myself & Irene
(DIRECTED BY PETER FARRELLY AND BOBBY FARRELLY; STARRING JIM CARREY, RENEE ZELLWEGER; 2000)

Me, Myself & Irene is a labored and sour comedy that rouses itself to create real humor, and then settles back glumly into an impenetrable plot and characters who keep repeating the same schtick, hoping maybe this time it will work. It stars Jim Carrey in a role that mires him in versions of the same gags, over and over. Renee Zellweger costars as a woman who stays at his side for no apparent reason except that the script requires her to.

The movie is by the Farrelly brothers, Peter and Bobby, whose *There's Something About Mary* still causes me to smile whenever I think about it, and whose *Kingpin* is a buried treasure. They worked with Carrey in *Dumb and Dumber,* which has some very big laughs in it, but this time their formula of scatology, sexuality, political incorrectness, and cheerful obscenity seems written by the numbers. The movie is as offensive as most of their work, which would be fine if it redeemed itself with humor. It doesn't. There is, for example, an extended passage making fun of an albino that is not funny at all, ever, in any part, but painfully drones on and on until the filmmakers cop out and make him the pal of the heroes.

Carrey plays a Rhode Island state trooper who puts up with shocking insults to his manhood and uniform and manages somehow to be a sunny Dr. Jeckyl, until he finally snaps and allows his Mr. Hyde to roam free. As the nice guy (named Charlie), he keeps smiling after his wife presents him with three black babies, fathered by a dwarf limo driver and Mensa member. He even keeps smiling when his neighbor allows his dog to defecate on his lawn, while the neighbor's wife steals his newspaper, and when the guys in the barbershop laugh at his attempts to enforce the law.

Years pass in this fashion. His wife runs off with the little genius. His sons stay with him, growing into enormous lads who are brilliant at school but use the MF-word as if it were punctuation. Since no one else in their lives uses it, the movie must think all African-Americans are required by statute or genetics to repeat the word ceaselessly (it might have been funnier to have all three boys talk like Sam Donaldson).

After the evil side of his personality ("Hank") breaks free, Carrey starts kicking butt and taking no prisoners. Through twists unnecessary to describe, he hooks up with the perky, pretty Irene (Renee Zellweger), and they become fugitives from the law, pursued by the evil Lt. Gerke (Chris Cooper) for reasons that have something to do with environmental scandals, country clubs, bribery, and cover-ups; the plot is so murky we abandon curiosity and simply accept that Carrey and Zellweger are on the run, and the bad guys are chasing them.

The movie has defecation jokes, urination jokes, dildo jokes, flasher jokes, and a chicken that must be thoroughly annoyed by the dilemma it finds itself in. Not many of the jokes are very funny, and some seem plain desperate. I did laugh a lot during a sequence when Carrey tries to put a wounded cow out of its misery, but most of the time I sat quietly reflecting that the Farrelly brand of humor is a high-wire act; it involves great risks and is a triumph if they get to the other side, but ugly when they fail.

Carrey has a plastic face and body, and does remarkable things with his expressions. As Charlie he's all toothy grins and friendliness. As Hank, his face twists into an evil scowl, and his voice is electronically lowered into a more menacing register. Problem is, although it's sort of funny to see Charlie reacting to the insulting ways people treat him, it is rarely funny to see him transform himself into Hank, who then takes revenge. Hank is not really a comic character, and it's a miscalculation to allow him to dominate most of the movie.

Irene, the Zellweger character, has not been invented fresh with a specific comic purpose, but is simply a recycled version of the character she usually plays. Her job is to be loyal and sensible, lay down the law, pout, smile, and be shocked. It is a thankless task; she's like the onscreen representative of the audience.

The Farrellys are gifted and have made me laugh as loudly as anyone since the golden age of Mel Brooks. They have scored before and will no doubt score again. This time they go for broke, and get there.

Men in Black II

(DIRECTED BY BARRY SONNENFELD; STARRING TOMMY LEE JONES, WILL SMITH; 2002) Some sequels continue a story. Others repeat it. *Men in Black II* creates a new threat for the MIB, but recycles the same premise, which is that mankind can defeat an alien invasion by assigning agents in Ray-Bans to shoot them into goo. This is a movie that fans of the original might enjoy in a diluted sort of way, but there is no need for it—except, of course, to take another haul at the box office, where the 1997 movie grossed nearly $600 million.

The astonishing success of the original *MIB* was partly because it was fun, partly because it was unexpected. We'd never seen anything like it, while with *MIB II* we've seen something exactly like it. In the original, Tommy Lee Jones played a no-nonsense veteran agent, Will Smith was his trainee, Rip Torn was their gruff boss, and makeup artist Rick Baker and a team of f/x wizards created a series of fanciful, grotesque aliens. Although the aliens had the technology for interplanetary travel, they were no match for the big guns of the MIB.

In *MIB II*, the guns are even bigger and the aliens are even slimier, although they do take sexy human form when one of them, Serleena, morphs into Lara Flynn Boyle. Another one, named Scrad (Johnny Knoxville), turns into a human who has a second neck with a smaller version of the same head, although that is not as amusing as you might hope.

The plot: The aliens are here to capture something, I'm not sure what, that will allow them to destroy Earth. The top MIB agent is now Jay (Smith), who needs the help of Kay (Jones), but Kay's memory has been erased by a "deneuralizer" and must be restored so that he can protect whatever it is the aliens want. Kay is currently working at the post office, which might have inspired more jokes than it does.

Smith and Jones fit comfortably in their roles and do what they can, but the movie doesn't give them much to work with. The biggest contribution is a dog named Frank (voice by Tim Blaney), whose role is much expanded from the first movie. Frank is human in everything but form, a tough-talking streetwise canine who keeps up a running commentary as the reunited MIB chase aliens through New York. One of the eyewitnesses they question is a pizza waitress named Laura, played by the beautiful Rosario Dawson, who Jay likes so much he forgets to deneuralize.

The special effects are good, but often pointless. As the movie throws strange aliens at us, we aren't much moved—more like mildly interested. There's a subway worm at the outset that eats most of a train without being anything more than an obvious special effect (we're looking at the technique, not the worm), and later there are other aliens who look more like doodles at a concept session than anything we can get much worked up about. There is, however, a very odd scene set in a train station locker, which is occupied by a chanting mob of little creatures who worship the key holder, and I would have liked to see more of them: What possible worldview do they have? If *Men in Black III* opens with the occupants of the locker, I will at least have hope for it.

Miss Congeniality 2: Armed and Fabulous

(DIRECTED BY JOHN PASQUIN; STARRING SANDRA BULLOCK, REGINA KING; 2005)

Having made the unnecessary *Miss Congeniality,* Sandra Bullock now returns with the doubly unnecessary *Miss Congeniality 2: Armed and Fabulous.* Perhaps it is not entirely unnecessary in the eyes of the producers, since the first film had a worldwide gross of $212 million, not counting home video, but it's unnecessary in the sense that there is no good reason to go and actually see it.

That despite the presence of Sandra Bullock, who remains a most agreeable actress and brings what charm she can to a character who never seems plausible enough to be funny. Does a character in a comedy need to be plausible? I think it helps. It is not enough for a character to "act funny." A lot of humor comes from tension between who the character is and what the character does, or is made to do. Since Miss Congeniality is never other than a ditz, that she acts like one is not hilarious.

You will recall that Gracie Hart (Bullock) is an FBI agent who in the first film impersonated a beauty pageant contestant in order to infiltrate—but enough about that plot, since all you need to know is that the publicity from the pageant has made her so famous that *MC2* opens with a bank robber recognizing her and aborting an FBI sting. Gracie is obviously too famous to function as an ordinary agent, so the FBI director makes her a public relations creature—the new "face of the bureau."

Since the Michael Caine character in the first film successfully groomed her into a beauty pageant finalist, you'd think Gracie had learned something about seemly behavior, but no, she's still a klutz. The bureau supplies her with Joel (Diedrich Bader), a Queer Guy for the Straight Agent, who gives her tips on deportment (no snorting as a form of laughter), manners (chew with your mouth closed), and fashion (dress like a Barbie doll). She is also assigned a new partner: Sam Fuller (Regina King), a tough agent with anger management issues, who likes to throw people around and is allegedly Gracie's bodyguard, assuming she doesn't kill her.

As Gracie is rolled out as the FBI's new face, there's a funny TV chat scene with Regis Philbin (Regis: "You don't look like J. Edgar Hoover." Gracie: "Really? Because this is his dress."). Then comes an emergency: Miss United States (Heather Burns), Gracie's buddy from the beauty pageant, is kidnapped in Las Vegas, along with the pageant manager (William Shatner).

Gracie and Sam fly to Vegas and humiliate the bureau by tackling the real Dolly Parton under the impression she is an imposter. Then they find themselves doing Tina Turner impersonations in a drag club. They also reenact the usual clichés of two partners who hate each other until they learn to love each other. And they impersonate Nancy Drew in their investigation, which leads to the thrilling rescue of Miss United States from the least likely place in the world where any kidnapper would think of hiding her.

Now a word about the name of Regina King's character, Sam Fuller. This is, of course, the same name as the famous movie director Sam Fuller

(*The Big Red One, Shock Corridor, The Naked Kiss*). Fuller (1912–1997) was an icon among other directors, who gave him countless cameo roles in their movies just because his presence was like a blessing; he appeared in films by Amos Gitai, Aki Kaurismaki, his brother Mika Kaurismaki, Larry Cohen, Claude Chabrol, Steven Spielberg, Alexandre Rockwell (twice), Wim Wenders (three times), and Jean-Luc Godard, the first to use him, in *Pierrot le Fou,* where he stood against a wall, puffed a cigar, and told the camera, "Film is like a battleground."

It may seem that I have strayed from the topic, but be honest: You are happier to learn these factoids about Sam Fuller than to find out which Las Vegas landmark the kidnappers use to imprison Miss United States and William Shatner. The only hint I will provide is that they almost drown, and Sandra Bullock almost drowns, too, as she did most famously in *Speed 2,* a movie about a runaway ocean liner. I traditionally end my reviews of the *Miss Congeniality* movies by noting that I was the only critic in the world who liked *Speed 2,* and I see no reason to abandon that tradition, especially since if there is a *Miss Congeniality 3* and it doesn't have Sam Fuller in it, I may be at a loss for words.

Monkeybone

(DIRECTED BY HENRY SELICK; STARRING BRENDAN FRASER, BRIDGET FONDA; 2001)

A character played by Brendan Fraser spends half of *Monkeybone* on life support, and so does the movie. Both try to stay alive with injections of nightmare juice. The movie labors hard, the special effects are admirable, no expense has been spared, and yet the movie never takes off; it's a bright idea the filmmakers were unable to breathe into life.

Fraser plays a cartoonist named Stu Miley ("S. Miley"—ho, ho). He's created a character named Monkeybone, which has become enormously popular and might soon star on its own TV show—except that Stu is one of those unsullied artists who shies away from success. He flees a fancy reception with his girlfriend Julie (Bridget Fonda), but as they're driving away a giant plastic Monkeybone toy in the back seat suddenly inflates, causing a crash. Julie is unharmed, but Stu goes into a coma, with his sister negotiating with the hospital about how soon they can pull the plug.

The coma is, in fact, action-packed. In his mind, Stu has taken an escalator to Downtown, a nightmare dreamland nightclub ruled by Hypnos (Giancarlo Esposito); it's not far from Thanatopolis, ruled by Death (Whoopi Goldberg). Here Monkeybone is the emcee, and exit passes are hard to come by. That leads to a scheme by Monkeybone ("I'm tired of being a figment!") to occupy Stu's body and escape from Downtown.

Meanwhile, on earth, Stu's time is drawing short and his sister has her hand on the plug. Julie scans a brain chart and intuits that Stu is trapped in a "nightmare loop." She thinks maybe an emergency injection of Nightmare Juice might scare him awake. Through a coincidental miracle of timing, Monkeybone leaves Downtown and possesses Stu's body just as the juice hits, so when he comes out of the coma and starts acting strangely, she blames it on the juice.

And so on. The plot is not exactly the issue here. *Monkeybone* was directed by Henry Selick, who also made *The Nightmare Before Christmas* and *James and the Giant Peach*. His ability to blend live action with makeup, special effects, and computer effects is about as good as it gets—and he leans away from computers and in the direction of bizarre sets and makeup and stop-action animation, which gives his work an eerie third-dimensionality unmatched by slicker computer effects.

Here he achieves technical marvels, but the movie just doesn't deliver. The Monkeybone character doesn't earn its screen time; it's just a noxious pest. Brendan Fraser has been at home before in cartoon roles (*George of the Jungle, Dudley Do-Right*), but here he seems more like the victim of the joke than the perpetrator, and Bridget Fonda's girlfriend is earnest and plucky, but not funny (she has to look concerned about Stu all the time).

One sequence made me smile. It involves Chris Kattan, from *Saturday Night Live*, as an organ transplant donor snatched from the hospital in mid-operation and lofted over the city by a hot air balloon, while spare parts fall from his incision and are greeted below by grateful dogs.

Downtown itself looks like the amusement park from (or in) Hell, and there's a lot of *Beetlejuice* in the inspiration for the strange creatures, one-eyed and otherwise, who live there. But strangeness is not enough. There must also be humor, and characters who exist for some reason other than to look bizarre. That rule would include Whoopi Goldberg's Death, who is sadly underwritten, and played by Whoopi as if we're supposed to keep repeating: "Wow! Look! Death is being played by Whoopi Goldberg!" It is a truth too often forgotten that casting a famous actor in a weird cameo is the setup of the joke, not the punch line.

Monster-in-Law

(DIRECTED BY ROBERT LUKETIC; STARRING JENNIFER LOPEZ, JANE FONDA; 2005)

Faithful readers will know I'm an admirer of Jennifer Lopez, and older readers will recall my admiration for Jane Fonda, whom I first met on the set of *Barbarella* (1968), so it has been all uphill ever since. Watching *Monster-in-Law*, I tried to transfer into Fan Mode, enjoying their presence while ignoring the movie. I did not succeed. My reveries were interrupted by bulletins from my conscious mind, which hated the movie.

I hated it above all because it wasted an opportunity. You do not keep Jane Fonda offscreen for fifteen years only to bring her back as a specimen of rabid Momism. You write a role for her. It makes sense. It fits her. You like her in it. It gives her a relationship with Jennifer Lopez that could plausibly exist in our time and space. It gives her a son who has not wandered over after the *E.R.* auditions. And it doesn't supply a supporting character who undercuts every scene she's in by being more on-topic than any of the leads.

No, you don't get rid of the supporting character, whose name is Ruby and who is played by Wanda Sykes. What you do is lift the whole plot up on rollers, and use heavy equipment to relocate it in Ruby's universe, which is a lot more promising than the rabbit hole this movie falls into. *Monster-in-Law* fails the Gene Siskel Test: "Is this film more interesting than a documentary of the same actors having lunch?"

The movie opens by establishing Charlotte "Charlie" Cantilini (Lopez) as an awfully nice person. She walks dogs, she works as a temp, she likes to cook, she's friendly and loyal, she roughs it on Venice Beach in an apartment that can't cost more than $2,950 a month, she has a gay neighbor who's her best bud. I enjoyed these scenes, right up until the Meet Cute with Young Dr. Kevin Fields (Michael Vartan), a surgeon who falls in love with her. She can't believe a guy like that would really like a girl like her, which is unlikely, since anyone who looks like Jennifer Lopez and walks dogs on the boardwalk has already been hit on by every dot-com entrepreneur and boy band dropout in Santa Monica, plus Donald Trump and Charlie Sheen.

Dr. Kevin's mother, Viola, played by Fonda, is not so much a clone of Barbara Walters as a rubbing. You get the outlines, but there's a lot of missing detail. In a flashback, we see that she was a famous television personality, fired under circumstances no one associated with this movie could possibly have thought were realistic—and then allowed to telecast one more program, when in fact security guards would be helping her carry cardboard boxes out to her car. Her last show goes badly when she attempts to kill her guest.

When we meet her, she's "fresh off the funny farm," guzzling booze, taking pills, and getting wake-up calls from Ruby, who is played by Sykes as if she thinks the movie needs an adult chaperone. Viola is seen as a possessive, egotistical, imperious monster who is, and I quote, "on the verge of a psychotic break." The far verge, I would say. When she learns that Dr. Kevin is engaged to marry Charlie, she begins a campaign to sabotage their romance, moaning, "My son the brilliant surgeon is going to marry a temp."

The movie's most peculiar scenes involve Charlie being steadfastly and heroically nice while Viola hurls rudeness and abuse at her. There is a sequence where Viola throws a "reception" for her prospective daughter-in-law and invites the most famous people in the world, so the little temp will be humiliated; Charlie is so serene in her self-confidence that even though she's dressed more for volleyball than diplomacy, she keeps her composure.

All during her monster act, we don't for a second believe Fonda's character because if she really were such a monster, she would fire Ruby, who insults her with a zeal approaching joy. Anyone who keeps Ruby on the payroll has her feet on the ground. Another problem is that Dr. Kevin is a world-class wimp, who actually proposes marriage to Charlie while his mother is standing right there. No doubt Dr. Phil will provide counsel in their wedding bed.

Eventually we realize that Fonda's character consists entirely of a scene waiting to happen: The scene where her heart melts, she realizes Charlie is terrific, and she accepts her. Everything else Viola does is an exercise in postponing that moment. The longer we wait, the more we wonder why (a) Charlie doesn't belt her, and (b) Charlie doesn't jump Dr. Kevin—actually, I meant to write "dump," but either will do. By the time the happy ending arrives, it's too late, because by then we don't want Charlie to marry Dr. Kevin. We want her to go back to walking the dogs. She was happier, we were happier, the dogs were happier.

Mr. Deeds

(DIRECTED BY STEVEN BRILL; STARRING ADAM SANDLER, WINONA RYDER; 2002)

At one point during the long ordeal of *Mr. Deeds,* it is said of the Adam Sandler character, "He doesn't share our sense of ironic detachment." Is this a private joke by the writer? If there's one thing Sandler's Mr. Deeds has, it's ironic detachment. Like so many Sandler characters, he seems fundamentally insincere, to be aiming for the laugh even at serious moments. Since the 1936 Frank Capra film *Mr. Deeds Goes to Town* was above all sincere, we wonder how this project was chosen; did Adam Sandler look at Gary Cooper and see a role for himself?

He plays Longfellow Deeds, pizzeria owner in the hamlet of Mandrake Falls, New Hampshire. The pizzeria is one of those establishments required in all comedies about small towns, where every single character in town gathers every single day to provide an audience for the hero, crossed with a Greek chorus. Nobody does anything in Mandrake Falls except sit in the pizzeria and talk about Deeds. When he leaves town, they watch him on the TV.

Turns out Deeds is the distant relative of an elderly zillionaire who freezes to death in the very act of conquering Everest. Control of his media empire and a $40 billion fortune goes to Deeds, who is obviously too good-hearted and simpleminded to deserve it, so a corporate executive named Cedar (Peter Gallagher) conspires to push him aside. Meanwhile, when Deeds hits New York, a trash TV show makes him its favorite target, and producer Babe Bennett (Winona Ryder) goes undercover, convinces Deeds she loves him, and sets him up for humiliation. Then she discovers she loves him, too late.

Frank Capra played this story straight. But the 2002 film doesn't really believe in it, and breaks the mood with absurdly inappropriate "comedy" scenes. Consider a scene where Deeds meets his new butler Emilio (John Turturro). Emilio has a foot fetish. Deeds doubts Emilio will like his right foot, which is pitch black after a childhood bout of frostbite. The foot has no feeling, Deeds says, inviting Emilio to pound it with a fireplace poker. When Deeds doesn't flinch, Turturro actually punctures the foot with the point of the poker, at which point I listened attentively for sounds of laughter in the theater and heard none.

There's no chemistry between Deeds and Babe, but then how could there be, considering that their characters have no existence except as the puppets in scenes of plot manipulation. After Deeds grows disillusioned with her, there is a reconciliation inspired after she falls through the ice on a pond and he breaks through to save her using the black foot. In story conferences, do they discuss scenes like this and nod approvingly? Tell me, for I want to know.

The moral center of the story is curious. The media empire, we learn, controls enormous resources and employs fifty thousand people. The evil Cedar wants to break it up. The good-hearted Deeds fights to keep it together so those fifty thousand people won't be out of work. This is essentially a movie that wants to win our hearts with a populist hero who risks his entire fortune in order to ensure the survival of Time-AOL-Warner-Disney-Murdoch. What would Frank Capra have thought about the little guy bravely standing up for the monolith?

Of the many notes I took during the film, one deserves to be shared with you. There is a scene in the movie where Deeds, the fire chief in Mandrake Falls, becomes a hero during a Manhattan fire. He scales the side of a building and rescues a woman's cats, since she refuses to be rescued before them. One after another, the cats are thrown onto a fireman's net. Finally there is a cat that is on fire. The blazing feline is tossed from the window and bounces into a bucket of water, emerging wet but intact, ho, ho, and then Deeds and the heavy-set cat lady jump together and crash through the net, but Deeds' fall is cushioned by the fat lady, who is also not harmed, ho ho, giving us a heartrending happy ending.

That is not what I wrote in my notes. It is only the setup. What I noted was that in the woman's kitchen, nothing is seen to be on fire except for a box of Special K cereal. This is a species of product placement previously unthinkable. In product placement conferences, do they discuss scenes like this and nod approvingly? Tell me, for oh, how I want to know.

National Lampoon's Van Wilder

(DIRECTED BY WALT BECKER; STARRING RYAN REYNOLDS, TARA REID; 2002)

Watching *National Lampoon's Van Wilder,* I grew nostalgic for the lost innocence of a movie like *American Pie,* in which human semen found itself in a pie. In *National Lampoon's Van Wilder,* dog semen is baked in a pastry. Is it only a matter of time until the heroes of teenage gross-out comedies are injecting turtle semen directly through their stomach walls?

National Lampoon's Van Wilder, a pale shadow of *National Lampoon's Animal House,* tells the story of Van Wilder (Ryan Reynolds), who has been the Biggest Man on Campus for seven glorious undergraduate years. He doesn't want to graduate, and why should he, since he has clout, fame, babes, and the adulation of the entire campus (except, of course, for the professor whose parking space he swipes, and the vile fraternity boy who is his sworn enemy).

Van Wilder is essentially a nice guy, which is a big risk for a movie like this to take; he raises funds for the swimming team, tries to restrain suicidal students, and throws legendary keg parties. Ryan Reynolds is, I suppose, the correct casting choice for Van Wilder, since the character is not a devious slacker but merely a permanent student. That makes him, alas, a little boring, and Reynolds (from ABC's *Two Guys and a Girl*) brings along no zing: He's a standard leading man when the movie cries out for a manic character actor. Jack Black in this role would have been a home run.

Is Van Wilder too good to be true? That's what Gwen (Tara Reid) wonders. She's a journalism student who wants to do an in-depth piece about Van for the campus paper. Of course she's the girlfriend of the vile frat boy, and of course her investigation inspires her to admire the real Van Wilder while deploring his public image. Tara Reid is remarkably attractive, as you may remember from *Josie and the Pussycats* and *American Pie 2,* but much of the time she simply seems to be imitating still photos of Renee Zellweger smiling.

That leaves, let's see, Kal Penn as Taj, the Indian-American student who lands the job as Van Wilder's assistant, and spends much of his time using a stereotyped accent while reciting lists of synonyms for oral sex. I cannot complain, since the hero's buddy in every movie in this genre is always a sex-crazed zealot, and at least this film uses nontraditional casting. (Casting directors face a Catch-22: They cast a white guy, and everybody wants to know why he had to be white. So they cast an ethnic guy, and everybody complains about the negative stereotype. Maybe the way out is to cast the ethnic guy as the hero and the white guy as the horny doofus.)

The movie is a barfathon that takes full advantage of the apparent MPAA guidelines in which you can do pretty much anything with bodily functions except involve them in healthy sex. The movie contains semen, bare breasts and butts, epic flatulence, bizarre forms of masturbation, public nudity, projectile vomiting, and an extended scene of explosive defecation with sound effects that resemble the daily duties of the Port-a-Loo serviceman, in reverse. There are also graphic shots of enormous testicles, which are allowed under the *National Geographic* loophole since they belong to Van Wilder's pet bulldog. Presumably the MPAA would not permit this if it had reason to believe there were dogs in the audience.

"On a scale of one to ten shots of bourbon needed to make a pledge ralph," writes Bob Patterson of the Web site Delusions of Adequacy, "this film will get a very strong five from most college-age film fans who are not offended by vulgar humor. Older filmgoers who might be offended by such offerings are encouraged to do something that is physically impossible (i.e., lift yourself up by your bootstraps)."

Although this is obviously the review the movie deserves, I confess the rating scale baffles me. Is it better or worse if a film makes you ralph? Patterson implies that older filmgoers might be offended by vulgar humor. There is a flaw in this reasoning: It is not age but humor that is the variable. Laughter for me was such a physical impossibility during *National Lampoon's Van Wilder* that had I not been pledged to sit through the film, I would have lifted myself up by my bootstraps and fled.

New York Minute

(DIRECTED BY DENNIE GORDON; STARRING MARY-KATE OLSEN, ASHLEY OLSEN; 2004)
They say baseball is popular because everyone thinks they can play it. Similar reasoning may explain the popularity of the Olsen twins: Teenage girls love them because they believe they could *be* them. What, after all, do Mary-Kate and Ashley do in *New York Minute* that could not be done by any reasonably presentable female adolescent? Their careers are founded not on what they do, but on the vicarious identification of their fans, who enjoy seeing two girls making millions for doing what just about anybody could do.

The movie offers the spectacle of two cheerful and attractive seventeen-year-olds who have the maturity of silly thirteen-year-olds, and romp through a day's adventures in Manhattan, a city that in this movie is populated entirely by hyperactive character actors. Nothing that happens to them has any relationship with anything else that happens to them, except for the unifying principle that it all happens to *them*. That explains how they happen to be (1) chased by a recreational vehicle through heavy traffic, (2) wading through the sewers of New York, (3) getting a beauty makeover in a Harlem salon, (4) in possession of a kidnapped dog, (5) pursued by music pirates, (6) in danger in Chinatown, and (7) . . . oh, never mind.

Given the inescapable fact that they are twins, the movie of course gives them completely opposite looks and personalities, and then leads us inexorably to the moment when one will have to impersonate the other. Mary-Kate Olsen plays Roxy Ryan, the sloppy girl who skips school and dreams of getting her demo tape backstage at a "punk rock" video shoot. Ashley Olsen plays Jane Ryan, a goody two-shoes who will win a four-year scholarship to Oxford University if she gives the winning speech in a competition at Columbia. Perhaps in England she will discover that the university is in the town of Oxford, and so can correct friends who plan to visit her in London. (I am sure the screenwriters knew the university was in Oxford, but were concerned that audience members might confuse "going to" Oxford and "being in" Oxford, and played it safe, since London is the only city in England many members of the audience will have heard of, if indeed they have.)

But I'm being mean, and this movie is harmless and as eager as a homeless puppy to make friends. In fact, it has a puppy. It also has a truant officer, played by Eugene Levy in a performance that will be valuable to film historians, since it demonstrates what Eugene Levy's irreducible essence is when he plays a character who is given absolutely nothing funny to say or do. His performance suggests that he stayed at home and phoned in his mannerisms. More inexplicable is Andy Richter's work as a limousine driver with sinister connections to music piracy rackets. He is given an accent, from where I could not guess, although I could guess why: At a story conference, the filmmakers looked in despair at his pointless character and said, "What the hell, maybe we should give him an accent."

Because the movie all takes place during one day and Roxy is being chased by a truant officer, it compares itself to *Ferris Bueller's Day Off*. It might as reasonably compare itself to *The Third Man* because they wade through sewers. *New York Minute* is a textbook example of a film created as a "vehicle," but without any ideas about where the vehicle should go. The Olsen twins are not children any longer, yet not quite poised to become adults, and so they're given the props and costumes of seventeen-year-olds, but carefully shielded from the reality. That any seventeen-year-old girl in America could take seriously the rock band that Roxy worships is beyond contemplation. It doesn't even look like a band to itself.

The events involving the big speaking competition are so labored that occasionally the twins seem to be looking back over their shoulders for the plot to catch up. Of course, there is a moment when all the characters and plot strands meet on the stage of the speech contest, with the other competitors looking on in bafflement, and of course (spoiler warning, ho, ho), Jane wins the scholarship. In fact (major spoiler warning), she does so without giving the speech, because the man who donates the scholarship reads her notes, which were dropped on the stage, and *knows* it would have been the winning speech had she only been able to deliver it. Unlikely as it seems that Jane could win in such a way, this scenario certainly sidesteps the difficulty of having her deliver a speech that would sound as if she could win.

The Next Best Thing

(DIRECTED BY JOHN SCHLESINGER; STARRING RUPERT EVERETT, MADONNA; 2000)

The Next Best Thing is a garage sale of gay issues, harnessed to a plot as exhausted as a junk man's horse. There are times when the characters don't know if they're living their lives, or enacting edifying little dramas for an educational film. The screenplay's so evenhanded it has *no* likable characters, either gay or straight; after seeing this film, I wanted to move to Garry Shandling's world in *What Planet Are You From?* where nobody has sex.

Not that anybody has a lot of sex in this PG-13 film. The story hinges on a murky event that takes place offscreen late one alcoholic night between Abbie (Madonna) and her gay best friend Robert (Rupert Everett). They were both in drunken blackouts, although of course by the next morning they're able to discuss their blackouts with wit and style, unlike your average person, who would be puking. Abbie gets pregnant and decides to have the baby, and Robert announces he will be a live-in father to the child, although he doesn't go so far as to become a husband to its mother.

Both Abbie and Robert are right up to date when it comes to sexual open-mindedness. Robert still dates, and Abbie's OK with that, although when Abbie meets a guy named Ben (Benjamin Bratt), Robert turns into a green-eyed monster. That's because Ben wants to marry Abbie and move to New York, and where would that leave Robert? If you think this movie, which begins as a sexual comedy, is going to end up as a stultifying docudrama about child custody, with big courtroom scenes before the obligatory stern black female judge, you are no more than ordinarily prescient.

The movie's problem is that it sees every side of all issues. It sides with Robert's need to be a father, and Benjamin's need to be a husband and lover, and Abbie's need to have a best friend, a husband, a lover, a son, and a lawyer. Luckily there is plenty of money for all of this, because Abbie is a yoga instructor and Robert is a gardener, and we know what piles of money you can make in those jobs, especially in the movies. I wish the film had scaled its lifestyles to the realities of service industry workers, instead of having the characters live in the kinds of places where they can dance around the living room to (I am not kidding) Fred Astaire's "Steppin' Out with My Baby" and have catered backyard birthday parties that I clock at $10,000, easy.

In describing the plot, I've deliberately left out two or three twists that had me stifling groans of disbelief. It's not that they're implausible; it's that they're not necessary. Any movie is bankrupt anyway when it depends on Perry Mason–style, last-minute, unexpected courtroom appearances to solve what should be an emotional choice.

Rupert Everett, "openly gay," as they say, must have had to grit his teeth to get through some of his scenes. Consider a sequence where, as Abbie's best friend, he is delegated to pick up her house keys after she breaks up with her early boyfriend, Kevin. ("I want to date less complicated women, Kevin tells her.") Kevin is a record producer, and we see him mixing the tracks for a rap group when Robert swishes in and pretends to be his ex-lover, while there are lots of yuks from the homophobic black rappers. Give the scene credit: At least it's not politically correct.

Madonna never emerges as a plausible human being in the movie; she's more like a spokesperson for a video on alternative parenting lifestyles. She begins the movie with a quasi-British accent, but by the halfway mark we get line readings like "we can be in each other's lifes" (a Brit, and indeed many an American, would say "lives").

This and other details should have been noticed by the director, John Schlesinger, whose career has included *Midnight Cowboy, Sunday Bloody Sunday, The Falcon and the Snowman, Madame Sousatzka,* and now . . . this?

Watching the movie, I asked myself why so many movies with homosexuals feel they need to be about homosexuality. Why can't a movie just get over it? I submit as evidence the magical new film *Wonder Boys,* in which the homosexuality of the character played by Robert Downey Jr. is completely absorbed into the much larger notion of who he is as a person. Nobody staggers backward and gasps out that his character is gay, because of course he's gay and everybody has known that for a long time and, hey, some people *are* gay, y'know? Watching *The Next Best Thing,* we suspect that if sexuality were banned as a topic of conversation, Abbie and Robert would be reduced to trading yoga and gardening tips.

No Such Thing

(DIRECTED BY HAL HARTLEY; STARRING SARAH POLLEY, ROBERT JOHN BURKE; 2002)

Hal Hartley has always marched in the avant garde, but this time he marches alone. Followers will have to be drafted. *No Such Thing* is inexplicable, shapeless, dull. It doesn't even rise to entertaining badness. Coming four years after his intriguing if unsuccessful *Henry Fool,* and filmed mostly on location in Iceland with Icelandic money, it suggests a film that was made primarily because he couldn't get anything else off the ground.

The film's original title was *Monster.* That this is a better title than *No Such Thing* is beyond debate. The story involves a monstrous beast who lives on an island off the Icelandic coast, and is immortal, short-tempered, and alcoholic. As the film opens the monster (Robert John Burke) has killed a TV news crew, which inspires a cynical New York network executive (Helen Mirren) to dispatch a young reporter (Sarah Polley) to interview him. Polley's fiancé was among the monster's victims.

Her plane crashes in the ocean, she is the sole survivor and therefore makes good news herself, and is nursed back to life by Julie Christie, in a role no more thankless than the others in this film. Since the filming, Julie Christie had a facelift and Helen Mirren won an Oscar nomination. Life moves on.

We seek in vain for shreds of recognizable human motivation. By the time she meets the monster, Polley seems to have forgotten he killed her fiancé. By the time she returns with the monster to New York, the world seems to have forgotten. The monster wants to go to New York to enlist the services of Dr. Artaud (Baltasar Kormakur), a scientist who can destroy matter and therefore perhaps can bring an end to the misery of the immortal beast. We are praying that in the case of this movie, matter includes celluloid.

Elements of the movie seem not merely half-baked, but never to have seen the inside of an oven. Helen Mirren's TV news program and its cynical values are treated with the satirical insights of callow undergraduates who will be happy with a C-plus in film class. Characterizations are so shallow they consist only of mannerisms; Mirren chain-smokes cigarettes, Dr. Artaud chain-smokes cigars, the monster swigs from a bottle. At a social reception late in the film, Sarah Polley turns up in a leather bondage dress with a push-up bra. Why, oh why?

Hal Hartley, still only forty-two, has proudly marched to his own drummer since I first met him at Sundance 1990 with *The Unbelievable Truth*, a good film that introduced two of his favorite actors, Adrienne Shelly and Robert Burke (now Robert John Burke, as the monster). Since then his titles have included *Trust* (1991), *Simple Men* (1992), *Amateur* (1994), *Flirt* (1995), and *Henry Fool*. My star ratings have wavered around 2 or 2½, and my reviews have mostly expressed interest and hope—hope that he will define what he's looking for and share it with us.

Now I'm beginning to wonder how long the wait will be. A Hartley film can be analyzed and justified, and a review can try to mold the intractable material into a more comprehensible form. But why does Hartley make us do all the heavy lifting? Can he consider a film that is self-evident and forthcoming? One that doesn't require us to plunder the quarterly film magazines for deconstruction? I don't mind heavy lifting when a film is challenging or fun, like *Mulholland Drive*. But not when all the weight is in the packing materials.

In *No Such Thing* we have promising elements. The relationship between the monster and the TV reporter suggests *Beauty and the Beast* (more the Cocteau than the Disney version), but that vein is not mined, and the TV news satire is too callow to connect in any way with real targets. Many of the characters, like Dr. Artaud, seem like houseguests given a costume and appearing in the host's play just to be good sports. That gifted actors appear here shows how desperate they are for challenging parts, and how willing to take chances. Hartley has let them down.

The One

(Directed by James Wong; starring Jet Li, Carla Gugino; 2001)

There is a vast question lurking at the center of *The One*, and the question is: Why? Assuming there are 124 universes and that you existed in all of them and could travel among them, why would you want to kill off the other 123 versions of you? This is, I submit, a good question, but not one discussed in any depth by Yulaw (Jet Li), the villain of the film. Jet Li also plays the film's hero and one of its victims, but neither of them understandably knows the answer.

The film opens with a narration informing us that there are parallel universes, and that "a force exists who seeks to destroy the balance so that he can become—*The One!*" Apparently every time one of your other selves dies, his power is distributed among the survivors. If Yulaw kills 123 selves, he has the power of 124. Follow this logic far enough, and retirement homes would be filled with elderly geezers who have outlived their others and now have the strength of 124, meaning they can bend canes with their bare hands and produce mighty bowel movements with scornful ease.

What does Yulaw hope to accomplish with his power? He might, the narrator suggests, become God—and thus, if killed, might bring all of creation to an end. A guy like this, you don't want him getting in fights and taking chances. But the God theory is theologically unsound, because God works from the top down and didn't get where he is by knocking off the competition. Maybe Yulaw is just a megalomaniac who gets off on being able to beat up everyone in the room. Maybe one of the differences between a good martial arts movie and one that is merely technically competent is that in the good ones, the characters have a motivation, and in the others life is just a competitive sport.

Yulaw defeats Lawless, one of his other selves, fairly early in the film, and then zeroes in on Gabe, who is a Los Angeles County sheriff's deputy. Gabe knows nothing of the multiverses, but is, under the rules, as strong as half of the dead men, and so a good match for Yulaw. Meanwhile, Yulaw is pursued from his home universe by Roedecker (Delroy Lindo) and Funsch (Jason Statham), agents of the Multiverse Bureau of Investigations. His wife, woman, girlfriend, or sidekick in all of these worlds is played by Carla Gugino.

The possibilities with this plot are endless. Alas, the movie is interested only in fight scenes, and uses the latest in computer-generated effects to show the various Jet Li characters as they throw enemies into the air, dodge bullets, hold a motorcycle in each hand and slam them together against an opponent, etc. The final epic confrontation features Jet Li fighting himself. Both are wearing black jumpsuits at the start of the fight, but the evil Jet Li shows consideration for the audience by stripping down to a blue top, so we can tell him apart from the good Jet Li.

This titanic closing fight, by the way, may use cutting-edge effects, but has been written with slavish respect for ancient clichés. It begins with the venerable It's Only a Cat Scene, in which a cat startles a character (but not the audience) by leaping at the lens. Then the characters retire to a Steam and Flame Factory, one of those Identikit movie sets filled with machines that produce copious quantities of steam, flames, and sparks. Where do they have their fight? On a catwalk, of course. Does anyone end up clinging by his fingertips? Don't make me laugh.

The movie offers brainless high-tech action without interesting dialogue, characters, motivation, or texture. In other words, it's sure to be popular.

On the Line

(DIRECTED BY ERIC BROSS; STARRING LANCE BASS, EMMANUELLE CHRIQUI; 2001)

Just when you think a dating movie can't conceivably involve more impossible coincidences and Idiot Plot situations, along comes another movie to prove you wrong. After *Serendipity,* here is *On the Line,* starring Lance Bass of 'N Sync in an agonizingly creaky movie that laboriously plods through a plot so contrived that the only thing real about it is its length. In both movies, a boy and a girl Meet Cute and instantly realize they are destined for each other, and then they plunge into a series of absurd contrivances designed to keep them apart.

Just once, could they meet and fall in love, and then the movie would be about their young lives together? I'm weary of romances about lovers who devote years to living far apart and barely missing chances to meet again. If this genre ever inspires a satire, it will end with the boy and girl sitting next to each other on an airplane—*still* not realizing they are together again, because by then they will be eighty, having spent sixty years missing each other by seconds.

Lance Bass plays Kevin Gibbons, a low-level Chicago ad executive who has no trouble with girls unless he really likes them. Then he freezes up and can't close the deal. One day on the L he meets Abbey (Emmanuelle

Chriqui), who has a sunny smile and a warm personality, and can recite all of the American presidents, in order! So can Lance! Somewhere between Buchanan and Bush they realize they are meant for each other. But Kevin just *can't* ask for her phone number. And despite decades of feminist advances, all Abbey can do is smile helplessly and leave their future in his hands. They part with rueful smiles. No, make that Rueful Smiles.

Later, Kevin kicks himself and moans to his roommates about the perfect girl who got away. These roommates include fellow 'N Sync-er Joey Fatone, as Rod, who sings in an open-mike saloon and specializes in kicking the amp; Eric (the comedian GQ), a devoted mope; and Randy (James Bulliard), the brains of the outfit. The four guys spend countless precious screen minutes hanging around their flat engaging in redundant dialogue while we desperately want the movie to *lose the roommates* and *bring back the girl!*

But no. Films for the teenage demographic are terrified of romance and intimacy between the sexes, and shyly specialize in boys plotting about girls and girls plotting about boys, with as few actual scenes between boys and girls as possible. So after Kevin papers the town with posters seeking the girl he met on the train, and dozens of calls flood in, the roommates divide up the calls and date the girls (not telling Kevin, of course).

Well, obviously, only the right girl would know she was not going out with Kevin. So when Eric dates Abbey and she knows he's not Kevin— *that's the girl!* Right? But no. Eric is dense to the point of perversity, and spends their date not saying the few obvious words that need to be said, while acting like a pig and giving Abbey the impression that Kevin planned this humiliation. This is the Idiot Plot gone berserk. One sentence—*one word!*—and all would be solved, but Eric and the screenplay contort themselves into grotesque evasions to avoid stating the crashingly obvious.

So of course Abbey is crushed, and so are we, because we realize we are in the grip of a power greater than ourselves—Hollywood's determination to make films at the level of remedial reading. No one involved in the making of this film is as stupid as the characters, so why do they think the audience is? Why not for once allow young lovers to be smart, curious, articulate, and quick?

It must be said that Lance Bass and Emmanuelle Chriqui have sweet chemistry together, in the few moments they are able to snatch away from the forces designed to separate them. Bass is likable (but then likability is the primary talent of 'N Sync), and Chriqui, from Montreal via *Snow Day* and *A.I.,* is warm and charming and has a great smile. I can imagine a lovely love story involving these two actors. Too bad *On the Line* goes to such lengths to avoid making it.

Pearl Harbor

(DIRECTED BY MICHAEL BAY; STARRING BEN AFFLECK, JOSH HARTNETT; 2001)

Pearl Harbor is a two-hour movie squeezed into three hours, about how on December 7, 1941, the Japanese staged a surprise attack on an American love triangle. Its centerpiece is forty minutes of redundant special effects, surrounded by a love story of stunning banality. The film has been directed without grace, vision, or originality, and although you may walk out quoting lines of dialogue, it will not be because you admire them.

The filmmakers seem to have aimed the film at an audience that may not have heard of Pearl Harbor or perhaps even of World War II. This is the *Weekly Reader* version. If you have the slightest knowledge of the events in the film, you will know more than it can tell you. There is no sense of history, strategy, or context; according to this movie, Japan attacked Pearl Harbor because America cut off its oil supply and they were down to an eighteen-month reserve. Would going to war restore the fuel sources? Did they perhaps also have imperialist designs? Movie doesn't say.

So shaky is the film's history that at the end, when Jimmy Doolittle's Tokyo raiders crash-land in China, they're shot at by Japanese patrols with only a murky throwaway explanation about the Sino-Japanese war already under way. I predict some viewers will leave the theater sincerely confused about why there were Japanese in China.

As for the movie's portrait of the Japanese themselves, it is so oblique that Japanese audiences will find little to complain about apart from the fact that they play such a small role in their own raid. There are several scenes where the Japanese high command debates military tactics, but all of their dialogue is strictly expository; they state facts but do not emerge with personalities or passions. Only Admiral Yamamoto (Mako) is seen as an individual, and his dialogue seems to have been singled out with the hindsight of history. Congratulated on a brilliant raid, he demurs, "A brilliant man would find a way not to fight a war." And later, "I fear all we have done is to awaken a sleeping giant."

Do you imagine at any point the Japanese high command engaged in the 1941 Japanese equivalent of exchanging high-fives and shouting "Yes!" while pumping their fists in the air? Not in this movie, where the Japanese seem to have been melancholy about the regrettable need to play such a negative role in such a positive Hollywood film.

The American side of the story centers on two childhood friends from Tennessee with the standard-issue screenplay names Rafe McCawley (Ben Affleck) and Danny Walker (Josh Hartnett). They enter the Army Air Corps and both fall in love with the same nurse, Evelyn Johnson (Kate Beckinsale)—first Rafe falls for her, and then, after he is reported dead, Danny. Their first date is subtitled "Three Months Later" and ends with Danny, having apparently read the subtitle, telling Evelyn, "Don't let it be three months before I see you again, OK?" That gets almost as big a laugh as her line to Rafe, "I'm gonna give Danny my whole heart, but I don't think I'll ever look at another sunset without thinking of you."

That kind of bad laugh would have been sidestepped in a more literate screenplay, but our hopes are not high after an early newsreel report that the Germans are bombing "downtown London"—a difficult target, since although there is such a place as "central London," at no time in two thousand years has London ever had anything described by anybody as a downtown.

There is not a shred of conviction or chemistry in the love triangle, which results after Rafe returns alive to Hawaii shortly before the raid on Pearl Harbor and is angry at Evelyn for falling in love with Danny, inspiring her timeless line, "I didn't even know until the day you turned up alive—and then all this happened."

Evelyn is a hero in the aftermath of the raid, performing triage by using her lipstick to separate the wounded who should be treated from those left to die. In a pointless stylistic choice, director Michael Bay and cinematographer John Schwartzman shoot some of the hospital scenes in soft focus, some in sharp focus, some blurred. Why? I understand it's to obscure details deemed too gory for the PG-13 rating. (Why should the carnage at Pearl Harbor be toned down to PG-13 in the first place?) In the newsreel sequences, the movies fades in and out of black-and-white with almost amusing haste, while the newsreel announcer sounds not like a period voice but like a Top 40 deejay in an echo chamber.

The most involving material in the film comes at the end, when Jimmy Doolittle (Alec Baldwin) leads his famous raid on Tokyo, flying Army bombers off the decks of Navy carriers and hoping to crash-land in China. He and his men were heroes, and their story would make a good movie (and indeed has: *Thirty Seconds Over Tokyo*). Another hero in the movie is the African-American cook Dorie Miller (Cuba Gooding Jr.), who because of his race was not allowed to touch a gun in the racist prewar Navy, but opens fire during the raid, shoots down two planes, and saves the life of his captain. Nice to see an African-American in the movie, but the almost total absence of Asians in 1941 Hawaii is inexplicable.

As for the raid itself, a little goes a long way. What is the point, really, of more than half an hour of planes bombing ships, of explosions and fireballs, of roars on the sound track and bodies flying through the air and people running away from fighters that are strafing them? How can it be entertaining or moving when it's simply about the most appalling slaughter? Why do the filmmakers think we want to see this, unrelieved by intelligence, viewpoint, or insight? It was a terrible, terrible day. Three thousand died in all. This is not a movie about them. It is an unremarkable action movie; Pearl Harbor supplies the subject, but not the inspiration.

The Perfect Man

(DIRECTED BY MARK ROSMAN; STARRING HILARY DUFF, HEATHER LOCKLEAR; 2005)

Is there no one to step forward and simply say that Heather Locklear's character in *The Perfect Man* is mad? I will volunteer. Locklear plays Jean Hamilton, a woman whose obsessive search for the "perfect man" inspires sudden and impulsive moves from one end of the country to another, always with her teenage daughter, Holly (Hilary Duff), and Holly's seven-year-old sister, Zoe (Aria Wallace). Apparently, there can only be one Perfect Man candidate per state.

As the movie opens, Holly is preparing to attend a prom in Wichita when her mother announces, "It's moving time!" Her latest boyfriend has broken up with her, so they all have to pile into the car and head for New York, where Mom providentially has a job lined up at a bakery—a job that pays well enough for them to move into an apartment that would rent for, oh, $4,000 a month.

Holly keeps an online blog named GirlOnTheMove.com, where she chronicles her mom's craziness for all the world. "Post me on Match.com," her mom tells Holly after they arrive in New York, but Holly thinks maybe it might be fun to see if her mom just—you know, *meets* someone. Jean's way of meeting someone is certainly direct: She attends a PTA meeting at Holly's new school, and suggests special PTA meetings for single parents and teachers. In desperation, Holly creates an imaginary online friend for her mom, who says all the things a woman wants to hear.

How does Holly know this is true? Because she's made a new friend at school (she's always making new friends, because she's always moving to new schools). This friend, named Amy (Vanessa Lengies) has an Uncle Ben (Chris Noth) who runs a bistro and is a bottomless well of information about what women want to hear, and what a Perfect Man consists of. Holly names the imaginary friend Ben, sends her mom Uncle Ben's photo and recycles what he tells her into the e-mail. Example of his wisdom: "When a woman gets an orchid, she feels like she's floating on a cloud of infinite possibility." If I met a woman who felt like she was floating on a cloud of infinite possibility after receiving an orchid, I would be afraid to give her anything else until she'd had a good physical.

The Perfect Man takes its idiotic plot and uses it as the excuse for scenes of awesome stupidity. For example, when Jean walks into Uncle Ben's restaurant and there is a danger they might meet, Holly sets off the sprinkler system. And when Holly thinks Ben is marrying another woman, she interrupts the wedding—while even we know, because of the tortured camera angles that strive not to reveal this, that Ben is only the best man.

Meanwhile, Jean has another prospect, a baker named Lenny (Mike O'Malley), who is a real nice guy but kind of homely, and invites her to a concert by a Styx tribute band. This involves driving to the concert in Lenny's pride and joy, a 1980 Pontiac Trans-Am two-door hardtop; Jean has to take off her shoes before entering the sacred precincts of this car. My personal opinion is that Lenny would be less boring after six months than the cloud of infinite possibilities guy.

The Perfect Man crawls hand over bloody hand up the stony face of this plot, while we in the audience do not laugh because it is not nice to laugh at those less fortunate than ourselves, and the people in this movie are less fortunate than the people in just about any other movie I can think of, simply because they are in it.

The Pink Panther

(DIRECTED BY SHAWN LEVY; STARRING STEVE MARTIN, KEVIN KLINE; 2006)

What is the moviegoer with a good memory to do when confronted with *The Pink Panther*, directed by Shawn Levy and starring Steve Martin? Is it possible to forget Blake Edwards and Peter Sellers? It is not. Their best Pink Panther movies did wonderfully what could not be done so well by anyone else, and not even, at the end, by them. (There was the sad *Trail of the Pink Panther* in 1982, cobbled together from outtakes after Sellers died in 1980.) Inspector Clouseau has been played by other actors before Martin (Alan Arkin and Roger Moore), but what's the point? The character isn't bigger than the actor, as Batman and maybe James Bond are. The character is the actor, and I had rather not see Steve Martin, who is himself inimitable, imitating Sellers.

Clouseau is wrong, and so is Kevin Kline as Inspector Dreyfus, the role that Herbert Lom made into a smoldering slow burn. Kline and Martin both wear the costumes and try the bad French accents, but it's like the high school production of something you saw at Steppenwolf, with the most gifted students in drama class playing the John Malkovich and Joan Allen roles. Within thirty seconds after Kline appeared on the screen, I was remembering the Kevin Kline Rule from my *Little Movie Glossary,* which observes that whenever Kline wears a mustache in a movie, he also has a foreign accent. Please do not write in with exceptions.

The movie credits Edwards as one of the sources of the story, which is fair enough, since the movie's ambition is to be precisely in the tradition of the Pink Panther movies. It's a prequel, taking place before *The Pink Panther* (1963), and showing Clouseau plucked from obscurity for his first big case. The French soccer coach has been murdered on the field in view of countless cheering fans, and the Pink Panther diamond has been stolen at the same time. The pressure is on Dreyfus to solve the case. His inspiration: Find the most incompetent inspector in France, announce his appointment, and use him as a decoy while the real investigation goes on secretly.

Clouseau, of course, qualifies as spectacularly incompetent, and his first meeting with Dreyfus begins unpromisingly when he succeeds in piercing the chief inspector's flesh with the pin on his badge. Clouseau is assigned Ponton (Jean Reno), an experienced gendarme, as his minder. Reno survives the movie by dialing down.

Clouseau, as before, has the ability to begin with a small mistake and build it into a catastrophe. Consider a scene where he drops a Viagra pill, and in trying to retrieve it, short-circuits the electricity in a hotel, sets it on fire, and falls through a floor. The mounting scale of each disaster is like a slapstick version of the death scenes in *Final Destination 3,* where a perfectly ordinary day in the stock room can end with a death by nail gun.

The Panther movies always featured beautiful women or, in the case of Capucine rumored to have been born a man, although I'll bet John Wayne hadn't heard that when they costarred in *North to Alaska.* The beauties this time are Beyonce, Emily Mortimer, and Kristin Chenoweth, and their task is essentially to regard Clouseau as if they have never seen such a phenomenon before in their lives.

Ponton in the meantime is subjected to the same kinds of attacks that Sellers used to unleash on Cato (Burt Kwouk), but I dunno: Even in purely physical scenes, something is missing. I think maybe the problem is that Steve Martin is sane and cannot lose himself entirely to idiocy. Sellers, who liked to say he had no personality, threw himself into a role as if desperate to grab all the behavior he could and run away with it and hide it under the bed.

There are moments that are funny in a mechanical way, as when Clouseau causes a giant world globe to roll out of an office and into the street, and it turns up much later to crash into a bicycle racer. But at every moment in the movie, I was aware that Peter Sellers was Clouseau, and Steve Martin was not. I hadn't realized how thoroughly Sellers and Edwards had colonized my memory. Despite Sean Connery, I was able to accept the other James Bonds, just as I understand that different actors might play Hamlet. But there is only one Clouseau, and zat ees zat.

Play It to the Bone

(Directed by Ron Shelton; starring Antonio Banderas, Woody Harrelson; 2000)

Play It to the Bone ends with a long, gruesome, brutal, bloody prizefight scene, which would be right at home in another movie but is a big miscalculation here, because it is between the two heroes of the story. We like them both. Therefore, we don't want either one to win, and we don't want either one to lose. What we basically want is for them to stop pounding one another. That isn't the way you want your audience to feel during a boxing movie.

The movie stars Antonio Banderas and Woody Harrelson as Cesar and Vince, a couple of has-been welterweights who get an emergency call from Las Vegas: Will they fight on the undercard before tonight's main event with Mike Tyson? Both slots have opened up after one of the scheduled fighters wiped himself out in a car crash and the other overdosed ("drugs are coming out of his ears"). Banderas and Harrelson are buddies and sparring partners who need a fresh start. The deal: They'll split $100,000, and the winner gets a shot at the title.

The movie was written and directed by Ron Shelton, an expert on sports movies; he wrote and directed *Bull Durham, White Men Can't Jump,* and *Cobb,* and wrote *Blue Chips.* One of his trademarks is expertise, and yet *Play It to the Bone* isn't an inside job on boxing but an assembly of ancient and familiar prizefight clichés (the corrupt promoter, the dubious contract, the ringside celebrities, the cut that may not stop bleeding, the "I coulda been a contender" scene). Even at that level it doesn't have enough of a boxing story to occupy the running time, and warms up with a prolonged and unnecessary road movie.

The setup: Neither fighter can afford airfare to Vegas. It doesn't occur to them to have the casino prepay their tickets. Instead, they convince Grace (Lolita Davidovich), who is Cesar's girlfriend, to drive them there in her vintage Oldsmobile convertible (all road movies involve classic cars, which drive down back roads with gas stations recycled from *The Grapes of Wrath*). When their credit card is rejected at a pit stop, they pick up Lia (Lucy Liu), a hitchhiker with funds.

The road trip involves many scenes intended to be colorful, including an obligatory fight between the two women. Shelton is good at comic conversation, but here the dialogue doesn't flow and sounds contrived, as when Cesar explains that he was once gay for a year, "but only exactly a year," because he was "trying all sorts of things." Vince, a Jesus freak, is shocked—but only, we sense, because the screenplay tells him he is. Both Cesar's sex life and Vince's spiritual visions are like first-draft ideas that don't flow convincingly from the characters. And what about Grace's motivation for the trip: Her hope of selling the rights to her gizmo inventions to high rollers? Uh, huh.

All leads up to the big fight, during which, as I've said, we want to hide our eyes. Shelton's approach is certainly novel: A match you want to stop before the fighters hit each other any more. It's bad enough that they're fighting, but why, in a silly comedy, did Shelton think he had to outdo *Raging Bull* in brutality? Vince and Cesar hammer each other until it is unlikely either fighter, in the real world, would still be conscious—or alive. It's a hideous spectacle, and we cringe because the movie doesn't know how odd it seems to cut from the bloodshed in the ring to the dialogue of the supporting players, who still think they're in a comedy.

Pootie Tang

(DIRECTED BY LOUIS C.K.; STARRING LANCE CROUTHER, JB SMOOVE; 2001)

Pootie Tang is not bad so much as inexplicable. You watch in puzzlement: How did this train wreck happen? How was this movie assembled out of such ill-fitting pieces? Who thought it was funny? Who thought it was finished? For that matter, was it finished? Take away the endless opening titles and end credits, and it's about seventy minutes long. The press notes say it "comes from the comedy laboratory of HBO's Emmy Award-winning *Chris Rock Show.*" It's like one of those lab experiments where the room smells like swamp gas and all the mice are dead.

Lance Crouther stars as Pootie Tang, a folk hero who has gained enormous popularity even though nobody can understand a word he says. He crusades against the evil Lecter Corp., which sells cigarettes, booze, drugs, and fast food to kids. Pootie is a regular character on *The Chris Rock Show,* and has a following, but he's more suited to skits than to a feature film—or at least to this feature film, which is disorganized, senseless, and chaotic.

Characters appear and disappear without pattern. Pootie has funny scenes, as when he dodges bullets, and other scenes, as when a woman eats a pie off his face, that seem left in the movie by accident. His secret weapon is his daddy's belt, which he uses against criminals. His daddy (Chris Rock) gave it to him on his deathbed, after being mauled by a gorilla at the steel mill. When the belt is stolen by an evil woman named Ireenie (Jennifer Coolidge), he loses his powers but is helped by a good woman named Biggie Shorty (Wanda Sykes, who provides more personality than the movie deserves).

Biggie Shorty is a hooker but spends most of her time boogying on street corners and encouraging Pootie Tang. She has a farm in Mississippi she loans Pootie, who, during his recuperation there, is encouraged by the white sheriff to date his daughter. This leads in the direction of a shotgun marriage, until the story thread evaporates and Pootie ends up in bed with Biggie. There is another villain named Dirty Dee (Reg E. Cathey), who is very dirty, and a villain, Dick Lecter, played by Robert Vaughn as if he may have a touch of lockjaw. Bob Costas plays an interviewer on one of those dreadful assignments where the writers thought it was funny simply *that* he was in the movie, instead of giving him anything funny to do.

Material this silly might at least be mindless entertainment for children, but *Pootie Tang* for no good reason includes a lot of language it has no need for. The studios put enormous pressure on the MPAA to award PG-13 ratings to what once would have been R-rated material, and the MPAA obliges. Here is dialogue your MPAA rates PG-13: "You can't hurt a ho with a belt. They like it." Women are routinely described as bitches and slapped around a lot (so are men). I have no problem with street language in movies with a use for the language. But why use it gratuitously in a movie that has no need for it, with a lead character whose TV exposure will attract younger viewers? What's the point?

Anyway, I'm not so much indignant as confused. Audiences will come out scratching their heads. The movie is half-baked, a shabby job of work. There are flashes of good stuff: a music video in the closing titles, some good songs on the sound track, Lance Crouther heroically making Pootie Tang an intriguing character even though the movie gives him no help. This movie is not in a releasable condition.

Princess Diaries

(Directed by Garry Marshall; starring Julie Andrews, Anne Hathaway; 2001)
Haven't I seen this movie before? *The Princess Diaries* is a march through the swamp of recycled ugly duckling stories, with occasional pauses in the marsh of sitcom clichés and the bog of Idiot Plots. You recall the Idiot Plot.

That's the plot that would be solved in an instant if anyone on the screen said what was obvious to the audience. A movie like this isn't entertainment. It's more like a party game that you lose if you say the secret word.

The film takes place in the present day, I guess, if through some kind of weird *Pleasantville* time warp the present day had the values and behavior of Andy Hardy movies. It is about a fifteen-year-old girl who doesn't realize she's really the princess of Genovia, which is "between France and Spain" and needs a heir from its royal bloodline if it is not to (a) go out of business, or (b) be taken over by the evil baron and baroness, I'm not sure which. Turns out that Mia Thermopolis (Anne Hathaway) is the daughter of the Prince of Genovia, but has never learned this fact, because her mother, Helen (Caroline Goodall), wanted to lead a normal life and thus left Genovia and her husband, never told Mia about her real father, and raised her normally—i.e., in a San Francisco firehouse where she slides down the pole every morning.

The prince has come to an untimely end, and now his mother comes to recruit Mia to take up her royal duties. The mother is Queen Clarisse Renaldi, played by Julie Andrews as a nice woman with very, very, very good manners. The suspense involves: Will Mia accept the throne? And will she choose as her boyfriend the snobbish jerk Josh (Erik Von Detten) or the nice Michael (Robert Schwartzman), older brother of her best friend, Lilly (Heather Matarazzo)? And, for that matter, is there any possibility that Josh will dump a glamorous cheerleader (Mandy Moore) after he sees how Mia looks once she takes off her glasses and does something with her hair? Anyone who doesn't immediately know the answers to these questions either lives in a cave, or wrote this screenplay.

The words "Why don't you do something about your hair?" have inspired movie transformation scenes since time immemorial, but rarely has the transformation been more of a setup than here. Garry Marshall, the director, hasn't had the nerve to cast a real fifteen-year-old as Mia, but supplies us instead with Anne Hathaway, who is almost twenty-one years old and is a classic beauty in the Daphne Zuniga tradition. We're expected to believe that this character gets so nervous in class that she throws up while trying to make a speech, and yet the rest of the time is as effortlessly verbal as a stand-up comedian.

One of the creaky problems thrown in the way of the plot is a "scandal" when Mia is photographed in what is not really a very scandalous situation at all, and so perhaps must renounce the throne. Queen Clarisse Renaldi seems reconciled to this. What do you think the chances are that the ruling family of a lucrative tax shelter—Monaco, for example—would abandon their principality because of a newspaper photo of the heir kissing a boy? In the interests of keeping the loot in the family, any heir—even Phoolan Devi, the late Bandit Queen of India—would be considered a viable candidate.

Garry Marshall made the wonderful *Pretty Woman,* but what was his thinking here? Some of the editing is plain sloppy. We are informed, for example, that when a kiss is magical, one of a girl's heels curls up off the floor. Cut to a heel curling up, but stuck to a strand of chewing gum. Whose heel? Whose gum? Nobody's. This is simply an isolated, self-contained shot. Later, at a dinner party, Marshall spends time establishing one of the guests as a drunk, but then the guest disappears without a payoff.

As *The Princess Diaries* creeps from one painfully obvious plot destination to another, we wait impatiently for the characters onscreen to arrive at what has long been clear to the audience. If the movie is determined to be this dim-witted, couldn't it at least move a little more quickly? The metronome is set too slow, as if everyone is acting and thinking in half time.

The Princess Diaries 2: Royal Engagement

(DIRECTED BY GARRY MARSHALL; STARRING JULIE ANDREWS, ANNE HATHAWAY; 2004)

The Princess Diaries 2: Royal Engagement offers the prudent critic with a choice. He can say what he really thinks about the movie, or he can play it safe by writing that it's sure to be loved by lots of young girls. But I avoid saying that anything is sure to be loved by anybody.

In this case, I am not a young girl, nor have I ever been, and so how would I know if one would like it? Of course, that's exactly the objection

I get in e-mails from young readers, who complain that no one like me can possibly like a movie like this. They are correct. I have spent a long time, starting at birth and continuing until this very moment, evolving into the kind of person who could not possibly like a movie like this, and I like to think the effort was not in vain.

So to girls who think they might like this movie, I say: Enjoy! Movies are for fun, among other things, and if you love *The Princess Diaries 2,* then I am happy for you, because I value the movies too much to want anyone to have a bad time at one.

But to Garry Marshall, the often-talented director of the original *Princess Diaries* as well as this sequel, I say: Did you deliberately assemble this movie from off-the-shelf parts, or did it just happen that way? The film is like an homage to the clichés and obligatory stereotypes of its genre. For someone like Marshall, it must have been like playing the scales.

The beautiful Anne Hathaway, still only twenty-two, stars as Princess Mia. You will remember that she was a typical American teenager whose mother raised her in a converted San Francisco firehouse, where she could slide down the pole every morning. Then a visit from Queen Clarisse of Genovia (Julie Andrews) revealed that she was, in fact, the queen's granddaughter and next in line to the throne.

In Part 2, she is the beloved Princess Mia of Genovia, a kingdom the size of a movie set, which is apparently located somewhere in Europe and populated by citizens who speak American English, except for a few snaky types with British accents. This kingdom has two peculiarities: (1) The shops and homes all seem to be three-fourth-scale models of the sorts of structures an American Girl doll would occupy; and (2) a great many of the extras get a few extra frames, in order to look uncannily as if they might be personal friends of the director. So many prosperous men in their sixties, so well barbered, groomed, and dressed, so Southern California in their very bearing, are unlikely to be visiting Genovia for any other reason, since the kingdom doesn't seem to have a golf course.

There's no need for me to spoil the plot; as I was saying just the other day about *The Village,* it spoils itself. If I were to describe the characters, you could instantly tell me what happens in the movie. Let's try that, as an experiment.

There is Princess Mia, who is given a deadline of one month to either marry or forfeit her rights to the throne. The evil Viscount Mabrey (John Rhys-Davies) wants to disqualify her because his nephew, Sir Nicholas (Chris Pine), is next in line to the throne. Desperate for a husband and learning that Queen Clarisse was perfectly happy in an arranged marriage, Mia decides to marry for the love of her country.

A suitable bachelor is discovered: nice Andrew Jacoby, duke of Kensington (Callum Blue). Mia accepts his proposal, despite, as she writes in her diary on the Web site, "He's everything a girl should want in a husband-to-be. It's . . . just that . . . something . . . you know." Meanwhile, of course, she hates the handsome young Sir Nicholas, who hangs around a lot and annoys her. "Dear Diary: Just look at him . . . all sneaky and smug and . . . and . . . cute."

OK now, given those clues, see if you can figure out who she ends up with. And for that matter, consider Joseph (Hector Elizondo), the chief of palace security. He has been in love with the widow Clarisse for years, and she knows it and is pleased. That provides us with a romance without closure that has persisted ever since the first movie, and if there is anything nature abhors more than a vacuum, it is a loving couple kept asunder when they should be sundering.

Director Marshall puts his cast and plot through their paces with the speed and deliberation of Minnesota Fats clearing the table. He even provides a fountain for two characters to stand beside, so they can illustrate Gene Siskel's maxim that nobody in a comedy ever comes within ten yards of water without falling in.

Yes, it's nice to see Julie Andrews looking great and performing a song, although the line "Give the queen a shout-out, and she'll sing" is one I doubt will ever be heard in Buckingham Palace. It is also rather original that at her slumber party, Mia and her friends don't get wasted at a private club, but engage in the jolly indoor sport of mattress surfing.

The Promise

(Directed by Chen Kaige; starring Cecilia Cheung, Jang Dong Gun; 2006)

The Promise is pretty much a mess of a movie; the acting is overwrought, the plot is too tangled to play like anything *but* a plot, and although I know you can create terrific special effects at home in the basement on your computer, the CGI work in this movie looks like it was done with a dial-up connection. What a disappointment from Chen Kaige, who has made great movies (*Farewell, My Concubine*) and no doubt will make them again.

The plot involves a touch of the crucial romantic misunderstanding in *Vertigo*. Princess Qingcheng (Cecilia Cheung) thinks she is in love with the great General Guangming (Hiroyuki Sanada), who has saved her life after she offended the king (Cheng Qian). But actually she is in love with the slave Kunlan (Jang Dong Gun), who is impersonating the general. Kunlan has been assigned to protect the king from an outlander assassin named Wuhuan (Nicolas Tse) and another assassin named Snow Wolf (Liu Te). This is all going to be on the final.

Qingcheng's love for the general (or Kunlan) is doomed whether or not she discovers that the former slave is impersonating his master. That is because in the early scenes of the movie, we saw Qingcheng as a child, being told by the Goddess Manshen (Hong Chen) that although she will have beauty and power and be a princess, she will lose every man she ever loves. This has possibilities. Since she loves Kunlan (thinking he is the general), what would happen if Kunlan were lost as per the prophecy, and she ended up with the real general? Would she then think she loved him and live happily ever after, not realizing he is not really the man she loves? Would her mistake grant him immunity? At some point I wanted James Stewart to appear and herd everybody up into a bell tower.

One of Kunlan's gifts is the ability to run really, really fast. I'm thinking of The Flash here. The problem with attaining that velocity is that Kunlan obviously must abandon the world of gravity and physical reality, and become a computer-generated graphic, and you know, it's a funny thing, CGI running may be faster than real running, but it never seems like anybody is really working at it. We're watching an effect instead of an achievement.

The CGI work in the movie is cheesy. One problem with CGI is that it inspires greed in directors. Chen Kaige reportedly had one thousand real extras for one of his battle scenes, and considering that Orson Welles put on a great battle in *Falstaff* with close-ups of about nine actors, that should have been plenty. But no. He uses CGI to multiply those soldiers until they take on all the reality of the hordes of *Troy*, who were so numerous that in one shot it was obvious they would all fit inside their city only by standing on each other's shoulders. Enough is enough.

Another difficulty is that the story is never organized clearly enough to generate much concern in our minds. The characters are not people but collections of attributes, and isn't it generally true that the more sensational an action scene, the less we care about the people in it? It's as if the scene signals us that it's about itself, and the characters are spectators just as we are.

I spent a fair amount of time puzzling over my notes and rummaging on the Web for hints about the details of the plot, and in the process discovered a new Movie Law. You are familiar with the Law of Symbolism: If you have to ask what something symbolized, it didn't. Now here is the Law of Plots: If you can't describe it with clarity, there wasn't one. I know someone will throw up *Syriana* as an objection, but there is a difference between a plot that is about confusion, and a plot that is merely confused.

Raise Your Voice

(Directed by Sean McNamara; starring Hilary Duff, Rita Wilson; 2004)

Hilary Duff has a great smile, and she proves it by smiling pretty much all the way through *Raise Your Voice,* except when there's a death in the family, or her roommate Denise says something mean to her, or she sees her kind-of boyfriend Jay kissing Robin after he said he'd broken up with her, or when her dad says she can't go to music camp. The rest of the time she smiles and smiles, and I love gazing upon her smile, although a still photo would achieve the same effect and be a time-saver.

She smiles in *Raise Your Voice,* a carefully constructed new movie that doesn't make her a contemporary teenager so much as surround her with them. She plays Terri Fletcher, a young music student, who after a personal tragedy wants to begin again by attending a three-week camp for gifted young musicians in Los Angeles. Her dad (David Keith) is against it: Terrible things can happen to a young woman in Los Angeles. Her mother (Rita Wilson) conspires with her artistic Aunt Nina (Rebecca De Mornay) to sneak her off to the camp while Dad thinks she's visiting Nina in Palm Desert. Aunt Nina is one of those artists who does alarming things up on stepladders with an acetylene torch.

All the kids are snobs at the camp, primarily so they can soften later. (If they soften right away, there goes the plot.) Terri's new roommate is Denise (Dana Davis), who plans to work hard for a scholarship, and resents Terri as a distraction. Sizing up Terri's wardrobe and her smile, Denise tells her: "You're like some kind of retro Brady Buncher." I hate it when a movie contains its own review. For that matter, earlier in the movie her brother tells her she's a "Stepford daughter," but he encourages her to go to the camp, direly predicting: "If you don't, you're going to end up doing *Cats* at the Y when you're forty."

Terri meets a nice kid named Jay (Oliver James), who has a British accent and is very encouraging and warm, and brings her out of herself and encourages her to sing with joy, and writes a song with her and says he doesn't date the bitchy Robin (Lauren C. Mayhew) anymore because she was "last summer." There is also an inspiring music teacher (John Corbett), who wants to find the best in her, and doesn't have to look very deep.

All of this plays out against the backdrop of Terri's deception of her dad, who is convinced she's in Palm Desert because Terri and Aunt Nina phone him on a conference call. Dad only wants the best for her, of course, but when he finds out about the deception, he declares, "I want her home, right now!"

Does that mean (a) she comes home, right now, or (b) her mom and Aunt Nina work on Dad, and, wouldn't you know, the auditorium door opens and Dad walks in just in time for his daughter to see him from the stage halfway through her big solo. The answer of course is (b), right down to the obligatory moment when the disapproving parent in the audience nods at the gifted child onstage and does the heartfelt little nod that means, "You were right, honey." But her dad was right about one thing. Something terrible did happen to her in Los Angeles. She made this movie.

Reign of Fire

(DIRECTED BY ROB BOWMAN; STARRING MATTHEW MCCONAUGHEY, CHRISTIAN BALE; 2002)

One regards *Reign of Fire* with awe. What a vast enterprise has been marshaled in the service of such a minute idea. Incredulity is our companion, and it is twofold: We cannot believe what happens in the movie, and we cannot believe that the movie was made.

Of course, in a story involving mankind's battle with fire-breathing dragons in the year 2020, there are a few factual matters you let slide. But the movie makes no sense on its own terms, let alone ours. And it is such a grim and dreary enterprise. One prays for a flower or a ray of sunshine as those grotty warriors clamber into their cellars and over their slag heaps. Not since *Battlefield Earth* has there been worse grooming.

The story: A tunnel beneath London breaks open an underground cavern filled with long-dormant fire-breathing dragons. They fly to the surface and attack mankind. When one is destroyed, countless more take its place. Man's weapons only increase the damage. Soon civilization has been all but wiped out; the heroes of the film cower in their underground hiding places and dream of defeating the dragons.

Along comes Van Zan (Matthew McConaughey), the Dragon Slayer. He is bald and bearded, and his zealot's eyes focus in the middle distance as he speaks. He's the kind of tough guy who smokes cigar butts.

Not cigars. Butts. He has a disagreement with Quinn Abercromby (Christian Bale), the leader of the group. I am not sure why they so ferociously oppose each other, but I believe their quarrel comes down to this: Van Zan thinks they have to fight the dragons, and Quinn thinks they have to fight the dragons but they have to look out real good, because those are dangerous dragons and might follow them home.

There's not much in the way of a plot. Alex (Izabella Scorupco) gets grubby and distraught while standing between the two men and trying to get them to stop shouting so much and listen to her scientific theories. Meanwhile, dragons attack, their animated wings beating as they fry their enemies. Their animation is fairly good, although at one point a dragon in the background flies past the ruined dome of St. Paul's, and you can see one through the other, or vice versa.

I'm wondering why, if civilization has been destroyed, do they have electricity and fuel? Not supposed to ask such questions. They're like, how come everybody has cigarettes in *Water World*? Van Zan figures out that the dragon's fire comes from the way they secrete the ingredients for "natural napalm" in their mouths. His plan: Get real close and fire an explosive arrow into their open mouth at the crucial moment, causing the napalm to blow up the dragon.

He has another bright idea. (Spoiler warning.) All of the dragons they see are females. Many of them carry eggs. Why no males? Because, Van Zan hypothesizes, the dragons are like fish and it only takes a single male to fertilize umpteen eggs. "We kill the male, we kill the species," he says.

Yeah, but . . . there are dragons everywhere. Do they only have one male, total, singular? How about those eggs? Any of them male? And also, after the male is dead, presumably all of the females are still alive, and they must be mad as hell now that they're not getting any action. How come they stop attacking?

I know I have probably been inattentive, and that some of these points are solved with elegant precision in the screenplay. But please do not write to explain, unless you can answer me this: Why are the last words in the movie "Thank God for evolution"? Could it be a ray of hope that the offspring of this movie may someday crawl up onto the land and develop a two-celled brain?

Reindeer Games

(DIRECTED BY JOHN FRANKENHEIMER; STARRING BEN AFFLECK, CHARLIZE THERON; 2000)

Reindeer Games is the first all-Talking Killer picture. After the setup, it consists mostly of characters explaining their actions to one another. I wish I'd had a stopwatch to clock how many minutes are spent while one character holds a gun to another character's head and gabs. Charlize Theron and Gary Sinise between them explain so much they reminded me of Gertrude Stein's line about Ezra Pound: "He was a village explainer, excellent if you were a village, but if you were not, not."

Just a nudge, and the movie would fall over into self-parody, and maybe work better. But I fear it is essentially serious, or as serious as such goofiness can be. It opens in prison with cellmates Rudy (Ben Affleck) and Nick (James Frain). Both are about to be set free. Nick has engaged in a steamy correspondence with Ashley (Theron), one of those women who have long-distance romances with convicts. His cell wall is plastered with photos that make her look like a model for cosmetics ads.

But then (I am not giving away as much as it seems, or perhaps even what it seems) Nick is knifed in a prison brawl, and when Rudy walks out of prison and lays eyes on Ashley—well, what would you do? That's what he does. "I'm Nick," Rudy tells her. Soon they make wild and passionate love, which inevitably involves knocking things over and falling out of bed and continuing on the floor. You'd think if people were that much into sex, they'd pay more attention to what they were doing.

Then there's a major reality shift, and perhaps you'd better stop reading if you don't want to know that . . . Ashley's brother Gabriel (Gary Sinise) heads a gang of scummy gunrunners who think Rudy used to work in an Indian casino in upstate Michigan—because, of course, they think Rudy is Nick, and that's what Nick told Ashley about himself. Gabriel and his gang try to squeeze info about the casino's security setup out of Rudy, who says he isn't Nick, and then says he is Nick after all, and then says he isn't, and has so many reasons for each of his answers that Gabriel gets very confused, and keeps deciding to kill him, and deciding not to kill him, and deciding to kill him after all, until both characters seem stuck in a time loop.

There are other surprises, too, a lot of them, each with its explanation, usually accompanied by an explanation of the previous explanation, which now has to be re-explained in light of the new explanation. They all got a lot of 'splainin' to do.

The movie's weakness is mostly in its ludicrous screenplay by Ehren Kruger. The director, John Frankenheimer, is expert at moving the action along and doing what can be done with scenes that hardly anything can be done with. Ben Affleck and Charlize Theron soldier through changes of pace so absurd it takes superb control to keep straight faces. Theron's character looks soft and sweet sometimes, then hard and cruel other times, switching back and forth so often I commend her for not just passing a hand up and down in front of her face: smile, frown, smile, frown.

Perhaps the movie was originally intended to open at Christmas. That would explain the title and the sequence where the casino, which looks like a former Target store, is stuck up by five Santas. But nothing can explain the upbeat final scene, in which, after blood seeps into the Michigan snow, we get a fit of Robin Hood sentimentality. The moment to improve *Reindeer Games* was at the screenplay stage, by choosing another one.

Resident Evil
(Directed by Paul Anderson; starring Milla Jovovich, Michelle Rodriguez; 2002)

Resident Evil is a zombie movie set in the twenty-first century and therefore reflects several advances over twentieth-century films. For example, in twentieth-century slasher movies, knife blades make a sharpening noise when being whisked through thin air. In the twenty-first century, large metallic objects make crashing noises just by being looked at.

The vast Umbrella Corporation, whose secret laboratory is the scene of the action, specializes in high-tech weapons and genetic cloning. It can turn a little DNA into a monster with a nine-foot tongue. Reminds me of the young man from Kent. You would think Umbrella could make a door that doesn't make a slamming noise when it closes, but its doors make slamming noises even when they're open. The narration tells us that Umbrella products are in "90 percent of American homes," so it finishes behind Morton salt.

The movie is *Dawn of the Dead* crossed with *John Carpenter's Ghosts of Mars,* with zombies not as ghoulish as the first and trains not as big as the second. The movie does however have Milla Jovovich and Michelle Rodriguez. According to the Internet Movie Database, Jovovich plays "Alice/Janus Prospero/Marsha Thompson," although I don't believe anybody ever calls her anything. I think some of those names come from the original video game. Rodriguez plays "Rain Ocampo," no relation to the Phoenix family. In pairing classical and literary references, the match of Alice and Janus Prospero is certainly the best name combo since Huckleberry P. Jones/Pa Hercules was portrayed by Ugh-Fudge Bwana in *Forbidden Zone* (1980).

The plot: Vials of something that looks like toy coils of plastic DNA models are being delicately manipulated behind thick shields in an airtight chamber by remote-controlled robot hands; when one of the coils is dropped, the factory automatically seals its exits and gasses and drowns everyone inside. Umbrella practices zero tolerance. We learn that the factory, code-named The Hive, is buried half a mile below the surface. Seven investigators go down to see what happened. Three are killed, but Alice/Janus Prospero/Marsha, Rain Ocampo, Matt, and Spence survive in order to be attacked for sixty minutes by the dead Hive employees, who have turned into zombies. Meanwhile, the monster with the nine-foot tongue is mutating. (Eventually, its tongue is nailed to the floor of a train car and it is dragged behind it on the third rail. I hate it when that happens.)

These zombies, like the *Dawn of the Dead* zombies, can be killed by shooting them, so there is a lot of zombie shooting, although not with the squishy green-goo effect of George Romero's 1978 film. The zombies are like vampires, since when one bites you it makes you a zombie. What I don't understand is why zombies are so graceless. They walk with the lurching shuffle of a drunk trying to skate through urped Slurpees to the men's room.

There is one neat effect when characters unwisely venture into a corridor and the door slams shut on them. Then a laser beam passes at head level, decapitating one. Another beam whizzes past at waist level, cutting the second in two while the others duck. A third laser pretends to be high but then switches to low, but the third character outsmarts it by jumping at the last minute. Then the fourth laser turns into a grid that dices its victim into pieces the size of a Big Mac. Since the grid is inescapable, what were the earlier lasers about? Does the corridor have a sense of humor?

Alice/Janus Prospero/Marsha Thompson and her colleagues are highly trained scientists, which leads to the following exchange when they stare at a pool of zombie blood on the floor.

ALICE/J.P./M.T./RAIN (I forget which): "It's coagulating!"

MATT/SPENCE (I forget which): "That's not possible!"

"Why not?!?"

"Because blood doesn't do that until you're dead!"

How does the blood on the floor know if you're dead? The answer to this question is so obvious I am surprised you would ask. Because it is zombie blood.

The characters have no small talk. Their dialogue consists of commands, explanations, exclamations, and ejaculations. Yes, an ejaculation can be dialogue. If you live long enough you may find that happening frequently.

Oh, and the film has a Digital Readout. The Hive is set to lock itself forever after sixty minutes have passed, so the characters are racing against time. In other words, after it shuts all of its doors and gasses and drowns everybody, it waits sixty minutes and *really* shuts its doors—big time. No wonder the steel doors make those slamming noises. In their imagination, they're practicing. Creative visualization, it's called. I became inspired and visualized the theater doors slamming behind me.

Resident Evil: Apocalypse

(DIRECTED BY ALEXANDER WITT; STARRING MILLA JOVOVICH, SIENNA GUILLORY;
    2004)

I'm trying to remember what the city was called in the original *Resident Evil* (2002). I don't think it was called anything, but in the new *Resident Evil: Apocalypse,* it's called Raccoon City, just like in the original video game. Call it what you will, it has the Toronto skyline. Toronto played Chicago in *Chicago* and now it plays Raccoon City. Some you win, some you lose.

The movie is an utterly meaningless waste of time. There was no reason to produce it except to make money, and there is no reason to see it except to spend money. It is a dead zone, a film without interest, wit, imagination, or even entertaining violence and special effects.

The original film involved the Umbrella Corp. and its underground research laboratory called The Hive. The experimental T-virus escaped, and to contain it, The Hive was flooded and locked. But its occupants survived as zombies and lurched about infecting others with their bites. Zombies can appear in interesting movies, as George Romero proved in *Dawn of the Dead* and Danny Boyle in *28 Days Later.* But zombies themselves are not interesting because all they do is stagger and moan. As I observed in my review of the first film, "they walk with the lurching shuffle of a drunk trying to skate through urped Slushies to the men's room."

Now time has passed and the Umbrella Corp. has decided to reopen The Hive. Well, wouldn't you know that the T-virus escapes *again,* and creates even more zombies? Most of the population of Raccoon City is infected, but can be easily contained because there is only one bridge out of town. The story involves three sexy women (Milla Jovovich, Sienna Guillory, and Sandrine Holt), the first a former Umbrella Corp. scientist, the second a renegade cop, the third a TV reporter. Picking up some guys along the way, they battle the zombies and try to rescue a little girl so her dad can pull some strings and get them out of the quarantined city before it is nuked.

We pause here for logistical discussions. In a scene where several characters are fighting zombies inside a church, the renegade scientist comes to the rescue by crashing her motorcycle through a stained-glass window and landing in the middle of the fight. This inspires the question: How did she know what was on the other side of the window? Was she crashing through the stained glass on spec?

My next logistical puzzlement involves killing the zombies. They die when you shoot them. Fine, except Umbrella Corp. has developed some mutants who wear bulletproof armor. Zillions of rounds of ammo bounce off this armor, but here's a funny thing: The mutants do not wear helmets, so we can see their ugly faces. So why not just shoot them in the head? Am I missing something here?

What I was missing were more of the mutants from the first picture, where they were little monsters with nine-foot tongues. They have a walk-on (or maybe a lick-on) in the sequel, but it's no big deal. *Resident Evil: Apocalypse* could have used them, but then this is a movie that could have used anything. The violence is all video-game target practice, the zombies are a bore, we never understand how Umbrella hopes to make money with a virus that kills everyone, and the characters are spectacularly shallow. Parents: If you encounter teenagers who say they liked this movie, do not let them date your children.

Rollerball
(DIRECTED BY JOHN McTIERNAN; STARRING CHRIS KLEIN, JEAN RENO; 2004)

Rollerball is an incoherent mess, a jumble of footage in search of plot, meaning, rhythm, and sense. There are bright colors and quick movement on the screen, which we can watch as a visual pattern that, in entertainment value, falls somewhere between a kaleidoscope and a lava lamp.

The movie stars Chris Klein, who shot to stardom, so to speak, in the *American Pie* movies and inhabits his violent action role as if struggling against the impulse to blurt out, "People, why can't we all just get along?" Klein is a nice kid. For this role, you need someone who has to shave three times a day.

The movie is set in 2005 in a Central Asian republic apparently somewhere between Uzbekistan and Mudville. Jean Reno plays Petrovich, owner of "the hottest sports start-up in the world," a Rollerball league that crowds both motorcycles and roller skaters on a figure eight track that at times looks like a Roller Derby crossed with demo derby, at other times like a cruddy video game. The sport involves catching a silver ball and throwing it at a big gong so that showers of sparks fly. One of the star players confesses she doesn't understand it, but so what: In the final game Petrovich suspends all rules, fouls, and penalties. This makes no difference that I could see.

Klein plays Jonathan Cross, an NHL draft pick who has to flee America in a hurry for the crime of racing suicidally down the hills of San Francisco flat on his back on what I think is a skateboard. His best friend is Marcus Ridley (LL Cool J), who convinces him to come to Podunkistan and sign for the big bucks. Jonathan is soon attracted to Aurora (Rebecca Romijn-Stamos, from *X-Men*).

"Your face isn't nearly as bad as you think," he compliments her. She has a scar over one eye, but is otherwise in great shape, as we can see because the locker rooms of the future are coed. Alas, the women athletes of the future still turn their backs to the camera at crucial moments, carry strategically placed towels, stand behind furniture, and in general follow the rules first established in 1950s nudist volleyball pictures.

I counted three games in the Rollerball season. The third is the championship. There is one road trip, to a rival team's Rollerball arena, which seems to have been prefabricated in the city dump. The games are announced by Paul Heyman, who keeps screaming, "What the hell is going on?" There is no one else in the booth with him. Yet when Aurora wants to show Jonathan that an injury was deliberate, she can call up instant replays from all the cameras on equipment thoughtfully provided in the locker room.

The funniest line in the movie belongs to Jean Reno, who bellows, "I'm this close to a North American cable deal!" North American cable carries Battling Bots, Iron Chefs, Howard Stern, and monster truck rallies. There isn't a person in the audience who couldn't get him that deal. Reno also has the second funniest line. After Jonathan engages in an all-night 120-mph motorcycle chase across the frozen steppes of Bankruptistan, while military planes drop armed Jeeps to chase him, and after he sees his best pal blown to bits *after* leaping across a suspension bridge that has been raised in the middle of the night for no apparent reason, Reno tells him, "Play well tonight."

Oh, and I almost forgot Aurora's breathless discovery after the suspicious death of one of the other players. "His chinstrap was cut!" she whispers fiercely to Jonathan. Neither she nor he notices that Jonathan makes it a point never to fasten his own chinstrap at any time during a game.

Someday this film may inspire a long, thoughtful book by John Wright, its editor. My guess is that something went dreadfully wrong early in the production. Maybe dysentery or mass hypnosis. And the director, John McTiernan (*Die Hard*), was unable to supply Wright with the shots he needed to make sense of the story. I saw a Russian documentary once where half the shots were blurred and overexposed because the KGB attacked the negative with X-rays. Maybe this movie was put through an MRI scan. Curiously, the signifiers have survived, but not the signified. Characters set up big revelations and then forget to make them. And the long, murky night sequence looks like it was shot, pointlessly, with the green-light NightShot feature on a consumer video camera.

One of the peculiarities of television of the future is a device titled "Instant Global Rating." This supplies a digital readout of how many viewers there are (except on North American cable systems, of course). Whenever something tremendously exciting happens during a game, the rating immediately goes up. This means that people who were not watching somehow sensed they had just missed something amazing and responded by tuning in. When *Rollerball* finally does get a North American cable deal, I predict the ratings will work in reverse.

Romeo Must Die

(Directed by Andrzej Bartkowiak; starring Jet Li, Aaliyah; 2000)

Shakespeare has been manhandled in countless modern-dress retreads, and I was looking forward to *Romeo Must Die*, billed as a war between Chinese and African-American families, based on *Romeo and Juliet*. After *China Girl* (1987), which sets the story in New York's Little Italy and Chinatown, and *Romeo + Juliet* (1996), which has a war between modern gangsters in a kind of CalMex strip city, why not a martial arts version in Oakland?

Alas, the film borrows one premise from Shakespeare (the children of enemy families fall in love), and buries the rest of the story in a creaky plot and wheezy dialogue. Much is made of the presence of Jet Li, the Hong Kong martial arts star (*Lethal Weapon 4*), but his scenes are so clearly computer-aided that his moves are about as impressive as Bugs Bunny doing the same things.

Li stars as Han Sing, once a cop, now taking the rap for a crime he didn't commit. He's in a Hong Kong prison as the movie opens. His brother is killed in Oakland after a fight at an African-American dance club, and Sing breaks out of prison to travel to America and avenge his brother. In Oakland, he meets Trish O'Day (Aaliyah, the singer) and they begin to fall in love while she helps him look into the death of his brother.

But what a coincidence! Her father, Isaak (Delroy Lindo), may know more about the death than he should, and soon the two lovers are in the middle of a war between Chinese and black organizations who are involved in a murky plot to buy up the waterfront for a new sports stadium. This real estate project exists primarily as a clothesline on which to hang elaborate martial arts sequences, including one Jackie Chan–style football game where Jet Li hammers half a dozen black guys and scores a touchdown, all at once.

It is a failing of mine that I persist in bringing logic to movies where it is not wanted. During *Romeo Must Die,* I began to speculate about the methods used to buy up the waterfront. All of the property owners (of clubs, little shops, crab houses, etc) are asked to sell, and when they refuse, they are variously murdered, torched, blown up, or have their faces stuck into vats of live crabs. Don't you think the press and the local authorities would notice this? Don't you imagine it would take the bloom off a stadium to know that dozens of victims were murdered to clear the land?

Never mind. The audience isn't in the theater for a film about property values, but to watch Jet Li and other martial arts warriors in action. *Romeo Must Die* has a lot of fight scenes, but key moments in them are so obviously special effects that they miss the point. When Jackie Chan does a stunt, it may look inelegant, but we know he's really doing it. Here Jet Li leaps six feet in the air and rotates clockwise while kicking three guys. It can't be done, we know it can't be done, we know he's not doing it, and so what's the point? In *The Matrix*, there's a reason the guy can fly.

There's a moment in Jackie Chan's *Rumble in the Bronx* when he uses grace and athletic ability to project his entire body through the swinging gate of a grocery cart, and we say, "Yes!" (pumping a fist into the air is optional). Here Jet Li tries the Chan practice of using whatever props come to hand, but the football game looks over-rehearsed and a sequence with a fire hose is underwhelming (anybody can knock guys off their feet with a fire hose).

Closing notes: Many windows are broken in the movie. Many people fall from great heights. There are a lot of rap songs on the sound track, which distract from the action because their lyrics occupy the foreground and replace dialogue. Killers on motorcycles once again forget it is dangerous for them to chase cars at high speed, because if they get thrown off their bikes, it will hurt. The reliable Motorcycle Opaque Helmet Rule is observed (when you can't see the face of a character because the visor is down, chances are—gasp!—it's a woman). No great romantic chemistry is generated between the young lovers, and there is something odd about a martial arts warrior hiding behind a girl's bedroom door so her daddy won't catch him. Delroy Lindo projects competence, calm, and strength in every scene. This movie needs a screenplay.

Running Free

(DIRECTED BY SERGEI BODROV; STARRING CHASE MOORE, JAN DECLEIR; 2000)
Running Free tells the life story of a horse in its own words. We do not find out much about horses in this process, alas, because the horse thinks and talks exactly like a young boy. The movie is another example, like Disney's *Dinosaur,* of a failure of nerve: Instead of challenging the audience to empathize with real animals, both movies supply them with the minds, vocabularies, and values of humans. What's the point?

As the film opens, the horse, later to be named Lucky, is born in the hold of a ship bound for German Southwest Africa, today's Namibia. It is 1911, and horses are needed to work in the mines. Lucky has to swim ashore while still a nursing colt. He glimpses daylight for the first time, and tells us, "I didn't see anything green in this desert land." Hello? Lucky has never seen anything green at all in his entire life.

But the movie keeps making that same mistake, breaking the logic of the point of view. Adopted by a young orphan stable boy named Richard (Chase Moore), Lucky finds himself in a stable of purebreds ruled by a stallion named Caesar. Lucky wants to make friends with the stallion's daughter, Beauty, but, "I was only the stable boy's horse. I wasn't good enough to play with his daughter." And when Lucky's long-missing mother turns up, Caesar attacks her, apparently in a fit of class prejudice, although you'd think a stallion would be intrigued by a new girl in town, despite her family connections.

Will the mother die from the attack? "I stayed with her all night, praying that she would survive," Lucky tells us. Praying? I wanted the movie to forget the story and explore this breakthrough in horse theology. I am weary of debates about whether our pets will be with us in heaven, and am eager to learn if trainers will be allowed into horse heaven.

The human characters in the movie are one-dimensional cartoons, including a town boss who speaks English with an Afrikaans accent, not likely in a German colony. His son is a little Fauntleroy with a telescope, which he uses to spy on Richard and Lucky. Soon all the Europeans evacuate the town after a bombing raid, which raises the curtain on World War I. The horses are left behind, and Lucky escapes to the mountains, where he finds a hidden lake. Returning to the town, he leads the other horses there, where at last they realize their birthright and Run Free.

Uh, huh. But there is not a twig of living vegetation in their desert hideout, and although I am assured by the movie's press materials that there are wild horses in Namibia to this day, I doubt they could forage for long in the barren wasteland shown in this film. What do they eat?

I ask because it is my responsibility: Of all the film critics reviewing this movie, I will arguably be the only one who has actually visited

Swakopmund and Walvis Bay, on the Diamond Coast of the Namib Desert, and even ridden on the very train tracks to the capital, Windhoek, that the movie shows us. I am therefore acutely aware that race relations in the area in 1911 (and more recently) would scarcely have supported the friendship between Richard and Nyka (Maria Geelbooi), who plays the bushman girl who treats Lucky's snakebite. But then a movie that fudges about which side is which in World War I is unlikely to pause for such niceties.

I seem to be developing a rule about talking animals: They can talk if they're cartoons or Muppets, but not if they're real. This movie might have been more persuasive if the boy had told the story of the horse, instead of the horse telling the story of the boy. It's perfectly possible to make a good movie about an animal that does not speak, as Jean-Jacques Annaud, the producer of this film, proved with his 1989 film *The Bear.*

I also recall *The Black Stallion* (1979) and *White Fang* (1991). Since both of those splendid movies were cowritten by Jeanne Rosenberg, the author of *Running Free,* I can only guess that the talking horse was pressed upon her by executives who have no faith in the intelligence of today's audiences. Perhaps *Running Free* would appeal to younger children who really like horses.

Rush Hour 2

(DIRECTED BY BRETT RATNER; STARRING JACKIE CHAN, CHRIS TUCKER; 2001)
Rush Hour (1998) earned untold millions of dollars, inspiring this sequel. The first film was built on a comic relationship between Jackie Chan and Chris Tucker, as odd-couple cops from Hong Kong and Los Angeles. It was funny because hard work went into the screenplay and the stunts. It was not funny because Chris Tucker is funny whenever he opens his mouth— something he proves abundantly in *Rush Hour 2,* where his endless rants are like an anchor around the ankles of the humor.

Jackie Chan complained, I hear, that the Hollywood filmmakers didn't give him time to compose his usual elaborately choreographed stunts in *Rush Hour 2,* preferring shorter bursts of action. Too bad Brett

Ratner, the director, didn't focus instead on shortening Tucker's dialogue scenes. Tucker plays an L.A. cop who, on the evidence of this movie, is a race-fixated motormouth who makes it a point of being as loud, offensive, and ignorant as he possibly can be.

There is a belief among some black comics that audiences find it funny when they launch extended insults against white people (see also Chris Rock's embarrassing outburst in *Jay and Silent Bob*). My feeling is that audiences of any race find such scenes awkward and unwelcome; I've never heard laughter during them, but have sensed an uncomfortable alertness in the theater. Accusing complete strangers of being racist is aggressive, hostile, and not funny, something Tucker demonstrates to a painful degree in this movie—where the filmmakers apparently lacked the nerve to request him to dial down.

There's one scene that really grated: The Tucker character finds himself in a Vegas casino. He throws a wad of money on a craps table and is given a stack of $500 chips. He is offended: It is racist for the casino to give him $500 chips instead of $1,000 chips, the dealer doesn't think a black man can afford $1,000 a throw, etc. He goes on and on in a shrill tirade against the dealer (an uncredited Saul Rubinek, I think). The dealer answers every verbal assault calmly and firmly. What's extraordinary about this scene is how we identify with the dealer, and how manifestly the Tucker character is acting like the seven-letter word for *jerk*. Rubinek wins the exchange.

The movie begins with Tucker and Jackie Chan going to Hong Kong on vacation after their adventures in the previous movie. Soon they're involved in a new case: A bomb has gone off in the American embassy, killing two people. Their investigation leads first to the leader of a local crime triad (John Lone) and then to an American Mr. Big (Alan King). Sex appeal is supplied by Roselyn Sanchez, as an undercover agent, and Zhang Ziyi, from *Crouching Tiger, Hidden Dragon,* as a martial arts fighter.

Jackie Chan is amazing as usual in the action sequences, and Zhang Ziyi has hand-to-hand combat with Chris Tucker in a scene of great energy. There are the usual Chan-style stunts, including one where the heroes dangle above city streets on a flexible bamboo pole. And a couple of those moments, over in a flash, where Chan combines grace, ability, and timing (in one, he slips through a teller's cage, and in another he seems to walk up a scaffolding). Given Chan's so-so command of English, it's ingenious to construct a sequence that silences him with a grenade taped inside his mouth.

But Tucker's scenes finally wear us down. How can a movie allow him to be so obnoxious and make no acknowledgment that his behavior is aberrant? In a nightclub run by Hong Kong gangsters, he jumps on a table and shouts, "OK, all the triads and ugly women on one side, and all the fine women on the other." He is the quintessential Ugly American, and that's not funny. One rule all comedians should know, and some have to learn the hard way, is that *they* aren't funny—it's the material that gets the laughs. Another rule is that if you're the top dog on a movie set, everybody is going to pretend to laugh at everything you do, so anyone who tells you it's not that funny is trying to do you a favor.

Sarah Silverman: Jesus Is Magic

(DIRECTED BY LIAM LYNCH; STARRING SARAH SILVERMAN, LA'VIN KIYANO; 2005)

Sarah Silverman: Jesus Is Magic is a movie that filled me with an urgent desire to see Sarah Silverman in a different movie. I liked everything about it except the writing, the direction, the editing, and the lack of a parent or adult guardian. There should have been somebody to stand up sadly after the first screening and say: "Sarah, honey, this isn't the movie you want people to see. Your material needs a lot of work; the musical scenes are deadly, except for the first one. And it looks like it was edited by someone fooling around with iMovie on a borrowed Mac."

Apparently the only person capable of telling Sarah Silverman such things is Sarah Silverman, and she obviously did not. Maybe the scene of her kissing herself in the mirror provides a clue. The result is a film that is going to make it hard to get people to come to the second Sarah Silverman film. Too bad, because Silverman is smart and funny and blindsides you with unexpected U-turns. She could be the instrument for abrasive and transgressive humor that would slice through the comedy club crap. But here, she isn't.

You have seen her before. She started on *Saturday Night Live* and has been in fifteen movies and a lot of TV shows. She's tall, brunette, and good-looking, and she says shocking things with the precise enunciation and poise of a girl who was brought up knowing how to make a good impression. The disconnect between what she says and how she says it is part of the effect. If she were crass and vulgar, her material would be insupportable: If you're going to use cancer, AIDS, and 9/11 as punch lines, you'd better know how to get the permission of the audience. She does it by seeming to be too well bred to realize what she's saying. She's always correcting herself. When she uses the word *retards* she immediately registers that it's non-PC and elaborates: "When I say 'retards,' I mean they can do anything."

So that's one of her lines. It would be a cheap shot for me to quote a dozen more, and do her act here in the review. Better to stand back and see why she's funny, but the movie doesn't work. The first problem is with timing. None of her riffs go on long enough to build. She gets a laugh, and then another one, maybe a third, and then she starts in a different direction. We want her to keep on, piling one offense on top of another. We want to see her on a roll.

That's in the concert documentary parts of the movie. She stands on a stage and does the material and there are cuts to the audience, but curiously not much of a connection; it doesn't seem to be *this* audience at *this* performance, but a generic audience. Then she cuts away from the doc stuff to little sketches. The first one, in which her sister (Laura Silverman) and her friend (Brian Posehn) brag about their recent accomplishments, is funny because she perfectly plays someone who has never accomplished anything and never will, and lies about it. Then we see her in a car, singing a song about getting a job and doing a show, and then she does a show. Fair enough.

But what's with the scene where she entertains the old folks at her grandma's rest home by singing a song telling them they will all die, soon? She is rescued by the apparent oblivion of the old folks, who seem so disconnected she could be working in blue screen. Then there's the scene where she angrily shakes the corpse of her grandmother in its casket. Here is a bulletin from the real world: Something like that is not intrinsically funny. Yes, you can probably find a way to set it up and write it to make it funny, but to simply do it, just plain do it, is pathetic. The audience, which has been laughing, grows watchful and sad.

To discuss the film's editing rhythm is to suggest it has one. There are artless and abrupt cuts between different kinds of material. She's on the stage, and then she's at the nursing home. There is a way to make that transition, but it doesn't involve a cut that feels like she was interrupted in the middle of something. And the ending comes abruptly, without any kind of acceleration and triumph in the material. Her act feels cut off at the knees. The running time, seventy minutes including end credits, is interesting, since if you subtract the offstage scenes that means we see less of her than a live audience would.

Now if Silverman had been ungifted or her material had lacked all humor, I would maybe not have bothered with a review. Why kick a movie when it's down? But she has a real talent, and she is sometimes very funny in a way that is particularly her own. Now she needs to work with a writer (not to provide the material but to shape and pace it), and a director who can build a scene, and an editor who can get her out of it, and a producer who can provide wise counsel.

On the basis of this movie, it will be her first exposure as a filmmaker to anyone like that.

Saving Silverman
(DIRECTED BY DENNIS DUGAN; STARRING JASON BIGGS, STEVE ZAHN; 2001)

Saving Silverman is so bad in so many different ways that perhaps you should see it as an example of the lowest slopes of the bell-shaped curve. This is the kind of movie that gives even its defenders fits of desperation.

Consider my friend James Berardinelli, the best of the Web-based critics. No doubt ten days of oxygen deprivation at the Sundance Film Festival helped inspire his three-star review, in which he reports optimistically, "*Saving Silverman* has its share of pratfalls and slapstick moments, but there's almost no flatulence." Here's a critical rule of thumb: You know you're in trouble when you're reduced to praising a movie for its absence of fart jokes, and have to add *almost.*

The movie is a male-bonding comedy in which three friends since grade school, now allegedly in their early twenties but looking in two cases suspiciously weathered for anyone under a hard-living thirty-two, are threatened by a romance. Darren Silverman (Jason Biggs), Wayne Le Fessier (Steve Zahn), and J. D. McNugent (Jack Black) grew up together sharing a common passion for the works of Neil Diamond; their sidewalk band, the Diamonds, performs his songs and then passes the hat.

The band is broken up, alas, when Darren is captured by Judith Snodgrass-Fessbeggler (Amanda Peet), a blond man-eater who immediately bans his friends and starts transforming him into a broken and tamed possession. "He's my puppet and I'm his puppet master!" she declares, proving that she is unfamiliar with the word *mistress,* which does not come as a surprise. In a movie so desperately in need of laughs, it's a mystery why the filmmakers didn't drag Ms. Snodgrass-Fessbeggler's parents onstage long enough to explain their decision to go with the hyphenated last name.

Wayne and J. D. concoct a desperate scheme to save Darren from marriage. They kidnap Judith, convince Darren she is dead, and arrange for him to meet the original love of his life, Sandy Perkus (Amanda Detmer), who is now studying to be a nun. She hasn't yet taken her vows, especially the one of chastity, and is a major babe in her form-fitting novice's habit.

I was going to write that the funniest character in the movie is the boys' former high school coach (R. Lee Ermey, a former marine drill sergeant). It would be more accurate to say the same character would be funny in another movie, but is stopped cold by this one, even though the screenplay tries. (When the boys ask Coach what to do with the kidnapped Judith, he replies, "Kill her.")

The lads don't idolize Neil Diamond merely in theory, but in the flesh, as well. Yes, Diamond himself appears in the film, kids himself, and sings a couple of songs. As a career decision, this ranks somewhere between being a good sport and professional suicide. Perhaps he should have reflected that the director, Dennis Dugan, has directed two Adam Sandler movies (both, it must be said, better than this).

Saving Silverman is Jason Biggs's fourth appearance in a row in a dumb sex comedy (in descending order of quality, they are *American Pie, Boys and Girls,* and *Loser*). It is time for him to strike out in a new direction; the announcement that he will appear in *American Pie II* does not seem to promise that.

Steve Zahn and Jack Black are, in the right movies, splendid comedy actors; Zahn was wonderful in *Happy, Texas,* and Jack Black stole his scenes in *High Fidelity* and *Jesus' Son.* Here they have approximately the charm of Wilson, the soccer ball. Amanda Peet and Amanda Detmer do no harm, although Peet is too nice to play a woman this mean. Lee Ermey is on a planet of his own. As for Neil Diamond, *Saving Silverman* is his first appearance in a fiction film since *The Jazz Singer* (1980), and one can only marvel that he waited twenty years to appear in a second film, and found one even worse than his first one.

Say It Isn't So

(DIRECTED BY JAMES B. ROGERS; STARRING CHRIS KLEIN, HEATHER GRAHAM; 2001)

Comedy characters can't be successfully embarrassed for more than a few seconds at a time. Even then, it's best if they don't know what they've done wrong—if the joke's on them, and they don't get it. The "hair gel" scenes in *There's Something About Mary* are a classic example of embarrassment done right. *Say It Isn't So,* on the other hand, keeps a character embarrassed in scene after scene, until he becomes an . . . embarrassment. The movie doesn't understand that embarrassment comes in a sudden painful flush of realization; drag it out, and it's not embarrassment anymore, but public humiliation, which is a different condition, and not funny.

The movie stars Heather Graham and Chris Klein as Jo and Gilly, a hairdresser and a dogcatcher who fall deeply in love and then discover they are brother and sister. Jo flees town to marry a millionaire jerk. Gilly lingers behind in public disgrace until he discovers they are not related after all. But since Jo's family wants her to marry the rich guy, everybody conspires to keep Gilly away. The movie tries for a long-running gag based on the fact that everybody in town mocks Gilly because he slept with his alleged sister. They even write rude remarks in the dust on his truck. This is not funny but merely repetitive.

The movie was produced by the Farrelly brothers, who in *There's Something About Mary* and *Kingpin* showed a finer understanding of the mechanics of comedy than they do here. *Say It Isn't So* was directed by James B. Rogers from a screenplay by Peter Gaulke and Gerry Swallow, who show they are students of Farrellyism but not yet graduates. They include obligatory elements like physical handicaps, sexual miscalculations, intestinal difficulties, and weird things done to animals, but few of the gags really work. They know the words but not the music.

Consider a scene in which Chris Klein, as Gilly, punches a cow and his arm becomes lodged in just that portion of the cow's anatomy where both Gilly and the cow would least hope to find it. I can understand intellectually that this could be funny. But to be funny, the character would have to have a great deal invested in *not* appearing like the kind of doofus who would pull such a stunt. Gilly has been established as such a simpleton he has nothing to lose. The cow scene is simply one more cross for him to bear. There is in the movie a legless pilot (Orlando Jones) who prides himself on his heroic aerial abilities. If he had gotten stuck in the cow and been pulled legless down the street—now that would have been funny. Tasteless, yes, and cruel. But not tiresome.

That leads us to another of the movie's miscalculations. Its characters are not smart enough to be properly embarrassed. To be Jo or Gilly is already to be beyond embarrassment, since they wake up already clueless. The genius of *There's Something About Mary* and *Kingpin* was that the characters played by Ben Stiller and Woody Harrelson were smart, clever, played the angles—and still got disgraced. To pick on Gilly and Jo is like shooting fish in a barrel.

Chris Klein's character seems like someone who never gets the joke, who keeps smiling bravely as if everyone can't be laughing at him. We feel sorry for him, which is fatal for a comedy. Better a sharp, edgy character who deserves his comeuppance. Heather Graham's Jo, whose principal character trait is a push-up bra, isn't really engaged by the plot at all, but is pushed hither and yon by the winds of fate.

That leaves three characters who are funny a lot of the time: Jo's parents, Valdine and Walter Wingfield (Sally Field and Richard Jenkins), and Dig McCaffey (Orlando Jones), the legless pilot. Valdine is a scheming, money-grubbing con woman who conceals from Gilly the fact that she is not his mother, so that Jo can marry the millionaire. And Walter is her terminally ill husband, communicating through an electronic voice amplifier, who bears a grudge against almost everyone he can see. These characters have the necessary meanness of spirit, and Dig McCaffey is so improbable, as a Jimi Hendrix look-alike, that he gets laughs by sheer incongruity.

On the TV clips, they show the scene where Jo gets so excited while cutting Gilly's hair that she takes a slice out of his ear. Since you have seen this scene, I will use it as an example of comic miscalculation. We see her scissors cutting through the flesh as they amputate an upper slope of his earlobe. This is not funny. It is cringe-inducing. Better to choose an angle where you can't see the actual cut at all, and then have his entire ear spring loose. Go for the laugh with the idea, not the sight, of grievous injury. And instead of giving Gilly an operation to reattach the missing flesh, have him go through the entire movie without an ear (make a subtle joke by having him always present his good ear to the camera). There are sound comic principles at work here, which *Say It Isn't So* doesn't seem to understand.

Note: The end credits include the usual obligatory outtakes from the movie. These are unique in that they are clearly real and authentic, not scripted. They demonstrate what we have suspected: that real outtakes are rarely funny.

Scary Movie 3

(DIRECTED BY DAVID ZUCKER; STARRING ANNA FARIS, CHARLIE SHEEN; 2003)

Scary Movie 3 understands the concept of a spoof but not the concept of a satire. It clicks off several popular movies (*Signs, The Sixth Sense, The Matrix, 8 Mile, The Ring*) and recycles scenes from them through a spoofalator, but it's feeding off these movies, not skewering them. The average issue of *Mad* magazine contains significantly smarter movie satire, because *Mad* goes for the vulnerable elements, and *Scary Movie 3* just wants to quote and kid.

Consider the material about *8 Mile*. Eminem is talented and I liked his movie, but he provides a target that *Scary Movie 3* misses by a mile. The Eminem clone is played by Simon Rex, whose material essentially consists of repeating what Eminem did in the original movie, at a lower level. He throws up in the john (on somebody else, ho, ho), he duels onstage with a black rapper, he preempts criticism by attacking himself as white, he pulls up the hood on his sweatshirt and it's shaped like a Ku Klux Klan hood, and so on. This is parody, not satire, and no points against Eminem are scored.

Same with the crop circles from *Signs,* where farmer Tom Logan (Charlie Sheen) finds a big crop circle with an arrow pointing to his house and the legend "Attack here." That's level one. Why not something about the way the movie extended silence as far as it could go? His parting scene with his wife (Denise Richards), who is being kept alive by the truck that has her pinned to a tree, is agonizingly labored.

The Ring material is barely different from *The Ring* itself; pop in the cassette, answer the phone, be doomed to die. *The Sixth Sense* stuff is funnier, as a psychic little kid walks through the movie relentlessly predicting everyone's secrets. Funny, but it doesn't build. Then there's an unpleasant scene at the home of newsreader Cindy Campbell (Anna Faris), involving a salivating priest who arrives to be a babysitter for her young son (ho, ho).

The movie is filled with famous and semifamous faces, although only two of them work for their laughs and get them. That would be in the pre-opening credits, where Jenny McCarthy and Pamela Anderson take the dumb blonde shtick about as far as it can possibly go, while their push-up bras do the same thing in another department.

Other cameos: Queen Latifah, Eddie Griffin, William Forsythe, Peter Boyle, Macy Gray, George Carlin, Ja Rule, Master P, and Leslie Nielsen, the Olivier of spoofs, playing the president. But to what avail? The movie has been directed by David Zucker, who with his brother Jerry and Jim Abrahams more or less invented the genre with the brilliant *Airplane!* (1980). Maybe the problem isn't with him. Maybe the problem is that the genre is over and done with and dead. *Scream* seemed to point in a new and funnier direction—the smart satire—but *Scary Movie 3* points right back again. It's like it has its own crop circle, with its own arrow pointing right at itself.

Scooby-Doo

(DIRECTED BY RAJA GOSNELL; STARRING MATTHEW LILLARD, FREDDIE PRINZE JR.; 2002)
I am not the person to review this movie. I have never seen the *Scooby-Doo* television program, and on the basis of the film I have no desire to start now. I feel no sympathy with any of the characters, I am unable to judge whether the live-action movie is a better idea than the all-cartoon TV approach, I am unable to generate the slightest interest in the plot, and I laughed not a single time, although I smiled more than once at the animated Scooby-Doo himself, an island of amusement in a wasteland of fecklessness.

What I can say, I think, is that a movie like this should in some sense be accessible to a nonfan like myself. I realize that every TV cartoon show has a cadre of fans that grew up with it, have seen every episode many times, and are alert to the nuances of the movie adaptation. But those people, however numerous they are, might perhaps find themselves going to a movie with people like myself—people who found, even at a very young age, that the world was filled with entertainment choices more stimulating than *Scooby-Doo*. If these people can't walk into the movie cold and understand it and get something out of it, then the movie has failed except as an in-joke.

As for myself, scrutinizing the screen helplessly for an angle of approach, one thing above caught my attention: the director, Raja Gosnell, has a thing about big boobs. I say this not only because of the revealing low-cut costumes of such principals as Sarah Michelle Gellar, but also because of the number of busty extras and background players, who drift by in crowd scenes with what Russ Meyer used to call "cleavage cantilevered on the same principle that made the Sydney Opera House possible." Just as Woody Allen's *Hollywood Ending* is a comedy about a movie director who forges ahead even though he is blind, *Scooby-Doo* could have been a comedy about how a Russ Meyer clone copes with being assigned a live-action adaptation of a kiddie cartoon show.

I did like the dog. Scooby-Doo so thoroughly upstages the live actors that I cannot understand why Warner Bros. didn't just go ahead and make the whole movie animated. While Matthew Lillard, Sarah Michelle Gellar, and Linda Cardellini show pluck in trying to outlast the material, Freddie Prinze Jr. seems completely at a loss to account for his presence in the movie, and the squinchy-faced Rowan (*Mr. Bean*) Atkinson plays the villain as a private joke.

I pray, dear readers, that you not send me mail explaining the genius of *Scooby-Doo* and attacking me for being ill-prepared to write this review. I have already turned myself in. Not only am I ill-prepared to review the movie, but I venture to guess that anyone who is not literally a member of a *Scooby-Doo* fan club would be equally incapable. This movie exists in a closed universe, and the rest of us are aliens. The Internet was invented so that you can find someone else's review of *Scooby-Doo*. Start surfing.

See Spot Run

(DIRECTED BY JOHN WHITESELL; STARRING DAVID ARQUETTE, MICHAEL CLARKE DUNCAN; 2001)

See Spot Run is pitched at the same intellectual level as the earlier stories involving Spot, which I found so immensely involving in the first grade. There are a few refinements. The characters this time are named Gordon, Stephanie, and James, instead of Dick and Jane. And I don't recall the Spot books describing the hero rolling around in doggy poo, or a gangster getting his testicles bitten off, but times change. The gangster is named Sonny Talia, in a heroic act of restraint by the filmmakers, who could have named him Gino with no trouble at all.

The movie is a fairly desperate PG-rated comedy about a dog that has been highly trained for the FBI's canine corps. After it bites off one of Talia's indispensables, the mob boss (Paul Sorvino) orders a hit on the dog, which is hustled into a version of the witness protection program, only to accidentally end up in the possession of young James (Angus T. Jones) and his babysitting neighbor, Gordon (David Arquette), who has a crush on James's mother, Stephanie (Leslie Bibb).

This is all setup for a series of slapstick comedy ventures, in which Gordon is humiliated and besmeared while the dog races about proving it is the most intelligent mammal in the picture. The most excruciating sequence has Gordon shinnying up a gutter pipe, which collapses (as all movie gutter pipes always do), tearing off his underpants and depositing him in one of Spot's large, damp, and voluminous gifts to the ecology. When Gordon is thoroughly smeared with caca, what do you think the odds are that (1) the lawn sprinkler system comes on, and (2) the police arrive and demand an explanation?

Another long sequence involves the destruction of a pet store, as mobsters chase the dog and Gordon gets encased in a large ball of bubble wrap, which is inflated by helium, causing him to . . . oh, never mind. And don't get me started on the scene where he lights the zebra fart.

Movies like this demonstrate that when it comes to stupidity and vulgarity, only the best will do for our children. There seems to be some kind of desperate downward trend in American taste, so that when we see a dog movie like this we think back nostalgically to the *Beethoven* dog pictures, which now represent a cultural high-water mark. Consider that there was a time in our society when children were entertained by the Lassie pictures, and you can see that the national taste is rapidly spiraling down to the level of a whoopee cushion.

And yes, of course, there are many jokes in *See Spot Run* involving the passing of gas and the placing of blame. Also a fight with two deaf women. Also an electrified dog collar that is activated by a TV channel changer, causing David Arquette to levitate while sparks fly out of his orifices. And a bus that slides over a cliff. And an FBI agent named "Cassavetes," which must be a masochistic in-joke by the filmmakers to remind themselves of how far they have fallen from their early ideals.

The one actor who emerges more or less unharmed is Michael Clarke Duncan, the gentle giant from *The Green Mile*, who is the dog's FBI handler and plays his scenes with the joy of a man whose stream of consciousness must run like this: *No matter how bad this movie is, at least it's better than working for the City of Chicago Department of Streets and Sanitation. I'm still wading through doggy do, but at least now I'm getting paid a movie star salary for doing it.*

Serendipity

(Directed by Peter Chelsom; starring John Cusack, Kate Beckinsale; 2001)
If we're meant to meet again, we will.

So says Sara Thomas to Jon Trager. This much has already happened: They have a Meet Cute while fighting over the same pair of cashmere gloves in Bloomingdale's. They feel, if not love, strong attraction at first sight. They go out for hot chocolate. They find out each is dating somebody else. They separate. They return—he for a scarf, she for a parcel. They meet again. He wants her phone number. But no. They must leave themselves in the hands of Fate.

Fate I have no problem with. Leaving themselves in the hands of this screenplay is another matter. It bounces them through so many amazing coincidences and serendipitous parallels and cosmic concordances that Fate is not merely knocking on the door, it has entered with a SWAT team and is banging their heads together and administering poppers.

Jon is played by John Cusack in what is either a bad career move or temporary insanity. Sara is played by Kate Beckinsale, who is a good actress, but not good enough to play this dumb. Jon and Sara have much in common; both are missing an *h*. The movie puts them through dramatic and romantic situations so close to parody as to make no difference; one more turn of the screw and this could be a satire of *Sleepless in Seattle*.

Consider. They want to be together. They like each other better than the people they are dating. But they toy with their happiness by setting a series of tests. For example: She says they'll get on separate elevators in a hotel and see if they both push the same button. Odds are about 30-to-1 against it. They do, however, both push the same button—but do not meet because of a little boy who pushes all the other buttons on Cusack's elevator. I consider this God's way of telling them, "Don't tempt me."

Another test. Jon will write his telephone number on a $5 bill and it will go out in the world, and she will see if it comes back to her. A third test. Sara will write her number in a copy of a novel by Gabriel Garcia Marquez, and if Jon finds it in a used-book store, well, there you are. (Marquez is fond of coincidences, but *Serendipity* elevates magic realism into the realm of three-card monte.) Jon searches in countless bookstores, having never heard of Bibliofind or Alibris, where for enough money every used-book seller in the world would be happy to have a peek inside his copies of the volume.

Years pass—two or three in the movie, more in the theater. Both are engaged to others. Some smiles are generated by her fiancé, a New Age musician (John Corbett) who illustrates the principle that men who chose to wear their hair very long after about 1980 are afflicted by delusional convictions that they are cooler than anyone else. The plot risks bursting under the strain of its coincidences, as Sara and Jon fly to opposite coasts at the same time and engage in a series of Idiot Plot moves so extreme and wrongheaded that even other characters in the same scene should start shouting helpful suggestions.

By the time these two people finally get together (if they do—I don't want to give anything away) I was thinking of new tests. What if she puts a personal ad in a paper and he has to guess which paper? How about dedicating a song to her, and trusting her to be listening to the radio at that moment, in that city? What about throwing a dart at a spinning world globe? I hope this movie never has a sequel, because Jon and Sara are destined to become the most boring married couple in history. For years to come, people at parties will be whispering, "See that couple over there? The Tragers? Jon and Sara? Whatever you do, don't ask them how they met."

Silent Hill

(DIRECTED BY CHRISTOPHE GANS; STARRING RADHA MITCHELL, SEAN BEAN; 2006)

I had a nice conversation with seven or eight people coming down on the escalator after we all saw *Silent Hill*. They wanted me to explain it to them. I said I didn't have a clue. They said, "You're supposed to be a movie critic, aren't you?" I said, "Supposed to be. But we work mostly with movies." "Yeah," said the girl in the Harley T-shirt, "I guess this was like a video game that you, like, had to play in order to, like, understand the movie."

I guess. I was out in Boulder, Colorado, last week on a panel about video games and whether they can be art, and a lot of the students said they were really looking forward to *Silent Hill* because it's one of the best games, and they read on the Internet that the movie was supposed to live up to the game. That was all speculation, of course, because Sony Pictures declined to preview the film for anybody, perhaps because they were concerned it would not live up to the game, or because they were afraid it would. When I told one student that the movie was not being previewed, there was real pain on his face, as if he had personally been devalued.

Not only can I not describe the plot of this movie, but I have a feeling the last scene reverses half of what I thought I knew (or didn't know). What I can say is that it's an incredibly good-looking film. The director, Christophe Gans, uses graphics and special effects and computers and grainy, scratchy film stock and surrealistic images and makes *Silent Hill* look more like an experimental art film than a horror film—except for the horror, of course. The visuals are terrific; credit also to cinematographer Dan Laustsen, production designer Carol Spier, and the art, set, and costume artists. But what are we to make of dialogue such as I will now describe?

A group of undead citizens of the ghost town of Silent Hill have gathered for some witch burning. The town was abandoned thirty years ago because of the fumes from mine fires, which still smolder beneath the surface. Gray ash falls like rain. "Something terrible happened here," a character says perceptively. The townspeople pile wood on a bonfire in the center of an abandoned church and tie an alleged witch to a ladder, which is then lowered over the flames until the victim's skin gets extra crispy. Next up: Little Sharon (Jodell Ferland), the daughter of the heroine, Rose (Radha Mitchell). She is tied to the ladder and prepared to be lowered and roasted, when her mother bursts into the church and cries out, and I quote, "It's OK, baby. Everything's gonna be OK!"

The people who live in Silent Hill are dead, I guess. Some of them glow like old embers on a fire, which is not a sign of life. They live in abandoned buildings and in the mines and in a Smoke and Flame Factory, which you will recall from my Little Movie Glossary is a factory-like location of uncertain purpose that generates a lot of smoke and flames. Also sharing their space are ratlike little CGI insects, who scurry around thinking they look a lot scarier than they do.

Rose has come here with her daughter Sharon because the girl has taken to sleepwalking at night, and standing on the edge of high cliffs while saying "Silent Hill" in her sleep. Obviously the correct treatment is to take her to the abandoned town itself. Rose and Sharon race off in the night, pursued by Rose's husband (Sean Bean) and a motorcycle cop (Laurie Holden) who is dressed like a leather mistress. The usual zombielike little girl turns up in the headlights, there is a crash, and then everybody wanders through the town for two hours while the art direction looks great. I especially liked the snakelike wires at the end that held people suspended in midair. I also liked it when Johnny Cash sang *Ring of Fire* on the sound track, since if there was ever a movie in need of a song about a ring of fire, this is that film.

Now here's a funny thing. Although I did not understand the story, I would have appreciated a great deal less explanation. All through the movie, characters are pausing in order to offer arcane back stories and historical perspectives and metaphysical insights and occult orientations. They talk and talk, and somehow their words do not light up any synapses in my brain, if my brain has synapses and they're supposed to light up, and if it doesn't and they're not, then they still don't make any sense.

Perhaps those who have played the game will understand the movie and enjoy it. Speaking of synapses, another member of that panel discussion at Boulder was Dr. Leonard Shlain, chairman of laparoscopic surgery at California Pacific Medical Center, and an author whose book *Art & Physics: Parallel Visions in Space, Time, and Light* makes you think that if anyone could understand *Silent Hill,* he could.

Dr. Shlain made the most interesting comment on the panel. He said they took some four- and five-year-olds and gave them video games and asked them to figure out how to play them without instructions. Then they watched the children's brain activity with real-time monitors. "At first, when they were figuring out the games," he said, "the whole brain lit up. But by the time they knew how to play the games, the brain went dark, except for one little point." Walking out after *Silent Hill,* I thought of that lonely pilot light, and I understood why I failed to understand the movie. My damn brain lit up too much.

Simpatico

(DIRECTED BY MATTHEW WARCHUS; STARRING NICK NOLTE, JEFF BRIDGES; 2000)

Simpatico is a long slog through perplexities and complexities that disguise what this really is: The kind of B-movie plot that used to clock in at seventy-five minutes on the bottom half of a double bill. It's based on a Sam Shepard play, unseen by me. Since Shepard is a good playwright, we're left with two possibilities: (1) It has been awkwardly adapted, or (2) it should have stayed in Shepard's desk drawer.

The plot involves a kind of exchange of personalities between Carter (Jeff Bridges), a rich Kentucky racehorse breeder, and Vinnie (Nick

Nolte), a shabby layabout who has been blackmailing him for years. They were once friends, long ago when they were young, and involved in a scheme to cheat at the track by switching horses. Vinnie has some photos that Carter would not want anyone to see, and that gives him leverage. This time, he interrupts Carter in the middle of negotiations to sell an expensive horse named Simpatico, demanding that he fly to California to get him out of a fix. Seems a supermarket cashier named Cecilia (Catherine Keener) is accusing him of sexual misconduct.

Oh, but it's a lot more complicated than that, and neither Cecilia nor her relationship with Vinnie is quite as described. Two other figures from the past also enter: Rosie (Sharon Stone), now Carter's boozy but colorful wife, and Simms (Albert Finney), once a racing commissioner, now a tracer of bloodlines. Students of noir will know that the contemporary story will stir up old ghosts.

Those who are not noir lovers won't be in the dark for long, since director Matthew Warchus and his cowriter, David Nicholls, supply flashbacks that incriminate some of the characters (although not, in this day and age, seriously enough to inspire the vast heavings of this leviathan plot). Nolte and Bridges are portrayed as young men by Shawn Hatosy and Liam Waite, a casting decision that adds to the murkiness, since Hatosy, who is supposed to be young Nolte, looks more like young Bridges, and Waite, who is supposed to be young Bridges, looks like nobody else in the movie. This theme is developed further, I suppose, as Nolte and Bridges subtly start to resemble each other.

It happens that I've just seen a complicated noir, Roman Polanski's *Chinatown*, which also involves sexual misconduct in the past and blackmail in the present. One reason it works so well is that the characters seem to drive the plot: Things turn out the way they do because the characters are who they are. The plot of *Simpatico* is like a clockwork mechanism that would tick whether or not anyone cared what time it was.

The Skulls

(DIRECTED BY ROB COHEN; STARRING JOSHUA JACKSON, PAUL WALKER; 2000)

I would give a great deal to be able to see *The Skulls* on opening night in New Haven in a movie theater full of Yale students, with gales of laughter rolling at the screen. It isn't a comedy, but that won't stop anyone. *The Skulls* is one of the great howlers, a film that bears comparison, yes, with *The Greek Tycoon* or even *The Scarlet Letter.* It's so ludicrous in so many different ways it achieves a kind of forlorn grandeur. It's in a category by itself.

The movie claims to rip the lid off a secret campus society named the Skulls, which is obviously inspired by the Yale society known as Skull and Bones. The real Skull and Bones has existed for two centuries and has counted presidents, tycoons, and CIA founders among its alumni. Membership was an honor—until now. After seeing this movie, members are likely to sneak out of the theater through the lavatory windows.

The story: Luke McNamara (Joshua Jackson) attends a university that is never mentioned by name. (Clues: It is in New Haven and has a lot of big Y's painted on its walls.) He is a townie, rides a bike, lost his father when he was one, is poor, works in the cafeteria. Yet he's tapped for membership in the Skulls because he is a star on the varsity rowing crew.

Luke's best friends are a black student journalist named Will Beckford (Hill Harper) and a rich girl named Chloe (Leslie Bibb). Luke secretly loves Chloe but keeps it a secret because "Chloe's parents own a private jet, and I've never even been in a jet." Another of Luke's friends is Caleb Mandrake (Paul Walker), whose father, Litten (Craig T. Nelson) is a Supreme Court candidate. With soap opera names like Caleb and Litten Mandrake (and Sen. Ames Levritt), the film contains an enormous mystery, which is, why doesn't Chloe have a last name? I suggest Worsthorne-Waugh.

Luke is tapped for the Skulls. This involves racing around campus to answer lots of ringing pay phones, after which he and the other new pledges are drugged, pass out, and awaken in coffins, ready to be reborn in their new lives. They go through "revealing ceremonies" inside the Skulls' campus clubhouse, a Gothic monument so filled with vistas and arches and caverns and halls and pools and verandahs that Dracula would have something along these lines if he could afford it.

Mel Brooks said it's good to be the king. It's better to be a Skull. Luke and his fellow tappees find $10,000 in their ATM accounts (later they get $100,000 checks). Beautiful women are supplied after an induction ceremony. They all get new sports cars. The Skulls insignia is branded on their wrists with a red-hot iron, but they get shiny new wristwatches to cover the scar. I'm thinking, how secret is a society when hookers are hired for the pledge class? Do they wear those watches in the shower? In this litigious age, is it safe to drug undergraduates into unconsciousness?

Each Skull is given a key to the clubhouse and a rule book. "There's a rule for all possible situations: they're told. I want that book. Rule One: Don't lose the rule book. Will, the journalist, steals Caleb's key and rule book and sneaks inside the clubhouse, and (I am now revealing certain plot secrets) is later found to have hanged himself. But was it really suicide? Luke thinks Caleb might know, and can ask him, because the Skulls have a bonding ceremony in which new members are assigned soul mates. You are locked in an iron cage with your soul mate and lowered into a pit in the floor, at which time you can ask him anything you want, and he has to answer truthfully, while the other Skulls listen to the words echoing through the crypt.

Many powerful adult men still take the Skulls very seriously. Not only Judge Litten Mandrake but Sen. Ames Levritt (William Petersen), who are involved in a power struggle of their own. They put pressure on Luke to end his curiosity about Will's death. The following dialogue occurs, which will have the New Haven audience baying with joy:

"This is your preacceptance to the law school of your choice."

"I haven't even applied yet."

"Imagine that!"

Chloe is enlisted as Luke's sidekick for some Hardy Boys capers, but soon Luke is subjected to a forcible psychiatric examination at the campus health clinic (no laughter here), and bundled off to a mental hospital where, so far-reaching is the influence of the Skulls, he is kept in a zombie state with drugs while the senator and the judge struggle over his future. Oh, and there's a car chase scene. Oh, and a duel, in broad daylight, with all the Skulls watching, in an outdoor pavilion on the Skulls' lawn that includes a marble platform apparently designed specifically for duels.

The real Skull and Bones numbers among its alumni former President Bush and his son. Of course, there's no connection between Skull and Bones and the fictional Skulls. Still, the next time George W. has a press conference, a reporter should ask to see under his wristwatch. Only kidding.

Slackers

(DIRECTED BY DEWEY NICKS; STARRING DEVON SAWA, JASON SCHWARTZMAN; 2002)
Slackers is a dirty movie. Not a sexy, erotic, steamy, or even smutty movie, but a just plain dirty movie. It made me feel unclean, and I'm the guy who liked *There's Something About Mary* and both *American Pie* movies. Oh, and *Booty Call*. This film knows no shame.

Consider a scene where the heroine's roommate, interrupted while masturbating, continues even while a man she has never met is in the room. Consider a scene where the hero's roommate sings a duet with a sock puppet on his penis. Consider a scene where we cut away from the hero and the heroine to join two roommates just long enough for a loud fart, and then cut back to the main story again.

And consider a scene where Mamie Van Doren, who is seventy-one years old, plays a hooker in a hospital bed who bares her breasts so that the movie's horny creep can give them a sponge bath. On the day when I saw *Slackers*, there were many things I expected and even wanted to see in a movie, but I confess Mamie Van Doren's breasts were not among them.

The movie is an exhausted retread of the old campus romance gag where the pretty girl almost believes the lies of the reprehensible schemer, instead of trusting the nice guy who loves her. The only originality the movie brings to this formula is to make it incomprehensible, through the lurching incompetence of its story structure. Details are labored while the big picture remains unpainted.

Slackers should not be confused with Richard Linklater's *Slacker* (1991), a film that will be treasured long after this one has been turned into landfill. *Slackers* stars the previously blameless Devon Sawa (*SLC Punk! Final Destination*) and Jason Schwartzman (*Rushmore*) as rivals for the attention of the beautiful Angela (James King, who despite her name is definitely a girl). Schwartzman plays Ethan, campus geek; Sawa is Dave, a professional cheater and con man. Ethan obsesses over Angela and blackmails Sawa by threatening to expose his exam-cheating scheme. He demands that Dave "deliver" the girl to him.

This demand cannot be met for a number of reasons. One of them is that Ethan is comprehensively creepy (he not only has an Angela doll made from strands of her hair, but does things with it I will not tire you by describing). Another reason is that Angela falls for Dave. The plot requires Angela to temporarily be blinded to Ethan's repulsiveness and to believe his lies about Dave. These goals are met by making Angela remarkably dense, and even then we don't believe her.

Watching *Slackers*, I was appalled by the poverty of its imagination. There is even a scene where Ethan approaches a girl from behind, thinking she is Angela, and of course she turns around and it is not Angela, but a girl who wears braces and smiles at him so widely and for so long we can almost hear the assistant director instructing her to be sure the camera can see those braces.

But back to the dirt. There is a kind of one-upmanship now at work in Hollywood, inspired by the success of several gross-out comedies, to elevate smut into an art form. This is not an entirely futile endeavor; it can be done, and when it is done well, it can be funny. But most of the wannabes fail to understand one thing: It is funny when a character is offensive *despite* himself, but not funny when he is *deliberately* offensive. The classic "hair gel" scene involving Ben Stiller and Cameron Diaz in *There's Something About Mary* was funny because neither one had the slightest idea what was going on.

Knowing that this movie will be block-booked into countless multiplexes, pitying the audiences that stumble into it, I want to stand in line with those kids and whisper the names of other movies now in release: *Monster's Ball, Black Hawk Down, Gosford Park, The Royal Tenenbaums, A Beautiful Mind, The Count of Monte Cristo.* Or even *Orange County*, also about screwed-up college students, but in an intelligent and amusing way. There are a lot of good movies in theaters right now. Why waste two hours (which you can never get back) seeing a rotten one?

Sleepover

(DIRECTED BY JOE NUSSBAUM; STARRING ALEXA VEGA, MIKA BOOREM; 2004)

I take it as a rule of nature that all American high schools are ruled by a pack of snobs, led by a supremely confident young woman who is blond, superficial, catty, and ripe for public humiliation. This character is followed everywhere by two friends who worship her and are a little bit shorter. Those schools also contain a group of friends who are not popular and do not think of themselves as pretty, although they are smarter, funnier, and altogether more likable than the catty-pack.

In the classic form of this formula, the reigning blonde dates a hunk whom the mousy outcast has a crush on, and everything gets cleared up at the prom when the hunk realizes the mouse is the real beauty, while the evil nature of the popular girl is exposed in a sensationally embarrassing way.

Sleepover, a lame and labored comedy, doesn't recycle this plot (the blonde gets dumped by her boyfriend) but works more as a series of riffs on the underlying themes. It moves the age group down a few years, so that the girls are all just entering high school. And it lowers the stakes—instead of competing for the football captain, the rivals enter into a struggle over desirable seating in the school's outdoor lunchroom. Winners get the "popular" table, losers have to sit by the Dumpster. That a school would locate a lunch area next to the garbage doesn't say much for its hygiene standards, but never mind.

Julie is the girl we're supposed to like. She's played by Alexa Vega, from *Spy Kids*. Staci (Sara Paxton) is the girl we're supposed to hate. Julie's posse includes Hannah (Mika Boorem), a good friend who is moving to Canada for no better reason, as far as I can tell, than to provide an attribute for a character with no other talking points; and Farrah (the wonderfully named Scout Taylor-Compton), who functions basically as an element useful to the cinematographer in composing groups of characters.

Julie decides to have a sleepover, and at the last minute invites poor Yancy (the also wonderfully named Kallie Flynn Childress), who is plump and self-conscious about her weight. Julie's invitation is so condescending it's a form of insult, something that doesn't seem to occur to the grateful Yancy. Julie's mom, the wonderfully named Gabby (Jane Lynch), lays down rules for the sleepover, all of which will be violated by the end of the evening without anything being noticed by her dad, Jay (Jeff Garlin), reinforcing the rule that the parents in teenage comedies would remain oblivious if their children moved the Ringling Bros., Barnum & Bailey Circus into their bedrooms.

Staci, the popular one, visits the slumber party to suggest a scavenger hunt, with the winner to get the desirable lunch table. So it's up to the girls to sneak out of the house and snatch all the trophies, including of course the boxer shorts of the high school hunk. There is a tradition in which movie teenagers almost always have bedrooms with windows opening onto roofs, porches, trellises, etc., which function perfectly as escape routes when necessary, but collapse instantly (a) when used by an unpopular character or (b) when the risk of discovery and betrayal needs to be fabricated.

What happens during the scavenger hunt I will leave to you to discover, if you are so unwise as to attend this movie in a season when *Mean Girls* is still in theaters. One of the movie's strangest scenes has Julie, who is about fourteen, sneaking into a bar because the scavenger hunt requires her to get a photo of herself being treated to a drink by a grown-up. This scene is outrageous even if she orders a Shirley Temple, but is even weirder because the guy she chooses is a teacher from her junior high, who must live in a wonderland of his own since he obviously has no idea of the professional hazards involved in buying a drink in public for one of his barely pubescent students, and then posing for a photo so she will have proof.

I don't require all high school (or junior high) comedies to involve smart, imaginative, articulate future leaders. But I am grateful when the movie at least devises something interesting for them to do, or expresses empathy with their real natures. The characters in *Sleepover* are shadows of shadows, diluted from countless better, even marginally better, movies. There was no reason to make this movie, and no reason to see it.

Snow Day

(DIRECTED BY CHRIS KOCH; STARRING MARK WEBBER, ZENA GREY; 2000)

Snow Day involves a very, very busy day in the life of an upstate New York teenager named Hal (Mark Webber), who is hopelessly in love with the unavailable school dreamboat, Claire (Emmanuelle Chriqui). He is, he believes, invisible to her, but that changes when a record snowfall forces the schools to close for a day, and gives him an opportunity to demonstrate what a unique and wonderful person he is—potentially, anyway.

The movie surrounds Hal with a large cast of supporting characters—too many probably for a two-hour movie, let alone this one that clocks at ninety minutes including end titles. There's his dad (Chevy Chase), a weatherman who resents having to wear silly costumes; and his mom (Jean Smart), a woman whose career keeps her so busy that she doesn't stop to smell the coffee or enjoy the snow.

And, let's see, his kid sister, Natalie (Zena Grey), and his best female friend, Lane (Schuyler Fisk), and, of course Snowplow Man (Chris Elliott), whose hated plow clears the streets and thus makes it possible to go to school—not that these kids don't wander all over town on the snow day. In a film top-heavy with plot and character, Snowplow Man should have been the first to go; played by Elliott as a clone of a Texas Chainsaw gang member, he is rumored to have made the snow chains for his tires out of the braces of the kids he's run down.

The arc of the movie is familiar. Hal yearns for Claire and is advised on his campaign by Lane, the loyal gal pal who perhaps represents true love right there under his very nose, were he not too blind, of course, to see it. He has to struggle against a school wiseguy on a high-powered snowmobile, who claims Claire for his own, while his weatherman dad has to wear hula skirts on the air in a fight for ratings with the top-rated local weather jerk. There's also a hated school principal and a square dee-jay at the ice rink (he likes Al Martino) and the programming executive (Pam Grier) who makes Chevy wear the silly costumes.

One of the inspirations for *Snow Day* is the 1983 classic *A Christmas Story*, also narrated by the hero, also with a kooky dad, also with a dream (a BB gun rather than a girl). But that was a real story, a memory that went somewhere and evoked rich nostalgia. *Snow Day* is an uninspired assembly of characters and story lines that interrupt one another, until the battle against Snowplow Man takes over just when we're hoping he will disappear from the movie and set free the teenage romance trapped inside it.

Acting Observation: Chris Elliott comes from a rich comic heritage (his father is Bob of Bob and Ray), but where his dad treasured droll understatement, Chris froths with overacting. There's a scene toward the end where he's tied to a children-crossing sign and laughs maniacally, like a madman, for absolutely no reason. Why is this funny? He has gone mad? Always was mad? It is funny to hear him laugh? We look curiously at the screen, regarding behavior without purpose.

Observation Two: Chevy Chase has been in what can charitably be called more than his share of bad movies, but at least he knows how to deliver a laugh when he's given one. (When his career-driven wife makes a rare appearance at dinner, he asks his son to "call security.") After the screening of *Snow Day*, I overheard another critic saying she couldn't believe she wished there had been more Chevy Chase, and I knew how she felt.

Third Observation: Through a coincidence in bookings, *Snow Day* and *Holy Smoke*, opening on the same day, both contain Pam Grier roles that inspire only the thought "What's Pam Grier doing in such a lousy role?" A year ago, she was in another lousy teenage movie, *Jawbreaker*. Is this the pay-off for her wonderful performance in *Jackie Brown* (1997)? What a thought-less place is Hollywood, and what talent it must feel free to waste.

Son of the Mask

(Directed by Lawrence Guterman; starring Jamie Kennedy, Alan Cumming; 2005)

One of the foundations of comedy is a character who must do what he doesn't want to do because of the logic of the situation. As Auden pointed out about limericks, they're funny not because they end with a dirty word, but because they have no choice but to end with the dirty word—by that point, it's the only word that rhymes and makes sense. Lucille Ball made a career out of finding herself in embarrassing situations and doing the next logical thing, however ridiculous.

Which brings us to *Son of the Mask* and its violations of this theory. The movie's premise is that if you wear a magical ancient mask, it will cause you to behave in strange ways. Good enough, and in Jim Carrey's original *The Mask* (1994), the premise worked. Carrey's elastic face was stretched into a caricature, he gained incredible powers, he exhausted himself with manic energy. But there were rules. There was a baseline of sanity from which the mania proceeded. *Son of the Mask* lacks a baseline. It is all mania, all the time; the behavior in the movie is not inappropriate, shocking, out of character, impolite, or anything else except behavior.

Both *Mask* movies are inspired by the zany world of classic cartoons. The hero of *Son of the Mask,* Tim Avery (Jamie Kennedy), is no doubt named after Tex Avery, the legendary Warner Bros. animator, although it is *One Froggy Evening* (1955), by the equally legendary Chuck Jones, that plays a role in the film. Their films all obeyed the Laws of Cartoon Thermodynamics, as established by the distinguished theoreticians Trevor Paquette and Lt. Justin D. Baldwin. (Examples: Law III: "Any body passing through solid matter will leave a perforation conforming to its perimeter"; Law IX: "Everything falls faster than an anvil.")

These laws, while seemingly arbitrary, are consistent in all cartoons. We know that Wile E. Coyote can chase the Road Runner off a cliff and keep going until he looks down; only then will he fall. And that the Road Runner can pass through a tunnel entrance in a rock wall, but Wile E. Coyote will smash into the wall. We instinctively understand Law VIII ("Any violent rearrangement of feline matter is impermanent").

Even cartoons know that if you don't have rules, you're playing tennis without a net.

The premise in *Son of the Mask* is that an ancient mask, found in the earlier movie, has gone missing again. It washes up on the banks of a little stream and is fetched by Otis the Dog (Bear), who brings it home to the Avery household, where we find Tim (Kennedy) and his wife, Tonya (Traylor Howard). Tim puts on the Mask, and is transformed into a whiz-kid at his advertising agency, able to create brilliant campaigns in a single bound. He also, perhaps unwisely, wears it to bed and engenders an infant son, Alvey, who is born with cartoonlike abilities and discovers them by watching the frog cartoon on TV.

Tim won an instant promotion to the big account, but without the Mask he is a disappointment. And the Mask cannot be found, because Otis has dragged it away and hidden it somewhere—although not before Otis snuffles at it until it attaches itself to his face, after which he is transformed into a cartoon dog and careens wildly around the yard and the sky, to his alarm.

A word about baby Alvey (played by the twins Liam and Ryan Falconer). I have never much liked movie babies who do not act like babies. I think they're scary. The first *Look Who's Talking* movie was cute, but the sequels were nasty, especially when the dog started talking. About *Baby's Day Out* (1994), in which Baby Bink set Joe Mantegna's crotch on fire, the less said the better.

I especially do not like Baby Alvey, who behaves not according to the rules for babies, but more like a shape-shifting creature in a Japanese anime. There may be a way this could be made funny, but *Son of the Mask* doesn't find it.

Meanwhile, powerful forces seek the Mask. The god Odin (Bob Hoskins) is furious with his son Loki (Alan Cumming) for having lost the Mask, and sends him down to Earth (or maybe these gods already live on Earth, I dunno) to get it back again. Loki, who is the god of mischief, has a spiky punk hairstyle that seems inspired by the jester's cap and bells, without the bells. He picks up the scent and causes no end of trouble for the Averys, although of course the dog isn't talking.

But my description makes the movie sound more sensible than it is. What we basically have here is a license for the filmmakers to do whatever they want to do with the special effects, while the plot, like Wile E. Coyote, keeps running into the wall.

Sorority Boys

(Directed by Wallace Wolodarsky; starring Barry Watson, Harland Williams; 2002)

One element of *Sorority Boys* is undeniably good, and that is the title. Pause by the poster on the way into the theater. That will be your high point. It has all you need for a brainless, autopilot, sitcom ripoff: a high concept that is right there in the title, easily grasped at the pitch meeting. The title suggests the poster art, the poster art gives you the movie, and story details can be sketched in by study of *Bosom Buddies, National Lampoon's Animal House*, and the shower scenes in any movie involving girls' dorms or sports teams.

What is unusual about *Sorority Boys* is how it caves in to the homophobia of the audience by not even *trying* to make its cross-dressing heroes look like halfway, even tenth-of-the-way, plausible girls. They look like college boys wearing cheap wigs and dresses they bought at Goodwill. They usually need a shave. One keeps his retro forward-thrusting sideburns and just combs a couple of locks of his wig forward to "cover" them. They look as feminine as the sailors wearing coconut brassieres in *South Pacific*.

Their absolute inability to pass as women leads to another curiosity about the movie, which is that all of the other characters are obviously mentally impaired. How else to explain fraternity brothers who don't recognize their own friends in drag? Sorority sisters who think these are real women and want to pledge them on first sight? A father who doesn't realize that's his *own son* he's trying to pick up?

I know. I'm being too literal. I should be a good sport and go along with the joke. But the joke is not funny. The movie is not funny. If it's this easy to get a screenplay filmed in Hollywood, why did they bother with that Project Greenlight contest? Why not ship all the entries directly to Larry Brezner and Walter Hamada, the producers of *Sorority Boys,* who must wear Santa suits to work?

The plot begins with three members of Kappa Omicron Kappa fraternity, who are thrown out of the KOK house for allegedly stealing party funds. Homeless and forlorn, they decide to pledge the Delta Omicron Gamma house after learning that the DOGs need new members. Dave (Barry Watson) becomes Daisy and is soon feeling chemistry with the DOG president, Leah (Melisa Sagemiller), who is supposed to be an intellectual feminist but can shower nude with him and not catch on he's a man.

Harland Williams and Michael Rosenbaum play the other two fugitive KOKs—roles that, should they become stars, will be invaluable as a source of clips at roasts in their honor. Among the DOGs is the invaluable Heather Matarazzo, who now has a lock on the geeky plain girl roles, even though she is in actual fact sweet and pretty. Just as Latina actresses have risen up in arms against Jennifer Connelly for taking the role of John Forbes Nash's El Salvadoran wife in *A Beautiful Mind,* so ugly girls should picket Heather Matarazzo.

Because the intelligence level of the characters must be low, very low, very very low, for the masquerade to work, the movie contains no wit, only labored gags involving falsies, lipstick, unruly erections, and straight guys who don't realize they're trying to pick up a man. (I imagine yokels in the audience responding with the Gradually Gathering Guffaw as they catch on. "Hey, Jethro! He don't know she's a guy! Haw! Haw! Haw!") The entire movie, times ten lacks the humor of a single line in the Bob Gibson/Shel Silverstein song "Mendocino Desperados." ("She was a he, but what the hell, honey/ Since you've already got my money . . .")

I'm curious about who would go to see this movie. Obviously moviegoers with a low opinion of their own taste. It's so obviously what it is that you would require a positive desire to throw away money in order to lose two hours of your life. *Sorority Boys* will be the worst movie playing in any multiplex in America this weekend, and, yes, I realize *Crossroads* is still out there.

Stealing Harvard
(DIRECTED BY BRUCE MCCULLOCH; STARRING JASON LEE, TOM GREEN; 2002)

The laugh in *Stealing Harvard* comes early, when we see the name of the company where the hero works. It's a home health care corporation named Homespital. That made me laugh. It made me smile again when the name turned up later. And on the laugh meter, that's about it. This is as lax and limp a comedy as I've seen in a while, a meander through worn-out material.

Jason Lee, who can be engaging in the right material (like *Chasing Amy* and *Almost Famous*), is bland and disposable here, as John Plummer, a young Homespital executive. The firm is owned by his fiancée's father (Dennis Farina), who subjects John to savage cross-examinations on whether he has slept with his daughter. He lies and says he hasn't. He might be telling the truth if he said he wishes he hadn't, since the fiancée, Elaine (Leslie Mann), inexplicably weeps during sex.

Despite his foray into the middle classes, John has not forgotten his super-slut sister Patty (Megan Mullally), who despite a life of untiring promiscuity has a daughter, Noreen (Tammy Blanchard), who has been accepted by Harvard. Carefully preserved home videos show John promising to help with her tuition, and as it happens Noreen needs $29,000— almost exactly the amount Elaine has insisted John have in the bank before she will marry him.

Crime is obviously the way to raise the money, according to John's best pal, Duff (Tom Green), who suggests a break-in at a house where the safe seems to stand open. The owner is, alas, at home, and there is a painfully unfunny sequence in which he forces John to dress in drag and "spoon" to remind him of his late wife. There's another botched robbery in which John and Duff, wearing ski masks, argue over which one gets to call himself Kyle, and so on.

Seeing Tom Green reminded me, how could it not, of his movie *Freddy Got Fingered* (2001), which was so poorly received by film critics that it received only one lonely, apologetic positive review on the Tomatometer. I gave it—let's see—no stars. Bad movie, especially the scene where Green was whirling the newborn infant around his head by its umbilical cord.

But the thing is, I remember *Freddy Got Fingered* more than a year later. I refer to it sometimes. It is a milestone. And for all its sins it was at least an ambitious movie, a go-for-broke attempt to accomplish something. It failed, but it has not left me convinced that Tom Green doesn't have good work in him. Anyone with his nerve and total lack of taste is sooner or later going to make a movie worth seeing.

Stealing Harvard, on the other hand, is a singularly unambitious product, content to paddle lazily in the shallows of sitcom formula. It has no edge, no hunger to be better than it is. It ambles pleasantly through its inanity, like a guest happy to be at a boring party. When you think of some of the weird stuff Jason Lee and Tom Green have been in over the years, you wonder what they did to amuse themselves during the filming.

Stealth

(Directed by Rob Cohen; starring Josh Lucas, Jessica Biel; 2005)

Stealth is an offense against taste, intelligence, and the noise pollution code—a dumbed-down *Top Gun* crossed with the HAL 9000 plot from *2001.* It might be of interest to you if you want to see lots of jet airplanes going real fast and making a lot of noise and if you don't care that the story doesn't merely defy logic, but strips logic bare, cremates it, and scatters its ashes. Here is a movie with the nerve to discuss a computer brain "like a quantum sponge" while violating Newton's laws of motion.

The plot: Navy fliers have been chosen to pilot a new generation of stealth fighter-bombers. They are Lt. Ben Gannon (Josh Lucas), Lt. Kara Wade (Jessica Biel), and Lt. Henry Purcell (Jamie Foxx, who in his speech on Oscar night should have thanked God this movie wasn't released while the voters were marking their ballots).

They're all aboard the aircraft carrier *Abraham Lincoln* in the Philippine Sea, under the command of Capt. George Cummings (Sam Shepard, who played the test pilot Chuck Yeager in *The Right Stuff*). In a movie like this, you're asking for trouble if you remind people of *2001, Top Gun,* and *The Right Stuff.*

The pilots believe that three is a lucky number, because it is a prime number. One helpfully explains to the others what a prime number is; I guess they didn't get to primes at Annapolis. In a movie that uses unexplained phrases such as "quantum sponge," why not just let the characters say "prime number" and not explain it? Many audience members will assume "prime number" is another one of those pseudo-scientific terms they're always thinking up for movies like this.

Capt. Cummings has bad news: They're being joined by a "fourth wingman." This is a UCAV (Unmanned Combat Aerial Vehicle) controlled by a computer. The pilots are unhappy, but not so unhappy that Gannon and Wade do not feel a powerful sexual attraction, although pilots are not supposed to fraternize. At one point Gannon visits Wade's cabin, where she has laundry hanging on the line, and is nearly struck by a wet brassiere. "Pardon my C-cup," she says, a line I doubt any human female would use in such a situation.

Suddenly the pilots have to scramble for an emergency: "Three terrorist cells are about to meet in twenty-four minutes in Rangoon," Capt. George tells them. Remarkable, that this information is so precise and yet so tardy. The pilots find they not only have time to take off from the aircraft carrier and fly to Burma, but to discuss their strategy via radio once they get there. The meeting is in a building that is still under construction. Computer simulations show that if it falls over, it will kill a lot of people on the ground. Amazing what computers can do these days. However, if the building is struck from directly above, it may fall down in its own footprint.

Alas, the rocket bombs carried by the planes do not achieve the necessary penetration velocity. Lt. Gannon decides that if he goes into a vertical dive, he can increase the velocity. The bomb is released, he pulls out of the dive low enough for everyone in Rangoon to get a good look at his plane, and the building collapses. It looks so much like the falling towers of the World Trade Center that I felt violated by the image.

Whoops! Another emergency. Lightning strikes the UCAV, which goes nuts and starts to download songs from the Internet. "How many? All of them." The computer also starts to think for itself and to make decisions that contradict orders. Meanwhile, the three human pilots, having participated in a mission that destroyed a skyscraper in Burma, may be on a worldwide most-wanted list, but they're immediately sent to Thailand for R&R. This gives Gannon a chance to photograph Wade in a bikini under a waterfall, while Purcell picks up a beautiful Thai girl. Soon all four of them are having lunch, and the three pilots are discussing military secrets in front of the Thai girl, who "doesn't speak English." Beautiful Thai girls who allow themselves to be picked up by U.S. pilots almost always speak English, but never mind. It's not that Purcell is too stupid to know that trusting her is dangerous; it's that the movie is too stupid.

How stupid? Nothing happens. The girl *can't* speak English.

Next mission: A nuclear crisis in Tajikistan! A warlord has nuclear bombs. The team flies off to the "former Soviet republic," where a nuclear cloud threatens five hundred thousand people, and Lt. Wade helpfully radios that they're going to need medical attention.

Various unexpected developments lead to a situation in which Lt. Wade's plane crashes in North Korea while Lt. Gannon is diverted to Alaska (they get such great fuel mileage on these babies, they must be hybrid vehicles). Then Gannon and the UCAV fly an unauthorized mission to rescue Wade, a mission that will succeed if the North Koreans have neglected to plant land mines in the part of the DMZ that Wade must cross.

Now about Newton's laws of motion. Let me try this out on you. A plane is about to explode. The pilot ejects. The plane explodes, and flaming debris falls out of the sky and threatens to hit the pilot and the parachute. If the plane is going at Mach One, Two, or Three, wouldn't the debris be falling miles away from the descent path of the pilot? I'm glad you asked. The parachute sucks up that flaming debris like a quantum sponge.

The Sweetest Thing

(DIRECTED BY ROGER KUMBLE; STARRING CAMERON DIAZ, CHRISTINA APPLEGATE; 2002)
I like Cameron Diaz. I just plain like her. She's able to convey bubble-brained zaniness about as well as anyone in the movies right now, and then she can switch gears and give you a scary dramatic performance in

something like *Vanilla Sky*. She's a beauty, but apparently without vanity; how else to account for her appearance in *Being John Malkovich*, or her adventures in *There's Something About Mary*? I don't think she gets halfway enough praise for her talent.

Consider her in *The Sweetest Thing*. This is not a good movie. It's deep-sixed by a compulsion to catalogue every bodily fluids gag in *There's Something About Mary* and devise a parallel clone-gag. It knows the words but not the music; while the Farrelly brothers got away with murder, *The Sweetest Thing* commits suicide.

And yet there were whole long stretches of it when I didn't much care how bad it was—at least, I wasn't brooding in anger about the film— because Cameron Diaz and her costars had thrown themselves into it with such heedless abandon. They don't walk the plank, they tap-dance.

The movie is about three girls who just wanna have fun. They hang out in clubs, they troll for cute guys, they dress like Maxim cover girls, they study paperback best-sellers on the rules of relationships, and frequently (this comes as no surprise), they end up weeping in each other's arms. Diaz's running mates, played by Christina Applegate and Selma Blair, are pals and confidantes, and a crisis for one is a crisis for all.

The movie's romance involves Diaz meeting Thomas Jane in a dance club; the chemistry is right but he doesn't quite accurately convey that the wedding he is attending on the weekend is his own. This leads to Diaz's ill-fated expedition into the wedding chapel, many misunderstandings, and the kind of Idiot Plot dialogue in which all problems could be instantly solved if the characters were not studiously avoiding stating the obvious.

The plot is merely the excuse, however, for an astonishing array of sex and body plumbing jokes, nearly all of which dream of hitting a home run like *There's Something About Mary*, but do not. Consider *Mary*'s scene where Diaz has what she thinks is gel in her hair. Funny—because she doesn't know what it really is, and we do. Now consider the scene in this movie where the girls go into a men's room and do not understand that in a men's room a hole in the wall is almost never merely an architectural detail. The payoff is sad, sticky, and depressing.

Or consider a scene where one of the roommates gets "stuck" while performing oral sex. This is intended as a rip-off of the "franks and beans" scene in *Mary*, but gets it all wrong. You simply cannot (I am pretty sure about this) get stuck in the way the movie suggests—no, not even if you've got piercings. More to the point, in *Mary* the victim is unseen, and we picture his dilemma. In *Sweetest Thing,* the victim is seen, sort of (careful framing preserves the R rating), and the image isn't funny. Then we get several dozen neighbors, all singing to inspire the girl to extricate herself; this might have looked good on the page, but it just plain doesn't work, especially not when embellished with the sobbing cop on the doorstep, the gay cop, and other flat notes.

More details. Sometimes it is funny when people do not know they may be consuming semen (as in *American Pie*) and sometimes it is not, as in the scene at the dry cleaners in this movie. How can you laugh when what you really want to do is hurl? And what about the scene in the ladies' room, where the other girls are curious about Applegate's boobs and she tells them she paid for them and invites them to have a feel, and they do, like shoppers at Kmart? Again, a funny concept. Again, destroyed by bad timing, bad framing, and overkill. Because the director, Roger Kumble, doesn't know how to set it up and pay it off with surgical precision, he simply has women pawing Applegate while the scene dies. An unfunny scene only grows worse by pounding in the concept as if we didn't get it.

So, as I say, I like Cameron Diaz. I like everyone in this movie (I must not neglect the invaluable Parker Posey, as a terrified bride). I like their energy. I like their willingness. I like the opening shot when Diaz comes sashaying up a San Francisco hill like a dancer from *In Living Color* who thinks she's still on the air. I like her mobile, comic face—she's smart in the way she plays dumb. But the movie I cannot like, because the movie doesn't know how to be liked. It doesn't even know how to be a movie.

Sweet November

(DIRECTED BY PAT O'CONNOR; STARRING KEANU REEVES, CHARLIZE THERON; 2001)

Sweet November passes off pathological behavior as romantic bliss. It's about two sick and twisted people playing mind games and calling it love. I don't know who I disliked more intensely—Nelson, the abrupt, insulting ad man played by Keanu Reeves, or Sara, Charlize Theron's narcissistic martyr. Reeves at least has the grace to look intensely uncomfortable during several scenes, including one involving a bag full of goodies, which we will get to later.

The movie is a remake of a 1968 film starring Sandy Dennis and Anthony Newley and, if memory serves, the same bed in a San Francisco bay window. Both films have the same conceit, which only a movie producer could believe: A beautiful girl takes men to her bed for one month at a time, to try to help and improve them. "You live in a box, and I can lift the lid," she explains. Why a month? "It's long enough to be meaningful and short enough to stay out of trouble," Sara says—wrong on both counts.

Read no further if you do not already know that she has another reason for term limits. She's dying. In the original movie the disease was described as "quite rare, but incurable." Here we get another clue, when Nelson opens Sara's medicine cabinet and finds, oh, I dunno, at a rough guess, 598 bottles of pills. The girl is obviously overmedicating. Give her a high colonic, send her to detox, and the movie is over.

Nelson is one of those insulting, conceited, impatient, coffee-drinking, cell phone–using, Jaguar-driving advertising executives that you find in only two places: the movies and real life. His motto is speed up and smell the coffee. Sara, on the other hand, acts like she has all the time in the world, even though (sob!) she does not. She sits on the hood of Nelson's car and commits other crimes against the male libido that a woman absolutely cannot get away with unless she looks exactly like Charlize Theron and insists on sleeping with you, and even then she's pushing it.

Nelson gradually learns to accept the gift of herself that she is offering. Actually, he accepts it quickly, the pig, but only gradually appreciates it. So warm, cheerful, perky, plucky, and seductive is Sara that Nelson, and the movie, completely forget for well over an hour that he has an apartment of his own and another girlfriend. By then the inexorable march of the rare but incurable disease is taking its toll, Sara has to go into the hospital, and Nelson finds out the Truth.

Will there be a scene where Sara, with a drip line plugged into every orifice, begs Nelson, "Get me out of here! Take me home!" Do bears eat gooseberries? Will there be a scene where Sara says, "Go away! I don't want you to see me like this!" Do iguanas like papayas? Will there be a scene where Sara's faithful gay friend (Jason Isaacs) bathes and comforts her? Yes, because it is a convention of movies like this that all sexy women have gay friends who materialize on demand to perform nursing and hygiene chores. (Advice to gay friend in next remake: Insist, "Unless I get two good scenes of my own, I've emptied my last bedpan.")

I almost forgot the scene involving the bag full of goodies. Keanu Reeves must have been phoning his agent between every take. The script requires him to climb in through Sara's window with a large bag that contains all of the presents he would ever want to give her, based on all the needs and desires she has ever expressed. I could get cheap laughs by listing the entire inventory of the bag, but that would be unfair. I will mention only one, the dishwashing machine. Logic may lead you to ask, "How can an automatic dishwasher fit inside a bag that Keanu Reeves can sling over his shoulder as he climbs through the window?" I would explain, but I hate it when movie reviews give everything away.

Swept Away

(DIRECTED BY GUY RITCHIE; STARRING MADONNA, ADRIANO GIANNINI; 2002)

Swept Away is a deserted island movie during which I desperately wished the characters had chosen one movie to take along if they were stranded on a deserted island, and were showing it to us instead of this one.

The movie is a relatively faithful remake of an incomparably superior 1976 movie with the lovely title, *Swept Away by an Unusual Destiny in the Blue Sea of August*. It knows the words but not the music. It strands two unattractive characters, one bitchy, one moronic, on an island where neither they, nor we, have anyone else to look at or listen to. It's harder for them than it is for us, because they have to go through the motions of an erotic attraction that seems to have become an impossibility the moment the roles were cast.

Madonna stars as Amber, the spoiled rich wife of a patient and long-suffering millionaire. They join two other couples in a cruise on a private yacht from Greece to Italy. The other five passengers recede into unwritten, even unthought-about roles, while Amber picks on Giuseppe (Adriano Giannini), the bearded deckhand. She has decided he is stupid and rude, and insults him mercilessly. So it was in the earlier film, but in this version Amber carries her behavior beyond all reason, until even the rudest and bitchiest rich woman imaginable would have called it a day.

Amber orders Giuseppe to take her out in the dinghy. He demurs: It looks like a storm. She insists. They run out of gas and begin to drift. She insults him some more, and when he succeeds after great effort in catching a fish for them to eat, she throws it overboard. Later she succeeds in putting a hole in the dinghy during a struggle for the flare gun. They drift at sea until they wash up on a deserted island, where the tables are turned and now it is Giuseppe who has the upper hand. Her husband's wealth is now no longer a factor, but his survival skills are priceless.

All of this is similar to the 1976 movie, even the business of the fish thrown overboard. What is utterly missing is any juice or life in the characters. Giancarlo Giannini and Mariangela Melato became stars on the basis of the original *Swept Away,* which was written and directed by Lina Wertmuller, one of the most successful Italian directors of the 1970s. She was a leftist but not a feminist, and aroused some controversy with a story where it turned out the rich woman liked being ordered around and slapped a little—liked it so much she encouraged the sailor to experiment with practices he could not even pronounce.

This new *Swept Away* is more sentimental, I'm afraid, and the two castaways fall into a more conventional form of love. I didn't believe it for a moment. They have nothing in common, but worse still, neither one has any conversation. They don't say a single interesting thing. That they have sex because they are stranded on the island I can believe. That they are not sleeping in separate caves by the time they are rescued I do not.

The problem with the Madonna character is that she starts out so hateful that she can never really turn it around. We dislike her intensely and thoroughly, and when she gets to the island we don't believe she has learned a lesson or turned nice—we believe she is behaving with this man as she does with all men, in the way best designed to get her what she wants. As for the sailor, does he *really* love her, as he says in that demeaning and pitiful speech toward the end of the film? What is there to love? They shared some interesting times together, but their minds never met.

The ending is particularly unsatisfactory, depending as it does on contrived irony that avoids all of the emotional issues on the table. If I have come this far with these two drips, and sailed with them, and been shipwrecked with them, and listened to their tiresome conversations, I demand that they arrive at some conclusion more rewarding than a misunderstanding based upon a misdelivered letter. This story was about something when Lina Wertmuller directed it, but now it's not about anything at all. It's lost the politics and the social observation and become just another situation romance about a couple of saps stuck in an inarticulate screenplay.

Taxi

(DIRECTED BY TIM STORY; STARRING QUEEN LATIFAH, JIMMY FALLON; 2004)

The taming of Queen Latifah continues in the dismal *Taxi*, as Queen, a force of nature in the right roles, is condemned to occupy a lamebrained action comedy. In a film that is wall-to-wall with idiocy, the most tiresome delusion is that car chases are funny. Movie audiences are bored to the

point of sullen exhaustion by car chases, especially those without motivation, and most especially those obviously created with a computer.

As the movie opens, Latifah plays a bicycle messenger who races
through Macy's, rattles down the steps of the subway, zips through a train
to the opposite platform, goes up a ramp, bounces off the back of a moving truck, lands on the sidewalk, jumps off a bridge onto the top of
another truck, and so on. This is, of course, not possible to do, and the
sequence ends with that ancient cliché in which the rider whips off a helmet and—why, it's Queen Latifah!

It's her last day on the job. She has finally qualified for her taxi license,
and before long we see the customized Yellow Cab she's been working on for
three years. In addition to the titanium supercharger given by her fellow bike
messengers as a farewell present (uh, huh), the car has more gimmicks than
a James Bond special; a custom job like this couldn't be touched at under
$500,000, which of course all bike messengers keep under the bed. Her
dream, she says, is to be a NASCAR driver. In her Yellow Cab?

Then we meet a cop named Washburn (Jimmy Fallon), who is spectacularly incompetent, blows drug busts, causes traffic accidents, and has
not his badge but his driver's license confiscated by his chief, Lt. Marta Robbins (Jennifer Esposito), who used to be his squeeze, but no more. When
he hears about a bank robbery, he commandeers Queen Latifah's cab, and
soon she is racing at speeds well over 100 mph down Manhattan streets in
pursuit of the robbers, who are, I kid you not, four supermodels who speak
Portuguese. Luckily, Queen Latifah speaks Portuguese, too, because, I
dunno, she used to be the delivery girl for a Portuguese take-out joint.

Oh, this is a bad movie. Why, oh why, was the lovely Ann-Margret
taken out of retirement to play Fallon's mother, an alcoholic with a blender
full of margaritas? Who among the writers (Ben Garant, Thomas Lennon,
and Jim Kouf) thought it would be funny to give Latifah and the cop
laughing gas, so they could talk funny? What's with Latifah's fiancé, Jesse
(Henry Simmons), who looks like a GQ cover boy and spends long hours
in fancy restaurants waiting for Queen Latifah, who is late because she is
chasing robbers, etc? Is there supposed to be subtle chemistry between
Latifah and the cop? It's so subtle, we can't tell. (He's afraid to drive

because he had a trauma during a driving lesson, so she coaches him to sing while he's driving, and he turns into a stunt driver and a pretty fair singer. Uh, huh.)

All these questions pale before the endless, tedious chase scenes, in which cars do things that cars cannot do, so that we lose all interest. If we were cartoons, our eyes would turn into X-marks. What is the *point* of showing a car doing 150 miles an hour through midtown Manhattan? Why is it funny that the cop causes a massive pile-up, with the cars in back leapfrogging onto the top of the pile? The stunt must have cost a couple of hundred thousand dollars; half a dozen indie films could have been made for that money. One of them could have starred Queen Latifah.

Latifah has been in movies since 1991 but first flowered in F. Gary Gray's *Set It Off* (1996), about four black working women who rob a bank. She was wonderful in *Living Out Loud* (1998), as a torch singer who has an unexpectedly touching conversation with a lovelorn elevator operator (Danny DeVito). She walked away with her scenes in *Chicago*.

Why was it thought, by Latifah or anyone, that she needed to make a movie as obviously without ambition, imagination, or purpose as *Taxi*? Doesn't she know that at this point in her career she should be looking for some lean and hungry Sundance type to put her in a zero-budget masterpiece that could win her the Oscar? True, it could turn out to be a flop. But better to flop while trying to do something good than flop in something that could not be good, was never going to be good, and only gets worse as it plows along.

Team America: World Police

(Directed by Trey Parker; starring Trey Parker, Matt Stone; 2004)
What're you rebelling against, Johnny?
Whaddya got?

— Marlon Brando in *The Wild One*

If this dialogue is not inscribed over the doors of Trey Parker and Matt Stone, it should be. Their *Team America: World Police* is an equal opportunity offender, and waves of unease will flow over first one segment of their audience, and then another. Like a cocky teenager who's had a couple of drinks before the party, they don't have a plan for who they want to offend, only an intention to be as offensive as possible.

Their strategy extends even to their decision to use puppets for all of their characters, a choice that will not be universally applauded. Their characters, one-third life-size, are clearly artificial, and yet there's something going on around the mouths and lips that looks halfway real, as if they were inhabited by the big faces with moving mouths from Conan O'Brien. There are times when the characters risk falling into the Uncanny Valley, that rift used by robot designers to describe robots that alarm us by looking too humanoid.

The plot seems like a collision at the screenplay factory between several half-baked world-in-crisis movies. Team America, a group not unlike the Thunderbirds, bases its rockets, jets, and helicopters inside Mount Rushmore, which is hollow, and race off to battle terrorism wherever it is suspected. In the opening sequence, they swoop down on Paris and fire on caricatures of Middle East desperadoes, missing most of them but managing to destroy the Eiffel Tower, the Arch of Triumph, and the Louvre.

Regrouping, the team's leader, Spottswoode (voice by Daran Norris), recruits a Broadway actor named Gary to go undercover for them. When first seen, Gary (voice by Parker) is starring in the musical *Lease,* and singing "Everyone has AIDS." Ho, ho. Spottswoode tells Gary: "You're an actor with a double major in theater and world languages! Hell, you're the perfect weapon!" There's a big laugh when Gary is told that, if captured, he may want to kill himself, and is supplied with a suicide device I will not reveal.

Spottswoode's plan: Terrorists are known to be planning to meet at "a bar in Cairo." The Team America helicopter will land in Cairo, and four uniformed team members will escort Gary, his face crudely altered to look "Middle Eastern," to the bar, where he will go inside and ask whazzup. As a satire on our inability to infiltrate other cultures, this will do, I suppose. It leads to an ill-advised adventure where in the name of fighting terrorism, Team America destroys the pyramids and the Sphinx. But it turns out the real threat comes from North Korea and its leader, Kim Jong Il (voice also by Parker), who plans to unleash "9/11 times 2,356."

Opposing Team America is the Film Actors Guild, or F.A.G., ho, ho, with puppets representing Alec Baldwin, Tim Robbins, Matt Damon, Susan Sarandon, and Sean Penn (who has written an angry letter about the movie to Parker and Stone about their comments, in *Rolling Stone*, that there is "no shame in not voting"). No real point is made about the actors' activism; they exist in the movie essentially to be ridiculed for existing at all, I guess. Hans Blix, the U.N. chief weapons inspector, also turns up, and has a fruitless encounter with the North Korean dictator. Some of the scenes are set to music, including such tunes as "*Pearl Harbor* Sucked and I Miss You" and "America—F***, Yeah!"

If I were asked to extract a political position from the movie, I'd be baffled. It is neither for nor against the war on terrorism, just dedicated to ridiculing those who wage it and those who oppose it. The White House gets a free pass, since the movie seems to think Team America makes its own policies without political direction.

I wasn't offended by the movie's content so much as by its nihilism. At a time when the world is in crisis and the country faces an important election, the response of Parker, Stone, and company is to sneer at both sides—indeed, at anyone who takes the current world situation seriously. They may be right that some of us are puppets, but they're wrong that all of us are fools and dead wrong that it doesn't matter.

The Texas Chainsaw Massacre

(DIRECTED BY MARCUS NISPEL; STARRING JESSICA BIEL, JONATHAN TUCKER; 2003)

The new version of *The Texas Chainsaw Massacre* is a contemptible film: vile, ugly, and brutal. There is not a shred of a reason to see it. Those who defend it will have to dance through mental hoops of their own devising, defining its meanness and despair as "style" or "vision" or "a commentary on our world." It is not a commentary on anything except the marriage of slick technology with the materials of a geek show.

The movie is a remake of, or was inspired by, the 1974 horror film by Tobe Hooper. That film at least had the raw power of its originality. It proceeded from Hooper's fascination with the story and his need to tell it. This new version, made by a man who has previously directed music videos, proceeds from nothing more than a desire to feed on the corpse of a once-living film. There is no worthy or defensible purpose in sight here: The filmmakers want to cause disgust and hopelessness in the audience. Ugly emotions are easier to evoke and often more commercial than those that contribute to the ongoing lives of the beholders.

The movie begins with grainy "newsreel" footage of a 1974 massacre (the same one as in the original film; there are some changes, but this is not a sequel). Then we plunge directly into the formula of a Dead Teenager Movie, which begins with living teenagers and kills them one by one. The formula can produce movies that are good, bad, funny, depressing, whatever. This movie, strewn with blood, bones, rats, fetishes, and severed limbs, photographed in murky darkness, scored with screams, wants to be a test: Can you sit through it? There were times when I intensely wanted to walk out of the theater and into the fresh air and look at the sky and buy an apple and sigh for our civilization, but I stuck it out. The ending, which is cynical and truncated, confirmed my suspicion that the movie was made by and for those with no attention span.

The movie doesn't tell a story in any useful sense, but is simply a series of gruesome events that finally are over. It probably helps to have seen the original film in order to understand what's going on, since there's so little exposition. Only from the earlier film do we have a vague idea of who the people are in this godforsaken house, and what their relationship is to one another. The movie is eager to start the gore and unwilling to pause for exposition.

I like good horror movies. They can exorcise our demons. *The Texas Chainsaw Massacre* doesn't want to exorcise anything. It wants to tramp crap through our imaginations and wipe its feet on our dreams. I think of filmgoers on a date, seeing this movie and then—what? I guess they'll have to laugh at it, irony being a fashionable response to the experience of being had.

Certainly they will not be frightened by it. It recycles the same old tired thriller tools that have been worn out in countless better movies. There is the scary noise that is only a cat. The device of loud sudden noises to underline the movements of half-seen shadows. The van that won't start. The truck that won't start. The car that won't start. The character who turns around and sees the slasher standing right behind her. One critic writes, "Best of all, there was not a single case of 'She's only doing that (falling, going into a scary space, not picking up the gun) because she's in a thriller.'" Huh? Nobody does anything in this movie for any other reason. There is no reality here. It's all a thriller.

There is a controversy involving Quentin Tarantino's *Kill Bill: Volume 1*, which some people feel is "too violent." I gave it four stars, found it kind of brilliant, felt it was an exhilarating exercise in nonstop action direction. The material was redeemed, justified, illustrated, and explained by the style. It was a meditation on the martial arts genre, done with intelligence and wit. *The Texas Chainsaw Massacre* is a meditation on the geekshow movie. Tarantino's film is made with grace and joy. This movie is made with venom and cynicism. I doubt that anybody involved in it will be surprised or disappointed if audience members vomit or flee. Do yourself a favor. There are a lot of good movies playing right now that can make you feel a little happier, smarter, sexier, funnier, more excited—or more scared, if that's what you want. This is not one of them. Don't let it kill ninety-eight minutes of your life.

13 Ghosts

(DIRECTED BY STEVE BECK; STARRING TONY SHALHOUB, EMBETH DAVIDTZ; 2001)

13 Ghosts is the loudest movie since *Armageddon.* Flash frames attack the eyeballs while the theater trembles with crashes, bangs, shatters, screams, rumbles, and roars. Forget about fighting the ghosts; they ought to attack the subwoofer.

The experience of watching the film is literally painful. It hurts the eyes and ears. Aware that their story was thin, that their characters were constantly retracing the same ground and repeating the same words, that the choppy editing is visually incoherent, maybe the filmmakers thought if they turned up the volume the audience might be deceived into thinking something was happening.

When the action pauses long enough for us to see what's on the screen, we have to admire the art direction, special effects, costumes, and makeup. This is a movie that is all craft and little art. It mostly takes place inside a house that is one of the best-looking horror sets I've seen, and the twelve ghosts look like pages from *Heavy Metal,* brought to grotesque life. (The thirteenth ghost is, of course, the key to the mystery.)

The screenplay, inspired by the 1960 William Castle film of the same name but written in a zone all its own, involves dead Uncle Cyrus (F. Murray Abraham), whose research into the occult included a medieval manuscript allegedly dictated by the devil. He leaves his house to his nephew Arthur (Tony Shalhoub), whose wife has tragically died; Arthur moves in with his son, Bobby (Alec Roberts), his daughter, Kathy (Shannon Elizabeth), and Maggie the Nanny (Rah Digga). They're joined by a wisecracking ghostbuster named Rafkin (Matthew Lillard) and Kalina (Embeth Davidtz), a paranormal who knows a lot about Uncle Cyrus, his research, and how the house works.

And does it ever work. Exterior steel panels slide up and down, revealing glass container cages inside that hold the twelve invisible ghosts, which Cyrus needed in order to . . . oh, never mind. What intrigues me is that this house—its shrieks of terror and its moving walls—attracts no attention at all from the neighbors, even late in the film when truly alarming things are happening. Maybe the neighbors read the screenplay.

The shatterproof glass cages, we learn, are engraved with "containment spells" that keep the ghosts inside. You can see the ghosts with special glasses, which the cast is issued; when they see them, we see them, usually in shots so maddeningly brief we don't get a good look. Our consolation, I guess, is that the cast has the glasses but we will have the Pause button when *13 Ghosts* comes out on DVD. The only button this movie needs more than Pause is Delete.

The house, Kalina explains, is really an infernal device: "We are in the middle of a machine designed by the devil and powered by the dead." Gears grind and levers smash up and down, looking really neat, and wheels turn within wheels as it's revealed that the purpose of this machine is to open the *"Oculorus Infernum."* When a character asks, "What's that?" the answer is not helpful: "It's Latin." Later we learn it is the Eye of Hell, and . . . oh, never mind.

If there are twelve ghosts there must, I suppose, be twelve containment cages, and yet when little Bobby wanders off to the subterranean area with the cages, he gets lost, and his father, sister, the nanny, the psychic, and the ghostbuster wander endlessly up and down what must be the same few corridors, shouting "Bobby! Bobby?" so very, very, very many times that I wanted to cheer when Rafkin finally said what we had all been thinking: "Screw the kid! We gotta get out of this basement!"

The production is first-rate; the executives included Joel Silver and Robert Zemeckis. The physical look of the picture is splendid. The screenplay is dead on arrival. The noise level is torture. I hope *13 Ghosts* plays mostly at multiplexes, because it's the kind of movie you want to watch from the next theater.

Thomas and the Magic Railroad

(DIRECTED BY BRITT ALLCROFT; STARRING ALEC BALDWIN, PETER FONDA; 2000)

Very early in *Thomas and the Magic Railroad,* Thomas the Tank Engine and another locomotive are having a conversation. Their eyes roll and we hear their voices—but their mouths do not move. No, not at all. This is such an odd effect that I could think of little else during their conversation. In an era when animated dinosaurs roam the Earth, ships climb two-hundred-foot walls of water, and Eddie Murphy can play five people in the same scene, is it too much to ask a tank engine to move its lips while speaking?

I think not. Either their mouths should move or their eyes should not roll. Take your pick. I felt like a grinch as I arrived at this conclusion, for Thomas was a cute tank engine and he steamed through a fanciful model countryside that was, as these things go, nice to look at. I was still filled with goodwill toward Thomas and his movie. That was before I met Burnett Stone.

He is the character played by Peter Fonda, and he spends much of his time in a cave deep within Muffle Mountain with Lady, a tank engine he has been trying to repair for years, but without luck: "I've never been able to bring her to life," he complains. "To make her steam." Fonda is so depressed by this failure that he mopes through the entire role, stoop-shouldered, eyes downcast, step faltering, voice sad, as if he had taken the screenplay too literally ("Burnett is depressed because he cannot get Lady to run") and did not realize that, hey, this is a kiddie movie!

Other actors are likewise adrift in the film. A few years ago Alec Baldwin was delivering the electrifying monologue in *Glengarry Glen Ross*. Now he is Mr. Conductor, about twelve inches tall, materializing in a cloud of sparkle dust in a geranium basket. I do not blame him for taking a role in a children's movie, not even a role twelve inches high. I do question his judgment in getting into this one.

Thomas and the Magic Railroad is an inept assembly of ill-matched plot points, meandering through a production that has attractive art direction (despite the immobile mouths). Many of the frames would make cheerful stills. Thomas and his fellow trains, even Evil Diesel, have a jolly energy to them, and I like the landscapes and trees and hamlets.

But what a lugubrious plot! What endless trips back and forth between the Isle of Sodor and the full-sized town of Shining Time! What inexplicable characters, such as Billy Twofeathers (Russell Means), who appear and disappear senselessly. What a slow, wordy, earnest enterprise this is, when it should be quick and sprightly.

That *Thomas and the Magic Railroad* made it into theaters at all is something of a mystery. This is a production with "straight to video" written all over it. Kids who like the Thomas books might—*might*—kinda like it. Especially younger kids. Real younger kids. Otherwise, no. Perhaps the success of the Harry Potter books has inspired hope that Thomas, also a British children's icon, will do some business. Not a chance. And in an age when even the cheapest Saturday morning cartoons find a way to make the lips move, what, oh what, was the reasoning behind Thomas's painted-on grin?

Thunderbirds

(DIRECTED BY JONATHAN FRAKES; STARRING BILL PAXTON, BEN KINGLSEY; 2004)

I run into Bill Paxton and Ben Kingsley occasionally, and have found them to be nice people. As actors they are in the first rank. It's easy to talk to them, and so the next time I run into one of them I think I'll just go ahead and ask what in the h-e-double-hockey-sticks they were *thinking* when they signed up for *Thunderbirds*. My bet is that Paxton will grin sheepishly and Kingsley will twinkle knowingly, and they'll both say the movie looked like fun, and gently steer the conversation toward other titles. *A Simple Plan*, say, or *House of Sand and Fog*.

This is a movie made for an audience that does not exist, at least in the land of North American multiplexes: fans of a British TV puppet show that ran from 1964 to 1966. "While its failure to secure a U.S. network sale caused the show to be canceled after thirty-two episodes, writes David Rooney in *Variety*, the 'Supermarionation' series still endures in reruns and on DVD for funky sci-fi geeks and pop culture nostalgists." I quote Rooney because I had never heard of the series and, let's face it, never have you. Still, I doubt that "funky" describes the subset of geeks and nostalgists who like it. The word "kooky" comes to mind, as in "kooky yo-yos."

Thunderbirds is to *Spy Kids* as Austin Powers is to James Bond. It recycles the formula in a campy 1960s send-up that is supposed to be funny. But how many members of the preteen audience for this PG movie are knowledgeable about the 1960s Formica and polyester look? How many care? If the film resembles anything in their universe, it may be the Jetsons.

A solemn narrator sets the scene. The Thunderbirds, we learn, are in real life the Tracy family. Dad is Jeff Tracy (Paxton), a billionaire who has built his "secret" headquarters on a South Pacific island, where his secret is safe because no one would notice spaceships taking off. His kids are named after astronauts: Scott, John, Virgil, and Gordon, and the youngest, Alan (Brady Corbet), who is the hero and thinks he is old enough to be trusted with the keys to the family rocket. His best friend, Fermat (Soren Fulton), is named after the theorem, but I am not sure if their best friend, Tin-Tin (Vanessa Anne Hudgens), is named after the French comic book hero or after another Tin-Tin. It's a common name.

The plot: The Hood (Kingsley) is a villain who (recite in unison) seeks world domination. His plan is to rob the Bank of London. The Thunderbirds are distracted when a Hood scheme endangers their permanently orbiting space station (did I mention Dad was a billionaire?), and when Dad and the older kids rocket off to save it, the coast is clear—unless plucky young Alan, Fermat, and Tin-Tin can pilot another rocket vehicle to London in time to foil them. In this they are helped by Lady Penelope (Sophia Myles) and her chauffeur (Ron Cook).

As the Tracys rocket off to rescue the space station, I was reminded of the Bob and Ray radio serial where an astronaut, stranded in orbit, is reassured that "our scientists are working to get you down with a giant magnet." Meanwhile, his mother makes sandwiches, which are rocketed up to orbit. ("Nuts!" he says. "She forgot the mayonnaise!")

Among the big *Thunderbirds* f/x scenes are one where the kids use their rocket ship to rescue a monorail train that has fallen into the Thames. This and everything else the Thunderbirds do seems to be covered on TV, but try to control yourself from wondering where the TV cameras can possibly be, and how they got there.

Paxton was in *Spy Kids 2* and at least knows this territory. Let it be said that he and Kingsley protect themselves, Paxton by playing a true-blue 1960s hero who doesn't know his lines are funny, and Sir Ben by trying his best to play no one at all while willing himself invisible. A movie like this is harmless, I suppose, except for the celluloid that was killed in the process of its manufacture, but as an entertainment it will send the kids tip-toeing through the multiplex to sneak into *Spider-Man 2*.

The Time Machine

(DIRECTED BY SIMON WELLS; STARRING GUY PEARCE, JEREMY IRONS; 2002)

The Time Machine is a witless recycling of the H. G. Wells story from 1895, with the absurdity intact but the wonderment missing. It makes use of computer-aided graphics to create a future race of grubby underground beasties who, like the characters in *Battleship Earth,* have evolved beyond the need for bathing and fingernail clippers. Because this race, the Morlocks, is allegedly a Darwinian offshoot of humans, and because they are remarkably unattractive, they call into question the theory that over a long period of time a race grows more attractive through natural selection. They are obviously the result of eight hundred thousand years of ugly brides.

The film stars Guy Pearce as Alexander Hartdegen, a brilliant mathematician who hopes to use Einstein's earliest theories to build a machine to travel through time. He is in love with the beautiful Emma (Sienna Guillory), but on the very night when he proposes marriage a tragedy happens, and he vows to travel back in time in his new machine and change the course of history.

The machine, which lacks so much as a seat belt, consists of whirling spheres encompassing a Victorian club chair. Convenient brass gauges spin to record the current date. Speed and direction are controlled by a joystick. The time machine has an uncanny ability to move in perfect synchronization with the Earth, so that it always lands in the same geographical spot, despite the fact that in the future large chunks of the moon (or all of it, according to the future race of Eloi) have fallen to the Earth, which should have had some effect on the orbit. Since it would be inconvenient if a time machine materialized miles in the air or deep underground, this is just as well.

We will not discuss paradoxes of time travel here, since such discussion makes any time travel movie impossible. Let us discuss instead an unintended journey which Hartdegen makes to eight thousand centuries in the future, when *Homo sapiens* have split in two, into the Eloi and Morlocks. The Morlocks evolved underground in the dark ages after the moon's fall, and attack on the surface by popping up through dusty sinkholes. They hunt the Eloi for food. The Eloi are an attractive race of brown-skinned people whose civilization seems modeled on paintings by Rousseau; their life is an idyll of leafy bowers, waterfalls, and elegant forest structures, but they are such fatalists about the Morlocks that instead of fighting them off they all but salt and pepper themselves.

Alexander meets a beautiful Eloi woman (Samantha Mumba) and her sturdy young brother, befriends them, and eventually journeys to the underworld to try to rescue her. This brings him into contact with the Uber Morlock, a chalk-faced Jeremy Irons, who did not learn his lesson after playing an evil Mage named Profion in *Dungeons & Dragons*.

In broad outline, this future world matches the one depicted in George Pal's 1960 film *The Time Machine*, although its blond, blue-eyed race of Eloi have been transformed into dusky sun people. One nevertheless tends to question romances between people who were born eight hundred thousand years apart and have few conversations on subjects other than not being eaten. Convenient that when humankind was splitting into two different races, both its branches continued to speak English.

The Morlocks and much of their world have been created by undistinguished animation. The Morlock hunters are supposed to be able to leap great distances with fearsome speed, but the animation turns them into cartoonish characters whose movements defy even the laws of gravity governing bodies in motion. Their movements are not remotely plausible, and it's disconcerting to see that while the Eloi are utterly unable to evade them, Hartdegen, a professor who has scarcely left his laboratory for four years, is able to duck out of the way, bean them with big tree branches, etc.

Guy Pearce, as the hero, makes the mistake of trying to give a good and realistic performance. Irons at least knows what kind of movie he's in and hams it up accordingly. Pearce seems thoughtful, introspective, quiet, morose. Surely the inventor of a time machine should have a few screws loose, and the glint in his eye should not be from tears. By the end of the movie, as he stands beside the beautiful Eloi woman and takes her hand, we are thinking not of their future together, but about how he got from the Morlock caverns to the top of that mountain ridge in time to watch an explosion that takes only a few seconds. A Morlock could cover that distance, but not a mathematician, unless he has discovered wormholes as well.

Tomcats

(DIRECTED BY GREGORY POIRIER; STARRING JERRY O'CONNELL, SHANNON ELIZABETH; 2001)

The men in *Tomcats* are surrounded by beautiful women, but they hate and fear them. That alone is enough to sink the film, since no reasonable person in the audience can understand why these guys are so weirdly twisted. But then the film humiliates the women, and we wince when it wants us to laugh. Here is a comedy positioned outside the normal range of human response.

The movie belongs to an old and tired movie tradition, in which guys are terrified that wedding bells may be breaking up that old gang of theirs (only last week we had *The Brothers,* an African-American version of the theme, but gentler and nicer). There is always one guy who is already (unhappily) married, one who is threatened with marriage, one who claims he will never marry, and then the hero, who wants to marry off the unmarriageable one to win a bet. This plot is engraved on a plaque in the men's room of the Old Writer's Retirement Home.

The twist this time: The guys all agree to pay into a mutual fund. The last one still single collects all the money. The fund quickly grows to nearly $500,000, so their fund must have bought hot tech stocks. (In the sequel, those same stocks—oh, never mind.)

The guy who vows never to marry is Kyle (Jake Busey). He likes to take his dates golfing and run over them with the cart. They bounce right up and keep smiling. The guy who wants to collect the money is Michael (Jerry O'Connell). He comes into a valuable piece of information: Kyle met one perfect woman, cruelly dumped her, and has always wondered if he made a mistake. Michael tracks down the woman, who is Natalie (Shannon Elizabeth) and enlists her in his scheme. She'll seduce and marry Kyle and get her revenge—oh, and she wants half the money, too.

The complication, which is so obvious it nearly precedes the setup, is that Michael and Natalie fall for each other. This despite the fact that by going along with his plan she reveals herself as a shameless vixen. The movie then runs through an assembly line of routine situations, including bad jokes about S&M and a proctologist who suspects his wife is a lesbian, before arriving at a sequence of astonishing bad taste.

Read no further if through reckless wrongheadedness you plan to see this movie. What happens is that Kyle develops testicular cancer and has to have surgery to remove one of his testicle teammates. During recovery he develops a nostalgia for the missing sphere, and sends Michael on a mission to the hospital's Medical Waste Storage room to steal back the treasure.

Alas, through a series of mishaps, it bounces around the hospital like the quarry in a handball game before ending up on the cafeteria plate of the surgeon who has just removed it, and now eats it, with relish. The surgeon is played by that accomplished actor David Ogden Stiers, my high school classmate, who also does Shakespeare and probably finds it easier.

The movie has other distasteful scenes, including a bachelor party where the star performer starts with ping-pong balls and works up to footballs. If the details are gross, the movie's overall tone is even more offensive. All sex comedies have scenes in which characters are embarrassed, but I can't remember one in which women are so consistently and venomously humiliated, as if they were some kind of hateful plague. The guys in the movie don't even seem to enjoy sex, except as a way of keeping score.

Tomcats was written and directed by Gregory Poirier, who also wrote *See Spot Run* and thus pulls off the neat trick, within one month, of placing two titles on my list of the worst movies of the year. There is a bright spot. He used up all his doggy-do-do ideas in the first picture.

Turn It Up

(DIRECTED BY ROBERT ADETUYI; STARRING PRAS MICHEL, JA RULE; 2000)

Turn It Up tells the story of a moral weakling who compromises his way through bloodbaths and drug deals while whining about his values. It's one of those movies where the more the characters demand respect, the less they deserve it. What's pathetic is that the movie halfway wants its hero to serve as a role model, but neither the hero nor the movie is prepared to walk the walk.

The rap singer Pras, of the Fugees, stars as Diamond, who dreams of becoming a superstar and spends hours in the studio, fine-tuning his tracks with small help from his cokehead mixer. Diamond's best friend is Gage (the rap singer Ja Rule), who finances the studio time by working as a runner for the drug dealer Mr. B (Jason Stratham). Diamond helps on deliveries, including one in the opening scene that leads to a shootout with a Chinese gang.

Dead bodies litter the screen, but there is not one word in the rest of the movie about whether Diamond and Gage are wanted by the police for questioning in the matter of perhaps a dozen deaths. By the end of the film, the two of them have killed, oh, I dunno, maybe six or eight other guys, but when we see the words "One Year Later" onscreen at the end, it is not to show Pras in prison but simply to share some sad nostalgia with him.

The movie is very seriously confused in its objectives, as if two or three story approaches are fighting for time on the same screen. Gage is an uncomplicated character—a sniveling weakling with a big gun who murders in cold blood. Diamond is more of a puzzle. He is loyal to Gage, and yet demurs at some of his buddy's activities ("She's pregnant," he protests, when Gage wants to kill a cleaning woman who witnessed one of their massacres). He seems to accept Gage's lowlife atrocities as the price of getting his studio time paid for and not having to actually work for a living.

The stuff involving Gage, Mr. B, and the significantly named music executive Mr. White (John Ralston) is standard drug-rap-ghetto-crime thriller material. But when Diamond's mother dies and his homeless, long-missing father (Vondie Curtis-Hall) turns up, another movie tries to get started. The father explains he abandoned his wife and son because he put his music first, and that was the start of his downfall. Now he sees his son doing the same thing. What he doesn't know is that Diamond has a pregnant girlfriend (Tamala Jones), and won't even give her his cell phone number because that's the first step on the long slide to enslavement by a woman.

Diamond's father listens to his demo tracks and abruptly drops a loud and clear message of music criticism into the movie: "Your music is too processed. You grew up on digitized music—you think that keyboard sample sounds like a real piano." Then his dad takes him to the American Conservatory of Music and plays classical music for him on a grand piano that apparently stands ready in a large empty space for the convenience of such visitors, and later tries to talk Diamond out of going along with Gage on a dangerous drug run.

Well, Diamond doesn't much want to go anyway. He keeps talking about how Gage should chill, and how he wants to get out of the drug and gun lifestyle, and how he loves his woman and wants to be a father to his unborn child, but he never really makes any of those hard decisions. It never occurs to him that he is living off of Gage's drug-soaked earnings— that his studio sessions are paid for by the exploitation of the very people he thinks his songs are about. He can't act on his qualms, I guess, because the movie needs him for the action scenes. *Turn It Up* says one thing and does another; Diamond frets and whines, while the movie lays on gunfire, torture, and bloodshed (the scene where Mr. B offers to run Gage's face through a meat slicer is memorable).

My guess is that Vondie Curtis-Hall had substantial input on his scenes, which have a different tone and sounder values than the rest of the movie. His advice to his son is good, and his performance is the best thing in the movie. But *Turn It Up* doesn't deserve it. Here is a film that goes out of its way to portray all the bad guys as white or Chinese, and doesn't have the nerve to point out that the heroes' worst enemies are themselves.

The Tuxedo

(DIRECTED BY KEVIN DONOVAN; STARRING JACKIE CHAN, JENNIFER LOVE HEWITT; 2002)
There is an ancient tradition in action movies that the first scene is a self-contained shocker with no relevance to the rest of the plot. James Bond parachutes from a mountainside, Clint Eastwood disarms a robber, etc. Jackie Chan's *The Tuxedo* opens with a deer urinating in a mountain stream. The deer, the urine, and the stream have nothing to do with the rest of the film.

The movie's plot does involve water. The bad guy wants to add an ingredient to the world's water supply that will cause victims to dehydrate and die. To save themselves, they will have to buy the villain's pure water. Since his opening gambit is to sabotage, I repeat, the *world's* water supply, he will dehydrate everyone except those already drinking only bottled water, and so will inherit a planet of health nuts, which is just as well, since all the fish and animals and birds will dehydrate too, and everyone will have to live on PowerBars.

I have been waiting for a dehydrating villain for some time. My wife is of the opinion that I do not drink enough water. She believes the proper amount is a minimum of eight glasses a day. She often regards me balefully and says, "You're not getting enough water." In hot climates her concern escalates. In Hawaii last summer she had the grandchildren so worked up they ran into the bedroom every morning to see if Grandpa Roger had turned to dust.

The movie's villain, whose name is Banning (Ritchie Coster), has a novel scheme for distributing the formula, or virus, or secret ingredient, or whatever it is, that will make water into a dehydrating agent. He plans to use water striders, those insects that can skate across the surface of a pond. In his secret laboratory he keeps his ultimate weapon, a powerful water strider queen.

Do water striders *have* queens, like bees and ants do? For an authoritative answer I turned to Dr. May Berenbaum, head of the Department of Entomology at the University of Illinois at Urbana-Champaign, and founder of the Insect Fear Film Festival, held every year at the great university.

She writes: "Water striders are true bugs (i.e., insects with piercing/sucking mouthparts) that run or skate on the surface of bodies of water, feeding on the insects that fall onto the water surface. There are about five hundred species of gerrids in the world and, as far as I know, not a single one of those five hundred species is eusocial (i.e., has a complex social structure with reproductive division of labor and cooperative brood care). I don't even know of an example of maternal care in the whole group. In short, the answer to your question is an emphatic 'No!' I can't wait to see this film. It definitely sounds like a candidate for a future Insect Fear Film Festival!"

More crushing evidence. Dr. Bruce P. Smith, expert entomologist at Ithaca College, writes me: "There is no known species of water striders that has queens. The most closely related insects that do are some colonial aphid species, and the most familiar (and much more distant relatives) are the ants, bees, wasps, and termites." He adds helpfully, "One mammal does have queens: the naked mole rats of Africa." Revealing himself as a student of insect films, he continues, "If my memory is correct, *Arachnophobia* has a king spider, but no queen—totally absurd!"

So there you have it. Professors Smith and Berenbaum have spoken. The evil Banning has spent untold millions on his secret plans for world domination, and thinks he possesses a water strider queen when he only has a lucky regular water strider living the life of Riley.

But back to *The Tuxedo*. Jackie Chan plays a taxi driver named Jimmy Tong, who is hired by Debi Mazar to be the chauffeur for Clark Devlin (Jason Isaacs), a multimillionaire secret agent whose $2 million tuxedo turns him into a fighting machine (also a dancer, kung-fu expert, etc). After Devlin is injured by a skateboard bomb, Jackie puts on the suit and soon partners with agent Del Blaine (Jennifer Love Hewitt), who realizes he has a strange accent for a man named Clark Devlin, but nevertheless joins him in battle against Banning.

The movie is silly beyond comprehension, and even if it weren't silly, it would still be beyond comprehension. It does have its moments, as when the tuxedo inadvertently cold-cocks James Brown, the Godfather of Soul, and Jackie Chan has to go onstage in place of the hardest working man in show business. He's very funny as James Brown, although not as funny as James Brown is.

There's something engaging about Jackie Chan. Even in a bad movie, I like him, because what you see is so obviously what you get. This time he goes light on the stunts, at least the stunts he obviously does himself, so that during the closing credits there are lots of flubbed lines and times when the actors break out laughing, but none of those spellbinding shots in which he misses the bridge, falls off the scaffold, etc. And some of the shots are computer-generated, which is kind of cheating isn't it, with Jackie Chan? Luckily, special effects are not frowned upon at the Insect Fear Film Festival.

Twisted

(DIRECTED BY PHILIP KAUFMAN; STARRING ASHLEY JUDD, SAMUEL L. JACKSON; 2004)

Phil Kaufman's *Twisted* walks like a thriller and talks like a thriller, but squawks like a turkey. And yet the elements are in place for a film that works—all until things start becoming clear and mysteries start being solved and we start shaking our heads, if we are well-mannered, or guffawing, if we are not.

Let me begin at the ending. The other day I employed the useful term *deus ex machina* in a review, and received several messages from readers who are not proficient in Latin. I have also received several messages from Latin scholars who helpfully translated obscure dialogue in *The Passion of the Christ* for me, and, as my Urbana High School Latin teacher Mrs. Link used to remind me, *In medio tutissimus ibis*.

But back to *deus ex machina*. This is a phrase you will want to study and master, not merely to amaze friends during long bus journeys but because it so perfectly describes what otherwise might take you thousands of words. Imagine a play on a stage. The hero is in a fix. The dragon is breathing fire, the hero's sword is broken, his leg is broken, his spirit is broken, and the playwright's imagination is broken. Suddenly there is the offstage noise of the grinding of gears, and invisible machinery lowers a god onto the stage, who slays the dragon, heals the hero, and fires the playwright. He is the "god from the machine."

Now travel with me to San Francisco. Ashley Judd plays Jessica Shepard, a new homicide detective who has a habit of picking up guys in bars and having rough sex with them. She drinks a lot. Maybe that goes without saying. Soon after getting her new job, she and her partner, Mike Delmarco (Andy Garcia), are assigned to a floater in the bay. She recognizes the dead man, who has been savagely beaten. It's someone she has slept with.

She reveals this information, but is kept on the case by the police commissioner (Samuel L. Jackson), who raised her as his own daughter after her own father went berserk and killed a slew of people, including her mother. The commissioner trusts her. Then another body turns up, also with the killer's brand (a cigarette burn). She slept with this guy, too. She's seeing the department shrink (David Strathairn), who understandably suggests she has to share this information with her partner. Then a third dead guy turns up. She slept with him, too. Wasn't it Oscar Wilde who said, "To kill one lover may be regarded as a misfortune. To kill three seems like carelessness?"

Det. Sheperd has a pattern. She goes home at night, drinks way too much red wine, and blacks out. The next day, her cell rings and she's summoned to the next corpse. Is she killing these guys in a blackout? Wasn't it Ann Landers who said that's one of the twenty danger signals of alcoholism? To be sure, Delmarco helpfully suggests at one point that she should drink less. Maybe only enough to maim?

So anyway, on a dark and isolated pier in San Francisco, three of the characters come together. I won't reveal who they are, although if one of them isn't Ashley Judd it wouldn't be much of an ending. Certain death seems about to ensue, and then with an offstage grinding noise . . . but I don't want to give away the ending. Find out for yourself.

And ask yourself this question: Assuming the premise of the first amazing development, how did the San Francisco police department know exactly which dark and isolated pier these three people were on, and how did they arrive in sixty seconds (by car, truck, motorcycle, and helicopter), and how come the cops who arrived were precisely the same cops who have already been established as characters in the story? And isn't it convenient that, fast as they arrived, they considerately left time for the Talking Killer scene, in which all is explained when all the Killer has to do is blow everyone away and beat it?

The movie does at least draw a moral: *Nemo repente fuit turpissimus.*

Undead

(DIRECTED BY MICHAEL SPIERIG AND PETER SPIERIG; STARRING FELICITY MASON, MUNGO MCKAY; 2005)

Undead is the kind of movie that would be so bad it's good, except it's not bad enough to be good enough. It's, let's see, the sixth zombie movie I've seen in the last few years, after *28 Days Later, Resident Evil,* the remake of *Dawn of the Dead, Shawn of the Dead,* and *George Romero's Land of the Dead.* That is a lot of lurching and screaming and heads blown off.

Undead is the work of two brothers from Australia, Michael Spierig and Peter Spierig, who wrote, directed, edited, and produced it, and are of the kitchen sink approach to filmmaking, in which zombies are not enough and we must also have aliens and inexplicable characters who seem to have wandered in from another movie without their name tags. It's comedy, horror, satire, and sci-fi, combined with that endearing Australian quality of finding their own country the nuttiest place on Earth. If the Australian cinema is accurate, once you leave the largest cities, the only people you meet are crazies, eccentrics, neurotics, parched wanderers in the Outback, and the occasional disk jockey who is actually a fish.

This tradition continues in *Undead,* which even includes some zombie fish. It takes place in the hamlet of Berkeley, in Queensland, a fishing mecca that has just held a beauty pageant to crown Miss Catch of the Day. This is Rene (Felicity Mason), an adornment to any bait store. Excitement such as the crowning of Miss Catch of the Day is interrupted by a meteor shower; rocks from space rain down upon Berkeley, some of them opening up platter-sized holes in the chests of the citizens, who stagger about with daylight showing through them, and have become zombies.

In the obligatory tradition of all zombie movies, a few healthy humans survive and try to fight off the zombies and preserve themselves. Rene is on her way out of town when the attack occurs; she has lost the mortgage on the family farm and is fleeing to the big city, or a larger hamlet, when she runs into a traffic jam. All attacks from outer space, natural or alien, immediately cause massive traffic pile-ups, of course, and the only functioning cars belong to the heroes.

In *War of the Worlds,* for example, Tom Cruise has the only car that works, after he and a friend peer under the hood and say, "It's the solenoid!" And so it is. This moment took me back to my youth, when cars could still be repaired without computers. They just had gas lines and spark plugs and things like that. I never understood anything about engines, but there were always kids in high school who would look under the hood and solemnly explain, "It's the solenoid." The solenoid, always the solenoid. You could impress girls with a line like that. "It's the solenoid." Works every time.

But I digress. Rene hits a traffic jam on the road out of town, and meets a bush pilot named Wayne (Rob Jenkins) and his girlfriend, Sallyanne (Lisa Cunningham), who was runner-up to Miss Catch of the Day, which means, I guess, you throw her back in. Sallyanne is preggers, so that she can do what all pregnant women in the movies and few pregnant women in life do, and hold her stomach with both hands most of the time. There is also a cop named Harrison (Dirk Hunter), who if you ask me should be named Dirk and played by Harrison Hunter, as Dirk is a better name than Harrison for a cop whose vocabulary consists of four-letter words and linking words.

They wander off the road and into the company of a local gun nut and survivalist named Marion (Mungo McKay), who if you ask me should be named Mungo and played by Marion McKay, as Mungo is a better name than Marion for a guy who has three shotguns yoked together so he can blast a zombie in two and leave its hips and legs lurching around with its bare spine sticking up in the air. For him, every shot is a trick shot; he'll throw two handguns into the air, kill a couple of zombies with a shotgun, and drop the shotgun in time to catch the handguns on the way down and kill some more.

Marion/Mungo hustles them all into his concrete-and-steel underground safe room, where their problems seem to be over until Marion announces, "There is no food or water." He didn't think of everything. Meanwhile, on the surface, the nature of the attack has changed, and some actual aliens appear. Who they are and what they want is a little unclear; I am not even absolutely certain if they were responsible for the meteorite attack that turned people into zombies, or have arrived shortly afterward by coincidence, making this the busiest day in local history, especially if you include the Miss Catch of the Day pageant.

There is a sense in which movies like *Undead* ask only to be accepted as silly fun, and I understand that sense and sympathize with it. But I don't think the Spierig brothers have adequately defined what they want to accomplish. They go for laughs with dialogue at times when verbal jokes are at right angles to simultaneous visual jokes. They give us gore that is intended as meaningless and funny, and then when the aliens arrive they seem to bring a new agenda. Eventually the story seems to move on beyond the central characters, who wander through new developments as if mutely wondering, hey, didn't this movie used to be about us?

Still, the horror genre continues to be an ideal calling card for young directors trying to launch their careers. Horror is the only non-porno genre where you don't need stars, because the genre is the star. *Undead* will launch the careers of the Spierigs, who are obviously talented and will be heard from again. Next time, with more resources, they won't have to repeat themselves. You see one set of hips and legs walking around with a spine sticking up out of them, you've seen them all.

Underclassman

(DIRECTED BY MARCOS SIEGA; STARRING NICK CANNON, ROSELYN SANCHEZ; 2005)

Underclassman doesn't even try to be good. It knows that it doesn't have to be. It stars Nick Cannon, who has a popular MTV show, and it's a combo cop movie, romance, thriller, and high school comedy. That makes the TV ads a slam dunk; they'll generate a Pavlovian response in viewers conditioned to react to their sales triggers (smartass young cop, basketball, sexy babes, fast cars, mockery of adults).

Cannon plays Tracy Stokes, a bike cop who screws up in the title sequence and is called on the carpet by his captain (Cheech Marin), who keeps a straight face while uttering exhausted clichés. ("You've got a long way to go before you're the detective your father was.") He gets a chance to redeem himself by working undercover at an exclusive L.A. prep school where a murder has been committed.

Turns out the murder is connected to a student car-theft ring, which is linked to drugs, which is an indictment of the rich students and their rich parents. It is a melancholy fact that a brilliant movie about high school criminals, Justin Lin's *Better Luck Tomorrow* (2002), got a fraction of the promotional support given to this lame formula film. If the teenagers going to *Underclassman* were to see *Better Luck Tomorrow,* they'd have something to think about and talk about and be interested in. *Underclassman* is a dead zone that will bore them silly while distracting them with the illusion that a lot of stuff is happening.

Why couldn't the movie have at least tried to do something unexpected, like making Tracy a good student? It's on autopilot: It makes him into a phenomenal basketball player (so good that most of his shots are special effects) and has him telling a classmate over dinner: "In my old neighborhood, crabs were not something you eat." Another food joke: A popular white student (Shawn Ashmore) mentions Benedict Arnold. "He makes good eggs," Tracy says. If he knows about eggs benedict, he knows about crab cakes. But never mind. He also gets involved in a linguistic discussion of the difference between "up their asses" and "on their asses."

The movie is multiethnic, but guess which ethnic group supplies the stooges, villains, and fall guys? There's a cute Asian cop (Kelly Hu) who helps Tracy a lot, and a sexy Latino teacher (Roselyn Sanchez) he wants to date (he's dying to tell her he's not really a student). And the plot asks us to believe that behind the murder is a conspiracy involving the local white establishment. Uh, huh. The white establishment in a rich Los Angeles neighborhood has ways to make (or steal) lots more money in business, without having to get involved in street crime.

Did anyone at any time during the talks leading up to this film say, "Gee, guys, doesn't it seem like we've seen this a million times before?" Did anyone think to create an African-American character who was an individual and not a wiseass stand-up with street smarts? Was there ever an impulse to nudge the movie in the direction of originality and ambition? Or was everybody simply dazed by the fact that they were making a film and were therefore presumably filmmakers?

Underclassman will probably open well, make its money, drop off quickly, go to video in a few months, and be forgotten. The sad thing is that Cannon, who is only twenty-five, showed real promise in *Drumline*. If he thinks *Underclassman* represents the direction his career should be taking, he needs to find himself a mentor.

The Village

(Directed by M. Night Shyamalan; starring Joaquin Phoenix, Bryce Dallas Howard; 2004)

The Village is a colossal miscalculation, a movie based on a premise that cannot support it, a premise so transparent it would be laughable were the movie not so deadly solemn. It's a flimsy excuse for a plot, with characters who move below the one-dimensional and enter Flatland. M. Night Shyamalan, the writer-director, has been successful in evoking horror from minimalist stories, as in *Signs*, which if you think about it rationally is absurd—but you get too involved to think rationally. He is a considerable director who evokes stories out of moods, but this time, alas, he took the day off.

Critics were enjoined after the screening to avoid revealing the plot secrets. That is not because we would spoil the movie for you. It's because if you knew them you wouldn't want to go. The whole enterprise is a shaggy-dog story, and in a way it is all secrets. I can hardly discuss it at all without being maddeningly vague.

Let us say that it takes place in an unspecified time and place, surrounded by a forest the characters never enter. The clothing of the characters and the absence of cars and telephones and suchlike suggests either the 1890s or an Amish community. Everyone speaks as if they had studied *Friendly Persuasion*. The chief civic virtues are probity and circumspection. Here is a village that desperately needs an East Village.

The story opens with a funeral attended by all the villagers, followed by a big outdoor meal at long tables groaning with corn on the cob and all the other fixin's. Everyone in the village does everything together, apparently, although it is never very clear what most of their jobs are. Some farming and baking goes on.

The movie is so somber, it's afraid to raise its voice in its own presence. That makes it dreary even during scenes of shameless melodrama. We meet the patriarch Edward Walker (William Hurt), who is so judicious in all things he sounds like a minister addressing the Rotary Club. His daughter Ivy (Bryce Dallas Howard) is blind but spunky. The stalwart young man, Lucius Hunt (Joaquin Phoenix), petitions the elders to let him take a look into the forest. His widowed mother, Alice (Sigourney Weaver), has feelings for Edward Walker. The village idiot (Adrien Brody), gambols about, and gamboling is not a word I use lightly. There is a good and true man (Brendan Gleeson). And a bridegroom who is afraid his shirt will get wrinkled.

Surrounding the village is the forest. In the forest live vile, hostile creatures who dress in red and have claws of twigs. They are known as Those We Do Not Speak Of (except when we want to end a designation with a preposition). We see Those We Do Not Speak Of only in brief glimpses, like the water-fixated aliens in *Signs*. They look better than the *Signs* aliens, who looked like large extras in long underwear, while Those We Do Not, etc., look like their costumes were designed at summer camp.

Watch towers guard the periphery of the village, and flares burn through the night. But not to fear: Those We Do, etc., have arrived at a truce. They stay in the forest and the villagers stay in the village. Lucius wants to go into the forest and petitions the elders, who frown at this desire. Ivy would like to marry Lucius and tells him so, but he is so reflective and funereal it will take him another movie to get worked up enough to deal with her. Still, they love each other. The village idiot also has a thing for Ivy, and sometimes they gambol together.

Something terrible happens to somebody. I dare not reveal what, and to which, and by whom. Edward Walker decides reluctantly to send someone to "the towns" to bring back medicine for whoever was injured. And off goes his daughter Ivy, a blind girl walking through the forest inhabited by Those Who, etc. She wears her yellow riding hood, and it takes us a superhuman effort to keep from thinking about Grandmother's House.

Solemn violin dirges permeate the sound track. It is autumn, overcast and chilly. Girls find a red flower and bury it. Everyone speaks in the passive voice. The vitality has been drained from the characters; these are the Stepford Pilgrims. The elders have meetings from which the young are excluded. Someone finds something under the floorboards. Wouldn't you just know it would be there, exactly where it was needed, in order for someone to do something he couldn't do without it.

Eventually the secret of Those, etc., is revealed. To call it an anticlimax would be an insult not only to climaxes but to prefixes. It's a crummy secret, about one step up the ladder of narrative originality from It Was All a Dream. It's so witless, in fact, that when we do discover the secret, we want to rewind the film so we don't know the secret anymore. And then keep on rewinding, and rewinding, until we're back at the beginning, and can get up from our seats and walk backward out of the theater and go down the up escalator and watch the money spring from the cash register into our pockets.

W

● ● ● ● ● ● ● ● ●

Waiting . . .

(DIRECTED BY ROB MCKITTRICK; STARRING RYAN REYNOLDS; 2005)

Waiting . . . is melancholy for a comedy. It's about dead-end lives at an early age and the gallows humor that makes them bearable. It takes place over a day at a chain restaurant named Shenaniganz (think Chili's crossed with Bennigan's), where the lives of the waiters and cooks revolve around the Penis Game. The rules are simple: Flash a fellow worker with the family jewels, and you get to kick him in the butt and call him a fag. Ho, ho.

Not long ago the restaurant was in the doldrums, morale was low, customers were rare. "The penis-showing game became a catalyst for change and improvement," says a cook named Bishop (Chi McBride). I dunno; to me it seems more like a catalyst for desperate shock value from a filmmaker who is trying to pump energy into a dead scenario.

I can imagine a good film based on the bored lives of retail workers whose sex lives afford them some relief. *The 40-Year-Old Virgin* is a splendid example, and given the slacker mentality of the waiters in *Waiting* . . . Kevin Smith's *Clerks* leaps to mind. Both of those films begin with fully seen characters who have personalities, possess problems, and express themselves with distinctive styles.

The characters in *Waiting* . . . seem like types, not people. What they do and say isn't funny because someone real doesn't seem to be doing or saying it. Everything that the John Belushi character did in *Animal House* proceeded directly from the core of his innermost being: He crushed beer cans against his forehead because he was a person who needed to, and often did, and enjoyed it, and found that it worked for him. You never got the idea he did it because it might be funny in a movie.

The central character in *Waiting* . . . is Monty (Ryan Reynolds), a veteran waiter who justifies his existence in hell by appointing himself its tour guide. He shows the ropes to a new employee named Mitch (John Francis Daley), beginning with the Penis Game and moving on to details about the kitchen, the table rotation, and the cultivation of customers. He also places great importance on the nightly parties where the employees get hammered.

Other staff members include the perpetually snarling Naomi (Alanna Ubach), who could make more money as the dominatrix she was born to play; Dan (David Koechner), the manager who has risen to the precipice of his ability, replacing the Penis Game with the Peter Principle; Serena (Anna Faris), who is way too pretty to be working at Shenaniganz and knows it; and Raddimus (Luis Guzman), the cook, who is a master at dropping food on the floor and seasoning it with snot, spit, and dandruff. The movie has a lesson for us, and it is: Do not get the food handlers mad at you.

The hero of sorts is Dean (Justin Long), who is discouraged to learn that while he's been making his $70 a day in tips, a high school classmate has become an electrical engineer. When the supercilious classmate leaves him a big tip, he feels worse than when a stiff leaves another waiter $2 on a $63 bill. The problem with the customers in both of those scenarios, and also with the lady customer who is relentlessly bitchy, is that there's nothing funny about them. They're mean and cruel and do not elevate their hatefulness to the level of satire but sullenly remain eight-letter words (in the plural form) beginning with *a*. Even the bitch's dinner companions are sick of her.

A subplot involves Natasha, the restaurant's sexy underage receptionist (Vanessa Lengies), who attracts both Monty and Dan the manager. I am trying to imagine how she could have been made funny, but no: The movie deals with her essentially as jailbait, something Monty is wise enough to just barely know and Dan reckless enough to overlook. I was also unable to see the joke involving Calvin (Robert Patrick Benedict), who (a) can't urinate because he's uptight that some guy may be trying to steal a glimpse of his jewels, but (b) is a champion at the Penis Game. There is a paradox here, but its solution doesn't seem promising.

What it comes down to is that Shenaniganz is a rotten place to work and a hazardous place to eat, and the people on both sides of the counter are miserable sods but at least the employees know they are. Watching the movie is like having one of these wretched jobs, with the difference that after work the employees can get wasted but we can only watch. It can actually be fun to work in a restaurant. Most of the waitpeople I have known or encountered have been competent, smart, and, if necessary, amusing. All the restaurant's a stage, and they but players on it. Customers can be friendly and entertaining. Tips can be OK. Genitals can be employed at the activities for which they were designed. There must be humor here somewhere.

Wasabi

(DIRECTED BY GERARD KRAWCZYK; STARRING JEAN RENO, RYOKO HIROSUE; 2002)

Jean Reno has the weary eyes and unshaven mug of a French Peter Falk, and some of the same sardonic humor, too. He sighs and smokes and slouches his way through thrillers where he sadly kills those who would kill him, and balefully regards women who want to make intimate demands on his time. In good movies (*The Crimson Rivers*) and bad (*Rollerball*), in the ambitious (Michelangelo Antonioni's *Beyond the Clouds*) and the avaricious (*Godzilla*), in comedies (*Just Visiting*) and thrillers (*Ronin*), he shares with Robert Mitchum the unmistakable quality of having seen it all.

Wasabi is not his worst movie and is far from his best. It is a thriller trapped inside a pop comedy set in Japan, and it gives Reno a chirpy young costar who bounces around him like a puppy on visiting day at the drunk tank. She plays his daughter, and he's supposed to like her, but sometimes he looks like he hopes she will turn into an aspirin.

The movie begins in Paris, where Reno plays Hubert Fiorentini, a Dirty Harry type who doesn't merely beat up suspects, but beats up people on the chance that he may suspect them later. During a raid on a nightclub, he makes the mistake of socking the police chief's son so hard the lad flies down a flight of stairs and ends up in a full-body cast. Hubert is ordered to take a vacation.

He shrugs and thinks to look up an old girlfriend (Carole Bouquet), but then his life takes a dramatic turn. He learns of the death in Japan of a woman he loved years earlier. Arriving for her funeral, he finds she has left him a mysterious key, a daughter he knew nothing about, and $200 million in the bank.

The daughter is named Yumi (Ryoko Hirosue). She is nineteen, has red hair, chooses her wardrobe colors from the Pokémon palate, and bounces crazily through scenes as if life is a music video and they're filming her right now.

The plot involves Yumi's plan to hire the Yakuza (Japanese Mafia) to get revenge for her mother's death. If there is a piece of fatherly advice that Hubert the veteran cop could have shared with her, it is that no one related to $200 million should do the least thing to attract the attention of the Yakuza. The plot then unfolds in bewildering alternation between pop comedy and action violence, with Hubert dancing in a video arcade one moment and blasting the bad guys the next.

There is no artistic purpose for this movie. It is product. Luc Besson, who wrote and produced it, has another movie out right now (*The Transporter*), and indeed has written, produced, or announced sixteen other movies since this one was made in far-ago 2001. Jean Reno does what he can in a thankless dilemma, the film ricochets from humor to violence and back again, and Ryoko Hirosue makes us wonder if she is always like that. If she is, I owe an apology to the Powerpuff Girls. I didn't know they were based on real life.

Wet Hot American Summer
(DIRECTED BY DAVID WAIN; STARRING JANEANE GAROFALO, DAVID HYDE PIERCE; 2001)

Hello muddah,
Hello fadduh—
Here I am at *Wet Hot American Summah*.

Wow I hate it
Something fierce—
Except the astrophysicist David Hyde Pierce.

He lives in a
Cottage nearby
And boy can he make Jeanane Garofolo sigh.

She's the director
Of Camp Firewood,
Which turns before our eyes into Camp Feelgood.

She is funny
As she's hurrying
Through the camper's names, including David Ben Gurion.

She dreams of bunking
David Hyde Pierce,
Who fears a falling Skylab will crush them first.

(*Chorus*)
Let me leave,
Oh mudduh faddah—
From this comic romp in Mother Nature . . .
Don't make me stay,
Oh mudduh faddah—
In this idiotic motion picture.

Every camper
And each counselor
Is horny, especially Michael Showalter.

He lusts after
Marguerite Moreau's bod,
But she prefers the lifeguard played by Paul Rudd.

The camp cook,
Chris Meloni,
Goes berserk because he feels attacked by phonies.

He talks to bean cans
And screams and moans
Periodically because of Post-Traumatic Anxiety Syndrome.

(*Chorus*)
I want to escape,
Oh mudduh faddah—
Life's too short for cinematic torture.
Comedies like this,
Oh mudduh faddah—
Inspire in me the critic as a vulture.

Ben and McKinley
Achieve their fame
As campers whose love dare not speak its name.

Ken Marino
Doesn't go rafting
Preferring Marisa Ryan, who is zaftig.

Watch David Wain's
Direction falter,
Despite the help of cowriter Showalter.

They did *The State*,
On MTV,
And of the two that is the one you should see.

Thoughts of *Meatballs*
Cruelly hamper
Attempts by us to watch as happy campers.

Allan Sherman
Sang on the telly.
I stole from him, and he from Ponchielli.

Whatever It Takes

(DIRECTED BY DAVID HUBBARD; STARRING SHANE WEST, JODI LYN O'KEEFE; 2000)
Whatever It Takes is still another movie arguing that the American teenager's IQ level hovers in the low nineties. It involves teenagers who have never existed, doing things no teenager has ever done, for reasons no teenager would understand. Of course, it's aimed at the teenage market. Maybe it's intended as escapism.

The screenplay is "loosely based on *Cyrano de Bergerac*," according to the credits. My guess is, it's based on the Cliff's Notes for *Cyrano*, studied only long enough to rip off the scene where Cyrano hides in the bushes and whispers lines for his friend to repeat to the beautiful Roxanne.

Cyrano in this version is the wonderfully named Ryan Woodman (Shane West), whose house is next door to Maggie (Marla Sokoloff). So close, indeed, that the balconies of their bedrooms almost touch, and they are in constant communication, although "only good friends." Ryan has a crush on Ashley (Jodi Lyn O'Keefe), the school sexpot. His best pal Chris (James Franco) warns him Ashley is beyond his grasp, but Ryan can dream.

If you know *Cyrano*, or have seen such splendid adaptations as Fred Schepisi's *Roxanne* (1987) with Steve Martin and Daryl Hannah, you can guess the key scene. Ryan talks Chris into going out with Maggie and then hides behind the scenery of a school play while prompting him with lines he knows Maggie will fall for. With Maggie neutralized, Ryan goes out with Ashley—who is a conceited, arrogant snob, of course, and will get her comeuppance in one of those cruel scenes reserved for stuck-up high school sexpots.

The film contains a funny scene, but it doesn't involve any of the leads. It's by Ryan's mom (Julia Sweeney), also the school nurse, who lectures the student body on safe sex, using a six-foot male reproductive organ as a visual aid. She is not Mrs. Woodman for nothing. As a responsible reporter I will also note that the film contains a nude shower scene, which observes all of the rules about nudity almost but not quite being shown.

And, let's see, there is a scene where Ashley gets drunk and throws up on her date, and a scene set in an old folks' home that makes use of enough flatulence to score a brief concerto. And a scene ripped off from *It's a Wonderful Life,* as the high school gym floor opens up during a dance to dunk the students in the swimming pool beneath. Forget about the situation inspired by *Cyrano*: Is there *anything* in this movie that isn't borrowed?

What Planet Are You From?

(DIRECTED BY MIKE NICHOLS; STARRING GARRY SHANDLING, ANNETTE BENING; 2000)
Here is the most uncomfortable movie of the new year, an exercise in feel-good smut. *What Planet Are You From?* starts out as a dirty comedy, but then abandons the comedy, followed by the dirt, and by the end is actually trying to be poignant. For that to work, we'd have to like the hero, and Garry Shandling makes that difficult. He begrudges every emotion, as if there's no more where that came from. That worked on TV's *Larry Sanders Show*—it's why his character was funny—but here he can't make the movie's U-turn into sentimentality.

He plays an alien from a distant planet, where the inhabitants have no emotions and no genitals. Possibly this goes hand in hand. He is outfitted with human reproductive equipment, given the name Harold Anderson, and sent to Earth to impregnate a human woman so that his race can conquer our planet. When Harold becomes aroused, a loud whirling noise emanates from his pants.

If I were a comedy writer I would deal with that alarming noise. I would assume that the other characters in the movie would find it extremely disturbing. I put it to my female readers: If you were on a date with a guy and every time he looked dreamy-eyed it sounded like an operating garbage disposal was secreted somewhere on his person, wouldn't you be thinking of ways to say you just wanted to be friends?

The lame joke in *What Planet Are You From?* is that women hear the noise, find it curious, and ask about it, and Harold makes feeble attempts to explain it away, and of course the more aroused he becomes the louder it hums, and when his ardor cools the volume drops. You understand. If you find this even slightly funny, you'd better see this movie, since the device is never likely to be employed again.

On Earth, Harold gets a job in a bank with the lecherous Perry (Greg Kinnear), and soon he is romancing a woman named Susan (Annette Bening) and contemplating the possibility of sex with Perry's wife, Helen (Linda Fiorentino). Fiorentino, of course, starred in the most unforgettable sexual put-down in recent movie history (in *The Last Seduction*, where she calls the bluff of a barroom braggart). There is a scene here with the same setup: She's sitting next to Harold in a bar, there is a humming from the nether regions of his wardrobe, etc., and I was wondering, is it too much to ask that the movie provide a hilarious homage? It was. Think of the lost possibilities.

Harold and Susan fly off to Vegas, get married, and have a honeymoon that consists of days of uninterrupted sex ("I had so many orgasms," she says, "that some are still stacked up and waiting to land"). Then she discovers Harold's only interest in her is as a breeder. She is crushed and angry, and the movie turns to cheap emotion during her pregnancy and inevitable live childbirth scene, after which Harold finds to his amazement that he may have emotions after all.

The film was directed by Mike Nichols, whose uneven career makes you wonder. Half of his films are good to great (his previous credit is *Primary Colors*) and the other half you're at a loss to account for. What went into the theory that *What Planet Are You From?* was filmable? Even if the screenplay by Garry Shandling and three other writers seemed promising on the page, why star Shandling in it? Why not an actor who projects joy of performance—why not Kinnear, for example?

Shandling's shtick is unavailability. His public persona is of a man unwilling to be in public. Words squeeze embarrassed from his lips as if he feels guilty to be talking. *Larry Sanders* used this presence brilliantly. But it depends on its limitations. If you're making a movie about a man who has a strange noise coming from his pants, you should cast an actor who looks different when it isn't.

What's the Worst That Can Happen?

(DIRECTED BY SAM WEISMAN; STARRING MARTIN LAWRENCE, DANNY DE VITO; 2001)

What's the Worst That Can Happen? has too many characters, not enough plot, and a disconnect between the two stars' acting styles. Danny De Vito plays a crooked millionaire, Martin Lawrence plays a smart thief, and they seem to be in different pictures. De Vito as always is taut, sharp, perfectly timed. Lawrence could play in the same key (and does, in an early scene during an art auction), but at other times he bursts into body language that's intended as funny but plays more like the early symptoms of St. Vitus's Dance.

There is an old comedy tradition in which the onlookers freeze while the star does his zany stuff. From Groucho Marx to Eddie Murphy to Robin Williams to Jim Carrey, there are scenes where the star does his shtick and the others wait for it to end, like extras in an opera. That only works in a movie that is about the star's shtick. *What's the Worst That Can Happen?* creates a world that plays by one set of comic rules (in which people pretend they're serious) and then Lawrence goes into mime and jive and odd wavings of his arms and verbal riffs, and maybe the people on the set were laughing but the audience doesn't, much.

The plot involves Lawrence as a clever thief named Kevin Caffery, who frequents auctions to find out what's worth stealing. At an art auction, he meets Amber Belhaven (Carmen Ejogo), who is in tears because she has to sell the painting her father left her; she needs money for the hotel bill. She has good reason to be in tears. The painting, described as a fine example of the Hudson River School, goes for $3,000; some members of the audience will be thinking that's at least $30,000 less than it's probably worth.

If Kevin is supplied with one love interest, Max Fairbanks (De Vito) has several, including his society wife (Nora Dunn), his adoring secretary (Glenne Headly), and Miss September. (When she disappears, Max's assistant, Earl [Larry Miller], observes there are "Eleven more months where she came from.") Kevin also has a criminal sidekick named Berger (John Leguizamo), and then there is his getaway driver Uncle Jack (Bernie Mac), and a Boston cop (William Fichtner) who is played for some reason as a flamboyant dandy. If I tell you there are several other characters with significant roles, you will guess that much of the movie is taken up with entrances and exits.

The plot involves Kevin's attempt to burgle Max's luxurious shore estate, which is supposed to be empty but in fact contains Max and Miss September. After the cops are called, Max steals from Kevin a ring given him by Amber Belhaven, and most of the rest of the movie involves Kevin's determination to get it back, intercut with Max's troubles with judges, lawyers, and accountants.

The jokes and the plots are freely and all too sloppily adapted from a Dortmunder novel by Donald E. Westlake, who once told me he really liked only one of the movies made from his books (*The Grifters*); he probably won't raise the count to two after this one. A comedy needs a strong narrative engine to pull the plot through to the end and firm directorial discipline to keep the actors from trying to act funny instead of simply being funny. At some point, when a movie like this doesn't work, it stops being a comedy and becomes a documentary about actors trying to make the material work. When you have so many characters played by so many recognizable actors in a movie that runs only ninety-five minutes, you guess that at some point they just cut their losses and gave up.

Note: Again this summer, movies are jumping through hoops to get the PG-13 rating and the under-seventeen demographic. That's why the battle scenes were toned down and blurred in *Pearl Harbor,* and no doubt it's why this movie steals one of the most famous closing lines in comedy history, and emasculates it. *The Front Page* ended with "The son of a bitch stole my watch!" This one ends with "Stop my lawyer! He stole my watch!" Not quite the same, you will agree.

White Chicks

(Directed by Keenen Ivory Wayans; starring Marlon Wayans, Shawn Wayans; 2004)

Various combinations of the Wayans family have produced a lot of cutting-edge comedy, but *White Chicks* uses the broad side of the knife. Here is a film so dreary and conventional that it took an act of will to keep me in the theater. Who was it made for? Who will it play to? Is there really still a market for fart jokes?

Marlon and Shawn Wayans play Marcus and Kevin Copeland, brothers who are FBI agents. Fired after a sting goes wrong, they're given a second chance. Their assignment: Protect Tiffany and Brittany Wilson (Anne Dudek and Maitland Ward), high-society bimbos who seem to be the target of a kidnapping scheme. The girls get tiny cuts in a car crash and are too vain to attend a big society bash in the Hamptons. Marcus and Kevin have the answer: They'll disguise themselves as the Wilsons and attend the party in drag.

Uh, huh. They call in experts who supply them with latex face masks, which fool everybody in the Hamptons but looked to me uncannily like the big faces with the talking lips on Conan O'Brien. There is also the problem that they're about six inches taller than the Wilsons. I suppose they're supposed to be, I dunno, Paris and Nicky Hilton, but at least the Hiltons look like clones of humans, not exhibits in a third-rate wax museum.

The gag is not so much that black men are playing white women as that men learn to understand women by stepping into their shoes and dishing with their girlfriends. Womanhood in this version involves not empowerment and liberation, but shopping, trading makeup and perfume tips, and checking out the cute guys at the party. "Tiffany" and "Brittany" pick up a posse of three friendly white girls, inherit the Wilsons' jealous enemies, and engage in the most unconvincing dance contest ever filmed, which they win with a break-dancing competition.

Meanwhile, a pro athlete named Latrell (Terry Crews) is the top bidder at a charity auction for Marcus, who represents his ideal: "A white chick with a black woman's ass!" This leads to all sorts of desperately unfunny situations in which Marcus tries to keep his secret while Latrell goes into heat. Also meanwhile, a labyrinthine plot unfolds about who is really behind the kidnapping, and why.

The fact that *White Chicks* actually devotes expository time to the kidnap plot shows how lamebrained it is, because no one in the audience can conceivably care in any way about its details. Audiences who see the TV commercials and attend *White Chicks* will want sharp, transgressive humor, which they will not find, instead of a wheezy story about off-the-shelf bad guys, which drags on and on in one complicated permutation after another.

Are there any insights about the races here? No. Are there any insights into the gender gap? No. As men or women, black or white, the Wayans brothers play exactly the same person: an interchangeable cog in a sitcom.

Because they look so odd in makeup, the effect is quease inducing. They fall victims, indeed, to the Uncanny Valley Effect. This phenomenon, named in 1978 by the Japanese robot expert Masahiro Mori, refers to the ways in which humans relate emotionally with robots. Up to a certain point, he found, our feelings grow more positive the more the robots resemble humans. But beyond a certain stage of reality, it works the other way: The closer they get to humans, the more we notice the differences and are repelled by them. In the same way, the not quite convincing faces of the two white chicks provide a distraction every moment they're on the screen. We're staring at them, not liking them, and paying no attention to the plot. Not that attention would help.

The Whole Ten Yards

(DIRECTED BY HOWARD DEUTCH; STARRING BRUCE WILLIS, MATTHEW PERRY; 2004)

A fog of gloom lowers over *The Whole Ten Yards,* as actors who know they're in a turkey try their best to prevail. We sense a certain desperation as dialogue mechanically grinds through unplayable scenes, and the characters arrive at moments that the movie thinks are funny but they suspect are not. This is one of those movies you look at quizzically: What did they think they were doing?

The movie is an unnecessary sequel to *The Whole Nine Yards* (2000), a movie in which many of the same actors sent completely different messages from the screen. "A subtle but unmistakable aura of jolliness sneaks from the screen," I wrote in my review of the earlier movie. "We suspect that the actors are barely suppressing giggles. This is the kind of standard material everyone could do in lockstep, but you sense inner smiles, and you suspect the actors are enjoying themselves."

The problem, I suspect, is that *The Whole Nine Yards* did everything that needed to be done with the characters and did it well. Now the characters are back again, blinking in the footlights, embarrassed by their curtain call. The movie has the hollow, aimless aura of a beach resort in winter: The geography is the same, but the weather has turned ugly.

You will recall that the earlier film starred Bruce Willis as Jimmy "The Tulip" Tudeski, a professional hit man who has moved in next door to a Montreal dentist named Oz (Matthew Perry). The dentist's receptionist was Jill (Amanda Peet), a woman whose greatest ambition in life was to become a hit woman. Jimmy was in hiding from a Chicago gangster named Janni Gogolak (Kevin Pollak), who wanted him whacked.

In *The Whole Ten Yards,* Jimmy the Tulip and Jill are married and hiding out in Mexico, where Jill finds employment as a hit woman while Jimmy masquerades as a house-husband. That puts Willis in an apron and a head cloth during the early scenes, as if such a disguise would do anything other than call attention to him. Oz, meanwhile, has moved to Los Angeles and is married to Cynthia (Natasha Henstridge), who used to be married to the Tulip. (His first wife, played in the earlier movie by Rosanna Arquette with a hilarious French-Canadian accent, might have been useful here.)

Janni Gogolak was made dead by Oz and the Tulip in the first picture, but now his father, the crime boss Laszlo Gogolak, has been released from prison and uses all of his power to find revenge against the two men; that fuels most of the plot, such as it is. Lazlo Gogolak is played by Kevin Pollak in one of the most singularly bad performances I have ever seen in a movie. It doesn't fail by omission, it fails by calling attention to its awfulness. His accent, his voice, his clothes, his clownish makeup—all conspire to create a character who brings the movie to a halt every time he appears on the screen. We stare in amazement, and I repeat: What did they think they were doing?

The movie's plot is without sense or purpose. It generates some action scenes that are supposed to be comic but are not, for the inescapable reason that we have not the slightest interest in the characters and therefore even less interest in their actions. The movie is instructive in the way it demonstrates how a film can succeed or fail not only because of the mechanics of its screenplay, but because of the spirit of its making.

The Whole Nine Yards was not a particularly inspired project, but it was made with spirit and good cheer, and you felt the actors almost visibly expanding on the screen; Amanda Peet in particular seemed possessed. Here we see the actors all but contracting, as if to make themselves smaller targets for the camera. That there will never be a movie named *The Whole Eleven Yards* looks like a safe bet.

Wolf Creek

(Directed by Greg McLean; starring John Jarratt, Nathan Phillips; 2005)

I had a hard time watching *Wolf Creek*. It is a film with one clear purpose: to establish the commercial credentials of its director by showing his skill at depicting the brutal tracking, torture, and mutilation of screaming young women. When the killer severs the spine of one of his victims and calls her "a head on a stick," I wanted to walk out of the theater and keep on walking.

It has an 82 percent "fresh" reading over at the Tomatometer. "Bound to give even the most seasoned thrill seeker nightmares" (*Hollywood Reporter*). "Will have Wes Craven bowing his head in shame" (Clint

Morris). "Must be giving Australia's outback tourism industry a bad case of heartburn" (Laura Clifford). "A vicious torrent of bloodletting. What more can we want?" (Harvey Karten). One critic who didn't like it was Matthew Leyland of the BBC: "The film's preference for female suffering gives it a misogynist undertow that's even more unsettling than the gore."

A "misogynist" is someone who hates women. I'm explaining that because most people who hate women don't know the word. I went to the Rotten Tomatoes roundup of critics not for tips for my own review, but hoping that someone somewhere simply said, "Made me want to vomit and cry at the same time."

I like horror films. Horror movies, even extreme ones, function primarily by scaring us or intriguing us. Consider *Three . . . Extremes* recently. *Wolf Creek* is more like the guy at the carnival sideshow who bites off chicken heads. No fun for us, no fun for the guy, no fun for the chicken. In the case of this film, it's fun for the guy.

I know, I know, my job as a critic is to praise the director for showing low-budget filmmaking skills and creating a tense atmosphere and evoking emptiness and menace in the outback, blah, blah. But in telling a story like this, the better he is, the worse the experience. Perhaps his job as a director is to make a movie I can sit through without dismay. To laugh through the movie, as midnight audiences are sometimes invited to do, is to suggest you are dehumanized, unevolved, or a slackwit. To read blasé speculation about the movie's effect on tourism makes me want to scream like Jerry Lewis: "Wake up, lady!"

There is a line, and this movie crosses it. I don't know where the line is, but it's way north of *Wolf Creek*. There is a role for violence in film, but what the hell is the purpose of this sadistic celebration of pain and cruelty? The theaters are crowded right now with wonderful, thrilling, funny, warmhearted, dramatic, artistic, inspiring, entertaining movies. If anyone you know says this is the one they want to see, my advice is: Don't know that person no more.

Oh, I forgot to mention: The movie doesn't open on December 23, like a lot of the "holiday pictures," but on Christmas Day. Maybe it would be an effective promo to have sneak previews at midnight on Christmas Eve.

Yours, Mine & Ours

(DIRECTED BY RAJA GOSNELL; STARRING DENNIS QUAID, RENE RUSSO; 2005)

Yours, Mine & Ours has one thing to be thankful for: Frank and Helen realize immediately that they're still in love, all these years after they were the prom king and queen in high school. They see each other, they dance, they talk while dancing, they kiss while talking, and in the next scene they're engaged to be married. That saves us the Idiot Plot device in which they're destined for each other but are kept apart by a series of misunderstandings. In this version, they're brought together by a series of misunderstandings, mostly on the part of the filmmakers, who thought they could remake the 1968 Henry Fonda/Lucille Ball film without its sweetness and charm.

The story: He is a Coast Guard admiral with eight children. She is a fashion designer with ten children. They were in love in high school and darn!—they shoulda gotten married then, if for no other reason than that they'd probably not have eighteen kids, although you never know, and some of hers are adopted. With a little willpower they could have merely starred in the sequel to *Cheaper by the Dozen*.

Frank likes everything shipshape. Helen is comfortable with a certain messiness. His kids line up for roll call and mess duty. Her kids are free spirits with a touch of hippie. Her family has a pig for a pet. I think his family has two dogs. That's how many I counted, about forty-five minutes into the movie, although as nearly as I can recall nobody ever claims them. Of course, I may have missed something. I wish I had missed more.

Dennis Quaid can be the most effortlessly charming of actors, but give him a break: It helps when he has effortlessly charming material. Here he has a formula to race through at breakneck speed, as if the director,

Raja Gosnell, is checking off obligatory scenes and wants to get home in time for the lottery drawing. Rene Russo can play a convincing and attractive mother of ten, but that's not what this material needs. It needs a ditzy madcap to contrast with the disciplined Coast Guard man. The earlier casting of Lucille Ball gives you an idea of what the role required, and Russo is simply too reasonable to provide it. If ever there was a role calling out "Goldie! Goldie!" this is the one.

No matter; we never get a sense of a real relationship between Frank and Helen. Their marriage seems like an extended Meet Cute. Gosnell and his writers, Ron Burch and David Kidd, crack the whip while making the characters jump through the obligatory hoops of the plot. We know, because we have seen one or two movies before this one, that it is necessary (a) for the two tribes of kids to become instant enemies, (b) for food fights to erupt on a moment's notice, (c) for there to be a Preliminary Crisis that threatens the marriage, and a Preliminary Solution, followed by (d) a Real Crisis and a Real Solution, and happily ever after, etc., with a farewell sight gag or two involving the pig. There is even a truce among the children, who oppose the marriage and have a plan: "We gotta stop fighting and get them to start."

There's not a moment in this story arc that is not predictable. Consider the outing on the sailboat. The *moment* Admiral Frank warns everybody that the boom can swing around and knock you overboard, I would have given 19 to 1 odds that the person knocked overboard would be— but you already know.

Now about those opening logos before the movie started. This one sets some kind of a record. In no particular order, I counted Columbia Pictures, Nickelodeon Movies, Paramount Pictures, and Metro-Goldwyn-Mayer. Why did no studio in Hollywood want to back a single one of last year's best picture nominees, and every studio in town wanted to get involved with this one? To be sure, Fox, Disney and Warner Bros. got left out. Too slow off the mark?

index